A Cultural History of the Chinese Character "*Ta* (她, She)"

This book offers a thorough examination of the history of a Chinese female pronoun – the Chinese character "*Ta* (她, She)" and demonstrates how the invention and social acceptance of this new word is inextricably intertwined with matters of sociocultural politics.

The Chinese character *Ta* for the third-person feminine singular pronoun was introduced in the late 1910s when the voices of women's liberation rang out in China. The invention and dissemination of this word not only reflected an ideological gendering of the Chinese script but also provoked heated academic and popular debate well into the 1930s. Thus, the history of *Ta* provides a prism through which to explore modern Chinese history. The author provides an ambitious and informed examination of how *Ta* was invented and promoted in relation to the gender equality movement, the politics of neologism, and other domestic elements and international catalysts.

This book is the first major work to survey *Ta*'s creation. It draws on diverse sources, including interviews with eight historians who experienced the popularisation of *Ta* as youths in the 1930s and 40s. This book will be an essential read for students and scholars of East Asian Studies, Chinese Cultural History, and those who are interested in the history of China.

Huang Xingtao is the Professor of the Institute of Qing History of Renmin University. He served as Dean of the Department of History and Director of the Institute of Qing History of Renmin University. He was a visiting scholar at the Harvard-Yenching Institute and Kobe University. His research interests include the history of the Qing Dynasty, modern Chinese ideological history, and social and cultural history. His works include *Reinventing China: A Study on the Concept of "the Chinese Nation" in Modern China, General History of Chinese Culture: the Republic of China Volume*, etc. He was awarded the Excellent Achievements Prize for Human and Social Sciences Research in National Normal High Education Institutions.

China Perspectives

The *China Perspectives* series focuses on translating and publishing works by leading Chinese scholars, writing about both global topics and China-related themes. It covers Humanities & Social Sciences, Education, Media, and Psychology, as well as many interdisciplinary themes.

This is the first time any of these books have been published in English for international readers. The series aims to put forward a Chinese perspective, give insights into cutting-edge academic thinking in China, and inspire researchers globally.

To submit proposals, please contact the Taylor & Francis Publisher for the China Publishing Programme, Lian Sun (Lian.Sun@informa.com).

Titles in History Currently Include

Contemporary Studies on Modern Chinese History III
Edited by Zeng Yeying

The Origin of East Asian Medieval Capital Construction System
The Ancient City of Ye
Niu Runzhen

The History of Chinese Presence in Nigeria (1950s–2010s)
Factories, Commodities, and Entrepreneurs
Shaonan Liu

The Indigenization of Christianity in China I
1807–1922
Qi Duan

A Cultural History of the Chinese Character "*Ta* (她, She)"
Invention and Adoption of a New Feminine Pronoun
Huang Xingtao

For more information, please visit www.routledge.com/China-Perspectives/book-series/CPH

A Cultural History of the Chinese Character "*Ta* (她, She)"
Invention and Adoption of a New Feminine Pronoun

Huang Xingtao

LONDON AND NEW YORK

First published in English 2023
by Routledge
4 Park Square, Milton Park, Abingdon, Oxon OX14 4RN

and by Routledge
605 Third Avenue, New York, NY 10158

Routledge is an imprint of the Taylor & Francis Group, an informa business

© 2023 Huang Xingtao

Translated by Darrell Dorrington

The right of Huang Xingtao to be identified as author of this work has been asserted in accordance with sections 77 and 78 of the Copyright, Designs and Patents Act 1988.

All rights reserved. No part of this book may be reprinted or reproduced or utilised in any form or by any electronic, mechanical, or other means, now known or hereafter invented, including photocopying and recording, or in any information storage or retrieval system, without permission in writing from the publishers.

Trademark notice: Product or corporate names may be trademarks or registered trademarks, and are used only for identification and explanation without intent to infringe.

English version by permission of Foreign Language Teaching and Research Publishing Co., Ltd.

British Library Cataloguing-in-Publication Data
A catalogue record for this book is available from the British Library

ISBN: 978-1-032-41724-0 (hbk)
ISBN: 978-1-032-41725-7 (pbk)
ISBN: 978-1-003-35944-9 (ebk)

DOI: 10.4324/9781003359449

Typeset in Times New Roman
by Apex CoVantage, LLC

Contents

List of Illustrations   *vii*
Preface   *xxi*

Introduction: The Character *Ta* 她, or She, and "Events in the History of Culture"   1

1   The Conundrum of the English Term *"She"*: A New Problem Arising From Contact With Western Languages   7

2   The Emergence of the Character *Ta* 她, plus *Ta'nü* 他女 and *Ta/To* 妥: The *New Youth* 《新青年》 Editorial Group's Early Discussions and the Experimentation Which It Engendered   15

3   An Account of the Early Written Use of the Character *Ta* 她 Before April 1920: A Survey of the Literary World   28

4   The Debate Over Preserving or Abolishing the Character *Ta* 她 and the Contest Between *Ta* 她 and *Yi* 伊: Adopters and Adoptees in the Linguistic Competition   49

5   Gender Confusion: Sensitivity Over "Female"-Related Terms: Concepts of Gender Equality and the Fate of the Character *Ta* 她   70

6   *Ta* (她, She), *Ta* (他, He), *Ta* (牠, It) and *Ta* (它, It): The Formation and Establishment of a New Pronoun Regime   97

7   The Socialisation of the Character *Ta* 她 after April 1920: An Examination of Its Deepening Acceptance and Popularisation   114

8 The Quest for Modernity and the Interaction Between
  Foreign Language Factors and Chinese Language
  Traditions: The Roots of *Ta* 她's Victory and Its
  Historical and Cultural Impact   144

Appendix I: Some Reflections on Cultural History Research   *175*
Appendix II: Revisiting the Question of the Character
  Ta 她 *and Understanding "Modernity": A Response to*
  Dr Yang Jianli 杨剑利   *184*
Appendix III: Illustrations and Figures   *199*
Afterword   *205*
Afterword to the Revised Edition   *209*
References   *211*
Index of Translated/Transliterated Titles Referred to
  in This Work   *225*
Index of Proper Names Used in This Work
  (in Pinyin Order)   *233*

Illustrations

Figure 0.1 A section of Zhen Xin's 枕薪 article "Miss" which opposes women labelling themselves as "Miss".

viii   *Illustrations*

Figure 0.2 In 1878, Guo Zansheng 郭赞生 translated the book *English School Grammar* 《文法初阶》, in which he first used the Chinese "他, 伊, 彼" to translate "he, she, it".

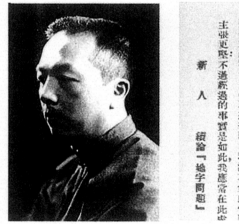
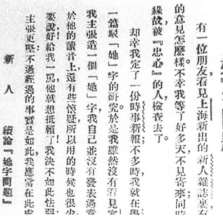

Figure 0.3 In 1917, Liu Bannong 刘半农 is the first editor of *New Youth* 《新青年》 magazine to propose the use of the word "*Ta* 她" but he is not the first practitioner. He elucidated the question systematically in his 1920 article "On the Question of the Character *Ta* 她" 《"她"字问题》.

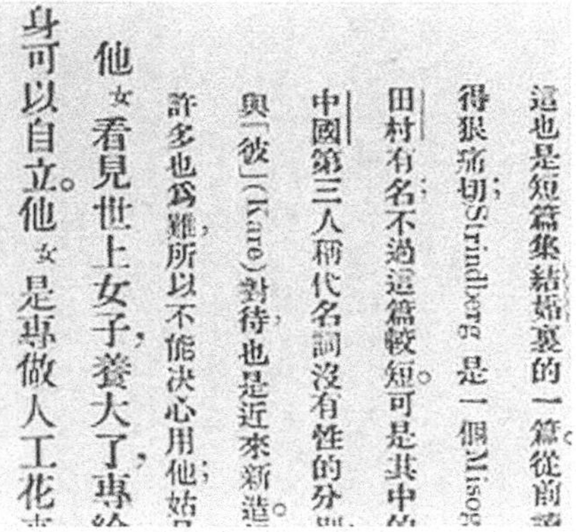

這也是短篇集結婚裏的一篇。從前讀
得狠痛切。Strindberg 是一個Misog
田村有名不過這篇較短。可是其中的
中國第三人稱代名詞沒有性的分
與「彼」(Kare)對待也是近來新造。
許多也爲難，所以不能決心用他姑
他女看見世上女子，養大了，專給
身可以自立。他女是專做人工花

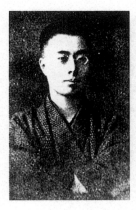

Figure 0.4 In 1918, Zhou Zuoren 周作人 was the first person to discuss the question of "*Ta* 她" publicly in *New Youth* 《新青年》 magazine. He also advocated imitating the Japanese translation of *Kanojo* 彼女 by using the two Chinese characters *ta'nü* 他女. Later Ye Shengtao 叶圣陶 et al. followed his creation and used *ta'nü* 他女.

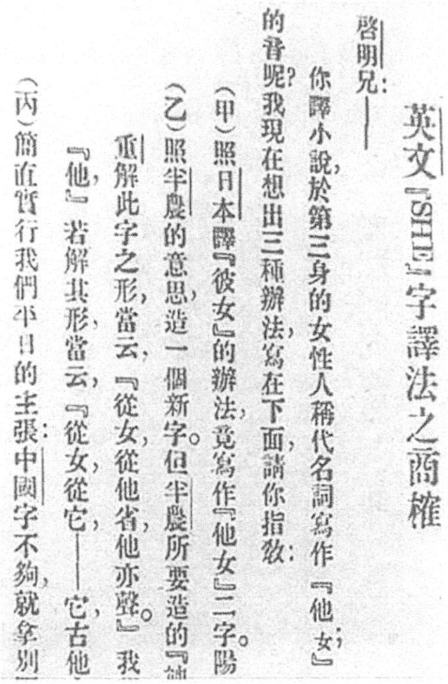

英文『SHE』字譯法之商榷

啓明兄：

你譯小說，於第三身的女性人稱代名詞寫作『他女』
的音呢？我現在想出三種辦法，寫在下面，請你指教：
(甲)照日本譯『彼女』的辦法，竟寫作『他女』二字。陽
(乙)照半農的意思，造一個新字。但半農所要造的『
重解此字之形，當云，『從女，從他省，他亦聲。』我
『他』，若解其形，當云，『從女，從它，——它，古他
(丙)簡直實行我們平日的主張：中國字不夠，就拿別

Figure 0.5 The article "The Discussion over the Translation of the English 'She'" 《英文 "she" 字译法之商榷》 published in *New Youth* 《新青年》 in April, 1919. Qian Xuantong 钱玄同 proposed creating a character *Ta*/*To* 妐 but Zhou Zuoren 周作人 argued that both "*Ta* 她" and "*To* 妐" shared the same pronunciation and so preferred to use *Yi* 伊. This idea had an enormous impact. Later *Ta* 她 and *Yi* 伊 began to compete in discussions and practice, resulting in *Yi* 伊 at one stage gaining the upper hand.

x *Illustrations*

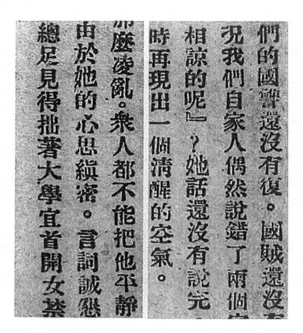

Figure 0.6 Two of the earliest formal uses of the *Ta* 她 word in Kang Baiqing 康白情's article "A Harbinger of Male-Female Relations in Peking's Student World" 《北京学生界男女交际之先声》, carried in the *Morning Post* 《晨报》, May 20, 1919.

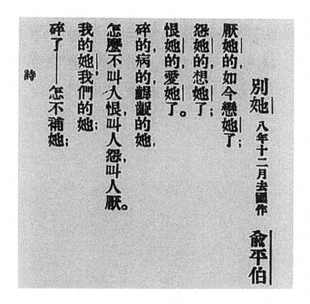

Figure 0.7 The poem "Bidding Her Farewell" 《别她》 is the first poem to refer to the nation as *Ta* 她 and was carried in *The Renaissance* 《新潮》, February 1920.

Illustrations xi

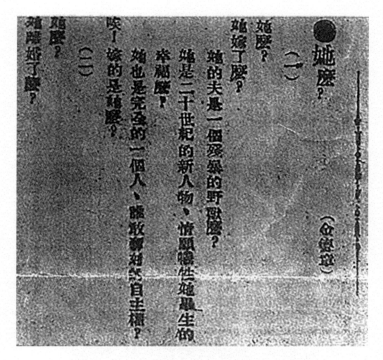

Figure 0.8 "She?" 《她么》 is the first new poem to use "*Ta* 她" in its title, written by Jin Dezhang 金德章 and carried in *The Republican Daily News* 《民国日报》, March 12, 1920.

Figure 0.9 Qian Xingcun 钱杏邨 published the poem "The Dahlia" 《大丽花》 (carried in *Emancipation Pictorial* 《解放画报》 Issue 13, July 30, 1921), and is an example of how the character *yi* 伊 was used in verse to represent the feminine third person.

xii *Illustrations*

Figure 0.10 "Whose Fault? Why Did She Commit Suicide?!" 《谁的罪,她为甚么要自杀?！》, drawn by Lin Xin 麟心, *Emancipation Pictorial* 《解放画报》 Issue 13, July 1921. This is probably the earliest work of art to use *ta* 她. The author denounces the banal feudal concept of being "faithful to one's husband unto death" which, like an evil apparition, was poisoning and devastating the women of China.

Figure 0.11 In 1921, *Emancipation Pictorial* 《解放画报》 used *ta* 她 as part of the Women's Liberation Movement to fight against the oppression and constraint of the old society.

Illustrations xiii

Figure 0.12 Emancipation Pictorial 《解放画报》 is the first magazine to use the character *ta* 她 in an illustration. This contributed greatly to the artistic practice of using the word *ta* 她.

xiv *Illustrations*

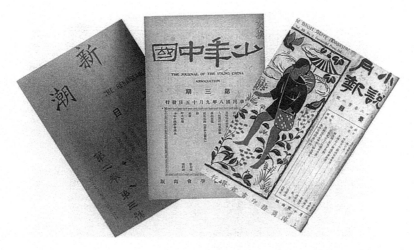

Figure 0.13 Such New Culture Movement magazines as *The Renaissance* 《新潮》, *The Journal of the Young China Association* 《少年中国》 and *The Short Story Magazine* 《小说月报》 were the largest contributors to the use of the word *ta* 她 in writing practice.

Figure 0.14 Female writers used *ta* 她 in their works before 1924: Lu Yin 庐隐 (top-left), Bing Xin 冰心 (top-middle), Chen Hengzhe 陈衡哲 (top-right), Feng Yuanjun 冯沅君 (bottom-left), Shi Pingmei 石评梅 (bottom-right).

Figure 0.15 Section of "Down with '*Yingci*'!" 《打倒"英雌"》, carried in *The Pei-yang Pictorial News* 《北洋画报》, Issue 1115, 1934.

Figure 0.16 "Ta (他), ta (她), ta (牠), and ta (它)" 《"他"、"她"、"牠"、"它"》, carried in *The Pei-yang Pictorial News* 《北洋画报》, Issue 1080, 1934.

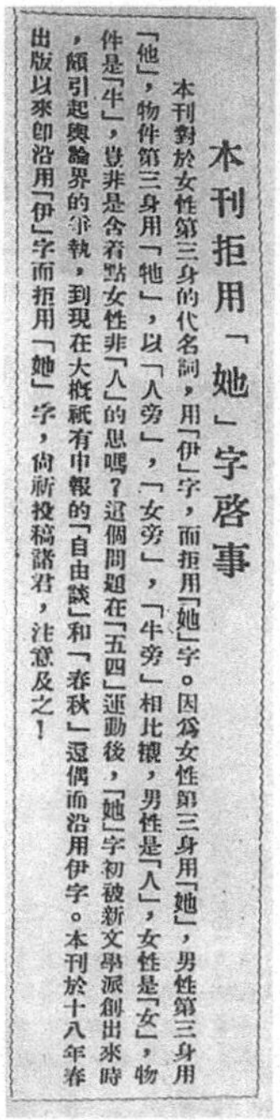

本刊拒用「她」字啓事

本刊對於女性第三身的代名詞，用「伊」字，而拒用「她」字。因爲女性第三身用「她」，男性第三身用「他」，物件第三身用「牠」，以「人旁」，「女旁」，「牛旁」相比擬，男性是「人」，女性是「女」，物件是「牛」，豈非是含着點女性非「人」的思嗎？這個問題在「五四」運動後，「她」字初被新文學派創出來時，頗引起輿論界的爭執，到現在大概祇有申報的「自由談」和「春秋」還偶而沿用伊字。本刊於十八年春出版以來即沿用「伊」字而拒用「她」字，尙祈投稿諸君，注意及之！

Figure 0.17 "Announcement: This Magazine Refuses to Use the Character *ta* 她" 《本刊拒用"她"字启事》, *Women's Voice* 《妇女共鸣》, 1934.

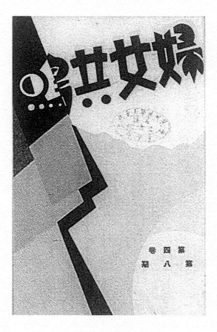

Figure 0.18 Cover of *Women's Voice* 《妇女共鸣》.

Figure 0.19 "'*Ta* 她' and the Women's Movement" 《"她"与妇运》, carried in *The Decameron* 《十日谈》, Issue 34, 1934, criticizing *Women's Voice* 《妇女共鸣》's refusal to use *ta* 她, arguing that this was grasping at shadows and abandoning the substantive.

Figure 0.20 Yang Gang 杨刚, "*Tiao* (frivolous) – Mei Lanfang" 《伩 – 梅兰芳》, *True Words* 《真话》, Issue 1, 1946. The writer satirically uses 伩 to refer in the third-person singular to a female character in Chinese opera.

Illustrations xix

Figure 0.21 Historian Chen Yinke's 陈寅恪, "Discussing National Language Examination Topics with Professor Liu Wendian" 《与刘文典教授论国文试题书》, carried in *The Critical Review* 《学衡》, Issue 79, in which he publicly opposes the use of *ta* 她 and states that he has never used the word *ta* 她 in his life.

Figure 0.22 Zhou Shoujuan 周瘦鹃, representative of the Mandarin Ducks and Butterflies School 鸳鸯蝴蝶派. He long opposed the use of *ta* 她 and advocated using *yi* 伊, only to surrender in 1943 and publicly use the word *ta* 她. See "Foreword to Violets" 《写在紫罗兰前头》, carried in *Violets* 《紫罗兰》 magazine, Issue 2, May 1943.

xx *Illustrations*

Figure 0.23 A section from Zhou Shoujuan's "Foreword to Violets" 《写在紫罗兰前头》, carried in *Violets* 《紫罗兰》 magazine, Issue 2, May 1943.

Preface

Some time ago I read with respect Xingtao's article on the character *ta* 她 in the Chinese language. Two years ago, he told me that he was meticulously researching the history of this character and planning to expand it into a book. I could not help mentally applauding the idea. My intuition and premonition (or perhaps my own research interest) told me that this kind of research would certainly be more meaningful than those nonsensical metanarratives of "post-colonialism" or "post-modernism". Every time I happened across those trendy, half-baked opuses, I would also ponder: why couldn't they calmly and methodically undertake some *real* research? *A Cultural History of the Chinese Character "Ta* (她, She)*" – Research on the Invention and Adoption of a New Feminine Pronoun* then, is the result of some very solid research.

    There is no doubt that there will be some who believe that writing a history of the character *ta* 她 is to make a mountain out of a molehill. I will not argue except to say that I am of the same mind as Xingtao: this is no minor topic. The depth of cultural history that the character *ta* 她 has reflected is truly rich. Naturally, here I am not only referring to the question of "seeing the bigger picture in the minutiae", a point on which this work already offers many brilliant insights, so we do not have to go over that again here. One very simple fact is that *ta* 她 involves half of humanity ("half the sky"), and *ta* 她, along with *ni* 你 and *wo* 我, are closely related, and that the joys and sorrows of mankind are largely related to "she/her" (*ta* 她) – so how can *ta* 她 not be important? Without "she/her" (*ta* 她), literature and the arts would lose their lustre; without "she/her" (*ta* 她) love songs and poems would be difficult to compose . . . Clearly, when I use the term "*ta* 她" here, I am making a general reference to all members of the fair sex in the history of culture. It was only 90 years ago that the character *ta* 她 appeared in China to represent the female sex, or to use the words of the author of this book, "If we are not simply looking at the character's outward appearance but at the internal logic of both form and meaning, then the fact remains that it was Liu Bannong who created and invented the singular third person pronoun *ta* 她". Someone like myself who has never researched the character *ta* 她 might quite naturally think of that poem by Liu Bannong 刘半农, "How Could I Not Think of Her" 《教我如何不想她》, even though many people might still not believe that this was the first actual appearance of the character *ta* 她 in verse.

The creation of the character *ta* 她 and the extremely lively debate around the design of the character, lead me to think of one opinion which was rife in the West from a very early stage and that was that the structure of Chinese characters was not suited to abstract thinking; that it was more conducive to visual intuitive thinking. Or, to put it another way, in contrast to the Western phonetic script, to a large extent Chinese characters are classified as ideographs and their meaning is largely evinced through script-based symbolism. Ideographs themselves can always be understood. Perhaps their pronunciation might have undergone changes across the long flow of history, or they might be pronounced differently in different dialects, but just as Arabic numerals are pronounced differently across different languages, the meaning that they carry is mostly obvious. It is precisely the ideographic character of the Chinese language that leads it to occupy a prominent position in the cultural and spiritual life of the Chinese people (of which Chinese calligraphy is only one expression). The early Western scholars of Chinese thought and language were already deeply committed to this type of rhetoric and moreover used this methodology to analyse the so-called Chinese way of thinking. Naturally, at the time, what they were faced with was classical and ancient Chinese and the conclusion of their linguistic comparison was that the logical thinking of the West was supported by the combinatorial syntax of its languages while an ideographic writing system led the Chinese people to value analogue thought. China's ancient philosophers were not good at making deductions from abstract concepts but rather were fond of using concrete examples to explain things; they were not fond of speculation but good at comparison. This was thus concrete, visual thinking.

As to the Chinese language, from very early times the West had differing opinions of which the previous was just one, albeit a very important one. Whether or not this formulation had merit is a matter of conjecture and a single paper perhaps might not be able to do it justice. But as far as the differing views of the creation of the character *ta* 她 is concerned, and the lively debate which erupted around its form, there is no room for doubt. In the very least it is one reason why this writer was so quick to be reminded of this type of thinking. The derivation of the *ta* 她 character from the *ta* 他 character and many, many other similar Chinese characters, informs us that the script had already incorporated reflection and that everything was encompassed within the physical form of the character.

All languages offer a basic methodology for thought and communication and all have their own unique rules and procedures for regulating that thought and communication. When people employ a certain type of language, they have virtually no way of discarding these unique rules. Which rules occupy a primary position and are fused into the structure of the language differs greatly between languages. Wilhelm von Humboldt presented a report entitled "On the Grammatical Structure of the Chinese Language" to the Berlin Science Academy on March 20, 1826, in which he analysed the advantages and disadvantages of the Chinese and Western languages. Despite his excessive "post-modern" or "post-colonial" point of view, Humboldt's questioning of the innate character of language is sound. His main thinking was that man's intelligence carries a responsibility to enunciate his thought and that without language, thought is impossible. However, he made a distinction between thought and language. To his mind, man has two intelligent behaviours; one directed at thought, and one directed at language. It goes without saying that Humboldt admired the logic and capability of the grammar of the main European languages and that Chinese (and let us stress again, we are here speaking of classical Chinese), because of an absence of grammar, was only capable of constructing simple syntaxes and incapable of constructing complex clauses or the vague concepts that populate philosophical reflection. Despite the fact that Humboldt was concentrating on the grammatical structure of the written language, he did not believe that the more complex a language's physical architecture was, the greater its functionality. Nor did he reject the idea that things which the Chinese language lacked in physical form might still exist in thought or that a deficiency in one area might mean a superiority in another. Because the form of Chinese characters does not change, the meaning of a sentence comes from the meaning of the words themselves, from the combination of words, their sequence and their context. Humboldt believed that the architecture of the Chinese language was capable of boosting man's delight in how concepts are arranged and daringly compiled and that this was even more conducive to linguistic imagination and creativity. I believe that the charm of China's ancient poetry can amply attest to this point, and naturally, not this alone.

Everyone is aware that Western epistemology is not suitable for application to all cultures and that Humboldt's reflection is only one of many. What requires explanation is that when Western scholars analyse the relationship between language and logic, they do not say that the Chinese language lacks logic, nor do they say that the Chinese people are incapable of logical thinking. What they do say is which languages are more conducive to logical thinking than others. Similarly, the Chinese tradition of not differentiating between male and female in the third person singular pronoun before the modern era, does not mean that it is incapable of indicating the gender of the third person. Nevertheless, one principle of linguistics is that the more compact and explicit the grammatical architecture is, the more easily can a given thought be expressed precisely. Here, the character *ta* 她 can be offered as an example. Similarly, when ancient Chinese is translated into the vernacular language according to the grammar of modern Chinese and a few characters are translated into a whole sentence, then we are able to observe this phenomenon.

In Western script, which is based on Latin and relies on letters of an alphabet and the sounds of speech, the creation of a new term is not a difficult process. Indeed, it is quite a common occurrence. This is not the case with Chinese (and here the transformation of traditional characters into simplified script is not included in the scope of the creation of characters). Newly created characters like *ta* 她 are among the few exceptions in Chinese. Since the middle of the 19th century, China has energetically persisted in translating and introducing a completely different Western knowledge and cultural matrix. In addition, it has attempted to marry Western scientific culture with the traditional Chinese culture. In this process, the translation and introduction of "Western learning" greatly enriched the academic vocabulary of modern Chinese. Many important terms and concepts in modern Chinese (and especially science, technology, and academic phraseology) indeed came into being in the second half of the 19th century and the beginning of the 20th century. Many terms also underwent a qualitative change during this period. New characters and new terms are an extremely complex phenomenon and are mainly expressed through vocabulary and semantics. Generally speaking, when people encounter a new value system or their traditional customs and rules are threatened or receive a shock, they will energetically seek out some new means of spiritual support, and any new discovery or value transformation can be expressed in language.

Following the Opium Wars, a serious inequality existed between Chinese and Western culture. This is an incontestable fact. However, can all the inventions and creativity that new discoveries in language gave rise to be seen as indicators of inequality? This question calls for some concrete analysis. Taking the character *ta* 她 as an example, Liu He 刘禾 in her *Translingual Practice* 《跨语际实践》 argues that treating the absence in Chinese of terms that corresponded to the third person feminine pronouns in European languages as "a type of flaw in the Chinese language itself" and even doing their best to make up for the deficiency, exemplifies the "inequality between languages" rather than any deficiency in the Chinese language. Because in the West, "when you translate the feminine plural *elles* from French into English, *they* carries no gender delineation yet people do not feel that there is any inconvenience caused". However, I believe that any linguistic transmutation or innovation operates by its own rules. No question of "equality" or "inequality" exists here, but simply a question of "existence" or "non-existence". The *elles* and *they* that exist respectively in French and English are idiomatic; in German the singular and plural feminine, as well as the common plural form, is *sie*, which is also dictated by grammar, so translation between them does not pose a problem. The creation of the character *ta* 她 is directly related to the contact between Chinese and Western languages and to translation. Since classical Chinese did not have equivalents for the English, French, German or Russian *she*, *elle*, *sie*, or *она*, it made sense to choose from within the existing lexicon but add a new meaning in order to cope with the situation (as many individuals did at the time). And if one felt that this method was not entirely optimal and that it would be preferable to create a new character, then that was also acceptable.

The creation of the character *ta* 她 and the debate around it cannot be said to have been brought on by Western cultural hegemony, but rather by the conscious action of many persons of knowledge and experience. No matter whether in Chinese or Western languages, the precondition for the creation of the majority of new words is that new objects and new concepts demand a new vocabulary. The emergence of a new age will inevitably turn language into a prime site for experimentation where new vocabulary appears in abundance. We can observe this phenomenon in François Rabelais, Pierre de Ronsard or Michel de Montaigne in France during the Renaissance, and the same can be seen amongst the worthies and scholars of modern and contemporary China. In many cases, new terms are formed by new explanations or understandings of existing words (lexical renewal) or a new arrangement of existing characters or terms. Whilst introducing Western learning to China in recent and modern times, there were many concepts which existed in the West but which we did not have, and this created difficulties for any accurate translation or introduction. It is for this reason that Yan Fu 严复 declared, "The establishment of a single name means days and months of hesitation." In response to the many initial critics of the character *ta* 她, Liu Bannong 刘半农 pointed out as the debate raged that if *ta* 她 could not in the end be established and popularised within the Chinese language, then its existence could at least be justified and found useful for the purpose of translating Western languages. When viewed in this manner, the creation of new terms can be seen as a question of necessity.

The interaction or collision of different languages will always to a greater or lesser extent leave marks. We do not deny that political and cultural power is able to lead to linguistic hegemony, however the coining of certain words or loanwords usually occurs within the "destination language" and the "source language" is simply a causal factor. For this reason, the creation of a newly coined word or the acceptance of a loanword is on the whole an act of the receiving party and not a surrender to linguistic hegemony. No matter whether it is newly created Chinese characters for chemical elements or the learning from and adoption of Western punctuation marking, or even perhaps an exploration of Chinese grammar, these are all an inevitable consequence of opening up to "Western learning" or "New learning" and necessary for the modernisation of the Chinese language. We can not only see in many translation activities and in linguistic practice the results that the diligent pursuit of the people at the time have achieved, but also a type of linguistic "survival of the fittest". When viewed from today's standpoint, we already cannot imagine modern Chinese without a *ta* 她 character in the same way that modern Chinese requires punctuation.

The view of the author of this work concerning the creation of the *ta* 她 character is quite apt:

> The legitimation of the *ta* 她 character in the Chinese language is basically not a result of any hegemonic attitude of the West, i.e., it is because it existed in Western languages that it therefore was a necessity in the Chinese language. It was embraced by the Chinese language because on a fundamental level it became associated with the modernist demands on the Chinese language that were kindled by the new age – or to put it another way, the demands of modernisation. Here the congress of the Western and modern natures of the *ta* 她 character is coincidental.

Apart from synthetically revealing its complex causal factors, the author especially stresses the function of the modernist demand for "precision" and "conciseness". It should be said that this view can not only be applied to the *ta* 她 character, but it can also be used to explain the many "newly minted" terms and concepts in Chinese a century or more ago.

As to whether the lack in ancient Chinese of a third person feminine pronoun similar to that which exists in Western languages was indeed "a type of defect in the Chinese language itself", that is another matter. Linguists are able to verify that certain languages are more suited to describing certain objects or situations. Examples of this type are numerous. For example, the French descriptions of certain objects or situations are much richer and more precise than those of other languages. The reason for this is that over the passage of history, thanks to unique conditions of social development, Frenchmen (when compared to people from other countries or regions) pay more attention to the minutiae and differences of certain objects or situations and they are therefore more meticulous and have access to more synonyms to choose from. As a result, when describing a certain object or situation, in French it is possible to describe it in the finest details while in other languages perhaps it can only be described roughly or in general terms. Naturally I could use any other language to make this point.

During the mutual exchange between people with differing mother tongues we can often hear the following statement, "Our language doesn't have the kind of expression you have in your language." This statement can amply reflect the difference between languages. I have personally, in a number of situations, declared that something is "untranslatable", which is what we are talking about. Among the languages that exist in the world today, the German capacity to create new concepts is perhaps the greatest. It is almost without restriction and therefore especially suited to philosophical reflection. The major 20th century thinker Martin Heidegger fully recognised, and moreover fully utilised, this facility. It is difficult to imagine him being able to come up with similar philosophical reflections in another language. To a significant extent it was German (Heidegger's German) that made much of his reasoning so complete.

Returning to *A Cultural History of the Chinese Character "Ta* (她, She)", I would like to address the relationship between this work and some methodological reflections – in other words, some research methods that occurred to me as I was reading the manuscript for the work.

This book reminded me immediately of "the archaeology of knowledge". Foucault saw his own research as an "archaeology of knowledge", which is in fact a type of linguistic analysis of a genre which explores "linguistic practice" or "linguistic events". Perhaps we could say that through focused research the serendipitous, fractious, and substantive nature of historical discourse can be stressed so as to demonstrate that objects are no longer perceived, described, executed, expressed, divided or recognised in the same manner. Naturally, linking to Foucault is only what personally occurred to me whilst reading the manuscript for this book and it is not to regard as important Foucault's archaeology of knowledge or the philosophical quest of the genealogical methodology and its strong deconstructionist flavour, but rather its literal meaning: *l'archéologie du savoir*.[1]

Additionally, the title of this book leads one to think immediately of Chen Yinke's 陈寅恪 saying that "exposition of an individual character is a work of cultural history". This was the author's clear methodological quest whilst researching the character *ta* 她, and it should be said that this quest has been successful. We are unquestionably witness to a brilliantly colored cultural history of the character *ta* 她. Naturally, to view Mr Chen's statement as a methodology and a directional orientation, to put it into practice would result in a very definitive study rather than the composition of a grand cultural history based on a single word. Such an undertaking would be unprecedented. In this example of the character *ta* 她, we see the "cultural history of this character", an event in the history of culture, or one chapter in the history of culture.

At the same time, as someone who has done some minor research into "the history of ideas" or "historical semantics", I will also most naturally connect the archaeology of the character *ta* 她 to historical semantics. This work holistically reveals the linguistic environment in which the character was born and the fabric of its growth and development. It also expands the analysis of this single term to an exploration of its lexical family, its conceptual architecture and its ideational network. Historical semantics not only analyses the "inherent meaning" and "application" of specific concepts or expressions, but it also surveys the relationship between similar, parallel, reciprocal, or associated concepts with a given concept and explores their multi-layered relationship, a process that can be seen to permeate this whole work.

Finally, what I would like to stress is the effort in terms of data that this book displays. No matter whether it is "the archaeology of knowledge" or "historical semantics", data is the be all and end all. Why else would you write a whole book about a single character if it was not for the fact that you were able to present a full range of data? Only with complete and accurate data can meaningful words be spoken, meaningful information imparted, or a task performed with ease. If we take the example of the great eight volume *Geschichtliche Grundbegriffe. Historisches Lexikon zur Politisch-sozialen Sprache in Deutschland (Basic Concepts in History. A Dictionary on Historical Principles of Political and Social Language in Germany)* (1972–1997) edited by Reinhart Koselleck, its basis was data. This "dictionary" is not a collection of "entries" in the traditional sense but rather a collection of articles discussing basic concepts, many of which exceed one hundred pages and could quite comfortably comprise a separate book in its own right. In addition, speaking of the German experience, to view social history, the history of thought or cultural history from the angle of the history of ideas, this is in the first instance the domain of the historian, and the greatest accomplishment is also theirs. Xingtao is a professor of history at the People's University. I remember several years ago the *Modern Chinese History Studies* 《近代史研究》 magazine sent a copy of his article "The Formation and Historical Practice of the Modern Concept of 'Civilization' and 'Culture' in the Late Qing and Early Republican Period" 《晚清民初现代"文明"和"文化"概念的形成及其历史实践》 to Germany for me to appraise anonymously. At the time I was deeply impressed. Apart from the article's novel perspective and viewpoints, I was impressed by the author's command and utilisation of a vast amount of data. I only learned the author's name after the article was published. I have since had the fortune to get to know Xingtao and with my deepening familiarity with his scholarship, that initial deep impression has slowly been transformed into a genuine conviction. I believe that even a reader who is unfamiliar with his work can guess that this book is the product of a historian and that the probing and command of the materials in many parts of this book truly demands one's admiration.

In recent years, Xingtao, with his reliance on solid data and his engagement in suggesting new trains of thought and new perspectives in the relevant research arenas, has undoubtedly opened up new horizons in historical research and offered new insights. In fact, this brilliant new gem, which is *A Cultural History of the Chinese Character "Ta* (她, She)", 《"她"字的文化史》 is not only Xingtao's masterful offering to historians, but it is also a cross-disciplinary achievement that has been anticipated by the humanities and social science circles, circles which will benefit from its reading. I am sure that it will be welcomed by all.

Fang Weigui

Note

1 The "archaeology of knowledge" that I cite in the text is the commonly accepted translation in academic circles in mainland China. The "l' archéologie du savoir" that Foucault uses can in fact be translated "knowledge archaeology". Despite the fact that in English-Chinese, French-Chinese and German-Chinese dictionaries archaeology, archéologie, or Archäologie are all translated as "archaeology", and that it is indeed a branch of learning, nevertheless in certain combinations (especially when combined with such abstract notions as "knowledge"), in Western languages this concept often refers to investigation or exploration. Wang Dewei 王德威 translated the title of Foucault's book as the *Excavation of Knowledge* 《知识的考掘》 (Maitian Publishing Company, Taiwan, 1993 edition), which is probably more apt.

Introduction

The Character *Ta* 她, or She, and "Events in the History of Culture"

It was reported in January 2000 that the American Dialect Society had conducted a survey on such topics as the "Word of the Past Millennium" and the 20th century's "Word of the Century". Among the entrants in the "Millennium" competition were "freedom", "truth", "science", "nature", "history", "OK", "book" and "she", and the finalists numbered only two, namely "science" and "she". In the end "she" defeated "science" by 35 votes to 27 to win the crown. Some commentators have deduced from this that the results of the competition "constitute an epoch-marking significance" and presages an "even more important role" for women in the 21st century.[1] Whether this prediction is well founded or not, I dare not hazard a guess. It nevertheless entices us to make Sino-Western cultural associations and whets our appetite to probe the academic delights associated with the historical question of the Chinese feminine third person pronoun *ta* 她, or she.

In many western languages, the history of gender distinction has been a long one. For example, in English, the marker of the feminine third person singular underwent a process of transformation from the old English "hēo" to the "she" of the Middle Ages. It is generally accepted that the word "she" probably took form in the 12th–13th century, making it a product of medieval English. However it did not simply morph from "hēo"; it was simultaneously influenced directly by the medieval English feminine definite article "sēo".[2] In Russian, the word "она" indicating the feminine third person singular, along with the masculine third person singular "он" and the neuter third person singular "оно" also arose relatively early, probably appearing during the "literary era" (11th–14th centuries), and their evolution is linked to the demonstrative pronoun "вон".[3] Whereas in the East – specifically in China, Japan, and Korea – the formation of the feminine third person singular pronoun *ta* "她", *kanojo* "彼女" (かのじょ) and *geu nyeo* "그녀" has a very short history. For example, the Japanese 彼女 has only been in circulation for approximately 120 years[4] while China's 她 character can only boast some 90 or more years, and the Korean 그녀 even less.[5] They are all products of the cultural interaction between the East and West in modern times.

In recent Chinese history the feminine third person singular character *ta* 她 has been recognised as "the most fascinating new word invented" by China during the May Fourth era.[6] Its creation, the debate, and its subsequent recognition and popularisation, is an archetypal linguistic phenomenon which made its appearance

DOI: 10.4324/9781003359449-1

following the East-West cultural contact. It is also a phenomenon of the new gender culture, while at the same time being a phenomenon of the metamorphosis in critical literary, ideological, and sociocultural history that is worthy of close scrutiny. In other words, it both historically participated in and influenced language, gender culture, literature, ideology and more throughout the process of the transformation of modern China. Therefore, its appearance, recognition, popularisation, and its very function can, to varying degrees, constitute a special object of study in such research fields as modern Chinese gender history, literature, and the history of writing, or even the history of ideas and of Sino-Western cultural interaction. I would even dare to venture that this type of research may perhaps constitute a vivid and unique historical resource for people today in their ruminations on inter-cultural contact and questions of modernity itself.

The famous English historian Peter Burke, whilst responding to questions by researchers on cultural history as to why we should specifically be mindful of linguistic matters, has clearly pointed out:

Why should scholars of cultural history involve themselves with language? Why shouldn't they leave it to the linguists to discuss? One of the reasons is that at any time, language is always a sensitive indicator. It can presage cultural transformation and not simply act as a reflector.[7]

This is one of the reasons why I was delighted to undertake research around the feminine singular third person pronoun *ta* 她, or "she".

Recently, certain scholars offered some original views on the idea of "events in the history of thought"[8] and inspired by this, I accept that there also exist "events in the history of culture". To my mind, so-called "events in the history of culture" should probably comprise two component parts: one would naturally be those major events which had an important and undeniable influence on cultural history such as the "May Fourth New Culture Movement" of modern China; the second would be incidents that have significant value as regards cultural reflection – an influence and significance which is not necessarily obvious, especially at the time they may have occurred, yet, with the passage of time, their rich cultural connotations and intrinsic significance is gradually perceived and further, individuals are lured into delving deeper, appreciating them, and expounding and reflecting on them. The creation of the feminine third person character *ta* 她, its recognition, cultural employment, and absorption into the national lexicon largely belongs to this latter category of "events in the history of culture".[9]

Earlier research on the character *ta* 她 has not been a blank canvas. The Chinese-American scholar Liu He 刘禾 has spoken briefly, yet with singular insightfulness, of the cultural significance of the invention of the feminine third person pronoun *ta* 她 from the perspective of translingual practice. Moreover, in her accompanying notes she specifically mentions several articles from *The China Times* 《时事新报》 and *New Man* 《新人》 magazines that discuss in 1920 the feminine *ta* 她 character.[10] Before and after Liu He 刘禾, there were scholars who, from the perspective of linguistic or biographical research, had, to varying degrees, cursorily touched on the question.¹¹ However, when compared to the rich historical trove attached to the character *ta* 她, most of the current research on the topic remains brief. Particularly scant is research on the debates which arose following the invention of the character along with the relevant circumstances relating to its popularisation and written practice. Also what has been under-studied is the general recognition of the character or the cultural effects that followed its entry into the Chinese lexicon. To this day, the academic world still lacks any penetrating research or analysis of these topics. In view of this, the present volume builds on previous research to undertake an even more comprehensive, meticulous, and thorough exploration and analysis of the early history of the character *ta* 她 and it is hoped as far as is possible to reveal the historical ideological and cultural underpinnings of the phenomenon.

In the mid-1930s the linguist Shen Jianshi 沈兼士 published an article entitled "Probing the Original Meaning of the Character *Gui* 鬼 [ghost]" 《"鬼"字原始意义之试探》 which won the highest approbation of the renowned historian Chen Yinke 陈寅恪. In his letter to the author Shen, Chen Yinke wrote:

> I have just read your grand work and I admire and respect it immensely. According to the current standards of classical scholarship, any exposition of an individual character is a work of cultural history. In my estimation this is the sole recent Chinese publication which unreservedly meets this criterion.¹²

Here "exposition of an individual character is a work of cultural history" is exactly the type of methodological determination of the feminine character *ta* 她 that this current work explores. Although I may not have achieved this, I have been determined to try. What is intriguing is that, during the Republican era, Chen Yinke 陈寅恪 himself was in fact a prominent opponent of the admission of the feminine character *ta* 她 into the Chinese lexicon. So, given the current circumstance, I think I would adopt Chen's methodology of approving the term whilst opposing his specific views on the subject. I wonder if the master scholar had been privy to what we know today what conclusion he would have come to?

Since I have regarded the feminine *ta* 她 as an "event in the history of culture", then the question of how we are to undertake an appropriate "narration" of this type of event must demand a response. Two years since this present work first appeared, I have already written in the preface to *In Search of a Cultural History*:

> How should an "event in the history of culture" really be narrated? This is a very divided question. I believe there are two principles of desegregation that should perhaps receive attention: one is that historians should draw upon a diverse range of culture history materials and spare no effort to clearly reconstruct the principal essence of the event, and by mobilizing one's own intellectual capacity, voluntarily and in a measured way, interpret its significance and associations. The other principle of desegregation is that historians should consciously communicate the incident's dynamic process of diverse competitive forces, concepts, even sounds jostling with one another, and link

4 *Introduction*

this with an analysis of the ultimately responsible social factors inherent in the incident along with some cultural reflection. If the narration of an "event in the history of culture" is always a megaphonic expression of the "victor" or is merely the unilateral deductions of the victor's logic, then as well as assuredly forfeiting any historical complexity, it will also lose any capacity to reflect on either history or culture.[13]

This work's investigation into the history of the feminine *ta* 她, its narration and its analysis, has to some extent employed the aforementioned principles, and I would respectfully invite the expert reader to feel free to proffer their judgement.

Notes

1 For the original report, refer to The American Dialect Society's web page: www.americandialect.org. Chen, Yaoming 陈耀明, "She: The 21st Century's Most Important Word"《她：21世纪最重要的一个字》, *Golden Age*《黄金时代》, Issue 4, 2000. Same or similarly titled works reporting this event were also penned by Xiao Yang 肖杨, Ge Luofu 葛洛夫 and others – see *Nanfang Daily*《南方日报》, January 10, 2001, and *Language and Literature World*《语文天地》, Issue 7, 2002.
2 See the entry "she" in *Webster's New Twentieth Century Dictionary of the English Language*, Unabridged, Second Edition and *The Oxford English Dictionary*, Second Edition, Volume XV, 1989. The latter's analysis of the process and the reasons for the historical transformation of the word "she", and especially its journey from "sēo" to "she" and not directly from "hēo" to "she" is quite detailed. The "English in the Middle Ages" section of *The Cambridge Encyclopaedia of the English Language* carries a section entitled "The SHE Puzzle" which details three different interpretations of the origins of the word "she". One holds that "she" was gradually formed through a series of transformations in sound from the original "hēo"; the second argues that it has its origin in the early English feminine form of the definite article "sēo"; and the third holds that while it arose from "sēo", it nevertheless chose a different phonetic pathway. (Crystal, David (ed.), *The Cambridge Encyclopaedia of the English Language*, Cambridge: Cambridge University Press, 1995, p. 43.)
3 The earliest extant Russian classics Повесть временных лет [*Tale of Bygone Years*]《往年纪事》, *Rus' Justice*《罗斯法典》 and *Tale of the Campaign of Igor*《伊戈尔远征记》 are works from this period and they all distinguish between the masculine and feminine. See Шахматов, А.А., *Историческая морфология русского языка*. М., 1957, с., 162–164. See also Иванов, В.В., *Историческая грамматика русского языка*. М., 1964 or Якубинский, Л.П., *История древнего русского языка*. М., 1953. For research and analysis of Russian language materials I have relied on the assistance of my colleague Dr Ye Bochuan 叶柏川, for which I express my sincere gratitude.
4 According to Mr Hida Yoshifumi's 飞田良文 authoritative research, the modern pronunciation of the term *kanojo* 彼女 had already appeared in the *Shūtei Sōzu Shōgakutokuhon* (Revised Illustrated Primary School Reader)《修订插图小学读本》 which was published in 1876, clearly indicating that it was a translation of the word "she". In 1885–1886 Tsubouchi Shōyō's 坪内逍遥 *Tōsei Shosei Kishitsu* (*The Disposition of Students in the Present Day*)《当世書生気質》 continued this work. Beginning in around 1888 the term *kanojo* 彼女 with the sense of "she" was gradually becoming more widespread throughout Japan. See Hida Yoshifumi's 飞田良文 *Meiji umare no nihongo* (New Japanese Linguistic Creations in the Meiji Period)《明治生まれの日本語》. Tankōsha 淡交社, May 2002, pp. 80–88. In addition, Mr Yanabu Akira's 柳父章 *Honyakugo "kare" "kanojo" no rekishi* (The History of the Translated Equivalent

of "he" and "she") 《翻訳語"彼""彼女"の歴史》 (See *Honyakugo seiritsu jijō* [The Emergence of a Language of Translation] 《翻訳語成立事情》), Iwanami Shoten 岩波書店, 1982, pp. 195–212) also delved into this question. For research and analysis of Japanese language materials, I have relied on the assistance of Mr Zhu Jingwei 朱京伟, Mr Tsuchiya Hiroshi 土屋洋, Mr Yamamoto Takuya 山本卓也, and others to whom I express my sincere gratitude.

5 The efforts of the Korean language to address the challenge of the western female third person pronoun largely began during the "New Fiction Period" "新小说时期" (1906–1917). Apparently, the novelist Jin Dongren 金东仁 was the first to employ the feminine third person pronoun in written form, whereupon *geu nyeo* formally entered the lexicon and by 1926 it appeared in Liang Zhudong's 梁柱东 *The Newlyweds* 《新婚记》 and became especially popular following the Korean War in 1954. See Ko, Kilseop 고길섶, "Word Games of Our Times: The Birth Story of the Odd [pronoun] 'she'" 『우리 시대의 언어게임: 괴짜 '그녀'의 탄생설화』 《怪物"她(*geu nyeo*)"的诞生故事》; see the work *Word Games of Our Times* 《我们时代的语言游戏》, Todam Publishers, 1995, pp. 169–177). My thanks to An Yuner 安允儿 for assistance with the Korean, and at the same time I would like to thank the Korean scholar Liang Yimo 梁一模 for his assistance.

6 See Liu, Lydia He 刘禾, *Translingual Practice* 《跨语际实践》, translated by Song, Weijie 宋伟杰 et al., Beijing: San Lian Bookstore, 2002, pp. 49–52.

7 Burke, Peter, *Languages and Communities in Early Modern Europe* 《语言的文化史 - 近代早期欧洲的语言和共同体》, translated by Li Xiaoxiang 李霄翔, Li Lu 李鲁 and Yang Yu 杨豫, Beijing: Peking University Press, September 2007. "Introduction", p. 1.

8 See Chen, Shaoming 陈少明, "What Is an 'Event in the History of Thought'" 《什么是 "思想史事件"》, *Jiangsu Social Sciences* 《江苏社会科学》, 2007, (1).

9 Regarding "Events in Cultural History", I have had some further thoughts since the original publication of the current work in 2009. I believe that:

> "Events in Cultural History" should possess two fundamental features: one is that they are not restricted to language, ideology, scholarship, art and literature, education, religion and other specific cultural categories, but will cross multiple categories. In other words, they are not simply an "event in the history of pedagogy", an "event in literary history" or an "event in art history". And related to this, their influence and function is capable of demonstrating some kind of cultural synthesis or continuity and carries some unique "significance in cultural history" that is worthy of thorough research or reflection. The second is that its occurrence is usually not the product of one point in time. It often must pass through a relatively long process over a considerably long period of time and its significance to cultural history at times may also require the reflective participation of subsequent scholars of the humanities before it can be manifest.

See "Author's Preface" to Huang, Xingtao 黄兴涛, *In Search of a Cultural History: Taking China in Recent Years as Our Prospect* 《文化史的追寻 – 以近世中国为视域》, Beijing: Renmin University Publishing House, 2011, p. 4.

10 See Liu, Lydia He 刘禾, *Translingual Practice* 《跨语际实践》, translated by Song, Weijie 宋伟杰 et al., Beijing: San Lian Bookstore, 2002, p. 70, Note 109.

11 For example, Meng, Shuhong 蒙树宏, "On '*Ta* 她'" 《说"她"》 (carried in *Lexicographical Studies* 《辞书研究》, 1981, (4)); Ling, Yuanzheng 凌远征, "The History of the Creation of the Character '*Ta* 她'" 《"她"字的创造历史》 (carried in *Linguistic Pedagogy and Research* 《语言教学与研究》, 1989 (4)); Gong, Shuming 贡树铭, "Liu Bannong and '*Ta* 她'" 《刘半农和"她"》 (carried in *On Chewing Words* 《咬文嚼字》, 2002, (4)); Zhu, Jinshun 朱金顺 "Two Historical Items Relating to the Creation of the Character '*Ta* 她'" 《有关"她"字创造的两件史料》 (carried

in *Green Earth* 《绿土》, April 1999 (38)); Yang, Jianmin 杨建民, "Liu Bannong and the Story of the Character '*Ta* 她'" 《刘半农与"她"字的故事》 (carried in *China Reading Weekly* 《中华读书报》, February 6, 2002) amongst others. In addition, a few biographies of Liu Bannong 刘半农 and Qian Xuantong 钱玄同 also sporadically touch on this topic.

12 Chen, Meiyan 陈美延 (ed.), *The Collected Works of Chen Yinke: Collected Letters* 《陈寅恪集·书信集》, Beijing: Sanlian Bookstore, 2001, pp. 172–173. Shen, Jianshi's 沈兼士, "Probing the Original Meaning of the Character '*Gui* 鬼'" 《"鬼"字原始意义之试探》 was earliest published in 1935 in *Chinese National Culture Quarterly* 《国学季刊》, Vol. 5, Issue 3.

13 See "Author's Preface" to Huang Xingtao 黄兴涛, *In Serarch of a Cultural History – Taking China in Recent Years as Our Prospect* 《文化史的追寻 – 以近世中国为视域》, Beijing: Renmin University Publishing House, 2011, pp. 4–5.

1 The Conundrum of the English Term "*She*"

A New Problem Arising From Contact With Western Languages

Before the modern era, China had no tradition of a pronoun which distinguishes between the masculine and feminine third person singular. For thousands of years, it seems that nobody felt the need to make this distinction. This question gradually appeared and rose to prominence after China came into contact with Western languages, and especially with the English language. Today we have long become accustomed to distinguishing between 他 (*ta* or "he") and 她 (*ta* or "she") whereas in fact this was a creative contribution by the New Culture devotees of the May Fourth era. And it is publicly acknowledged that the use of 她 or 伊 (*yi*) to represent the female third person singular or "she" and its other Western language equivalents was thanks to the advocacy of people like Liu Bannong 刘半农 and Zhou Zuoren 周作人, amongst others.

While the modernist *ta* 她 character formally appeared in the May Fourth period, nevertheless, questions of distinguishing between the masculine and feminine third person singular had already surfaced in China from the beginning of the 19th century or even earlier. The adoption of the character *yi* 伊 to clearly translate the English pronoun "she" and thus invest in the character a feminine meaning while at the same time using the character 他 with its traditionally indeterminate gendering and giving it an exclusively masculine meaning was not necessarily the exclusive affair of the May Fourth period that people usually attribute it to. As far as this writer has been able to ascertain, by the end of the 1870s at least, this had already been suggested. This long-held historical misconception must be confronted and clarified.

1 China's Earliest Attempt to Confront the Quandary of the Word "She"

In 1822, the first protestant missionary to visit China, Robert Morrison, in his *A Dictionary of the Chinese Language* 《英华字典》 already clearly touched on the question of there being no way of using an existing Chinese term to accurately translate the English word "she". He used English to introduce the word "she", "SHE, the female pronoun demonstrative, has no corresponding word in Chinese, 他 *ta*, is He, she, or it. The woman before mentioned, 该妇 kae foo [*gai fu*]." See Figure 1.1.

DOI: 10.4324/9781003359449-2

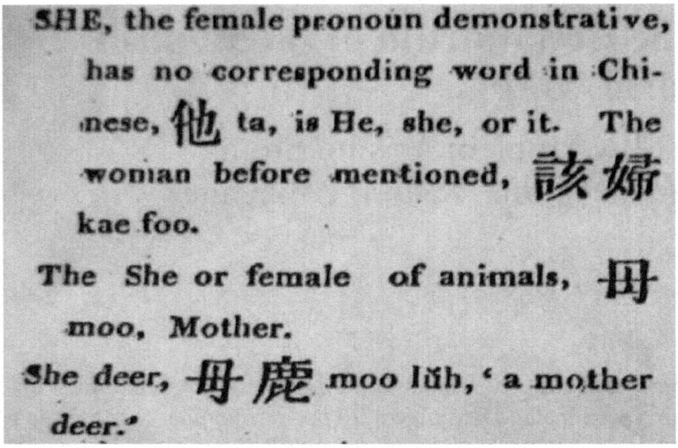

8 *The Conundrum of the English Term "She"*

> SHE, the female pronoun demonstrative, has no corresponding word in Chinese, 他 ta, is He, she, or it. The woman before mentioned, 該婦 kae foo.
>
> The She or female of animals, 母 moo, Mother.
>
> She deer, 母鹿 moo lŭh, 'a mother deer.'

Figure 1.1 The Chinese translation of the word "she", Robert Morrison, *A Dictionary of the Chinese Language*, 1822 edition, reprint from the 1996 Japanese version, Vol. 6, p. 388.

Figure 1.2 Morrison and his assistants.

In 1823 Morrison published the first Chinese book on English grammar, *A Grammar of the English Language* 《英国文语凡例传》, where he once again highlighted the fact that there was no Chinese equivalent for the English word "she". He translated the words he, she, and it respectively as 他男 (*ta nan* [male]), 他女

(*ta nü* [female]), and 他物 (*ta wu* [object]), and translated his, her, and its as 他男的 (*ta nan de* [that man's]), 他女的 (*ta nü de* [that woman's]), and 该物的 (*gai wu de* [that object's]) respectively. At the same time, he translated "I saw her" as 我见他（妇人）(*wo jian ta* [*fu ren*] [I saw that individual (woman)]); "This is his", he translated as 这个是他（男人）的 (*zhe ge shi ta* (*nan ren*) *de* [This is that individual (man)'s]); and translated "That is hers" as 那个是他（妇人）的 (*na ge shi ta* (*nü ren*) *de* [That is that individual (woman)'s]).[1] This type of parenthetical method indicating precisely the gendered value of the character *ta* (他) in a situation where there was no specific term to distinguish gender was indeed an act of necessity. In 1879, when Yang Shaoping 杨少坪, who was versed in pidgin English, encountered this type of situation in his work *A Guide to the English Language* 《英字指南》, he had no other choice (or had no alternative) but to treat it in a similar fashion.[2]

In 1864 when the English missionary Wilhelm Lobscheid 罗存德 published his *Chinese-English Grammar* 《英话文法小引》 in Hong Kong, he was probably influenced by the Cantonese or Hakka dialect of the day and thus rendered all third person signifiers as *kui* 佢. See Plate 3.

Chinese-English Grammar is a bilingual Chinese-English work especially designed for the teachers at the church's girls' schools and other elementary schools to teach English grammar. When introducing how gender was delineated in English, Lobscheid translated "gender" as *yin yang lei zi* (阴阳类字 or "terms relating to the *yin* [feminine] and *yang* [masculine] categories"). He further used the terms *nan*

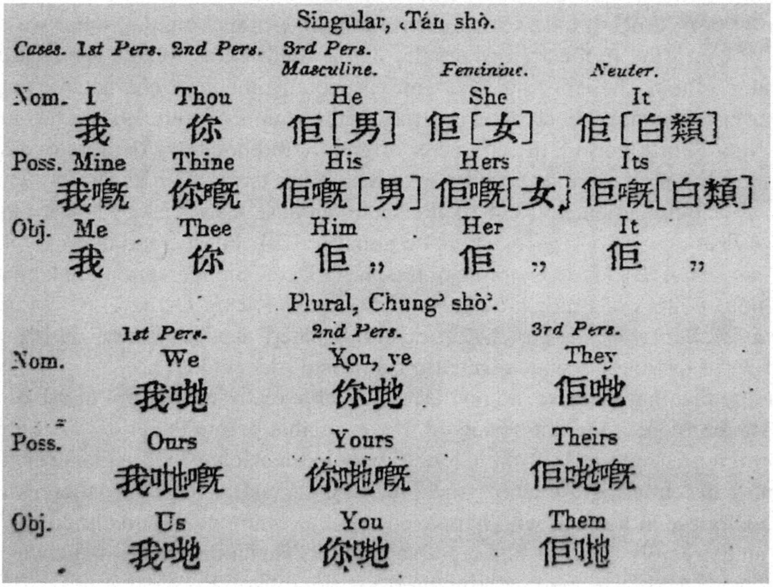

Singular, ˏTán shò.

Cases.	1st Pers.	2nd Pers.	3rd Pers. Masculine.	Feminine.	Neuter.
Nom.	I 我	Thou 你	He 佢[男]	She 佢[女]	It 佢[白類]
Poss.	Mine 我嘅	Thine 你嘅	His 佢嘅[男]	Hers 佢嘅[女]	Its 佢嘅[白類]
Obj.	Me 我	Thee 你	Him 佢 ,,	Her 佢 ,,	It 佢 ,,

Plural, Chungˀ shòˀ.

	1st Pers.	2nd Pers.	3rd Pers.
Nom.	We 我哋	You, ye 你哋	They 佢哋
Poss.	Ours 我哋嘅	Yours 你哋嘅	Theirs 佢哋嘅
Obj.	Us 我哋	You 你哋	Them 佢哋

Figure 1.3 Wilhelm Lobscheid's translation of "she", "he", and "it" in his *Chinese-English Grammar* 《英话文法小引》. See the 1864 Hong Kong edition of this work, Section 2, p. 7.

zi (男字 or "masculine term"), nü zi (女字 or "feminine term"), and bai zi (白字 or "neuter term"). Alternatively, he would use *yang lei zi* (阳类字 or "term for the masculine category"), *yin lei zi* (阴类字 or "term for the feminine category"), and *bai lei zi* (白类字 or "term for the neuter category"). At times he went further and used *nan shu* (男属 or "male category"), *nü shu* (女属 or "female category"), etc.[3] to distinguish between the masculine, feminine, and neuter. One of the relevant passages reads as follows:

> The *kui* 佢 character is translated as "he, she, it, they". And why? Foreign languages are different to Chinese. There are three types of pronouns: one is masculine (男字), one is feminine (女字), and one is neuter (白字). For example, 佢 (*qu*, he) refers to brothers; 佢 (*qu*, she) refers to sisters; 佢 (*qu*, it) refers to a child; and 佢 (*qu*, they) refers to many. So, you can see from this that the English language is more precise than Chinese.[4]

Thus, we can see that, when faced with the different renditions in English and Chinese of the third person pronoun, Lobscheid not only had no answer, but he also clearly harbored some feeling of superiority toward the English language. To him, the Chinese language was obviously not as clear and intelligible as English. This was a commonly held preconception amongst the British and Americans in China at the time, and it reflected an already long-established attitude of cultural discrimination.

Traditionally, in Chinese, apart from such characters as "*ta* 他", "*kui* 佢", "*qu* 渠" and "*bi* 彼", being used to represent the third person singular, there was also the *yi* 伊 character. In the area where the *Wu* 吴 dialect was spoken (i.e., southern Jiangsu, northern Zhejiang, and Shanghai) especially, the *yi* 伊 character was quite popular in colloquial speech. And contrary to the claims of some during the subsequent May Fourth period, the character originally did not carry definite overtones of gender differentiation, as was the case with other terms such as 他, 佢, 渠, and so on. The publication in 1874 of the Shanghainese Cao Xiang 曹骧's famous *English Primer* 《英字入门》 where he translated all "he, she and it" as *yi* 伊 and "they" as *yimen* 伊们 is an example of this. In 1875 the pioneer among independent indigenous editors of English-Chinese dictionaries, Kuang Qizhao 邝其照, in his *Integrated Dictionary* 《字典集成》 also translated "she" as "*ta* 他, *yi* 伊, *qi* 其 (referring to females)",[5] which can also stand as direct evidence.

But the fact that Chinese did not have a suitable ready-made term to use did not mean the problem could not be solved. If we say that before the mid-1870s neither the foreign missionaries nor the Chinese people themselves had an answer to the challenge of rendering the word "she", then by the end of the 1870s there was indeed a Chinese individual who happened upon a commendable methodology and made an extremely valuable and creative attempt. This individual's name was Guo Zansheng 郭赞生. He made a structured yet flexible and proactive effort to take all the terms already existing in Chinese that were capable of expressing the third person singular such as "他", "伊", and "彼", and ventured a clear demarcation and precise gendered application of the terms. Albeit, today, Guo Zansheng and his *English School Grammar* 《文法初阶》 which contained the fruits of his creativity have all but been forgotten. This is not unrelated to the fact that to this day research on the early dissemination of English and other foreign languages within China has not been afforded the attention it deserves.[6]

2   The Unique Creativity of *English School Grammar* 《文法初阶》 and Its Limitations

From the late Qing Dynasty, with the continued deepening of China's language exchange with the West, people had no choice but to vigorously create new characters (such as several chemical elements), or perhaps change some traditional applications of Chinese characters in order to express certain terms in Western languages. In 1878, when Guo Zansheng translated and published his work *English School Grammar*, on the question of confining the use of the traditional *yi* 伊 character to represent the female gender, he took an extremely creative step.

In this work he not only repeatedly and consciously employed *yi* 伊 and *ta* 他 to define gender, but he also clearly translated "he, him" as *ta* 他; translated "she, her" as *yi* 伊; translated "it" as *bi* 彼; and translated "his, her, its" as *ta de* 他的, *yi de* 伊的, and *bi de* 彼的. What is more, when translating certain specific sentences that included "she" and "he", he was at pains to distinguish between the two, for example, "He is in the garden, but she is in school" he translated as *"ta* (他) . . ., but *yi* (伊) . . .", etc.[7] From the following translated section and the two plates which I have photographed, we can see even more clearly the consciousness of the translator:

> *Man* means HE (*ta* 他) and is of the masculine gender; *Woman* means SHE (*yi* 伊) and is of the feminine gender; *Boy* means HE (*ta* 他) and is masculine; and *Girl* means SHE (*yi* 伊) and is feminine.[8]

In this way, Guo Zansheng became the first Chinese scholar to take certain characters which originally carried no gender differentiation and imbued them with meaning to define gender. Here he boldly and manifestly attributed femininity to the character *yi* 伊 and allowed *ta* 他 to express masculinity. Later history confirms that this was an inspired choice on the part of Mr Guo, as well as being extremely imaginative.

But who was Guo Zansheng? I am restricted in my knowledge of him and am only aware that he was also known as Guo Luogui 郭罗贵; that he was a native of Guangzhou (or Yangcheng 羊城); that he proof-read Tan Daxuan's 谭达轩 *English-Chinese Dictionary* 《英汉字典》; and that he published the Chinese-English bilingual business reference work *Trade Essentials* 《通商须知》 in 1899. The "Postscript" to *Trade Essentials* described him thus, "Mr Guo Zansheng was conversant with both Chinese and Western literature and an excellent writer. He studied in an English school for many years and also had a long career in the Customs Department in Guangdong".[9] From the English works that he had edited and compiled, it is obvious that Mr Guo indeed had a good command of

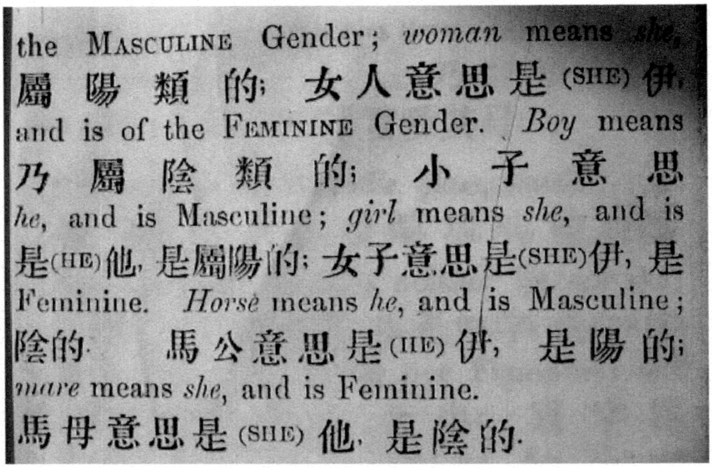

12 *The Conundrum of the English Term "She"*

> the MASCULINE Gender; *woman* means *she*,
> 屬 陽 類 的; 女人意思是 (SHE) 伊,
> and is of the FEMININE Gender. *Boy* means
> 乃 屬 陰 類 的; 小 子 意 思
> *he*, and is Masculine; *girl* means *she*, and is
> 是 (HE) 他, 是屬陽的; 女子意思是 (SHE) 伊, 是
> Feminine. *Horse* means *he*, and is Masculine;
> 陰的. 馬公意思是 (HE) 伊, 是 陽 的;
> *mare* means *she*, and is Feminine.
> 馬母意思是 (SHE) 他, 是 陰 的.

Figure 1.4 English School Grammar 《文法初阶》 clearly translates "she", "he", and "it" as *ta* 他, *yi* 伊, and *bi* 彼 in order to address gender distinction. But he reverses the terms when he applies them to animals. From the context, it appears that this is but a slip of the pen.

English. The English original of *English School Grammar* was an inspirational volume aimed at introducing English children to their language, and there is one trait that stands out in Guo Zansheng's translation of the work, namely that he adopted a rigorous comparative technique of the two languages and paid the utmost attention to basic concepts of grammar and terminology and applied this to his translation. He also was at great pains not to allow those terms which were difficult to translate to be glossed over and treated ambiguously. This is why he was able to creatively translate the terms "he, she, and it". In his translation work, Guo Zansheng also frequently experimented with the practice of writing from left to right and was the first Chinese writer to use Western style punctuation. This predates the accepted scholarly wisdom that Yan Fu's 严复 1904 *English Grammar Explained* 《英文汉诂》 was the "earliest experimentation" in this area by a full 36 years![10]

What is worth noting is that *English School Grammar* was published in Hong Kong and that the author was not actually a member of the *Wu* dialectical community. It is therefore obvious that the area mentioned previously that used the *yi* 伊 character was unquestionably much broader than scholars have previously imagined.[11]

Based on a relatively accurate recognition of the gender distinction in the English language, Guo Zansheng translated "gender" as "intrinsic gender" (生性) or "*yin* or *yang*" and "male or female classification" (男女分类), but he had not yet clearly conveyed the meaning of the "neuter or neutral gender". How we now translate "gender" (性别) is actually the Japanese translation and is reasonably accurate. After the entry "SHE 伊", Guo Zansheng specifically clarifies that this refers to the "female" (女子), which he adds in brackets,[12] because he knows all too well that the use of the character *yi* 伊 to refer exclusively to the female sex was still just a convention that he had personally adopted. In the same work, while he similarly indicated in many instances this self-awareness, he was still not able to maintain this attitude throughout. In some places where he was not so thorough, he still uses the character *ta* 他 to translate the word "she", so we can see that even Mr Guo himself was not yet able to establish conclusively the conditions under which he should use either of the terms. This is completely understandable given the linguistic context of the Chinese language at the time.

There is currently a lack of textual evidence to determine one way or the other whether Guo Zansheng's approach influenced the subsequent advocacy of some in the May Fourth period for the use of *yi* 伊 to translate the word "she", a topic that will be discussed in more detail later. However, the fact that in the Late Qing and around the May Fourth period there were multiple people using the *yi* 伊 character simultaneously to represent the feminine third person singular does at least show that in the traditional Chinese language, the character *yi* 伊 did have the potential to correspond to the word "she".

So far, we have used the exclusive example of English to examine how Chinese people of the late Qing as well as foreigners in China approached the question of representing the feminine third person singular in Chinese. In the late Qing, of all the Western languages, English was the language that had the greatest influence on the Chinese language. Apart from English, while other Western languages did to varying degrees also present similar issues in translation, it appears that they failed to have any noticeable effect. I have indeed done my best to appraise myself of the situation regarding other Western languages, but the results have been scant.

Take French, for example: at the time several important French-Chinese dictionaries were published. However, in introducing the feminine third person singular "*elle*", none of them indicated definitively that the Chinese language lacked a precise linguistic counterpart.[13] In fact it was not until 1922 when the Commercial Press published the *Model French-Chinese Dictionary* 《模范法华辞典》 edited by Xiao Ziqin 萧子琴 et al. that "*elle*" was variously translated as *bi* 彼, *ta* 他 (indicating the female gender), or *ta* 她,[14] and by this time the character *ta* 她 had already been invented to represent the feminine third person singular and had achieved a certain amount of currency.

Notes

1 Morrison, Robert, *A Grammar of the English Language*, Macau, 1823, pp. 64–66. See Huang, Xingtao 黄兴涛, "The First Chinese-English Work on English Grammar – *A Grammar of the English Language*" 《第一部中英文对照的英语文法书 –〈英国文语凡例传〉》, carried in *Wen Shi Zhi Shi* 《文史知识》, 2006 (3).
2 Yang, Shaoping 杨少坪, *A Guide to the English Language* 《英字指南》, Vol. 6, Shanghai: Fifth year of the Guangxu era (1879), pp. 3–5.
3 Lobscheid, Wilhelm 罗存德, *Chinese-English Grammar* 《英话文法小引》, Hong Kong, 1864. Part 1, pp. 15–16, 31–32; Part 2, p. 7.

4 Lobscheid, Wilhelm 罗存德, *Chinese-English Grammar* 《英话文法小引》, Hong Kong, 1864. Part 1, pp. 15–16. The work *Chinese-English Grammar* has been extremely difficult to source in mainland China and I am eternally grateful to Mr Shen Guowei 沈国威 for providing a facsimile copy.
5 Kuang, Qizhao邝其照 (ed.), *An Integrated Dictionary* 《字典集成》, Hong Kong, 1875, p. 281.
6 Huang, Xingtao 黄兴涛, "*'Mandarin Grammar' and 'English School Grammar' (The Earliest Dissemination of a Knowledge of English Grammar in the Late Qing Dynasty)*" Part II 《〈文学书官话〉与"文法初阶"（晚清英文语法知识的最早传播）》（之二）, carried in *Wen Shi Zhi Shi* 《文史知识》, 2006 (4).
7 Guo, Zansheng 郭赞生 (trans.), *English School Grammar* 《文法初阶》, Hong Kong: Fourth Year of the Guangxu Era (1878), pp. 40, 90, 48.
8 Guo, Zansheng 郭赞生 (trans.), *English School Grammar* 《文法初阶》, Hong Kong: Fourth year of the Guangxu era, 1878, pp. 63–64.
9 See Ma, Huabao's 马华宝, *Postscript* to *Trade Essentials* 《通商须知》, typeset using movable type by the Wenyutang Bookstore 文裕堂书局, Hong Kong, 1899. The cover of the work is signed Guo Luogui 郭罗贵 while the author's preface is signed Guo Zansheng 郭赞生, otherwise known as a native of "Panyu in South China 岭南番禺".
10 Huang, Xingtao 黄兴涛, "*'Mandarin Grammar' and 'English School Grammar' (The Earliest Dissemination of a Knowledge of English Grammar in the Late Qing Dynasty)*" Part II 《〈文学书官话〉与〈文法初阶〉（晚清英文语法知识的最早传播）》（之二）, carried in *Wen Shi Zhi Shi* 《文史知识》, 2006 (4).
11 In *A Portuguese Chinese Dictionary* 《葡汉辞典》 which was probably completed in 1583–1588 and possibly co-edited by Michele Ruggieri 罗明坚 and Matteo Ricci 利玛窦, the parallel use of *ta* 他 and *yi* 伊 had already made an appearance – for example, in the translation of *Terrispeito* as "respect him (*ta* 他) or envy her (*yi* 伊)". See the section in the following work which displays original dictionary text: Wei, Ruowang 魏若望 (Editor in Chief), arranged and published by the National Library of Portugal and the Ricci Institute for Chinese-Western Cultural History et al., *A Portuguese Chinese Dictionary* 《葡汉辞典》, 2001, p. 148. My thanks to Mr Zhang Xiping 张西平 for providing me with a facsimile copy of this dictionary.
12 Guo, Zansheng 郭赞生译 (trans.), *English School Grammar* 《文法初阶》, Hong Kong: Fourth year of the Guangxu era, 1878, p. 53.
13 Professor of Chemistry at the Tong Wen Guan, Beijing, A. A. Billequin (ed.), *Dictionnaire Francais-Chinois* 《汉法合璧字典》, Beijing: Beitang Publishing House, 1891 translates "elle" as "他，其，伊，渠". See p. 213 of the work. In addition, one of the three great European translators, the French Jesuit missionary Séraphin Couvreur in 1890 in his *Dictionnaire Chinois-Francais* 《汉法字典》, published in 1890 by the Hejianfu 河间府 translates "*ta* 他" as "il, elle, lui, autre". See p. 711 of the work. The *New French-Chinese Dictionary* edited and translated by Lu Bohong 陆伯鸿 et al. and published by the Commercial Press in 1914 translates "elle" as "*ta* 他，*bi* 彼". See p. 174 of the dictionary. Besides these, there are several dictionaries that treat the terms in a similar fashion. My thanks to Han Hua 韩华 from the Peking Library for his relevant assistance regarding materials in French.
14 Xiao, Ziqin 萧子琴 et al. (eds.), *Model French-Chinese Dictionary* 《模范法华辞典》, Shanghai: Commercial Press, 1922, p. 229.

2 The Emergence of the Character *Ta* 她, plus *Ta'nü* 他女 and *Ta/To* 牠

The *New Youth* 《新青年》 Editorial Group's Early Discussions and the Experimentation Which It Engendered

During the time of the May Fourth culture movement, the editors and writers for the *New Youth* 《新青年》 magazine, who were passionate about introducing the new international literature to China, whilst adopting an intense attitude of reflection and criticism of China's traditional culture, exhibited an indomitable positive attitude and courageous and creative spirit in confronting the question of how to deal with the gender distinction of the third person in the West and how to translate the word "she". The *ta* 她 character was born out of precisely this need to express the feminine third person singular in Chinese.

1 The Proposal of the *Ta* 她 Character and the Early Deployment of *Ta'nü* 他女

Beginning in 1917, such members of the *New Youth* editorial group as Liu Bannong 刘半农 and Zhou Zuoren 周作人 had already begun to discuss the question of translating the word "she" and in the process, Liu Bannong was first to suggest that the character *ta* 她 be invented. However, while before 1920 he did entertain this unconventional idea, he had yet to express his opinion unequivocally in printed form. I have to this day failed to identify any clear proof of him using the character *ta* 她 in any prior formal context. At the beginning of 1920, in his article "On the Question of the Character *Ta* 她" 《"她"字问题》, Liu Bannong himself declared:

> When I originally suggested that we create a character *ta* 她, I myself did not publish my idea. It was only in the works of Mr Zhou Zuoren that it was raised. And because I personally still had some reservations as to the pronunciation of the character, I very rarely used it (it seems I might still have not used it. I can't really recall).[1]

Liu Bannong was never one to hide the truth or afraid to take responsibility, so his recollection at the time deserves to be taken seriously by us today. Some say that Liu Bannong had already, in 1917, in such works as *The Soul of the Violin* 《琴魂》, tried to use the *ta* 她 character, but to my mind, this type of statement I fear should largely be classified as erroneous or misinformed.[2]

DOI: 10.4324/9781003359449-3

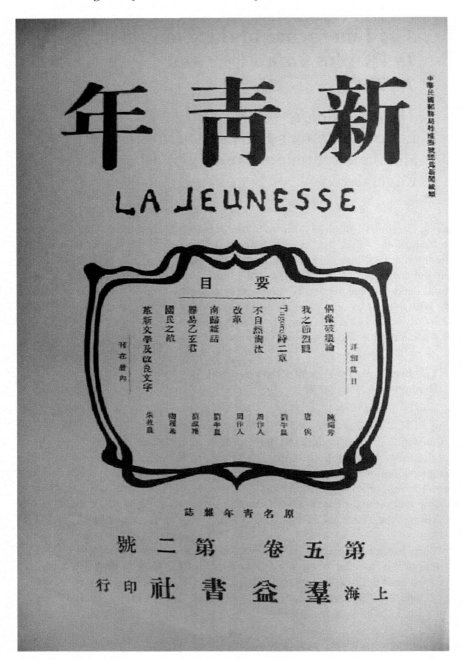

Figure 2.1 Cover of *New Youth*, Vol. 5, No. 2, 1918.

In fact, the first to officially raise and discuss this question should be Zhou Zuoren. On August 15, 1918, Mr Zhou published his translated work "Reform" 《改革》 in *New Youth* (the original author was the famous Swedish playwright August Strindberg), which carried two paragraphs of explanation, the second of which reads:

> The Chinese third person pronoun has no gender distinction, which is quite inconvenient. [Liu] Bannong has proposed the creation of the character *ta* 她 to be used in contrast to the character *ta* 他 which was an excellent idea. The Japanese use *Kanojo* 彼女 and *Kare* 彼 to deal with this situation, but this too is a recent invention. Initially this also felt a little wooden, but over time it seems OK. My only fear at the moment is that a *nü* 女 radical added to a *ye* 也 character is not in the printer's typesetting kit and if we were to have to cast a goodly number of these characters then it might be difficult, so I have not been able to decide to use it. I have therefore come up with a temporary solution and that is to use the *ta* 他 character followed up with a subscript *nü* 女 character. This matter needs to be considered at length.[3]

Here Zhou Zuoren not only reveals to the world for the first time Liu Bannong's suggestion of creating a new character *ta* 她, but that he is also, theoretically at least, in basic agreement. It is only that in the application of the concept, printing would pose a problem, and so he emulated the Japanese practice and adopted the temporary solution of adding a *nü* 女 character after the *ta* 他 character. Thus, when Liu Bannong mentions that Zhou Zuoren raised the question, there is no doubt that he is referring to the work "Reform".

In several issues of *New Youth* following August 1918, whenever Zhou Zuoren needed to translate the feminine third person singular, he always used *ta'nü* 他女. For example, in his translation of Hans Christian Andersen's *The Little Match Girl* or Chekhov's *The Darling*,[4] he always adopted this practice. This was not unlike Morrison's earlier approach in his *A Grammar of the English Language* mentioned previously. However, *The Little Match Girl* was a Danish story and *The Darling* was Russian, so it is obvious that he did not only have his sights set on the English word "she" but rather all the feminine third person singular pronouns in other Western languages as well.

Nowadays, we may find the cumbersome *ta'nü* 他女 that Zhou Zuoren consistently used in his translations of foreign fiction appears and reads awkwardly. One could also imagine how it would have grated with readers of the day: no matter whether a supporter or a critic of the practice, there is no doubt that all readers must have been left with an indelible impression. As part of the editorial group of *New Youth*, Hu Shi 胡适 and Qian Xuantong 钱玄同 were the first to come out publicly and reflect on this situation. Hu Shi published consecutively his translation of Guy de Maupassant's short story "A Parricide" 《弑父之儿》 in Issues 6 and 7 of *Weekly Critic* 《每周评论》 on January 26 and February 2, 1919, in which, apart from using the character *ta* 他, he also used the expression "that woman/girl" 那女的 as well. At the end of the translation, he adds a note, saying, "I do not

18 *The Emergence of the Character Ta* 她, *plus Ta'nü* 他女 *and Ta/To* 妳

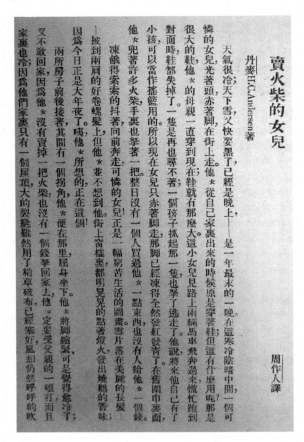

Figure 2.2 Zhou Zuoren's relatively early use of ta'nü 他女 as published in his translation of *The Little Match Girl* in January-February 1919.

approve of using the *ta* 他 character followed by the nü 女 character in subscript, so I have not used it in this item."[5] Unfortunately Hu Shi failed to mention exactly why he opposed this practice. In response to Hu Shi's declaration, Liu Bannong in his subsequent essay "On the Question of the Character *Ta* 她" 《"她"字问题》 refers obliquely to it, "If we follow Hu Shi's practice of using 'that woman/girl' in place of 'she' (see *Weekly Critic*, I am not sure which issue), . . . while the meaning might be correct, the tonal sensitivity, the linguistic dexterity and the complexity of the task all leave something to be desired."

However, at the time Zhou Zuoren's creativity also had its supporters. Whilst leafing through another important magazine of the New Culture movement, *The Renaissance* 《新潮》, I was amused to discover the father of modern Chinese children's tales, grand novelist and member of the The Renaissance Society 新潮社 Ye Shaojun 叶绍钧 (Ye Shengtao 叶圣陶) had been an enthusiastic practitioner of *ta'nü* 他女. He not only led the way in using *ta'nü* 他女 in his articles on "women's liberation" where women were struggling for recognition, but he may be the first author to use *ta'nü* 他女 in a published piece of fiction (before this Zhou Zuoren had mainly used the expression in his translations). On February 1, March 1, and May 1, 1919, Ye Shaojun published consecutively "On the Dignity of Women" 《女子人格问题》 as well as the short stories "Is this a Person Too?" 《这也是一个人?》 and "Spring Excursion" 《春游》 in the aforementioned magazine in which he followed Zhou Zuoren by using *ta'nü* 他女 to represent the feminine third person pronoun.

From "On the Dignity of Women" 《女子人格问题》 we can clearly see Ye Shaojun's obvious support for women in their struggle for independence and equal rights with men. In other words, for Mr Ye the expression *ta'nü* is a symbol of feminine independence and equality with men. The article stresses, "Dignity is a spirit which any individual within a group should be possessed of", and that "the spirit of a robust and independent member of any group" is, without doubt, a spirit that women, like men, should be possessed of. Expanding on this, the author strenuously criticises male-dominated society for ravaging and ruining women's dignity and denounces "The three cardinal guides and the five constant virtues" (纲常名教) as well as "The Three Obediences and Four Virtues" (三从四德) for their insistence on so-called "chastity and virtue" (贞操节烈). As a male writer, the author further displays a quite rare spirit of self-criticism. The article attacks the men of this male-dominated society who were oppressing women in the following terms:

> Men only have two types of principles (主义) in their relationship with women. One is to call them all kinds of wonderful names, leading them to be duped and to abandon their (*ta'nü* 他女) individual dignity. This is called

Figure 2.3 Responding to Zhou Zuoren's suggestion, the New Literature writer Ye Shaojun (Ye Shengtao) is the first to employ the term ta'nü 他女 in a work of fiction.

"enticement". The other is when a man sees a woman as inferior to himself, when he despises her (ta'nü 他女) and fails to accept that she (ta'nü 他女) is as equally "human" (ren 人) as himself and therefore fails to recognise her (ta'nü 他女) dignity. This is called "chauvinism".

The two short stories "Is This a Person Too?" and "Spring Excursion" clearly have as their main theme the revelation of the cruel fate of women in contemporary China and an advocacy for female independence and equality with men. The first work depicts a tragic female figure who is forced to act as a beast of burden in the household of her husband, regularly beaten and scolded, with no dignity or respect. Her child dies prematurely and her husband's family berate her for her recalcitrance. She escapes to work as a servant in the city but she is discovered and dragged back. Her husband dies of an illness and she is eventually sold off to defray the husband's funerary expenses.[6] This is quite similar to the later image of Lu Xun's 鲁迅 Sister Xianglin 祥林嫂. "Spring Excursion" is less than a thousand characters in length, yet manages some 31 occurrences of ta'nü 他女. It is a story that chronicles the experience of a woman totally subject to her husband's turns of mood and who eventually, during a spring excursion, experiences for the first time a genuine feeling of personal reality, "She (ta'nü 他女) simply felt that she had long melded with the scenery, nature, vivacity and nobility that surrounded her."[7] The concealed meaning of the author was that a woman only had to walk out of that constricted circle of the home in order to attain true independence. Not only would she enter the domain of "nature", but she could also attain a previously unimagined independence, and as a consequence she would reduce her own state of dependence.

Ye Shaojun's aforementioned unique and ideologically elucidatory literary practice leads us to understand how the expression ta'nü 他女, at its birth in fact already bore the solemn and enlightened May Fourth period mission of "women's liberation".

What needs to be explained is that when "Spring Excursion" and other items were included in Ye Shaojun's collection of short stories entitled "Barriers" 《隔膜》, all occurrences of the expression ta'nü 他女 had been converted to the character yi 伊, and so now-a-days, whoever reads his Collected Works or Complete Works is unaware of the fact that he had enthusiastically used the expression ta'nü 他女 in the past (it is my humble belief that any editor of Collected Works – and especially Complete Works – worth his/her salt should check the edition of any article or work included in the collection and ideally use the original as his/her source). Additionally, it is possible that when the construct ta'nü 他女 appeared, it gave people an excessively strange feeling or that the typesetters were not willing or perhaps not accustomed to such special treatment and so on some occasions in the relevant work the nü 女 character in the ta'nü 他女 construct was left out or consciously omitted. For example, in the work "Is This a Person Too?", apart from the first ta'nü 他女 in the work, all subsequent occurrences were mistakenly rendered as ta 他. This, from a practical point of

The Emergence of the Character Ta 她, *plus Ta'nü* 他女 *and Ta/To* 牠

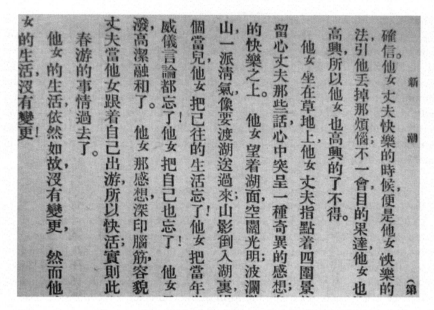

Figure 2.4 A section of Ye Shaojun's "Spring Excursion" 《春游》 where he employs the term "*ta'nü*" 他女.

view, would appear to indicate that the character *ta'nü* 他女 did not have a very reassuring future.[8]

In early 1920, Guo Moruo 郭沫若 also specifically employed a similar expression, namely *ta (nü)* 他 (女). For example, on January 26 of that year in the short story "Mouse Plague" 《鼠灾》, published in the supplement *Light of Learning* 《学灯》 to *The China Times* 《时事新报》, Guo Moruo audaciously employed the expression *ta (nü)* 他 (女) on multiple occasions, leaving a deep impression on the readers. Having read it, readers could easily come to the strong realisation that, from the context of his linguistic construction, it was absolutely necessary to come up with an appropriate character to represent the feminine third person in order to differentiate it from the masculine.[9]

2 Qian Xuantong 钱玄同, Zhou Zuoren 周作人 and the Initial Discussion around the Translation of the Word "She"

On the question of the attention of people at large being drawn to the character *ta* 她, February 15, 1919 is a date worthy of closer attention. On this day, the magazine *New Youth* 《新青年》, which had drawn the avid attention of the new guard at the time, published Qian Xuantong and Zhou Zuoren's article

"The Discussion over the Translation of the English 'She'" 《英文"she"字译法之商榷》, which was the first to publicly discuss the topic. In the article, Qian Xuantong suggests three methods of translating the word: one was to translate it like Zhou Zuoren did in imitating the Japanese translation of *Kanojo* 彼女, namely translating it using the two characters *ta'nü* 他女 and retaining the character *ta* 他 to represent the masculine third person pronoun. The second method was to follow Liu Bannong's lead and create a new character. However, he thought that the *ta* 她 character that Liu Bannong had constructed was "not ideal" and therefore suggested creating a character *ta/to* "牠" instead. Qian Xuantong's argument was:

> If the *ye* 也 element that is on the right-hand side of this (*ta*) 她 character is used to represent the third person, then according to Xu Shuzhong's 许叔重 (Xu Shen's 许慎 courtesy name) explanation of its form, he would say, "Use the [feminine] radical *nü* '女' and adopt this element from the *ta* 他 character but maintain the original pronunciation *ta*." I think that if we are to follow this line of thinking, wouldn't it be better to create a character *ta/to* 牠? The character *ta* 他 was traditionally written as *ta* 它, so we could use "它" to replace "他". Then to explain the form of the character, we could say, "Use *nü* 女 with its inherent meaning plus *ta* 它 with its meaning; the character *ta* 它 was the original form of *ta* 他, so we can also use the *ta* 它 pronunciation." In this way, the new character will fully incorporate the meaning of both *ta* 他 and *nü* 女.

The third method was, to their mind, the most logical method, "If Chinese doesn't have an appropriate character, then just take the foreign word and use it; there is no necessity to create a new character, just simply use the [English] word *she*." However, if this method was adopted, then the *ta* 他 character, which originally encompassed the three genders of masculine, feminine, and neuter, with the feminine removed from its scope, its meaning would narrow and the remaining masculine and neuter would be expressed using the *ta* 他 character. However, Liu Bannong felt this was "also not all that satisfactory". He therefore went further to suggest that we go for broke and simply adopt the three English words *he*, *she*, and *it* into the Chinese language and be done with it, or, rather than English, might not the *li*, *si*, and *gi* of Esperanto be even more appropriate?

As to Qian Xuantong's personal assessment of the previous three methods, he felt that the first was "not all that appropriate" because the meaning of the Japanese *Kanojo* 彼女 was "*that* female" and that while linguistically it might be without fault, nevertheless, if in Chinese it was rendered as the two characters *ta'nü* 他女, then it would be "ungainly" and readers would have trouble dealing with it. Should it actually be read with the same sound as *ta* 他? Or should *ta'nü* 他女 be read as two separate characters? As for the second method, Qian Xuantong felt that it was "serviceable", but at the same time he was concerned that each time several *ta/to* "牠" characters would have to be specially cast and "in practice, this might present a problem – it is hard to know". What is more, at the time Qian, Zhou and

The Emergence of the Character Ta 她, plus Ta'nü 他女 and Ta/To 牠 23

Figure 2.5 The linguist Qian Xuantong who was the first to engage in the discussion of the question of the character *ta* 她.

others were obsessed with getting rid of Chinese characters because they felt that "Chinese characters were not really an appropriate medium for use and that to go and construct new ones would appear to be a futile exercise." At the time, he was therefore inclined towards the third option, feeling that there was "no obstacle whatsoever" to adopting it, even arguing that while even more people would not be able to understand it, still "that should not be a bother." In any case, the creation of a new character would only be useful to "youthful students" and not to "illiterates" or "kitchen maids and farmhands". "From now on, students who genuinely seek learning will undoubtedly all be able to understand foreign languages". His biased and improper contemptuous attitude towards the lower classes and despising of the traditional language is clear for all to see.

In response to Qian Xuantong's February 8, 1919 interrogatory letter, Zhou Zuoren responded some five days later. He first explained in detail his actual thinking regarding his previous use of the construct *ta'nü* 他女. As it happens, his motivation for creating this strange character which "incorporated the feminine, conformed to the third person, but retained the sound *ta*" was three-fold:

> On the one hand it was important that it be serviceable in performing translation, while on the other the convenience of the printery needed to be considered. Finally, it must be a method whereby the Chinese reader would

pronounce the word as *ta* 他 while at the same time their mind would register the female *nü* 女 concept, which in combination would form a pronoun for the female third person.

He confirmed that the two characters *ta'nü* 他女 should be pronounced in the same manner as the *ta* 他 character, and that the *nü* 女 character here should be seen for the moment as an unspoken symbol. At the same time, he also clearly indicated that he himself was not completely satisfied with the innovation, mainly because:

It is convenient as a visual character but not as an audible one; if one were to pronounce the character and not view it, then it would not be understood. This is indeed one of its drawbacks. But as to the ungainly form of the character, this is secondary.

Following on from this, whilst assessing Qian Xuantong's three earlier suggested methodologies, Zhou Zuoren again comprehensively rejected his own methodology, acknowledging that the *ta'nü* 他女 approach was "impractical". "Not only is it not a proper word, but it in fact runs contrary to the original meaning of the pronoun". He pointed out that the Chinese classics carried such expressions as "the young man . . . something or other" or "the female . . . something or other". But the "young man" and "female" here were both used as nouns, so they could not be used as pronouns. "If a noun can double as a pronoun, what use would we have for pronouns?" Carrying on from this, he "thought of the Japanese *Kanojo* 彼女, but that wasn't particularly appropriate either." In fact, this equates to rejecting the previously mentioned methodology that Hu Shi had already adopted. Thus, it must be said that Zhou Zuoren had truly advanced awareness of the question considerably.[10]

Zhou Zuoren in fact did not approve of importing either the English word "she" or the relevant related words from Esperanto. Despite the fact that, at the time, he, like Liu Bannong, was enthusiastic about phonetic notation and reform of the national language, to the point of hoping that China might ultimately adopt Esperanto, nevertheless he recognised that "Until the new edifice is constructed, the occupants of the old dwelling must continue to patch it up as best they can" and that it was necessary to learn from abroad in some critical aspects. But if such building bricks as pronouns were adopted comprehensively from abroad, then it would be a mammoth task, so he proposed the simpler option of first inventing a few new "strange characters" from within the scope of the Chinese language. At the same time, Mr Zhou stressed that this type of pronoun would "not only be used in translation, but it would also be indispensable to 'kitchen maids and farmhands' when they were writing letters or reading". In sum, he indicated that while Liu Bannong's advocacy for the pronoun *ta* 她 which he had created, along with the character *ta/to* 佗 which Qian Xuantong promoted, did have merit, nevertheless he also recognised that in terms of pronunciation, because neither of them were distinguishable from the character *ta* 他, then neither of them could be said to be ideal. Weighing up the situation, would it not be preferable to mandate the exclusive use of the original native Chinese expression indicative of the third person, namely the character *yi* 伊? Zhou Zuoren argued:

> Since I have split up the character *ta* 她 and written it as *ta'nü* 他女, if we were to use this character, then there should be no argument. But if as you say we create a character *ta/to* 牠, the philological justification would be even stronger, and it would also have my strong support. But this is still the visual character; it still falls short of the goal. Therefore, it must be assigned a sound that is different to the *ta* 他 character for it to be satisfactory. The day before yesterday you said to me that one approach would be for 他 to be pronounced *ta*, and for 牠 to be pronounced *to*. But then I thought of the character *yi* 伊 in the classics, which, apart from names like Yi Yin (伊尹) or Sun Hongyi (孙洪伊), is very rarely used, and dialectically still carries quite a number of heritage pronunciations, why then don't we simply take this character *yi* 伊 and decide to use it for the third person feminine pronoun? We would then not have to ask the printery to cast another symbol and we could distinguish it from the sound of the character *ta* 他. It would be killing two birds with the one stone!

Zhou Zuoren's view met with Qian Xuantong's instant and enthusiastic approval. In his letter in reply the following day, Mr Qian added several other reasons why the *ta/to* 牠 and *ta* 她 characters should be abandoned and the *yi* 伊 character exclusively employed:

> Thinking more deeply about creating a *ta/to* 牠 or *ta* 她 character, and pronouncing them with the classical pronunciation *tuo* 拖, this is not ideal. For one reason, we would be advocating putting limits on a Chinese character while at the same time we would be adding a newly created Chinese character. I just feel uneasy about this. Secondly, if we were to create a new character out of older ones yet pronounce the new character according to the old custom, isn't that a bit pedantic? Third: if we insist on forging a new character then I fear the printery may give us grief. If we are to avoid these three issues, then it is best just to use the *yi* 伊 character.... If in our written work we were to adopt the use of the character *ta* 他 for the masculine and *yi* 伊 for the feminine, etc., then when this gradually becomes a habit, I feel that they would eventually cease being used interchangeably. I am therefore much in favour of employing the *yi* 伊 character.[11]

As mentioned previously by the late Qing, some had already adopted the use of *yi* 伊 to translate the word "she". However, after the appearance of the character *ta* 她, the conscious selection of *yi* 伊, because it differed in pronunciation from *ta* 他, and the rejection of *ta* 她 confirmed that *ta* 他 should be reserved for the exclusive use of the masculine third person. Moreover, its use in literary circles both before and after May Fourth was extremely influential, and in this it cannot be denied that Zhou Zuoren and Qian Xuantong were pioneers. Still, the discussion around the character *ta* 她 did not cease despite the consensus temporarily achieved by these two pioneers. Qian and Zhou's particular fondness for *yi* 伊 had one year later momentarily inspired even more writers and scholars, however the ultimate conclusion of history did not accord with the will and logic of dismissing *ta* 她 and embracing *yi* 伊.

Notes

1 Liu, Bannong 刘半农, "On the Question of the Character *Ta* 她" 《"她"字问题》, originally carried in *Light of Learning* 《学灯》, 1920 Issue 8, and reprinted in *New Man* 《新人》, No. 6.
2 Some articles such as Meng, Shuhong 蒙树宏, "On '*Ta* 她'" 《说"她"》, carried in *Lexicographical studies* 《辞书研究》, 1981 (4); Di, Hua 翟华, *Western Men and Women Are Different* 《西式男女有别》, carried in *Youth Reference* 《青年参考》, May 28 1999 ; Xiao, Yang 肖杨, *She: The Most Important Word of the 21st Century* 《她：21世纪最重要的一个字》 (carried in *Nanfang Daily* 《南方日报》, January 10 2001) and others all state that Liu Bannong used the *ta* 她 character that he had invented in his 1917 translation of the British play *The Soul of the Violin* 《琴魂》 (erroneously referred to as *Meng Hun* 《梦魂》). So, I have inspected the original text of the earliest publication of *The Soul of the Violin* 《琴魂》 in *New Youth* 《新青年》 in 1917 and *ta* 他 is used in all the relevant places. It is therefore obvious that this statement is incorrect. I assume that the mistake stems from *Essays of [Liu] Bannong* 《半农杂文》 Volume 1 published in June 1934 by the Xingyuntang 星云堂 Bookstore in which not only were all instances of *ta* 他 changed to the character *ta* 她, but the *ta* 它 character also appears even though it was not included in the original text. The same thing occurs in other articles of his which were published after 1917, despite the fact that the publication date of the articles is included at the end of each work without change. This easily gives rise to misunderstanding. Apart from the fact that the character *ta* 她 was already in wide circulation at the time, the reason why Liu Bannong dealt with it in this manner in 1934 could be that after 1917 he already had a mind to propose the *ta* 她 character. So, from this we can see that in researching new terms, questions of edition and publication date are important elements that cannot be ignored.
3 Zhou, Zuoren trans., "Reform" 《改革》, carried in *New Youth* 《新青年》, Vol. 5, Issue 2.
4 The two articles were carried separately in *New Youth* 《新青年》, Vol. 6, Issue 1 (January 15, 1919) and *New Youth* 《新青年》, Vol. 6, Issue 2 (February 15, 1919) respectively. When *Light of Learning* 《学灯》 republished *Little Match Girl* 《卖火柴的女儿》 on March 21, 1919, after its original publication in *New Youth* 《新青年》, *ta'nü* 他女 had been changed to the character *ta* 他.
5 When Zhou Zuoren's 周作人 "Reform" 《改革》 was included in 1920 in *Fragments* 《点滴》 (compiled and translated by Zhou Zuoren 周作人 and published by Xinchao Press in its August 1920 first edition as the third in the series *The Renaissance Collection* 《新潮丛书》), the text explaining the character *ta* 她 was excised and *ta'nü* 他女 was substituted with the character *yi* 伊. In 1928 when "Reform" 《改革》 was included in Zhou Zuoren's collected translation works under the title *The Empty Drum* 《空大鼓》, the explanation for the character *ta* 她 was similarly omitted. In 1919 when Hu Shi's 胡适 *A Parricide* 《弑父之儿》 was included in *Short Stories* (Volume I) (first edition October 1919 by the East Asia Library) the margin notes concerning *ta'nü* 他女 were also omitted. Mr Zhu Jinshun 朱金顺 especially wrote *"Two Historical Items Relating to the Creation of the Character 'Ta* 她 *(she)'"* 《有关"她"字创造的两件史料》 [carried in *Green Earth* 《绿土》, 1999 (38)] to make the above historical facts public so as "not to have the relevant documents obliterated by history".

The Emergence of the Character Ta 她*, plus Ta'nü* 他女 *and Ta/To* 牠   27

6   Ye, Shaojun 叶绍钧 (Shengtao 圣陶), "Is This a Person Too?" 《这也是一个人？》, carried in *The Renaissance* 《新潮》 on March 1, 1919, in Vol. 1, Issue 3.
7   Ye, Shaojun 叶绍钧, "Spring Excursion" 《春游》, carried in *The Renaissance* 《新潮》 on May 1, 1919, in Vol. 1, Issue 5.
8   In Ye, Shaojun's 叶绍钧 "Is This a Person Too?" 《这也是一个人？》, the opening sentence reads: "She (他女) was born to a rural household and did not have the fortune to 'call maids and serving girls' or to 'apply face powder and lipstick'". However, apart from this sentence, whenever the feminine third person singular is encountered in the remaining text, *ta'nü* 他女 fails to appear and the character *ta* 他 is used instead. This would appear to be an omission in typesetting. As to the phenomenon of the *nü* 女 character in *ta'nü* 他女 being typeset in large font, this occurred the first time Ye Shengtao 叶圣陶 employed the expression in "The Question of Women's Personality" 《女子人格问题》 (carried in *The Renaissance* 《新潮》 on February 1, 1919, in Vol. 1, Issue 2). This can be seen from the quoted portion of the original text.
9   For example, "Mouse Plague" 《鼠灾》 reads: "She (*ta* 他 [his woman 他的女人]) must have been thinking she (*ta* 他 [*nü* 女]) had placed her clothes in his (Pingfu – the male protagonist's) canvas case.... If he (*ta* 他) returns home and she (*ta* 他 [*nü* 女]) is crying, or she is irritable as if (she) had lost something, he (*ta* 他) as usual would then certainly comfort her (*ta* 他 [*nü* 女])." See Deng, Niudun 邓牛顿 (comp.), "Missing Pages from Guo Moruo's 'Goddess' (1919–1921)" 《郭沫若（女神）集外佚文 (1919–1921)》, carried in the *Journal of Nankai University* 《南开大学学报》, 1978 (3).
10 After this, the practice of using *ta'nü* 他女 did not cease completely, but there were some who proposed that the two characters *ta* (他) and *nü* (女) be combined into a single character. However, the meaning was already different. For example, in 1933 some wrote and pointed out:

> In this world there are those who dislike the two characters *ta* 她 and *ta* 牠 for their inability to describe three or more people if there is a mix of both male and female, and thus have created the *ta'nü* 他女 construction (see a certain gentleman's translation in Commercial Press's *Literature and Art Series* 《文艺丛刊》). This is odd in the extreme, and the reasons for it cannot be fathomed. It really makes one draw a long breath! If this ethos were to spread more widely then the typesetters and our readership would die of over-work. What can one say?

(see Li, Xiaotong 厉筱通, "The Question of the Vulgar Scripted 她 and 牠" 《"她"和"牠"的俗书问题》, *Current Opinion* 《时代公论》, No. 114.)
11 For the contents of the previous conversation between Qian 钱 and Zhou 周, see: "The Discussion over the Translation of the English 'She'" 《英文"she"字译法之商榷》, carried in *New Youth* 《新青年》, February 1919, Vol. 6, Issue 2.

3 An Account of the Early Written Use of the Character *Ta* 她 Before April 1920

A Survey of the Literary World

Following the publication of the exchange between Qian 钱 and Zhou 周 over the translation of the English word "she", no others were immediately encouraged to participate in open discussion. Nevertheless, there were members of society who had already been influenced by the exchange, including the earlier Zhou Zuoren 周作人 in his note of clarification, written prior to his August 1918 translated work *Reform* 《改革》, when he began to successively employ *yi* 伊 and *ta* 她 for the feminine third person pronoun. As for the character *ta* 她, such notable pioneers of the new literature as Kang Baiqing 康白情, Yu Pingbo 俞平伯, Wang Tongzhao 王统照, Tian Han 田汉 and others consciously became early adopters of the character in the written script.[1]

1 Kang Baiqing 康白情, Yu Pingbo 俞平伯 et al. and the Early Entry of *ta* 她 Into the New Literature

As far as I have been able to establish, on May 20, 1919, just sixteen days after the May Fourth Movement erupted, the 24-year-old Peking University student Kang Baiqing 康白情 published an article entitled "A Harbinger of Male-Female Relations in Peking's Student World" 《北京学生界男女交际之先声》 in *The Morning Post* 《晨报》 in which on two occasions he employed the character *ta* 她 as the female third person pronoun. Moreover, for the next four months, in other words before October 1919, it appears that he alone in the whole country was enamored of the character *ta* 她, so it would not be an exaggeration to name Kang Baiqing as the first adopter of the character *ta* 她 in China.[2]

Kang Baiqing with his special affection for the character *ta* 她 was born in 1895 in Anyue County 安岳县 in Sichuan. In 1917, at age 22, he entered the Philosophy Department of Peking University, and at the end of 1918, along with Fu Sinian 傅斯年, Luo Jialun 罗家伦 and others, formed the The Renaissance Society 新潮社 and quickly became one of the leading figures among the New Literature youth and the student movement of the day. After the Young China Youth Association 少年中国学会 was formally established on July 1, 1919, he also became an important member of this association. Before Guo Moruo's 郭沫若 *Goddess* 《女神》 appeared, Kang Baiqing and Yu Pingbo could be said to have been the two most outstanding and influential new young vernacular poets of the day. If we were to

Use of the Character Ta 她 *Before April 1920* 29

Figure 3.1 A portrait of some members of the Young China Association. Fifth from the right is Kang Baiqing, the earliest and most comprehensive adopter of the character *ta* 她.

acknowledge this point, then perhaps it might help us understand how the character *ta* 她 gained traction in its application and practice under the penmanship of Kang.

1.1 "Co-Education" and Kang Baiqing's Earliest Adoption of the Character *ta* 她

Although Kang Baiqing, champion of the new culture movement and brave and innovative "new youth", took the lead in grasping Liu Bannong's 刘半农 vision and creatively and unhesitatingly utilised the character *ta* 她. Nevertheless, the reason why he was able at this time to resolutely make such a move does have an ideological back-story worth mentioning, namely the new trending calls for "co-education" and "proper male-female social intercourse" which were vigorously springing up in May Fourth Beijing and elsewhere.

In April 1919, before the May Fourth movement had erupted, Kang Baiqing participated in the discussion in the pages of the *Women's Magazine* 《妇女杂志》 on the question of "co-education", and how male and female students should maintain proper and fair relations. On the day of May Fourth, Kang Baiqing's The Renaissance Society fellow-traveler, Xu Yanzhi 徐彦之, published his "Random Thoughts on the Question of Male-Female Relations" 《男女交际问题杂感》 in *The Morning Post* 《晨报》. From May 6 to May 10, Kang Baiqing's "Universities Should Take the Lead in Lifting the Ban on Female Students" 《大学宜首开

女禁论》 also ran in *The Morning Post* 《晨报》 in which he stressed that "this question of banning women is just as alien as the 'question of slavery'". He called on men who occupied "the status of conqueror" to "abandon (their) special position, offer (their) full sympathy, and support this righteous war in order to resolve the situation." The following day, Luo Jialun 罗家伦 entered the fray, publishing his "Universities Should be Open to Women" 《大学应为女子开放》 also in *The Morning Post*, adding his support. Thus, the call for "co-education" gradually surged through society and its influence burgeoned.

In the eyes of such individuals as Kang Baiqing, "co-education" and instituting "proper and pure male-female relations with mutual respect for the dignity of the other" was, without a doubt, first and foremost a demand for the human right of "gender equality". Secondly, it was also part of the innate need of the two genders for mutual inclusivity and nurturing. Or to use Mr Kang's words:

> From the point of view of form, when men and women interact, all conventions that are capable of restraining wanton behavior will naturally come into play. . . . So, in spirit, male-female relations certainly have the capacity to engender moral integrity.

What is both interesting and worth noting in the magazine article in which Kang Baiqing first used the female character *ta* 她 is his personal experience of involving himself in the organisation of the Peking Middle and Higher Schools Student Association 北京中等以上学校学生联合会 and the strength of the independent women with whom he interacted. It is this which informed his ideological advocacy regarding male-female relations.

In his article "A Harbinger of Male-Female Relations in Peking's Student World" 《北京学生界男女交际之先声》,[3] Kang Baiqing informed his readers that on May 13, 1919, the Peking Middle and Higher Schools Student Association convened a meeting to discuss the question of how to further develop the May Fourth Movement. After the meeting commenced and before they could effectively launch into the main topic, he was dismayed to find everyone debating incessantly and at length an inappropriate article and two questionable expressions by certain individuals. Eventually, a young woman by the name of Fei Xingzhi 费兴智 could not take it any longer and stood up to speak, reminding everyone:

> Our meeting is meant to discuss how to save the nation – how to rectify the current state of affairs, and not waste time arguing over trivialities. We have not yet avenged our nation, nor have we banished our national traitors – in fact sometimes we even pardon them. In any case, even our own people occasionally speak erroneously and recognise their mistake, so what more is there to forgive?

On hearing Miss Fei rationally and pointedly re-focus on the bigger picture, speaking simply and concisely, the whole audience, including Kang Baiqing, could not but be deeply moved. The following day, when Kang Baiqing was recounting the event, having got to this scene, a pronoun brim full of respect for the dignity of the opposite sex and respect for their ability and insight – the character *ta* 她 – finally emerged cogently from his brush, bursting onto the stage, "She (她) was yet to finish speaking when the applause of the room as a whole assaulted my eardrums and the meeting came alive momentarily." This is the first time the feminine pronoun *ta* 她, or "she", was formally used in China.

In the process of explaining why this speech by Miss Fei, whose life today is still much of a mystery, was so hugely effective, a second *ta* 她 character soon followed from the pen of Kang Baiqing:

> Just imagine how chaotic that meeting was and the fact that no one was able to bring it to order. So why were Miss Fei's scant words able to affect a resolution? It is because her [again the character *ta* 她 is used] mind was focused and her expression sincere, but also "gender" played a major part. This goes to show that what I referred to in my essay "Universities Should Take the Lead in Lifting the Ban on Female Students" 《大学宜首开女禁论》 was certainly not just idle prattle.

In this essay Kang Baiqing was especially impressed by the female participants in the May Fourth movement. In their quest to save the nation, they had amply fulfilled their social obligation and had begun to gradually participate in society. They had also established and participated in various types of social organisations. He approved of their activities in "being very disciplined and conscientious, something that even the early republican women's suffrage movement couldn't match" and believed that

> This is something that is motivated by their belief that they are equal with men, something that is clearly exemplified by the fact that they have renounced seclusion and demand equal intercourse with men. This is also a first step towards a recognition by men that they are entitled to an equal measure of human dignity.

At the same time, they also confirmed that this was the "Harbinger of Male-Female Relations in Peking's Student World" that they had hoped for, and which society expected.

From the previous description of Kang Baiqing's first use of the character *ta* 她 it is not difficult to see that co-education and the first steps towards improved male-female social intercourse were both the precondition and the immediate opportunity for the feminine *ta* 她 to emerge shoulder to shoulder with the male *ta* 他 onto the social stage.

1.2 *A Review of the Initial Entry of Ta* 她 *Into the New Literature*

Kang Baiqing is not only the first person to formally use the character *ta* 她 in a newspaper or magazine, but he is also the first practitioner to formally use the

32 *Use of the Character Ta* 她 *Before April 1920*

character in the New May Fourth Cultural Movement's new poetry and fiction, and even in literary criticism.

From August through September 1919, in the *New Art and Literature* "新文艺" column of the *Light of Learning* 《学灯》 as well as in *The Journal of the Young China Association* 《少年中国》, he published the poem "Seeing Mu Han off to Paris" 《送慕韩往巴黎》 at virtually the same time. In this work he referred metaphorically to a steamboat that was about to embark by employing the third person feminine character *ta* 她. In September that same year, *The Journal of the Young China Association* 《少年中国》 further published his short story "Society" 《社会》, the poem "South of the Yangtze" 《江南》, and "My View on the New Poetry" 《新诗底我见》, and in each of them he used the character *ta* 她 as a feminine pronoun. Of these, "Society" 《社会》 was the first piece of creative fiction to use *ta* 她. The work consisted of a mere 400 characters or so, yet *ta* 她 appeared some 18 times. Using the female pronoun *ta* 她 throughout the whole text, Kang Baiqing created the image of an unnamed young married woman whom he had seen whilst visiting West Lake: she was elegant and refined, unadorned and timid, extremely preoccupied yet

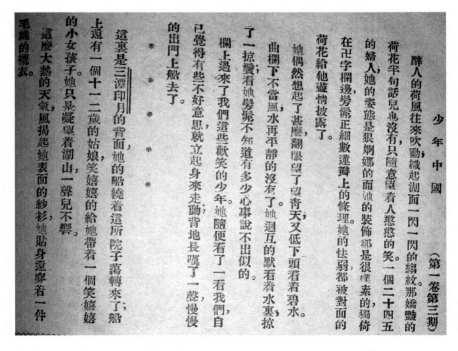

Figure 3.2 A section from the earliest short story to use the character *ta* 她 in the creative process – Kang Baiqing's "Society" 《社会》.

kind-hearted and traditional. This would appear to be the first literary depiction of a traditional Chinese female by a writer of the new literature, sketched using the character *ta* 她.[4]

In October 1919, the *The Renaissance* 《新潮》 magazine carried Kang Baiqing's poem "Farewelling a Guest on the Huangpu" 《送客黄浦》 and Yu Pingbo's short story "Around the Stove" 《炉景》 in which they each separately deployed the character *ta* 她.[5] Similarly, both men published simultaneously in *The Renaissance* in February 1920, including Kang's poem "The Question" 《疑问》 and Yu's short stories "Dogs and Badges of Honor" 《狗和褒章》 and "Reflections on a Week in Shanghai" 《一星期在上海的感想》, along with the poem "Bidding Her Farewell" 《别她》. All these works employed the character *ta* 她.[6] A little earlier, in December 1919, Yu Pingbo had also published the long poem "Chrysanthemum" 《菊》 in Volume 2, Issue 2 of *The Renaissance* in which he declares his complex and sincere adoration for "her" (她), the chrysanthemum. It could be said that in this work the *ta* 她 character is over-used, to the point of tedium (reaching some 20 instances), and one can well imagine the extent to which the poem might have attracted the attention of readers when it first appeared.

In 1920, Kang Baiqing went on to use the character *ta* 她 in a number of vernacular poems including "East of the Yalu" 《鸭绿江以东》, "Lushan Travel Diary: 2nd of 37 Pieces" 《庐山纪游三十七首之二》, and others. Of these, the poem "The Question" 《疑问》, mentioned previously, was rather poetic and nostalgic. Its second verse reads:

Petals in the pond;
Figure in the mirror;
She [*ta* 她] is in my heart.
My only care is that I may not be in her's [*ta* 她底].[7]

Amongst the early and innovative New Literature users of *ta* 她, apart from Kang Baiqing, his fellow Renaissance Society member Yu Pingbo 俞平伯 is most worthy of mention. Of the New Culture community, Yu is certainly one of the most enamored of using the character *ta* 她 before April 1920, i.e., before the character became hotly debated in China. He was also one of the most prolific users of the term (and the richest in terms of connotations that the character conveyed) as well as the most adept. What is more, his level of consciousness with respect to his innovation was also extremely elevated. In his opening remarks on the poem "Chrysanthemum" 《菊》 in which he refers to the chrysanthemum as "she" (*ta* 她), he specifically notes:

Many have written poems about chrysanthemums in the past and the topic has virtually been done to death. My writing this poem can be seen as "the new staging of an old play", but when those old fogies and young conservatives see it, they will certainly stroke their beards – although the young conservatives don't have beards – then sigh and say, "culture has hit rock bottom"!

One of the key things in this "new staging of an old play" is undoubtedly the use of the character for "she" (*ta* 她) to refer to the chrysanthemum flower. He utilises the technique of anthropomorphism to bestow on the flower a distinctly feminine quality and thereby ferment an unusual kind of poetic blending of the object and the self. This is the first such occurrence in the history of Chinese literature.[8]

From the materials currently available to the present author, Yu Pingbo is one of the earliest practiced users of the character *ta* 她 in fiction as well as one of the earliest poets to use the character in the title of a vernacular poem. His use of *ta* 她 in his short stories "Around the Stove" 《炉景》 and "Dogs and Badges of Honor" 《狗和褒章》 was both most skilful and successful. "Around the Stove" 《炉景》 was published in October 1919 with a complete text of less than 700 characters and is a simple story in which the author vividly depicts a rich man about to take a young concubine and who, eventually through deception and intimidation, forces his wife to comply and accept the concubine. "Dogs and Badges of Honor" 《狗和褒章》 was published in February 1920, and while not very lengthy, its composition is ingenious with the name of the main protagonist absent for the duration of the entire text; instead, the character *ta* 她 is used. The text employs the character *ta* 她 some 40 times from beginning to end as it vividly, distinctly, and archetypically presents the tragic image of a married woman who spends a lifetime of living alone, lonely, and silent yet sensitive and mistrustful, a dog her only company for the entire day. Eventually she is able to glimpse her memorial

Figure 3.3 Yu Pingbo 俞平伯, who was a relatively early adopter of the character *ta* 她 in literary creation.

arch in honor of a chaste widow and thus die content. This is a kind of conscious literary riposte to the devastation which had been imperceptibly wrought by the traditional Confucian code of ethics on Chinese women. The constant appearance of the character *ta* 她 powerfully highlights the tragedy of the female sex and its lifelong defense of its chastity which admirably heightens the artistic expressive power of the narrative. This is an early masterpiece of creative new literature which takes as its theme the opposition to the old feudal ethics with the character *ta* 她 as its radiant symbol. Previous critiques have all basically ignored the distinctive epochal nature of Yu Pingbo's employment of the character *ta* 她 in so far as none have paid any attention to this aspect of any of the aforementioned works.

Another relatively early adopter of the character *ta* 她 in fiction and poetry was the writer Wang Tongzhao 王统照. On December 1, 1919, he published his short story "Why She Died" 《她为什么死》 in Issue 2, Volume 1 of the magazine *The Dawn* 《曙光》, which he helped establish. Employing the character *ta* 她 some 88 times, he vividly recounts the tragic love story of a woman called Huiru 慧如 from Qufu, the county town of Shandong, and powerfully promotes the new literary theme of women's liberation. "Why She Died" 《她为什么死》 can also be said to be the first Chinese short story to directly insert the character *ta* 她 into the title. Wang Tongzhao's short story "Remorse" 《忏悔》 published in February 1920, closely followed by "Murdered by Art" 《是艺术杀了他》 and others, as well as such poems as "The Voice of the 20th Century" 《二十世纪的声》 published on February 5, 1920, in *The Morning Post* 《晨报》, all made copious use of the female pronoun *ta* 她.

As for magazines, the greatest contribution in terms of employment and popularisation of the character *ta* 她 was when the promulgators of the new culture established *The Journal of the Young China Association* 《少年中国》, *The Renaissance* 《新潮》, and the supplement *Light of Learning* 《学灯》 to the magazine *The China Times* 《时事新报》. This was especially true of *The Journal of the Young China Association* 《少年中国》 which was edited by the Young China Association 少年中国学会. The magazine was established on July 1, 1919, by the outstandingly creative devotees of China's new culture. From Issue 3, Volume 1 in September of that year, the magazine began to publish a string of poems, short stories, plays and other literature which employed the *ta* 她 character. Its main authors and translators, Kang Baiqing 康白情, Tian Han 田汉, Huang Zhongsu 黄仲苏, Zhou Wu 周无, Zheng Boqi 郑伯奇, and others were all some of the earliest adopters of the character *ta* 她, and especially the renowned poet and playwright Tian Han 田汉. From the start of 1920 he maintained his practice of using the *ta* 她 character in the pages of the magazine for some four years. For example, between February and June 1920, he published such items as "Poets and Labor" 《诗人与劳动问题》, "Ideology in Goethe's Poetry" 《歌德诗中所表现的思想》 and "New Romanticism and Other Things" 《新罗曼主义及其他》 in *The Journal of the Young China Association* 《少年中国》 where he uniformly and liberally employed the character *ta* 她.[9] Following this, he also consciously experimented with the use of *ta* 她 in the plays that he wrote and translated such as "The Violin and the Rose" 《环球璘与蔷薇》, "Salome" 《沙乐美》, "Hamlet"

36 *Use of the Character Ta* 她 *Before April 1920*

Figure 3.4 The novelist Wang Tongzhao 王统照, a relatively early experimenter in the use of the character *ta* 她 in creative writing.

《哈姆雷特》, and "Romeo and Juliet" 《罗密欧与朱丽叶》. It is worth mentioning the German poem that he quoted in his March 1920 "Ideology in Goethe's Poetry" 《歌德诗中所表现的思想》 which his good friend Guo Moruo 郭沫若 had helped him translate. This poem also used the character *ta* 她 quite frequently and so it is possible that by this time at least Guo Moruo might also have been sporadically using the character *ta* 她 in his creative writing.[10]

Among the relatively early users of the character *ta* 她 in the pages of *The Journal of the Young China Association* 《少年中国》 before April 1920 were the prominent members of the Young China Association 少年中国学会 Zhou Wu 周无, Huang Zhongsu 黄仲苏 et al. For example, in December 1919, Zhou Wu published a poem entitled "August 15 Last Year" 《去年八月十五》 in the magazine, using the character *ta* 她 some ten times.[11] However, the same individual in the same magazine switched to using *yi* 伊 in 1920,[12] revealing a certain indecision. Nor was this condition rare in the early period. Again, on February 3, 1920, Huang Zhongsu published such translated poems as "Seventeen Poems by Tagore" 《泰戈尔的诗十七首》 and "Six Poems by Tagore" 《泰戈尔的诗六首》 in the same magazine along with such original vernacular poems as "Seeing Association Friends Wei Shizhen, Wang Ruoyu, Chen Jianxiu and Xu Chuseng off to Study in Europe" 《送会友魏时珍、王若愚、陈剑修、许楚僧赴欧留学》[13] which all skillfully employed the character *ta* 她 to explore poetic landscapes and flavours.

From April 1920 through 1921, the number of new style authors who employed the character *ta* 她 in the pages of *The Journal of the Young China Association* 《少年中国》 increased even further, including such individuals as Zheng Boqi 郑伯奇, Yun Zhen 恽震, Yuan Bi 袁弼, Shen Zemin 沈泽民 and others, with the poets the most proactive and prominent. In fact, amongst the earliest adopters of the character *ta* 她, poetry continued to be the most important experimental domain and of course it was also the literary form most heavily influenced by the character. Because of the heightened requirement for brevity in poetry and its special demands for expressing emotion and symbolism, it offered a boundless and expansive ground for the feminine pronoun *ta* 她.

Apart from poetry, fiction, including in translation, was also fertile soil for experimentation with the character *ta* 她. Before April 1920, such widely read publications as *Shen Bao* 《申报》 also began to use the character *ta* 她 in its translated literature. For example, on February 15, 1920, *Shen Bao* 《申报》 published Lujiangfengsheng's 庐江凤生 translation of the renowned Russian playwright Chekhov's short story "Old Age" 《暮年》 (at the time entitled "A Short Work on Grief" 哀情短篇) from Russian in which he used the character *ta* 她 more than 49 times, leaving a deep impression on the reader.[14]

2 *Ta's* 她 Earliest Appearance in Poetry and Some of Its Early Uses

A commonly held belief is that the first time the character *ta* 她 entered the poetic realm was in Liu Bannong's famous "How Could I Not Think of Her" 《教我如何不想她》,[15] but this is in fact most incorrect. Liu Bannong could not have written this poem any earlier than August 1920[16] and its formal publication appears to be even later. The earliest openly published edition of this poem that I have seen is in *The Morning Post Supplement* 《晨报副刊》 on September 16, 1923, under the title "Love Song" 《情歌》. What is more, this publication was not at the instigation of Liu Bannong himself. It was published as an expression of "abject adoration" without Liu Bannong's permission. As far as I have been able to ascertain, the "besotted admirer" who was responsible for the poem's publication was "Hong Xi" 洪熙, the later comparatively famous republican author Zhang Yiping 章衣萍.

I have not yet found anyone who has raised this point, so you will perhaps indulge my inclusion of Zhang Yiping's postscript to the publication of the poem in order to assist our literature specialists to undertake a more in-depth investigation:

> This poem was given to me by my deceased friend SY some six months ago (he copied it from a letter that Mr Liu Fu 刘复 had written to his uncle). The style and creativity of the poem is rare in the field of new poetry and scarcely a day goes by in which I do not recite it in its entirety. I am publishing it here to introduce it to any youth who may have lost a lover and I trust that no one will take offence.
>
> (The evening of September 12, Hong Xi 洪熙)

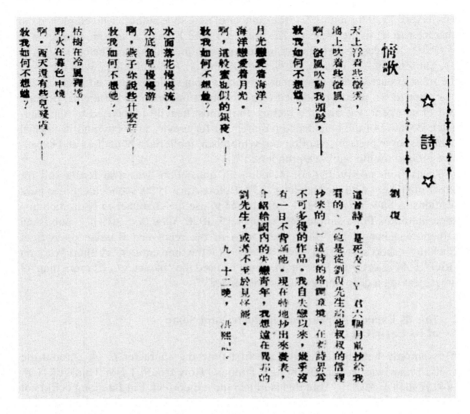

Figure 3.5 Liu Fu (Liu Bannong)'s "Love Song" 《情歌》 carried in *The Morning Post Supplement* 《晨报副刊》, 1923.

Zhang Yiping, also known as Hong Xi, was from Jixi County in Anhui Province. He had had frequent dealings with his fellow-countryman Hu Shi 胡适 and loved to speak of "My friend Hu Shizhi 胡适之". He had also established such publications as *Yu Si* 《语丝》 with Lu Xun 鲁迅 and others. His later publications *Love Letters Vol. 1* 《情书一束》 and *Love Letters Vol. 2* 《情书二束》 were best-sellers. After editing his *Letters Between Two* 《两地书》, Lu Xun jokingly told Li Jiye 李霁野 that he was going to edit a volume of "love letters," and this is probably how the idea originated. When the affectionate yet lovelorn Zhang Yiping saw Liu Bannong's poem, he decided to view it as a love poem. While he may have been quite discerning, nevertheless the title "Love Song" 《情歌》 always left people with the suspicion that this wasn't Liu Bannong's original intention but rather Mr Zhang's attempt at being clever. In September 1926 when Liu Bannong published his collection *Raising the Whip* 《扬鞭集》, this poem was included under the title "How Could I Not Think of Her" 《教我如何不想她》, and with that, its different import was clear to all.

"How Could I Not Think of Her" 《教我如何不想她》 was not only the earliest poem to introduce the term *ta* 她, it is also far from being the first poem to use the term in its title. Apart from the aforementioned "Bidding Her Farewell" 《别她》 by Yu Pingbo, the *Enlightenment Magazine* 《觉悟》, a supplement to *The Republican Daily News* 《民国日报》, had published on March 12, 1920, a new poem by the famed Jin Dezhang 金德章 entitled "She?" 《她么》,[17] which reads:

1

She [她]?
Is she married?
    Is her husband a vicious brute?
    She is a new 20th century individual; is she willing to sacrifice her whole happiness?
Alas! Is it she who is married?

2

She?
Is she divorced?
    Did her brother force her to marry?
    Now that she is awake, does her brother disapprove?
    While she might have escaped that bitterness, how can she be free?
Alas! Is it she who is divorced?

3

She?
Did she die?
Was she so miserable?
    She was such a philosophical young person, could she have died for the old code of ethics?
    She struggled to the end; was it glorious or humiliating?
Alas! Was it she who died?

This poem utilised the image of "her" marriage, divorce and ultimately "her" despondent death to express sympathy for the uniquely tragic fate of Chinese women who were not free to marry as they wished. It is indeed an unprecedented offering and moves the reader powerfully. In the work, the frequent utilisation of the feminine pronoun *ta* (她), its constant reappearance, naturally and artistically transcended the individual woman and gave enhanced prominence to the significance of the female sex as a whole, expressing the intense solicitude of the age towards the movement for "women's liberation".

We can be sure that while Liu Bannong may have been the earliest creator of the *ta* 她 character, yet while the various individuals mentioned previously were busily introducing the term into poetry, prose, and fiction, he remained watching from the sidelines. We can see this from the poetry that he published prior to the beginning of 1920 along with the various people mentioned previously in such journals as *New Youth* 《新青年》 or *The Renaissance* 《新潮》. The poem in which Liu Bannong first introduced the term *ta* 她 into poetry in the pages of *New Youth* 《新青年》 was called "Evening in a Small Peasant Household" 《一个小农家的暮》. This poem in the vernacular language employed the newly minted character *ta* 她 to depict a peasant wife, guileless and natural, while reserving the traditional pronoun *ta* 他 to refer to the husband and *tamen* 他们 to refer to the collective children, portraying a singularly ordinary, homely peasant family evening. The poem reads:

> She [她] prepares the meal by the stove,
> The newly cut firewood crackles.
> The fire blazes in the grate,
> Flickering across her crimson face,
> And adding a red glow to her dark garments.
> He [他] cradles an old pipe,
> And slowly returns from the fields;
> Hanging his hoe in the corner of the room,
> He sits on the straw bed,
> And teases an affectionate puppy.
> Then he strides over to the railing,
> And inspects his beast,
> Then he turns to her and says:
> "Eh?
> The new wine that we just brewed?"
> On the tops of the green mountains opposite their door,
> The tips of the pine trees
> Already reveal a crescent moon.
> The children are there gazing at the moon,
> And counting the stars in the sky:
> "One, two, three, four . . ."
> "Five, eight, six, two . . ."
> They [他们] count, and they sing:
> "When there are lots of people around, one cannot be calm.
> When there are lots of stars in the sky, the moon is not bright."
>
> (London, February 7, 1921)

In fact, "Evening in a Small Peasant Household" 《一个小农家的暮》 has already been acknowledged as an extremely elegant and mature new vernacular poem, but it was not published until August 1, 1921.[18] It should be said that in terms of the utilisation of the character *ta* 她, Liu Bannong can only be counted as one of the laggards. In the pages of *New Youth* 《新青年》, other "new youths" such as Yu Pingbo were already using the character in poetry. For example, on November 1, 1920, Yu Pingbo published his new poem "Inscription on a Photograph Taken at Keyan in Shaoxing" 《题在绍兴柯严照的相片》 in *New Youth* 《新青年》[19] where he used the character *ta* 她 extensively. The poem reads:

She [她] cradles the so-called me;
But I inhabit a different she.
Do I exist? Is that her?
That. Can it be known?
And this. Can it be known?
Who has the patience to concern themselves with these things?
And I'm afraid if I were to add anything she wouldn't be interested,
And would only mince away and make excuses.
"Ahhh! I *would* be willing – who said I wouldn't?"
"Sure! Forgive me, please!"

This is the first poem to contain the character *ta* 她 in *New Youth* 《新青年》 and the first time the magazine formally used the character. Still, on the whole, *New Youth* 《新青年》 was not entirely committed to using *ta* 她 prior to 1921, which was a far cry from such other publications as *The Journal of the Young China Association* 《少年中国》 or *The Renaissance* 《新潮》 which promoted the new culture.

Was the first instance where the character *ta* 她 was used to refer to and symbolise the mother country the poem by Liu Bannong entitled "How Could I Not Think of Her" 《教我如何不想她》, as some imagine?[20] This in fact is untrue as well. Yu Pingbo's poem "Bidding Her Farewell" 《别她》 published in *The Renaissance* 《新潮》 in February 1920, which I have referred to above, clearly used *ta* 她 to refer to China. The poem, written prior to leaving for study in Britain, expressed his complex emotions regarding his passion for his country and his determination to repay her by reforming himself. This writer believes that the poem "Bidding Her Farewell" 《别她》 is probably also the first poem which unequivocally referred to the country as *ta* 她 or "she" and pointedly gave vent to his deep emotion for his country in poetic form. Since the poem has in the past been largely unfamiliar to most, the reader will forgive me if I quote it here in full:

Bidding Her [她] *Farewell (Written on My Departure From the Country in December 1919)*[21]

Those who loathed her [她] now long for her,
Those who decried her now miss her;
Those who hated her, now love her.
Shattered, ill, filthy,
How could one not hate her, blame her, loathe her?
My her, our her;

Shattered – why not then make her whole?
Ill – why not then save her?
Filthy – why not then wash her?
Is this not my duty?
What have I said?
Do I want to run away? Am I afraid of a little pain?
How dare I!
I think – I think she is mine, and I am hers;
If I love myself, then I must love her, and if I want to save myself, then I must save her.
Take it easy, sweet dreams,
Coward! Drunkard!
Is this how I should treat myself?
Is this how I should treat myself for her sake?
I pick up my luggage and step out;
Go! Go! Go quickly!
Many have already – or are in the process of – saving their own "she".

This feminisation of the nation expressed a sentiment that had heretofore been unfamiliar to Chinese readers and was both an innovative transformation in terms of poetic theme as well as a novel experiment in patriotic literature. It is a pity that to date these phenomena have attracted little attention in modern Chinese literary research.

In fact, not only had people begun to use the character *ta* 她 to represent the mother country before April 1920, but similarly it was used to refer to many things of beauty and objects of an author's affection such as works of literature that they adored or flowers and plants in the natural world, the moon, a place, and more. We have already referred previously to Yu Pingbo's use of *ta* 她 to refer to a chrysanthemum in his poetic practice, and he also used the same character to refer to Shanghai, this "very first fashionable and open" modern metropolis.[22] In the utilisation of the character *ta* 她, the early Kang Baiqing 康白情 was even more innovative. As early as late 1919 he had already used the character *ta* 她 to refer to his own work.[23] At the same time he also used the character to refer to a departing ship and the moon.

On February 5, 1920, the *New Literature* column of *The Morning Post* 《晨报》 carried a new poem entitled "Light of the Full Moon" 《满月的光》 by the author "TT" which used *ta* 她 to refer to the moon.[24] Not only was it new and original in form, but it was also deeply poetic. The poem reads:

    A wonderful expanse of alabaster moonlight,
 Silently rests on the earth!
    The thin shadows of the wizened trees
    Shimmer their lively form.
It seems that all that she [她] illuminates
Shimmer in a congruent vivacity;

Glistening inside and out with the same radiance,
All blemishes dismissed.
Oh, moon! Would that I could steep myself in your bright sea forever
And grow to be as pure and lustrous as yourself![25]

As to the use of *ta* 她 to represent the crystallisation of one's own ideal or treasured objects, we can point to a relatively earlier example. For example, in May 1920 a student from the Tsinghua University 清华学校 refers to the Truth Association 唯真学会 which they had helped establish with the aim of reforming society and advancing the "cultural movement" as "she" (*ta* 她), declaring with fulsome affection:

The future of the Truth Association 唯真学会 can be imagined from the traces of the vicissitudes of her [她] past . . . . However, the progress of our Association is not her own progress. She must rely on her Association friends in order to be transformed, and if her Association friends continue to progress daily, then she will certainly also continue to progress. This is my confident assertion.[26]

We can thus see that of the new youth who employed the character *ta* 她, there were already some who on an emotional level, whether consciously or unconsciously, linked it to the cause of the new culture movement itself.[27]

Next, we will glance again at the circumstances surrounding the earliest use of the character *yi* 伊 in modern literature.

As noted previously, the use of the character *yi* 伊 to translate the Western third person singular pronoun had already surfaced during the late Qing. The move to consciously use *yi* 伊 to represent the third person singular in translation and creative writing by and large coincided with the use of *ta* 她. I have not specifically delved into the circumstances surrounding the earliest appearance of the character *yi* 伊 before or after May Fourth; however, it can be asserted that at a minimum, following *New Youth*'s 《新青年》 publication of the discussion of the English word "she" at the beginning of 1919, Zhou Zuoren and others had already begun to use *yi* 伊 relatively consciously in the sense of the female third person singular in their literary practice. For example, on November 1, 1919, Zhou Zuoren published his "Three Dreams in the Desert" 《沙漠间的三个梦》 in the Sixth issue of Volume 6 of *New Youth* 《新青年》 in which he consciously used the character *yi* 伊 in contrast to the [male] character *ta* 他 (see Plate 14). From this juncture until the end of 1923, he continued to use the *yi* 伊 character. And Zhou Zuoren's elder brother Lu Xun 鲁迅 had a largely similar approach to the use of the character *yi* 伊. In his "A Small Incident" 《一件小事》 he had already used the *yi* 伊 character to represent the feminine third person. This piece had already been published in the annual supplement to *The Morning Post* 《晨报》 on December 1, 1919. However, as far as I have been able to ascertain, in June 1919 a writer signing themselves Liaozuobuyi 辽左布衣 in their short story entitled "Brilliant Sister of Mine" 《慧姐》 was already using *yi* 伊 as the feminine third person

44 *Use of the Character Ta* 她 *Before April 1920*

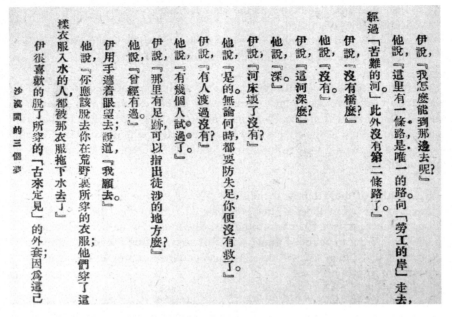

Figure 3.6 An extract from Zhou Zuoren's relatively early translated work "Three Dreams in the Desert" 《沙漠間的三个梦》 in which he used *yi* 伊 as the feminine third person pronoun.

pronoun.[28] This is some five months earlier than the Zhou brothers' official use of the term.

Apart from *New Youth* 《新青年》, many periodicals including *The Morning Post* 《晨报》, *The Eastern Miscellany* 《东方杂志》, and *The Renaissance* 《新潮》 also frequently saw *yi* 伊 deployed to act as the feminine third person pronoun prior to April 1920. Mao Dun 茅盾, Hu Yuzhi 胡愈之, Ye Shengtao 叶圣陶 and others were also early exploratory users of the *yi* 伊 character in modern works. As for the period following this up until the 1930s, the use of the *yi* 伊 character as the third person singular female pronoun became even more popular, even for a time surpassing the alternative *ta* 她, as we shall discuss in the following chapters.

Notes

1 For the modern-style poems that Guo Moruo 郭沫若 wrote from 1919 to the beginning of 1920, if we only look at his various Collected Works, Complete Works, or early poetry collections, then it would be easy to mistakenly believe that he was already by that time using the *ta* 她 character. For example, in the poem "The Lure of Death" 《死的诱惑》 which he published on September 29, 1919 in the supplement *Light of Learning* 《学灯》 to Shanghai's *The China Times* 《时事新报》, as well as in the

two poems "Taking One's Leave" 《别离》 and "At the Performance" 《演奏会上》 which were published in the *Light of Learning* 《学灯》 on January 8 and 9, 1920 respectively, the *ta* 他 character that he used in the original has been consistently changed to the *ta* 她 character without any clarification. The current *Complete Works of Bingxin* 《冰心全集》 (Haixia Wenyi Publishing House, 1994) is similar. Even the newly published *Complete Works of Fu Sinian* 《傅斯年全集》 (Hunan Education Publishing House, 2003) is the same. For example, all the *ta* 他 characters that Fu Sinian used in his poem "From Arrogance to Deference" 《前倨后恭》 which was published on May 1, 1919, in *The Renaissance* 《新潮》 have, in his *Complete Works* been changed to *ta* 她. Hence, whilst researching relevant questions of linguistic culture, many *Collected Works* or *Complete Works* edited by current individuals cannot be relied on (often the responsibility does not lie with the editors, but the publishing house editors who obviously think they should be altered). We must, without fail, return to the original "site" of their activity or to their use of the *ta* 她 character. This without doubt adds a layer of difficulty to our research.

2 The attribution reads "Article submitted by Kang Baiqing". For relevant conclusions regarding Kang Baiqing's earliest employment of *ta* 她, see the results of my research from the end of 2006 and the beginning of 2007. My humble work "The Story of the Character *Ta* 她: Invention, Debate and Early Circulation" 《"她"字的故事：女性新代词符号的发明、论争与早期流播》 may be consulted. Yang, Nianqun 杨念群 (ed.), *New History* 《新史学》, Vol. 1, Beijing: Zhonghua Shuju, 2007, pp. 115–164.

3 This work was originally carried in *The Morning Post* 《晨报》, May 20, 1919. It also used the term "May Fourth Movement" 五四运动, so the common perception that Luo Jialun 罗家伦 invented the term on May 26, 1919, is not accurate. This perception originates from Hu Shi's 胡适 1935 essay "Commemorating 'May Four'" 《纪念"五四"》 in which he determined that the earliest use of the term "May Fourth Movement" 五四运动 was in a piece entitled "The Spirit of the May Fourth Movement" 《五四运动的精神》 attributed to "Yi" 毅 (published in *Weekly Critic* 《每周评论》, May 26, 1919). Later scholars discovered that "Yi" 毅 was Luo Jialun's *nom de plume*. The saying "Invented by Luo Jialun" subsequently began to spread. In recent years some have investigated the situation and raised an objection. Some argue that the term appeared on May 18, 1919 in "Declaration of a Student Strike" 《罢课宣言》 published by the "Peking Middle and Higher Schools Student Association" 北京中等以上学校学生联合会 [see Kong, Fanling 孔凡岭, "The Earliest Appearance of the Term May Fourth Movement and its Connotations" 《"五四运动"一词的最早出现及其涵义》 in *History Teaching* 《历史教学》 2000 (7)]; others believe that the expression appeared first in "Telegram to the Teams in All Provinces" 《致各省各团体电》 issued on May 14, 1919 by this same "Peking Middle and Higher Schools Student Association" [See Yang, Hu 杨琥, "An Investigation into the Origin of the Name 'May Fourth Movement'" 《"五四运动"名称溯源》, *Journal of Peking University* 《北京大学学报》, 2006(3)]. What is worth noting is that these declarations and telegrams were all issued by the "Peking Middle and Higher Schools Student Association" and that the president of the Association at the time was Peking University student Duan Xipeng 段锡朋. Representing Peking University at subsequent meetings as alternate participants, apart from Duan were Deng Zhongxia 邓中夏, Huang Rikui 黄日葵, Xu Deheng 许德珩, Yi Keyi 易克嶷, Zhang Guotao 张国焘, Kang Baiqing 康白情 and Chen Bao'e 陈宝锷 – and Luo Jialun 罗家伦 was not among them. This fact can also be attested to by Luo Jialun's memoirs of the May Fourth Movement (and besides, given Mr Luo's own disposition, if it really had been of his making then I fear that he would not have held back from 'recognizing' this fact). We know from Kang Baiqing's "A Harbinger of Male-Female Relations in Peking's Student World" 《北京学生界男女交际之先声》 which was published on

May 20, 1919 that it was he who represented Peking University at the relevant Association meeting on May 13, 1919, and it is possible that he was an important drafter of the "Declaration" or "Telegram" of the following day. These documents also reveal that they were drafted on May 14, 1919, and the opening lines of these documents read "Following the 'May Fourth Movement' a Peking Middle and Higher Schools Student Association was convened, and a significant number from the female middle school fraternity also participated." Hence, I boldly surmise that the term "May Fourth Movement" could actually have been first invented by Kang Baiqing and that his fellow student and friend Luo Jialun and others were influenced by this. Of course, the term could also have been a result of mutual deliberations amongst the various new youth of Peking University and that Kang was the first to use it.

4 Kang Baiqing's 康白情 "Society" 《社会》 published in *The Journal of the Young China Association* 《少年中国》 Vol. 1, No. 3, September 1919.
5 Carried in *The Renaissance* 《新潮》, Vol. 2, No. 1.
6 Carried in *The Renaissance* 《新潮》, Vol. 2, No. 3.
7 Carried in *The Renaissance* 《新潮》, Vol. 2, No. 3. What is worth noting is that Kang Baiqing's 康白情 poem "The Question" 《疑问》 in which he experimented with the character *ta* 她 had by that time already been published at least three times. In February 1920 it was published in *The Journal of the Young China Association* 《少年中国》, Vol. 1, No. 8, and in the same month it was carried in *Light of Learning* 《学灯》, followed by a repeat publication in *The Renaissance* 《新潮》.
8 While Yu, Pingbo 俞平伯 used *ta* 她 so effusively in "Chrysanthemum" 《菊花》, Hu Shi continued to use *ta* 他 to represent the female sex in his "Story of Li Chao" 《李超传》 in the very same issue of *The Renaissance* 《新潮》.
9 The three works "Poets and Labor" 《诗人与劳动问题》, "Ideology in Goethe's Poetry" 《歌德诗中所表现的思想》 and "New Romanticism and Other Things" 《新罗曼主义及其他》 by Tian, Han 田汉 were carried separately in *The Journal of the Young China Association* 《少年中国》 Vol. 1, Issues 8–9.
10 As far as I am aware, Guo, Moruo's 郭沫若 four poems published as "My Prose Poetry" 《我的散文诗》 in December 1920 in *Light of Learning* 《学灯》 supplement to *The China Times* 《时事新报》 already included two items which clearly used the *ta* 她 character, one being "She and He" 《她与他》, and the other "Female Corpse" 《女尸》. See Deng, Niudun 邓牛顿 (comp.), "Missing Items from Guo Moruo's *Goddess Collection*" 《郭沫若〈女神〉集外佚文》 (1919–1921), carried in *Nankai Univeristy Journal* 《南开大学学报》, 1978 (3).
11 Zhou, Wu 周无, "August 15 Last Year" 《去年八月十五》, carried in *The Journal of the Young China Association* 《少年中国》, Vol. 1, No. 6.
12 For example, in the French poem "Happiness" 《幸福》 translated by Zhou Wu 周无 and published in October 1920 in *The Journal of the Young China Association* 《少年中国》 Vol. 2, Issue 4, the magazine changed to using *yi* 伊 to represent the feminine third person singular.
13 Various poems by Huang Zhongsu 黄仲苏 carried in *The Journal of the Young China Association* 《少年中国》, Vol. 1, Nos 8–9.
14 Lujiangfengsheng's 庐江凤生 translation of the Russian playwright's work "Old Age" 《暮年》 was carried in *Shen Bao* 《申报》, February 15, 1920, p. 15.
15 Cai, Ying 蔡瑛, "Liu Bannong's *Ta* 她 [She]" 《刘半农的 "她"》, carried in *CPPCC (Chinese People's Political Consultative Conference) Daily* 《人民政协报》, July 27 2006. A relevant search on the *Baidu* 百度 platform reveals that similar inaccurate statements may be found throughout the search results. There are also those who believe that Liu Bannong's "How Could I Not Think of Her" 《教我如何不想她》 is still the earliest official use of the character *ta* 她. This mistaken opinion is similarly widespread. I will not repeat these sources here, however, I trust that my research will be sufficient to assist in rectifying these inaccurate statements.

16 According to Liu Xiaohui's 刘小蕙 *My Father Liu Bannong* 《父亲刘半农》, Liu Bannong's "How Could I Not Think of Her" 《教我如何不想她》 was written on September 4, 1920. There is also another common belief that it was written on August 16, 1920. This awaits further research.
17 "She?" 《她么》, the original poem was carried in the *Enlightenment Magazine* 《觉悟》 supplement to *The Republican Daily News* 《民国日报》 published on March 12, 1920.
18 The same issue (Vol. 9 No. 4) of *New Youth* 《新青年》 published a translated poem by Liu Bannong under the title "Summer Daybreak" 《夏天的黎明》 which also liberally employed the character *ta* 她. Liu Bannong notes that this poem, as well as "Evening in a Small Peasant Household" 《一个小农家的暮》, were both composed in London and the dates of composition were separately recorded as April 2, 1921.
19 Yu Pingbo's 俞平伯 poem "Inscription on a Photograph Taken at Keyan in Shaoxing" 《题在绍兴柯严照的相片》, carried in *New Youth* 《新青年》, Vol. 8, No. 3.
20 Questions have been raised as to whether Liu Bannong's 刘半农 "How Could I Not Think of Her" 《教我如何不想她》 originally referred to his lover or indeed to his mother country. His daughter Liu Xiaohui 刘小蕙 in her work *My Father Liu Bannong* 《父亲刘半农》 stressed: "At the time, the *ta* 她 referred to in all of my father's poetry was our mother country and not some female friend that he may have been thinking of." He was later eulogised by Zhao Yuanren 赵元任 in song: "It expressed the unbounded longing they both had for the mother country." See *My Father Liu Bannong* 《父亲刘半农》, Shanghai: People's Publishing House, 2000, p. 57. The work also argues that this poem was the "first instance of using the character *ta* 她 in a poem" (*My Father Liu Bannong*, p. 158). Such a statement is mistaken as we have shown previously. Zhao Yuanren and others also believe that the first use of *ta* 她 was in reference to the mother country.
21 Yu Pingbo's 俞平伯 poem "Bidding Her Farewell" 《别她》, originally carried in *The Renaissance* 《新潮》 Vol. 2, No. 3, February 1920.
22 See Yu, Pingbo 俞平伯, "Reflections on a Week in Shanghai" 《一星期在上海的感想》, namely:

> Before I get into the text proper, I'd like to say a little about her [她] background. Shanghai is on the lower reaches of the Yangtze River and traded with foreign countries at a very early stage, so South China's industrial and commercial circles are all concentrated there. Euro-America and Japan also made her [她] the grand base camp for their industrial and commercial wars. Thus, Shanghai on the one hand was the crystallization of South China's material world, while on the other it was the rump of Euro-America's material world. She [她] could be said in the main to be China's first fashionable and open city. But nowadays, her [她] sisters have all awakened and started rising while she [她] sleeps, blindly running after others. Isn't this rather strange?

(Carried in *The Renaissance* 《新潮》 Vol. 2, No. 3, February 1920)

23 See "Kang Baiqing Notice" 《康白情启事》, carried in *The Renaissance* 《新潮》, Vol. 2, No. 1, October 1919.
24 "Light of the Full Moon" 《满月的光》 was also published in Issue 5, 1920 of *La Studentaro de la Stata Pekin-Universitato* 《北京大学学生周刊》, authored by Zhu Ziqing 朱自清.
25 A relatively early poem that uses the character *ta* 她 to refer to the moon is the poem "Seeking the Moon" 《找月亮》 by Yang Baosan 杨宝三 in *The Morning Post* 《晨报》 on May 8, 1920.
26 Ming, Xi 鸣希, "The Past and the Present of the Truth Association" 《唯真学会的过去与现在》, carried in the inaugural issue of *Truth* 《唯真》, May 1920, published by Tsinghua Truth Society, p. 59.

27 A little later, on October 10, 1921, in the Foreword to the inaugural issue of *Advance Together* 《共进》 magazine, the character *ta* 她 was also used in this manner. See Vol. 2, Part B of *Introduction to Periodicals of the May Fourth Era* 《五四时期期刊介绍》, People's Publishing House, 1959 (1979 impression), pp. 611–612.
28 Liaozuobuyi 辽左布衣, "Brilliant Sister of Mine" 《慧姐》, carried in the "Fiction" column of *The Morning Post* 《晨报》, June 5, 1919.

4 The Debate Over Preserving or Abolishing the Character *Ta* 她 and the Contest Between *Ta* 她 and *Yi* 伊

Adopters and Adoptees in the Linguistic Competition

Perhaps having been stimulated by works employing the characters *ta* 她 and *yi* 伊, and one year after the discussion between Liu Bannong and Zhou Zuoren on how to translate the word "she", the critics began to pay attention to the term *ta* 她 and began a heated debate over whether to retain or reject the term.

1 Should the Newly Coined Character *Ta* 她 Be Abandoned?

On April 3, 1920, the monthly magazine *New Man* 《新人》 published an article entitled "This is Liu Bannong's Error" 《这是刘半农的错》 by Han Bing 寒冰. In no uncertain terms, the writer named, and took to task, the evil originator of the character *ta* 她. He uncompromisingly opposed the use of the character, arguing that it amounted to blindly following Western grammar, that it had already become an "impediment to the culture movement", and proposed that it be abandoned immediately, a stance which elicited a significant response.[1]

In the second half of the month following the publication of Han Bing's[2] article, Sun Zuji 孙祖基 followed it up with a rebuttal entitled "Research on the Character *Ta* 她 – Is Liu Bannong Really Wrong?" 《"她"字的研究 – 刘半农果真是错么?》 in *Light of Learning* 《学灯》, the supplement to *The China Times* 《时事新报》. Some days later Han Bing published a further article entitled "Refuting the Research on the Character *Ta* 她 – If Liu Bannong Is Not Wrong Then Who Is?" 《驳"她"字的研究 – 刘半农不错是谁错?》 to which Sun Zuji then responded with the piece "Against 'Refuting the Research on the Character *Ta* 她'" 《非 "驳'她'字的研究"》, whereupon the two proceeded to trade blows in the pages of *Light of Learning* 《学灯》. At the same time, Zou Zhengjian 邹政坚, Meng Shen 梦沈 and others also penned pieces in *Light of Learning* 《学灯》, taking Han Bing to task, whereupon Han Bing was emboldened and responded with two articles, "A Detailed Critique of the Question of the Character *Ta* 她" 《关于"她"字问题的申论》 and "Refuting again the 'Research on the Character *Ta* 她'" 《再驳<"她"字的研究>》, in which he continued his engagement with the debate.[3] In April 1920, the debate over the question of the character *ta* 她 reached a climax and it was not long before the principal editor of *New Man* 《新人》 magazine, Wang Wuwei 王无为,

DOI: 10.4324/9781003359449-5

Figure 4.1 Compilation of previous articles discussing the character *ta* 她, *New Man* 《新人》 magazine, Vol. 2.

collated all the main articles in the discussion and offered them for discussion, which extended the momentum of the debate until the following summer and into the fall.

After June 1920, Liu Bannong, who had been studying in Europe, also joined the debate. He wrote his article, "On the Question of the Character *Ta* 她" 《"她"字问题》, and posted it back to China where it was published in the August 9 issue of the magazine *Light of Learning* 《学灯》 in which he, for the first time, comprehensively laid out his reasons for advocating for the character *ta* 她. Han Bing, however, remained resolute and wrote "Further Discussion on 'the Question of the Character *Ta* 她'" 《续论"她字问题"》 which was carried some three days later in *Light of Learning* 《学灯》 and in which he delivered a spirited response, insisting on the soundness of his stance and showing an unwillingness to concede an inch.

Apart from *New Man* 《新人》 and *Light of Learning* 《学灯》, *The Republican Daily News* 《民国日报》 and its supplement *Enlightenment Magazine* 《觉悟》, amongst others, joined the debate. Those participating directly or tangentially, apart from those mentioned previously, included Shao Lizi 邵力子, Chen Wangdao 陈望道, Cai Yuanpei 蔡元培, Da Tong 大同, Zhuang Fu 壮甫 and more. The period from late 1920 to 1922 can be said to constitute the aftermath of the debate about "The differentiation of the character '*ta* 他'", which included numerous questions about the character *ta* 她.

Before the primary opponent of the character *ta* 她 during the high tide of the debate, Han Bing, crossed swords directly with Liu Bannong 刘半农, his principal reasons for his rejection may be summarised in the following points: the first was that "the most lofty aim of a script is to meet the needs of a people", and whether or not a script has met that need "is premised on the fact that it has been able to win the recognition of the populace at large." "At present the populace has already accepted that the existing *ta* 他 character has already met that need, so therefore there is no need for change". Second, from the point of view of time, the utility of a script for a people demands that the more convenient and the less bothersome the better. When people currently view the *ta* 他 character, they recognise it immediately; they do not need to spend time thinking about it. But if they were to encounter the character *ta* 她, they would look it up in the dictionary only to find that it was "not found" or "absent" and in fact would waste valuable contemplative time. This would lead to fruitless consternation. Third, if we were to change the third person feminine pronoun to *ta* 她 then when women refer to themselves as *wo* 我, *wu* 吾, or *yu* 余, or when other people refer to a female as *ni* 你, *yi* 伊,[4] *ru* 汝, and so on, then these would all have to be changed as well so as to demonstrate difference. Now isn't that just too bothersome? Fourth, classical Chinese had a *ta* 她 character:

> According to the *Yupian* 《玉篇》, 她 is the ancient form of 姐. Quoting the *Shuowen* 《说文》, the people from Sichuan refer to mother as 姐 and according to the *Huainan[zi]* 《淮南》 they use 社, 她 or 媸. Quoting the *Liushugu* 《六书故》, 姐 is an ancient character, pronounced like *ye* 也 and written 她, or pronounced as *zhe* 者 and written 媸.

Han Bing also pointed out two further classical pronunciations of the character. In the ensuing debate, he clearly declared that the reason why he was highlighting the origin of the character *ta* 她 was not to comprehensively oppose the modern use of classical script, but rather to show that, "The character *ta* 她 was not personally invented by Liu Bannong; it was dug up from a millennia-old tomb." Moreover, the character *ta* 她 in the classical language already had a defined meaning and it was not appropriate to use it in a new context.[5] Fifth, he stressed that *ta* 她 and *ta* 他 were pronounced the same, so that "any reform brought about by using the *ta* 她 character could only demonstrate difference through script and that gender could never be delineated orally; the difference can be seen but not heard." There is no value in it to speak of (this is in fact a repetition of the point made by Zhou Zuoren earlier). Han Bing went even further to note that visually the differentiation afforded by the character *ta* 她 was not great. And the reader must read the context in any case; if they did read the written context, then even if the undifferentiated *ta* 他 character was used, it would still be possible to work out to whom it referred, so why go to the trouble and insist on using *ta* 她?[6] And if the context was not taken into account, then not only would it not be obvious who the gender-determining *ta* 他 or *ta* 她 referred to, but even who the "me" and "you", the first and second persons, referred to would not be as clear as people imagine.[7]

During the continuing debate, Han Bing gradually realised that the main reason why he was advocating the abandonment of the character *ta* 她 in fact relied on the following two points:

> The fact that there is no way of distinguishing auditorily between *ta* 她 and *ta* 他 is a disadvantage; the *ta* 她 character has a prescribed meaning in the *Shuo Wen* 《说文》 dictionary and hence it would easily give rise to misunderstanding. These are two shortcomings. Given these two shortcomings, naturally we must quickly abandon the project and come up with a new methodology and solve the difficulty in the written script. This is something we must do, so why must we accept this nasty *ta* 她 medicine and force it down our throats?[8]

In response to Han Bing's aforementioned arguments for abandoning *ta* 她, Sun Zuji 孙祖基, Zou Zhengjian 邹政坚, Meng Shen 梦沈, Da Tong 大同, Liu Bannong 刘半农 and others individually and from their own points of view either expressed doubt or offered a rebuttal to varying degrees.[9] They pointed out that it is precisely to meet the needs of the people that it is necessary to create the character *ta* 她 or some other appropriate character to represent the feminine gender. In some circumstances, no matter how well you may understand the context, you may still be unable to identify to whom the *ta* 他 might refer.[10] Admittedly, the non-gendered *ta* 他 has satisfied the needs of people in the past and gained recognition, however the reform as represented by the character *ta* 她 accords more closely with the requirements of present-day and future readers and will, in a short amount of time, be commonly recognised and become listed in all dictionaries, just as the character *ta* 他 has in the past made the transition from absence to presence. Moreover, the object of employing the character *ta* 她 was to offer clear differentiation and to save valuable time, and while some initial unfamiliarity is unavoidable, over time the anticipated outcome can be achieved. The female third person pronoun is different to the first or second person, so the necessity for *ta* 她 to distinguish between the sexes cannot be denied, based on a totally misleading premise because

> The first and second person pronouns represent the speaker and the direct audience who are of necessity most proximate, whereas the third person represents someone being spoken about and is therefore further removed from the action. And there is another consideration: the speaker and the audience can alternate but are fixed in number, but a person being referred to [a third person] can be a single person or many.[11]

Additionally, they pointed out that although a character *ta* 她 existed in the classics, it has all but been forgotten by people today, which does not mean that people nowadays cannot use it if it were infused with a new meaning. And while verbally *ta* 她 cannot be distinguished from *ta* 他, nevertheless, in the written form, because it is able to give prominence to a gender difference and "put an end to ambiguity;"[12] surely this was a significant consideration.

On the issue of defending the character *ta* 她, the view that Liu Bannong expressed in his belated article "On the Question of the Character *Ta* 她" 《"她"字问题》[13] on the whole can be said to appear even more mature. He insisted that a "third person feminine pronoun" was a new necessity for the Chinese language. In the past, Chinese people did not have such a pronoun, but "with a bit of effort surveying the context, the meaning of *ta* 他 can be ascertained with a minimal chance of misinterpretation." Currently, we are in contact with languages of various countries in the world, and despite the fact that it may not be used all that frequently in our own script, "It, at the very least, could serve a useful purpose in the task of translation". To this end, he offered some examples arising from translation which provided concrete proof of his argument.

As to Han Bing's rejection of the argument that, having accepted *wo* (我, me) and *ni* (你, you) for the first and second persons, "why not then also differentiate according to gender"? Along with the view that it was unnecessary to make a gendered distinction in the case of the third person, Liu Bannong's riposte "displayed an even loftier standard". Apart from summarizing the views of his predecessors and applying the two criteria of "distance" and the "number of people being referred to" in order to distinguish and explain it, he also argued that this rhetorical question of Han Bing's was "excellent" and that it raised an important question. He did not "'make fun of his misunderstanding, but rather applied a rigorous analysis to it." Prior to Liu Bannong, Sun Zuji 孙祖基, who had spiritedly faced off with Han Bing, had taken the example of how in English the first and second person could not be gender-distinguished like the third person in order to ridicule Han Bing's "naivete" and "ignorance", to the extent that he ignorantly maintained that "no matter which language, the reality is the same".[14] This quickly riled Han Bing who declared that this was blatantly "taking English as the official standard".[15] Nevertheless, with his limited experience, the still smarting Han Bing was unable to offer any contrary evidence. Liu Bannong, on the other hand, had indeed studied in France, was experienced and knowledgeable, and understood the complexity of the myriad of world languages, so on the one hand he adroitly conceded, "In French and German, inanimate objects are all distinguished by gender, while in English the names of countries, ships, or most abstract names are all considered feminine, while in Arabic, the second person pronoun is divided into masculine and feminine."[16] (I would argue that had Han Bing been aware of these facts, then he would no doubt have already taken it as a reason to oppose the character *ta* 她). Meanwhile, he quick-wittedly pointed out the distinction between "necessity" 需要 and "blindly following" 盲从, stressing that "These phenomena are relics of the history of languages, so if we really were to 'blindly follow', why not advocate to actively adopt them?" The implication was that if we were to adopt and use *ta* 她 then it does not equate to blindly following English, French, German or any other languages; that it was an intelligent and conscious choice made in response to a new necessity.

Liu Bannong went on to argue that "The script of any nation's language invariably expands through the ages and is never static"; "Of the function words (including conjunctions and pronouns) that we use in our essays, nine out of ten no longer carry their original meaning"; and the original pronunciation of many characters in classical Chinese had long since changed. According to these three arguments, Liu debunked the idea that new characters cannot be created or that the original meaning or pronunciation of characters cannot be changed. He went on to deftly point out that:

> Having considered these three arguments, we can state that, because of a real need and because this symbol is extremely similar to the *ta* 他 character, is easily recognised and yet clearly different which would avoid any confusion, we should therefore use it. If it has never existed, let us just say that we created it; and if it has existed in the past but is not much used now-a-days and has become superfluous, then just say that we have borrowed it.

Perhaps Liu Bannong did not fully realise that the character *ta* 她 already existed when he first introduced it, so at this stage it appears that he was not too willing to simply accept this fact. To him, even if historically it had existed, it nevertheless had not been used very much and had long since been forgotten as a "superfluous character". This is why in his own essays he continued to call the *ta* 她 character a "new invention".

To Liu Bannong, the only regret he had about the character *ta* 她 was that there was no way of differentiating it from the character *ta* 他 in terms of pronunciation. Compared to the character *yi* 伊, this was an unavoidable drawback. But at the same time, *ta* 她 had some advantages over *yi* 伊. Liu Bannong put it this way:

> Auditorily, the difference between *yi* 伊 and *ta* 他 is quite clear, however it does not match *ta* 她 in several respects: 1. Verbally the opportunity to use the *yi* 伊 character as the third person pronoun is limited and it would find difficulty in gaining much popularity; 2. The *yi* 伊 character is not able to demonstrate the feminine gender as clearly as *ta* 她; 3. The *yi* 伊 character has classical overtones, so it does not sit comfortably in the vernacular.

For these reasons, Liu Bannong came to the conclusion that "It is best just to use *ta* 她 and to alter the pronunciation ever so slightly."

So, how exactly could the pronunciation be altered in a rational and convenient manner? Liu Bannong believed that the English so-called "hard/strong" and "soft/weak" pronunciation method was an "excellent model" worth exploring. In this case, *ta* 他 could be pronounced as "*ta*", and one could perhaps shorten the newly created *ta* 她 character to "*te*" or lengthen it a little to pronounce it

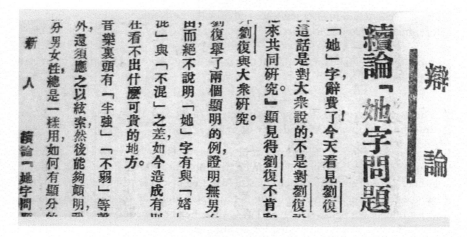

Figure 4.2 A section of Han Bing's article "Further Discussion on 'the Question of the Character *Ta* 她'" 《续论"她字问题"》 in which he rejected the use of *ta* 她.

"*taj*". This means of altering the sound of a word is indeed a difficult task, but not impossible.[17]

However, Liu Bannong's opinion did not convince Han Bing, but rather elicited an even stronger backlash. In his "Further Discussion on 'the Question of the Character *Ta* 她'" 《续论"她字问题"》,[18] Han Bing launched a spirited tit-for-tat rebuttal from several different angles. He first of all criticised Liu Bannong's failure to mention the fact that the character *ta* 她 had long existed already, and added to that there was "the problem that the character *ta* 她 was often confused with the characters *jie* 媎 and *jie* 姐". He believed that if a character that was easily confused with other characters was created and had to be used with extreme "caution" and was incapable of offering complete clarity, then the character "really represented nothing of value." And secondly, he rejected the feasibility of using the English weak/strong pronunciation methodology to differentiate the pronunciation between the two characters. He maintained that under normal circumstances in speech "criteria for accentuation are non-existent", so when a word was actually pronounced, he feared that there would still be no way of distinguishing between them. Additionally, Han Bing stressed, "If you are to create or adapt a character, then there are three criteria: first, the sound must be appropriate; second, it must be practical; and third, it should not be forced," and if we were to follow Liu Bannong's method of creating a character and altering the sound, then:

> The sound of the *ta* 她 character could not indicate what character it was; because it cannot be pronounced, it is not practical; and if it is divided up

along stressed and unstressed lines only for the convenience of translating a foreign text, then it is too forced.

For these reasons, Han Bing believed that there was no way that the *ta* 她 character could be accepted.

2 The Tussle Between the Two Characters *Ta* 她 and *Yi* 伊, and the Temporary Ascendancy of *Yi* 伊

Before Liu Bannong made a direct reply, in the debates between Han Bing and Sun Zuji et al., Han had already changed his mind: at first, he insisted on a single *ta* 他 character, arguing that there was no need whatsoever to imitate the English insistence on gender distinction in the third person, and that this would be creating a rod for one's own back. However, later, while he continued to oppose *ta* 她 passionately, he nevertheless adjusted his position ever so slightly, advocating for the use of *yi* 伊, accepting the view that it was necessary to distinguish between the genders. By the time he clashed directly with Liu Bannong, he had already turned into a fierce advocate for *yi* 伊. Thus, the thing that eventually most caught people's attention in Han Bing's refutation of Liu Bannong was his support of *yi* 伊 and his rejection of *ta* 她.

But did not Liu Bannong insist that "verbally the opportunity to use the *yi* 伊 character as the third person pronoun is limited and it would find difficulty in gaining much popularity"? Han Bing, meanwhile, declared that *yi* 伊 in fact enjoyed considerable popularity:

> Jiangsu, Zhejiang, Fujian and some parts of Jiangxi and Sichuan commonly use *yi* 伊, and it is not completely unfamiliar in Anhui, Hunan and Hubei. If we were to make an effort to popularise the term, it would not be difficult to reach unanimity across the country.

And did not Liu Bannong argue that *yi* 伊 was not able to convey the feminine as clearly as *ta* 她 could? To which Han Bing unequivocally declared:

> In the past, nine times out of ten *yi* 伊 has been used to represent the feminine in poetry and song lyrics, and that convention has continued down to the present without change. So now, if we take *yi* 伊 to represent the feminine *ta* 他, it will be based on tradition and will be accepted more widely as a result. Even though it does not include a female *nü* 女 radical, its feminine credentials still remain obvious!

Not only did he frame it in this way, but Han Bing illustrated his point with an example, arguing that whether or not femininity is obvious bears no direct relationship to the presence of the feminine *nü* 女 radical, "It is not that with the *nü* 女 we are able to be clear and that without the *nü* 女 we cannot be clear". What is important is that "In the past, if a character was created then the experience of the ancients was always preserved in some way." For example:

> The character *nu* 奴 [slave] incorporates the *nü* 女 or female radical, but customarily everyone accepts that it represents the masculine! And if we want it to represent the feminine, then we all add a *nü* 女 and end up with "*nü nu* 女奴" [female slave]!

Or considering other expressions such as *ling ping* 伶俜 [lonely/solitary], "anyone would naturally say that it represents the female demeanor, so why must we use *nü* 女 as part of the character to make that clear!"

Such an impassioned defense of the character *yi* 伊 by Han Bing was of course not unreasonable, but it also left many with significant misgivings. Setting aside the question as to whether 伶俜 specifically refers to the female only, or whether the word 奴 only refers to the male, his two assertions, namely that the geographical range of the character 伊 is extremely broad and that this character has traditionally been used "nine times out of ten to refer to the feminine" in poetry were not entirely convincing. As to the question of the area in which the character *yi* 伊 was used, some of the academics who advocated for *ta* 她 either claimed that it was restricted to "certain parts of Jiangxi and Zhejiang Provinces" only,[19] and some claimed that it was restricted to "such areas as the southeast of Jiangsu or Fujian and Zhejiang".[20] In general, they all believed that the area in question was not terribly broad, a point that even the advocates for *yi* 伊 on the whole also conceded. As to the claim that "nine times out of ten" the character *yi* 伊 when used in poetry and song lyrics had in the past referred to women, the claim was even less able to be substantiated. The real situation remained that the character *yi* 伊 in the past never fundamentally carried a gendered meaning.

Apart from this, there was another important reason why Han Bing argued for the use of *yi* 伊 and rejected the character *ta* 她, which is, to his mind, in the literary circles of the time, that the adoption of *yi* 伊 had already displayed a certain pragmatic superiority. He thus confidently declared, "In actuality, most of the newspapers and magazines that are available to us are using *yi* 伊 and not *ta* 她, so it is obvious that *yi* 伊 holds the promise of unity while *ta* 她 does not."[21]

In sum, in the years between 1920 and 1922, in the discussion around the question of the character *ta* 她, the opposition to its use from the point of view of language itself was restricted to two streams: one stream which arose from the principle of linguistic simplicity, convenience and effectiveness completely opposed using the third person pronoun to distinguish gender; and the other stream, whilst accepting the distinction, nevertheless opposed the character *ta* 她 and remained enamoured of the character *yi* 伊. And individuals like Han Bing who had migrated from the first stream to the second were good examples of the process.

At the time, the number of individuals publicly supporting the first stream was not great, but it was not without its important proponents. For example, Cai Yuanpei 蔡元培 who was well versed in both Chinese and Western scholarship in June 1920 published his "Speech to the Beijing National Language Pedagogical Institute" 《北京国语传习所的演说》 in which he clearly expressed his opposition to gender differentiation in third person pronouns. He declared:

> Recently some have insisted that the third person pronoun exhibit differentiation: some would have us use the character *ta* 她, while others would have us use the *yi* 伊 character. However, I would argue that there is no need to differentiate in such a way. For example, if we have a situation where we have a man and a woman and we use 他 and 她 to differentiate between them, then of course this is all well and good; but if we encounter two men or two women, then of what use is such a distinction?[22]

Obviously, Cai Yuanpei had not at that time noticed that some were already using 伊们 or 她们. He was coming from the standpoint that grammar should, as far as possible, be succinct. It is precisely for this reason that he criticised the numerical and adjectival variations in English, French, German, and other languages as well as changes for number, tense, word endings, and so on as being unnecessarily complex and inferior to the simplicity of the Chinese language.[23] What he was inferring was that the absence of a gendered distinction in the Chinese third person pronoun was much simpler and more convenient than that of Western languages.

At the time, besides Cai Yuanpei, those opposing a gendered distinction in the third person pronoun included such figures as Chen Dabei 陈大悲 and Sun Xunqun 孙逊群. In the early summer of 1921, the renowned contemporary playwright Chen Dabei in his essay entitled "*Yi* 伊 and *ta* 她 in Theatrical Scripts" 《剧本中的"伊"和"她"》, which was published in *The Theater* 《戏剧》, from the point of view of both script and performance, unequivocally opposed the use of 她 and 伊 to differentiate gender, arguing that "To make a distinction like in Western languages is both inconvenient and meddlesome".[24]

Sun Xunqun 孙逊群 expressed similar dissenting views, instigating an extreme rebuttal after many proposals for "differentiating the character *ta* 他" had been suggested. In October 1921, commencing from the utility of the pronoun, he argued that a single *ta* 他 was sufficient for the Chinese language; that there was no necessity for further differentiation. This was similar to Han Bing's earlier view, but there were also slight differences. To Mr Sun's mind, mastering the use of pronouns indeed represented progress in terms of language and script; it could lead to economy in terms of language – in other words, the rather verbose expression "that antecedent character" (本字) or "that antecedent name" (本名) (referring to an item that had previously appeared in the work) could be dispensed with. And this is precisely why, if "that antecedent character" or "that antecedent name" could be replaced by a pronoun, and we use *ta* 他 to refer to them, then we will always be able to indicate clearly what

The Debate Over the Character Ta 她   59

Figure 4.3 Magazine cartoons continue to use the character *ta* 他 to refer to women. Taken from Issue 5, September 1920 of *Emancipation Pictorial* 《解放画报》.

we are referring to and therefore there is no need for further derivatives of *ta* 他. He argued:

> If we were to work on the form of a character and change or add a symbol, then what use would we have for a pronoun? Would it not be better to just go ahead and use the original character and be done with it? If we say that foreign languages make many distinctions with the third person pronoun and we should follow suit, then that is no reason. They have their own reasons for needing to make the distinction. If we were to use our *ta* 他 without differentiating, then we would cope, and it is precisely because our *ta* 他 is so versatile that we can do this.[25]

Nevertheless, Mr Sun failed to elaborate exactly why he thought the utility of the Chinese *ta* 他 character was so superior.

There is another reason why Sun Xunqun was opposed to a gendered differentiation of the character *ta* 他, and that is that he believed that "It is not true that Chinese script is imprecise. In fact, it is *too* precise and so its cultural dissemination has been somewhat slow." We only have to look at the "*Shuowen Jiezi* 《说文解字》 or at dictionaries where the differentiation between emphasis and casualness, complexity and simplicity is extremely fine" to realise this. For this reason, the highest priority at the moment should be to "Eliminate the many unnecessary distinctions that have existed in the language", and not to actively go out and create more new distinctions.[26]

In response to these views of Mr Sun, the linguist Gong Dengchao 龚登朝 raised a point of debate. He published an article in *Light of Learning* 《学灯》, noting that in simple conversation and essays it is possible to "insist on indiscriminately using" the *ta* 他 character, but that this was definitely not possible in more complex articles. Naturally, the use of a gender-distinguishing third person pronoun would ultimately have limits. In other words, there would always be the possibility that it would "not be entirely practical" or "no matter how much it was reformed, there would always be difficult circumstances". However, when such truly difficult and special circumstances arise, it might be best not to use a pronoun at all, and instead use the original noun. This is not to say that pronouns might not be useful. Pronouns, after all, are both precise and convenient and therefore should be used in much of our conversation and writing. At the same time, Mr Gong conceded that while "Classical Chinese does incorporate many distinguishing characters that are extremely illogical, the vernacular language should simply discard them". For example, animals like pigs and goats have different terms for different years in their life cycle and terms for relatives are differentiated with much precision and detail, and so on. These pedantic differentiating terms may need to be discarded and the imprecise third person pronoun in Chinese may need to be improved, but this is not to say that these two things are incompatible.[27]

On February 27, 1922, the *Common Sense* 《常识》 supplement to *Shen Bao* 《申报》 which was presided over by Yang Yinhang 杨荫杭 published the article "Regarding *Ta* 她" 《说她》 under the pseudonym *Zhen* 箴 or "Warning". The article summed up the opinions of such individuals as Han Bing and others and added the writer's own thoughts, openly declaring his/her allegiance to the camp of those who opposed the character *ta* 她. In the body of the text, the author pointed out that the character *ta* 她 could be found in the *Yupian: The Female Radical Section* 《玉篇·女部》 and that it was used to represent the character *jie* 姐 [older sister] in days gone by. It was also pronounced as a combination of the consonant of the character 兹 *zi* and the vowel of 也 *ye*, that is, *zie*. In the distant past it was also sometimes rendered *zie* 馳 while Sichuanese called their mother *jie* 姐, so therefore "the three characters *jie* 姐, *ta* 她, and *zie* 馳 were all pronounced *zie*, meaning mother". Thus, when "those who now advocate the New Literature" use the character *ta* 她 specifically to represent the feminine, feeling that it is some "new" word and that it is a novelty, the truth is otherwise. At the same time, he also solemnly yet humorously "warned" the reader:

> If all women were to be called "mother", then a strong woman would voice her disapproval angrily, and if she was weak, her facial expression might betray her anger. If she was a vulgar woman she might perhaps curse and

swear or want to slap your face. Meanwhile, those advocates of the New Literature would, out of their great loathing for traditional culture and having not thought about it thoroughly, point at all women and call them mother, albeit without meaning to be disparaging. They simply do this out of ignorance!

The author continues:

Perhaps we should ask people now-a-days why we use *xiaojie* 小姐 to address an unmarried woman? Calling an unmarried woman *xiaojie* 小姐 is similar to calling a man who has a father *shaoye* 少爺. The term *shaoye* 少爺 respects both the father and the son. Similarly, the term *xiaojie* 小姐 respects both the mother and the daughter. The meaning [of the terms] is unmistakeable because *xiaojie* 小姐 is a deferential appellation while *dajie* 大姐 in contrast is contemptuous. Since *ta* 她 has the same pronunciation and meaning as *jie* 姐 and *zie* 馳, if we were to use *ta* 她 to replace *ta* 他 when referring to a female then it would be extremely vulgar!

The original form of the *ta* 他 character was *ta* 它, which is the ancient form of the word for "snake" (*she* 蛇). In ancient times, thatched dwellings suffered greatly from the presence of snakes, so people would ask each other "Do you have any snakes"? Later people borrowed the *tuo* 佗 character (as in "burden/load") to refer to a man whilst retaining the *ta* 它 sound; it took the consonant from *tu* 徒 and the vowel from *he* 何 to form the homophone *ta*. In modern-day Wuxi it still carries the original sound. The common form of *ta* 他 is indicative of a "human being", but there is no indication of the sound. What is more, this word has long been in use, appearing as early as in the *Yu Pian* 《玉篇》. If we consider the composite character that incorporates both *ren* 人 and *ye* 也 as a compound ideographic construct, then the *ye* 也 character originally referred to a female; so *zie* 馳 must refer to a woman rather than a man. Moreover, men and women are both human beings, and we are after all advocating equality of the sexes, so why shouldn't we just use the *ta* 他 character for both? If we insist on replacing *ta* 他 with *ta* 她, then it will cause confusion whereby we would be calling a woman mother, and what could be gained from that?![28]

Unfortunately, I have so far been unable to determine the real name of this author who regularly published short "Idle Talk" (常谈) pieces in the "Common Sense" (常识) supplement to the *Shen Bao* 《申报》during 1920–1924.

In summary, of the openly published discussions during the period from 1920 to 1922, the supporters of the view that it was necessary to have a gender distinction in the third person pronoun still clearly occupied the dominant position. And among the advocates for a gendered distinction, those who championed the character *yi* 伊 were more or less in the ascendancy. At the end of April, 1920, before *New Man* 《新人》 magazine published (under the title "The Debate Over the Question of the Character '*Ta* 她'" 《"她"字问题的辩论》) its compilation of articles involved in the debate which Han Bing's article "This Is Liu Bannong's Error"

《这是刘牛农的错》 had triggered, the magazine's editor in chief Wang Wuwei 王无为 added a special "Editor's note" in which he advanced an interim summary of the debate which tended to reflect the view of the observers of the debate that the character *ta* 她 was already wavering and that *yi* 伊 had temporarily occupied the more advantageous position. He writes:

> On the question of the character *ta* 她, from the moment Han Bing advocated for its overthrow, there was a ferocious and substantive response. Currently both sides of the debate have taken a brief pause. The result is that the *ta* 她 character that Liu Bannong created has been fundamentally shaken whilst Han Bing's launchpad for attacking it has also undergone some changes. Now, such esteemed colleagues as [Sun] Zuji 祖基 and Mengshen 梦沈 who had expressed their lack of faith in Han Bing, are inclining towards using *yi* 伊. So, whether or not *ta* 她 has value is no longer a major issue. The question now is whether it is appropriate or not to use *yi* 伊 as the feminine pronoun and what character should be used to represent non-defined objects and thus create an appropriate totality or end point. I sincerely hope that our esteemed colleagues will continue to prosecute the debate.[29]

Apart from those mentioned previously, the arguments that the advocates for the superiority of *yi* 伊 over the alternative *ta* 她 at the time included a further two lines of reasoning which are worth mentioning. One was where some stressed that in traditional Chinese the *yi* 伊 character could act like the earlier *zhen* 朕 which mutated from a broad to a narrow meaning. *Zhen* 朕 was able to be transformed from "a personal pronoun that could be used by everyone" to later habitually being seen as a personal pronoun used exclusively by the emperor. Thus, for the *yi* 伊 character to be transformed from "a pronoun that is commonly used for the third person of both genders" to become "exclusively used as a third person singular pronoun for the female sex" would be logical.[30] The second line refers to some who had begun to look at the two characters from the point of view of their radicals and believed that the structure of the *yi* 伊 character more reasonably reflected the spirit of gender equality than did the *ta* 她 character.[31]

Nevertheless, despite there being multiple attacks by the advocates of *yi* 伊 on *ta* 她, internal contradictions were unavoidable. For example, certain crucial debaters (such as Han Bing) invariably emphasised the antiquity of the *ta* 她 character and hence the ease with which it could be confused with its original meaning. On the other hand, the majority of those advocating for *yi* 伊 (such as Chen Wangdao et al.) were mindful of Zhou Zuoren's original misgivings and criticised *ta* 她 for its recent fabrication since "presses would certainly need to cast new blocks, adding a layer of inconvenience to the printing process."[32] This contradiction is to this day not without a certain value to historians when contemplating the question of the nature of *ta* 她 immediately following its appearance.

In contrast to the advocates of *yi* 伊, one of the main complicating factors for the proponents of *ta* 她 was the question of pronunciation. The vast majority recognised the impossibility of distinguishing between *ta* 她 and *ta* 他 in terms of

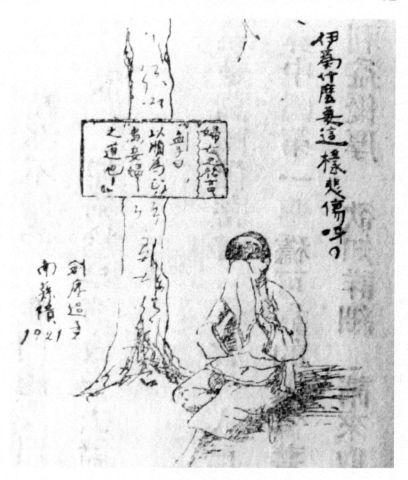

Figure 4.4 The *yi* 伊 character is used to specifically refer to the feminine and to illustrate the plight of women. Originally carried in the May 1921 Issue 11 of *Emancipation Pictorial* 《解放画报》.

pronunciation as being a defect or inadequacy. Nor were they able to suggest a consistent strategy for changing the sound that could win acceptance. Some, like Zou Zhengjian 邹政坚, as a consequence even suggested pronouncing *ta* 她 like *yi* 伊,[33] thereupon encountering the rebuke of many of the advocates of *yi* 伊. In the words of the linguist Chen Wangdao 陈望道, "If *ta* 她 is pronounced like *ta* 他, then the sound would be the same; and if it was pronounced as *yi* 伊, then why not just use *yi* 伊 and be done with it?!"[34]

Earlier, Liu Bannong, Qian Xuantong 钱玄同 and Zhou Zuoren had suggested a similar change to pronounce *ta* 他 as *tuo* 拖, however they quickly realised that this was somewhat pretentious and dropped it. Han Bing's aforementioned multi-pronged attack on Liu Bannong regarding the pronunciation of *ta* 她 also exemplifies the fact that in the competition with *yi* 伊, since the supporters of *ta* 她 championed a pronunciation that differed with *ta* 他, they in fact placed themselves momentarily in a passive and distinctly disadvantageous position.

In fact, not only did *yi* 伊 take a leading position for a time in the formal debate, but it also displayed its superiority in the actual process of application. When I employed a statistical methodology to the frequency of *yi* 伊 and *ta* 她 to the magazines and literature of the May Fourth period, I was clearly struck by the fact that *yi* 伊 outnumbered the occurrence of *ta* 她 by a considerable margin in the period 1919 to 1922 as a representation of the third person singular. Besides the brothers Lu Xun and Zhou Zuoren, as well as Qian Xuantong, Mao Dun 茅盾 (Shen Yanbing 沈雁冰) also occasionally used *ta* 她 throughout 1920. However, prior to 1921 in most instances they all consciously used *yi* 伊. After abandoning *ta'nü* 他女 and prior to July 1922, Ye Shengtao 叶圣陶 mostly used *yi* 伊, as did Zhu Ziqing 朱自清 from 1919 to July 1922. Li Dazhao 李大钊, Shao Lizi 邵力子, Li Hanjun 李汉俊, Liang Zongdai 梁宗岱, Chen Wangdao 陈望道, Liu Dabai 刘大白, Li Jinxi 黎锦熙 and other figures who were active in the commentary and linguistics fields also consciously used *yi* 伊 in the period 1919 through 1922, and many of them continued to use the term even much longer.

Perhaps we might take the poem "The Dahlia" 《大丽花》 [35] by Qian Xingcun 钱杏邨 (A Ying 阿英), published in July 1921, as an example and give a snapshot of how the character *yi* 伊 was used in verse to represent the feminine third person:

The Dahlia

Red – a bright red ball gown,
    Graces her [伊] beautiful form.
    Accentuating her [伊] face – white as snow;
    Her [伊] hair – golden.
    A demure visage,
    Tilted towards a rosy setting sun. . . .
"Wind Aunt" is here,
    She [伊] bursts into a vigorous dance;
    She [伊] – she [伊] falters,
    Trembling – trembling uncontrollably.
    How she [伊] longs for me,
    How I pity her [伊],
    I kiss her [伊] passionately,
    She [伊] – she [伊] dips her [伊] head in silence and we embrace tenderly. –
    A guileless affection trembles nervously,
    A beguiling gaze stares vacantly. . . .
    The faint tracks of tears;
    Deep in meditation.

While replete with poetic qualities – or perhaps to the lovers of the "new literature" at the time, this poem might exemplify the poetic zenith of the day – I have simply chosen it to illustrate the use of *yi* 伊 to represent the third person in literature.

In view of the previous situation, it is not surprising that between September and November, 1920, Han Bing, who opposed *ta* 她 and advocated for *yi* 伊, determined that the vast majority of newspapers and magazines all used *yi* 伊 and not *ta* 她, declaring that the *yi* 伊 character enjoyed "universal promise" and used this as a riposte to Liu Bannong. Meanwhile, at the time, Han Bing was not alone in holding this view. In June 1921, throwing himself into the fray, Da Tong 大同 put pen to paper and declared, "It is most appropriate to use the *yi* 伊 character. While no-one has decreed it so, still its use has slowly become universal in literary circles."[36] In November 1922, Qian Xuantong declared even more convincingly:

> Recently Li Jinxi 黎锦熙 and I have deliberated and found that not only has the use of *yi* 伊 for the feminine already become the norm, but there is some basis in classical literature for it, so there is no need for further adjustment.[37]

However, what these individuals failed to realise is that the emphatic position of *yi* 伊 in terms of practice and confirmation was not to last long, and less than two years later the scene had experienced a reversal, with the final result now common knowledge.

Notes

1 *New Man* 《新人》 was a magazine that was established in April 1920 by Wang Wuwei 王无为 and his associates of the New Man Society 新人社. Its purpose was to criticise the current situation within the new culture movement in an attempt to affect an expansion of the movement. The core members of the Society were committed to the movement for the liberation of women and were dissatisfied with the dogmatic nature of Chen Duxiu 陈独秀, the leader of the new culture movement, and certain specific proposals of the New Youth faction 新青年派 that he led. When the journal was launched, it consciously focused on the issue of the word "she", which was quite a sensational move.

2 Han, Bing's 寒冰 original name was Sun Yuqi 孙毓麒. He was only 18 years of age when he joined the New Man Society and published this article. At the time, he was a student at Fudan University 复旦大学, later gaining fame as Sun Hanbing 孙寒冰 and travelling to the USA where he studied politics. On his return, he taught at Fudan University where he served first as Dean and then Provost of the Law School. The work "This Is Liu Bannong's Error" 《这是刘半农的错》 was drafted and signed by Han Bing 寒冰, however it incorporated the views of two other members of the New Man Society (using the pen names "Xiu Shui" 秀水 and "Ji Shi" 积石), so we can see that it also expressed the shared attitudes and views of his colleagues.

3 The texts of this debate were originally carried in *Light of Leaning* 《学灯》 on April 18, 20, 24, 25, and 27, 1920.

4 Han Bing knew that apart from the character *yi* 伊 acting as a third person pronoun, in ancient times it had been used for the second person, much like *ni* 你. Later many

66 *The Debate Over the Character Ta* 她

linguists like Mr Lü Shuxiang 吕叔湘 pointed out that in the Jin and Yuan periods *yi* 伊 was used in this manner, indicating the second person.

5 Han, Bing 寒冰, "This is Liu Bannong's Error" 《这是刘半农的错》 (carried in *New Man* 《新人》 Vol. 1, Issue 1, April 1920), "A Detailed Critique of the Question of the Character *Ta* 她" 《关于"她"字问题的申论》 (carried in *Light of Learning* 《学灯》 on April 27, 1920, and reprinted in *New Man* 《新人》, Vol. 1, Issue 2, 1920.

6 Han Bing's original words were:

> Texts are structured, and any text that contains the character *ta* 他 must have a contextual basis. Therefore, people who read the text will naturally understand the meaning of *ta* 他 and know that what it represents is male, female or neuter, so there is no need for reform.

For this text together with his fifth reason, see the two items: "This is Liu Bannong's Error" 《这是刘半农的错》 and "Refuting the Research on the Character *Ta* 她 – If Liu Bannong Is Not Wrong Then Who Is?" 《驳"她"字的研究 – 刘半农不错是谁错？》 – the latter text was carried in *Light of Learning* 《学灯》 on April 20, 1920 and reprinted in *New Man* 《新人》 Issue 2.

7 Han, Bing 寒冰, "A Detailed Critique of the Question of the Character *Ta* 她" 《关于"她"字问题的申论》, carried in *Light of Learning* 《学灯》 on April 27, 1920.

8 Ibid.

9 In sum, this argument remains relatively rational, and might be fair and reasonable, but in the exchange between Han Bing and Sun Zuji there are often attacks mocking the other party as "ignorant of logic", "not erudite enough", "offering shallow reasoning", "cacophonous", "using reasoning that holds no value for debate" and so on.

10 For example, Meng Shen 梦沈 writes in "Refuting the Research on the Character *Ta* 她: Could It Be That Liu Bannong Is Wrong?" 《驳"她"字的研究：难道是刘半农错么》：

> Of course, you need to look at the context since you want to find the source, but if you do not use the character *ta* 她 to represent the female in some places, you can arrange the context as carefully as you like, but unfortunately other people will not be able to understand you.

Quoted from *Light of Leaning* 《学灯》 April 25, 1920.

11 This view is the result of Liu Bannong's synthesis of the relevant arguments in his "On the Question of the Character *Ta* 她." Before Liu, Sun Zuji 孙祖基 had already pointed out:

> The first and second persons involve a face-to-face conversation and everything is clear. There is no problem with the attributes of pronouns. However, it is somewhat difficult to use the third person, because the third person is often not there when the first and second person speak. It is therefore necessary to make use of this difference in order to reveal the true intent of the text.

(See Sun, Zuji 孙祖基, "Against 'Refuting the Research on the Character *Ta* 她'" 《非"驳'她'字的研究"》, carried in *Light of Learning* 《学灯》 April 24, 1920 in the "Youth Club" "青年俱乐部" column; or alternatively see *New Man* 《新人》 Issue 2.) Meanwhile, Meng Shen 梦沈 stressed the following from another angle: "You" (*ni* 你) and "I" (*wo* 我) are both just single persons, so we cannot make a mistake, however "he/she/it" (*ta* 他) represents a third person and "the third person comprises numerous others, so one must make a distinction." (See Meng, Shen 梦沈, "Refuting the Research on the Character *Ta* 她: Could It Be That Liu Bannong Is Wrong?" 《驳"她"字的研究：难道是刘半农错么？》, originally carried in *Light of Learning* 《学灯》 April 25, 1920.)

12 Da, Tong 大同, "Research on the 'Third Person Pronoun'" 《"第三身代名词"底研究》, reprinted in *New Man* 《新人》 Issue 2.

13 Liu Bannong's 刘半农 article "On the Question of the Character *Ta* 她" 《"她"字问题》 was first carried in *Light of Learning* 《学灯》 on August 9, 1920, and was later reprinted by *New Man* 《新人》 in its Issue 6.
14 See Sun Zuji's 孙祖基 two articles "Research on the Character *Ta* 她 – Is Liu Bannong Really Wrong?" 《"她"字的研究：刘半农果真是错吗？》 and "Against 'Refuting the Research on the Character *Ta* 她'" 《非"驳·她'字的研究"》.
15 Han, Bing 寒冰, "Refuting the Research on the Character *Ta* 她 – If Liu Bannong Is Not Wrong Then Who Is?" 《驳"她"字的研究 – 刘半农不错是谁错？》.
16 In 1935 when Liu Bannong 刘半农 published his *Essays of [Liu] Bannong* 《半农杂文》 the article "On the Question of the Character *Ta* 她" 《"她"字问题》 which was included in the collection saw the deletion of the reference to German in the section "In French and German . . ." as well as the reference to "plural" in the section "In English . . . the abstract name for the plural . . . ." in order to avoid any ambiguity and to ensure accuracy.
17 See Liu, Bannong 刘半农, "On the Question of the Character *Ta* 她" 《"她"字问题》. The article indicates that it was composed in London on June 6, 1920 and carried in the column "Discussion and Debate" "讨论·商榷" in *Light of Learning* on August 9, 1920, while Han Bing's 寒冰 "Further Discussion on 'the Question of the Character *Ta* 她'" 《续论"她字问题"》 was published on August 12 in *Light of Learning* 《学灯》 and later reprinted in Issue 6 of *New Man* 《新人》 with Liu Bannong's article included in the same issue of *New Man* 《新人》 as an "Appendix". However it must be pointed out that in 1935 when Liu Bannong 刘半农 included his "On the Question of the Character *Ta* 她" 《"她"字问题》 in his *Essays of [Liu] Bannong* 《半农杂文》, he had completely revised his proposition in the original text that the "strong form" and "weak form" in English pronunciation be imitated, and pointed out that:

> The character *ta* 他 in the common language carries two readings: one being *tá*, which is used in speech and the other, *tuó*, which is used for reading. I am not averse to establishing "他" as "*tá*" and "她" as "*tuó*". To change the pronunciation is indeed a difficult task, but I don't think it would be too difficult to insist on a pronunciation that already exists within the language.

But this change left some of Han Bing's refutations without a target. *Essays of [Liu] Bannong* 《半农杂文》 indicates that the original version of this piece was carried in *The China Times: Light of Learning* 《时事新报·学灯》 on August 9, 1920, and this important change was not mentioned. Other changes that were not mentioned included his introduction of the 它 element (this will be discussed later). Because people have subsequently understood his proposals from those that were included in his "On the Question of the Character *Ta* 她" 《"她"字问题》 as published in *Essays of [Liu] Bannong* 《半农杂文》, there are many who misrepresent him. For example, Liu He 刘禾 makes a similar mistake when she quotes Liu Bannong 刘半农. See the Chinese translation of Liu He 刘禾, *Translingual Practice* 《跨语际实践》 quoted previously, p. 51.
18 Han, Bing 寒冰, "Further Discussion on 'the Question of the Character *Ta* 她'" 《续论"她字问题"》, originally carried in *Light of Learning* 《学灯》, August 12, 1920, and later reprinted by *New Man* 《新人》 Issue 6.
19 Jin, Fushen 金福申, "The Pronoun *Ta* (他, he) and *Ta* (她, she)" 《代名词他(he)同她(she)》, carried in the *Discussion* 讨论 column of *The Morning Post Supplement* 《晨报副刊》, March 18, 1921.
20 Chen, Sibai 陈斯白, "Opinions on the Differentiation of the Character *Ta* 他 (he)" 《"他" 字分化的意见》, carried in *Light of Learning* 《学灯》, October 8, 1921.
21 Han, Bing 寒冰, "Further Discussion on 'the Question of the Character *Ta* 她'" 《续论"她字问题"》, reprinted in *New Man* 《新人》 Issue 6.

22 This article by Cai Yuanpei 蔡元培 was carried consecutively in *Enlightenment Magazine* 《觉悟》 June 27–28, 1920. I would like to thank Shen Jie 沈洁 in Shanghai for his valuable assistance whilst I was consulting both *Enlightenment Magazine* 《觉悟》 and *Light of Learning* 《学灯》.
23 See previous reference to Cai, Yuanpei 蔡元培, "Speech to the Beijing National Language Pedagogical Institute" 《北京国语传习所的演说》.
24 See Da, Tong 大同, "The Third Person Feminine Pronoun in Drama" 《戏剧里第三身女性代名词》. In this article, Da Tong quotes Chen Dabei's 陈大悲 specific objection to the character *ta* 她 as follows: "While in the script readers can distinguish between the masculine and feminine, however, when performed on stage, the audience will not be able to understand"; meanwhile, if *yi* 伊 was used, only a handful of people will understand unless the country as a whole gives the order that "'from a certain month or day, all 400,000,000 citizens must only use *yi* 伊 to represent the third person feminine and not *ta* 他.' Only under these circumstances might it be successful." The subtext being that it was impossible. Da Tong also criticised Chen Dabei 陈大悲 for, on the one hand opposing the use of a pronoun to distinguish gender in the third person, while on the other hand, whilst translating *Silver Box* 《银盒》 himself used *ta* 她, which was at odds with what he had espoused. This article was carried in the *Correspondence* 通信 column of *Enlightenment Magazine* 《觉悟》, June 7, 1921.
25 Sun, Xunqun 孙逊群, "A Discussion of '*Ta*, 他'" 《"他"的讨论》, carried in the *Youth Club* "青年俱乐部" column of *Light of Learning* 《学灯》, October 27, 1921.
26 Ibid.
27 Gong, Dengchao 龚登朝, "The Debate over How to Read '*Ta*, 他'" 《读"他"的讨论》, *Light of Learning* 《学灯》, November 2, 1921.
28 Zhen 箴, "Regarding *Ta* 她" 《说她》, carried in *Shen Bao* 《申报》, February 27, 1922, p. 17. The attitude of this author is similar to that of Zhou Shoujuan 周瘦鹃 who presided over this issue of *Shen Bao: Free Talk* 《申报·自由谈》 and was an author and representative of the Mandarin Ducks and Butterflies School 鸳鸯蝴蝶派.
29 Carried in *New Man* 《新人》 Issue 2, May to July 1920. Strictly speaking, the main aim of Sun Zuji 孙祖基 and his fellow travelers was to oppose any wholesale return to a use of the character *ta* 他 which made no distinction along gender lines. As to whether *yi* 伊 or *ta* 她 was preferable, they were not overly concerned. As Sun Zuji 孙祖基 argued, Han Bing's advocacy for "the restoration of the *ta* 他 character and the cancellation of the *ta* 她 character cannot be tolerated, however, whether at a later date the character *ta* 她 may be challenged, that is another matter. I believe that this *ta* 她 character can for the moment be used in the transition between *ta* 他 and some X character. In any event, a new character must be created."

(Sun, Zuji 孙祖基, "Research on the Character *Ta* 她 – Is Liu Bannong Really Wrong?" 《"她"字的研究 – 刘半农果真是错吗？》)

Thus, we can say that Sun Zuji was not totally convinced of the value of *ta* 她. However, it is not completely accurate to say that he, like Meng Shen 梦沈 and others "was on a trajectory to adopt the character *yi* 伊."
30 Da, Tong 大同, "Research on the 'Third Person Pronoun'" 《"第三身代名词"底研究》. Chen Wangdao 陈望道 in "The Female Third Person 'Pronoun'" 《女子性第三身"身次代名词"》 also believed that "There is a solid historical basis for narrowing the scope of personal pronouns. We have therefore chosen *yi* 伊 and not *ta* 她", carried in *Enlightenment Magazine* 《觉悟》, May 3, 1920.
31 The author sought the help of Dr Shen Wei 沈巍 to make a copy of this illustration which uses the character *yi* 伊 to represent the feminine third person pronoun along with the preceding few illustrations that use *ta* 他 or *ta* 她 for the same purpose when I published my article "The Story of the Character '*Ta*' 她" 《"她"字的故事》. When I published the present work, I had them re-photographed with the help of Chen Yiming 陈一鸣.

32 Chen, Wangdao 陈望道, "The Female Third Person 'Pronoun'" 《女子性第三身 "身次代名词"》, carried in *Enlightenment Magazine* 《觉悟》, supplement to *The Republican Daily News* 《民国日报》 on May 3, 1920.
33 Zou, Zhengjian 邹政坚, "The Debate over 'Refuting the Research on the Character *Ta* 她'" 《"驳她字的研究" 的讨论》, carried in *Light of Learning* 《学灯》, April 24, 1920.
34 Chen, Wangdao 陈望道, "The Female Third Person 'Pronoun'" 《女子性第三身 "身次代名词"》. Han Bing, Da Tong and others also offered similar words of censure. For example, Da Tong pointed out:

> Since the character *ye* 也 was written *ta* 它 in the ancient past, and *ta* 他 was actually the ancient written character for *ta* 它, therefore, by analogy *ta* 她 is the same as *ta* 他. Thus, there is no reason to pronounce *ta* 她 as *yi* 伊, so *yi* 伊 should be used instead.
> (See Da, Tong 大同, "Research on the 'Third Person Pronoun'" 《"第三身代名词" 底研究》 referenced previously.)

35 "The Dahlia" 《大丽花》, carried in *Emancipation Pictorial* 《解放画报》 Issue 13, July 30, 1921.
36 Da, Tong 大同, "The Third Person Feminine Pronoun in Drama" 《戏剧里第三身女性代名词》, carried in *Enlightenment Magazine* 《觉悟》, June 7, 1921, in its *Correspondence* 通信 column.
37 Qian, Xuantong 钱玄同, "Discussion of the Differentiation between the Two terms 'He' (*ta*, 他) and 'They' (*tamen*, 他们)" 《"他"和"他们"两个词儿的分化之讨论》, carried in *National Language Monthly* 《国语月刊》, Vol. 1, Issue 10, November 20, 1922.

5 Gender Confusion: Sensitivity Over "Female"-Related Terms

Concepts of Gender Equality and the Fate of the Character *Ta* 她

The character *ta* (她, or "she") was born during the May Fourth period and was initially nurtured amongst the ranks of the devotees of *New Youth* 《新青年》. It was boldly trialed by the "new youth" at Peking University and other institutes of higher learning who were committed to a literary revolution and to getting on board the "The Renaissance". It was initially employed when domestically the calls for "co-education" and "women's liberation" were ringing out and internationally the movement for female participation in politics was at its zenith.... All these things naturally led people to ruminate over the legitimate debate between the contemporary concept of equality of the sexes and the appearance of the feminine character *ta* 她 or "she", and the historical relationship between the two. In today's eyes, or at least in the eyes of the present imaginatively challenged author, when compared to the sense of feminine delicacy and endearment that the character *yi* 伊 so easily conveys, the feminine *ta* 她, similar in sound and form with the (now masculine) *ta* 他, would appear to evoke a more "independent" and "liberated" feminine image which stands equal to men and furthermore, is associated even more intimately with the "New May Fourth Woman" in the historical imagination.

However, despite any analysis from the point of view of historical background, the coining and popularisation of the feminine character *ta* 她 undoubtedly did bear an intimate and subtle relationship with its potential utility to the modern consciousness. This would appear to be the obvious and natural conclusion we must draw in explaining the birth of the feminine character *ta* 她. But in fact, in thumbing through the relevant historical documents which address this question, I am yet to identify any formal text which openly and legitimately argues for the character from the modern standpoint of equality of the sexes. On the contrary, this concept in fact forms the most important and most powerful ideological basis for many contemporaries' opposition to the character.

1 Three Instances of Using Equality of the Sexes to Oppose the Feminine *Ta* 她

One instance is the use of concepts such as gender equality to fundamentally oppose the gendered delineation of the "third person". This can be illustrated by an open letter from an individual named Zhuang Fu 壯甫 which was published in

DOI: 10.4324/9781003359449-6

Enlightenment Magazine 《觉悟》 on April 16, 1920, at the height of the debate over the question of the feminine character *ta* 她. The letter reads:

> On the question of women's liberation, aren't most of those who currently advocate the new culture clamoring loudly with such super stylish phrases as "cutting the hair", "discarding the skirt", "abandoning personal adornment", "public concourse of communication" or "co-education"? And what is the reason they spare no effort to advocate thus? It is none other than to dismantle any distinctions between men and women, to break down any delineation, and to declare that, apart from any physiological considerations, there is no distinction between men and women and that we are all relegated to the status of "human beings". If this is so, then there is one matter that I cannot understand.
>
> Does this character *ta* 她 refer to a female version of the character *ta* 他? If yes, then I have a slight objection: 1. Perhaps this feminine *ta* 她 character is seen to imitate the meaning of the English "She", or 2. Perhaps it was already part of our national script. Of these two scenarios, no matter what, I vehemently disapprove. And why? If we say that it has been learned from abroad, then I dare to say that these individuals who would learn from the West have not done a very good job! At this time of striving to obliterate all traces of gender, in marking it out with this new styled feminine *ta* 她 character, and making the delineation between male and female so crystal clear, isn't this just too ridiculous? And if we were to say that it already existed in our national script, then why was it never thus described in the classics? So, if it were to be resolved in this manner then the rituals and manners of many thousands of years would all need to be discarded. Should not such an unnecessary thing as this then also be discarded?[1]

Those who held such a view were certainly not an insignificant minority – in fact they were quite common. For example, just two months later another by the name of Yixuan 忆萱 wrote to Shao Lizi 邵力子, editor of *The Republican Daily News* 《民国日报》, expressing doubt and dissatisfaction at *Enlightenment Magazine's* 《觉悟》 consistent rendering of *ta* 他 as *ta* 她 in order to distinguish between the masculine and feminine third person. The letter reads:

> Do not the columns of *Enlightenment* advocate for abolition of the distinction between men and women? I recall that previously some were critical of addressing women as "Miss"! Isn't using *ta* 她 doing exactly the same thing? So if we are to make the distinction in this way, then . . . shouldn't we add a feminine *nü* 女 radical to all pronouns relating to the female sex, and wouldn't that too be counted as new culture? Shouldn't this practice be promoted?[2]

Naturally this type of opinion was subsequently refuted. After Zhuang Fu's 壯甫 letter appeared, Da Tong 大同 who had advocated distinguishing between the masculine and feminine third person singular quickly counter-attacked:

We are currently investigating the written confluence of the masculine and feminine third person singular; we are not attempting to advocate for any distinction between men and women. This is a misunderstanding on the part of Master Zhuang Fu 壯甫! According to Zhuang Fu's opinion, the two characters "male" and "female" should be extirpated, and a new omni-gendered character used instead. Such a character might be manufactured but it would require all humanity to become omni-gendered, and that cannot be achieved.[3]

In his open letter in reply to Yi Xuan 忆萱, Shao Lizi expressed a similar sentiment. He wrote:

The feminine and masculine third person singular, like the feminine and masculine genders, are different, and it is easy to distinguish between them in the written word. This presents no obstruction to breaking down the barriers between men and women. Many have outlined the reason for this. Many have also discussed the absence of the necessity to add a feminine *nü* 女 radical to the first and third person feminine pronouns . . . . However, we must recognize that this is wholly a question of script and that it has nothing to do with the delineation between male and female.[4]

The second expression of the influence of the May Fourth concept of gender equality on the question of the character *ta* 她 is that some advocated for the retention of the *ta* 他 character as the common symbol representing both men and women, but following the *ta* 他 character with a qualifying male *nan* 男 or female *nü* 女 character. In other words, they would be distinguished in script as *ta'nan* 他男 or *ta'nü* 他女. This view deliberately differs with the earlier proposal by Zhou Zuoren 周作人 of retaining the original *ta* 他 to represent masculinity and adopting *ta'nü* 他女 to represent femininity, a proposal which was obviously also based on the principle of gender equality. However, in the final analysis, in the contest with the alternative feminine *ta* 她 character, the view at the time was that it was clumsy and was rejected and had little impact.[5]

At the time, the most powerful move to use the concept of gender equality to oppose the character *ta* 她, and the one which had the most enduring influence, was the hype surrounding the use of the gendered radical component of the characters *ta* 她 and *ta* 他, and the accompanying strong support for the use of *yi* 伊 for the feminine third person singular. For this reason, some in the feminist movement in fact for a long period of time openly refused to use the character *ta* 她.

Not surprisingly, leading the charge to consider the question from this point of view was none other than Han Bing 寒冰, who had taken the lead in publicly opposing the feminine *ta* 她. In his "A Detailed Critique of the Question of the Character *Ta* 她" 《关于"她"字问题的申论》in April 1920, whilst explaining

Gender Confusion: Sensitivity Over "Female"-Related Terms 73

that it would be better to "use the *yi* 伊 character directly" rather than pronounce the feminine *ta* 她 character with the *yi* 伊 sound, he pointed out:

> Since the character *ta* 他 has a *human* 人 radical, as does the character *yi* 伊, therefore, from the point of view of gender equality, this would appear to be fair, and it would avoid the use of an extremely pretentious form, so on balance it is preferable.

Because this was not Han Bing's 寒冰 primary argument, he was unable to expand on the point and I am yet to identify anyone who offered a timely rebuttal to it. In February 1922, Zhou Shoujuan 周瘦鹃, whom I have mentioned previously, offered a similar opinion from the standpoint of the demand for gender equality.

From the various relevant records of the time, dissenting views and sentiments were in fact quite rife throughout society. For example, in the September 1922 *Modern Woman* 《现代妇女》 supplement to *The China Times* 《时事新报》 stated:

> A certain gentleman in a certain publication wrote an article in which he used the character 男也 a number of times, taxing the typesetters such that their sweat fell like rain . . . . Apparently, this was an act of vengeance on behalf of the character *ta* 她.[6]

Figure 5.1 You Luan 友鸾 uses the character "男也" and the word "男士" in the work "'Miss [女士]' and 'She [她]'".

Naturally, this was also an expression of the concept of gender equality.

In July 1924, the third annual conference of the China Education Reform Society 中华教育改进社 was especially convened to discuss the motion that "such pronouns and adjectives as *ta* 她, *ta* 牠 and *na* 哪 be adopted and that their pronunciation be confirmed in order to reform the national language." Mr Zhu Ziqing 朱自清 who had participated in this discussion, recorded with humor the relevant content of the discussion and at the same time revealed the genuine existence of the viewpoints previously mentioned. Since Mr Zhu's notes are so moving and indicative, we must quote them at length:

> (This case) The main focus of the discussion was women, and specifically on the character *ta* 她 or "she". "Humanity" or 人, and "beasts" 牛 can be left to stand as radicals. The only thing that we are having an issue with is "woman", the female *nü* 女 radical that stands beside the *ta* 她 or "she" character! And so the arguments started. One professor says, "In my 'experience', all female students detest the *ta* 她 character – the male *ta* 他 simply sports a 'human' *ren* 人 radical, but the female *ta* 她 insists on a *nü* 女, or female radical, signaling that it is a woman that is being referred to. This is what they are upset about! When I distribute my lecture notes, they often change any *ta* 他 characters by changing the *ren* 人 or human radical into a *nan* 男 or male radical to make their revenge obvious." When the audience heard this, they all chuckled as if it was quite amusing. Then another speaker rose to refute her, "I also teach a female class and I have not experienced this!" Heidegger's law then sprang into action: the reconciliation brigade arrived, saying, "It looks like we have two camps. Those who use classical Chinese are happy to use the *yi* 伊 character – like Mr Zhou Zuoren 周作人; and those who use the vernacular prefer to use the *ta* 她 character, with the users of *yi* 伊 numbering slightly less. But in fact, the two characters are identical." The sentence "Those who use classical Chinese are happy to use the *yi* 伊 character" is really interesting! It is true that classical Chinese certainly does use the *yi* 伊 character; but if we say that those *yi*'s are all women, then we cannot avoid offending quite a number of men! It is true that Mr Zhou Zuoren advocated using the *yi* 伊 word, but only in the vernacular; I can guarantee you that he never mentioned "using classical Chinese" . . . that would be doing Mr Zhou an even greater disservice! So, the reconciliation was ineffectual. A female teacher leaped to her feet, and everyone pricked up their ears because this concerned them personally and she must have some brilliant contribution to make! She spoke quite quickly, so I was only able to catch one arresting sentence, "Historically, all characters that have borne the *nü* 女 radical have been bad characters; we can never use the female *ta* 她 character!" Then a "he" immediately rose to his feet to retort,
>
> "Doesn't the *hao* 好 or 'good' character have a female *nü* 女 radical?" Everyone burst out laughing, and amidst the laughter a venerable voice suddenly interjected, "As I see it, the *ta* 他 character is like all of us common people riding in the third-class carriage; if the *ta* 她 character adds the

feminine *nü* 女 radical, then it's like inviting our female colleagues to sit in the second-class, and what's wrong with that?" At that the whole auditorium broke into laughter and the eyes of several in the audience glistened as if they were about to burst into tears. It really was a case of "laugh 'til one cries". After that, things got a little confused, probably because the meeting closed with the laughter ringing around them, whereupon the curtain closed on the fun. This "second-class", "third-class" analogy was indeed refreshing, perfectly capable of opening a new frontier in rhetoric and has left me with an enduring feeling of delight . . . . But this "second-third class distinction" also comes with exceptions: that evening as I was leaving Nanking, there in third-class I clearly spotted three "she's"! I thought to myself: why doesn't "she" and "she" and "she" sit in the second-class carriage? Could it be that they were too polite? – So, what that objector had said in the meeting must be true after all![7]

There is indeed much to ponder in Zhu Ziqing's account. Take for example the feminist teacher who opposed the feminised character *ta* 她. Of course, she angrily points out that historically no Chinese character that has borne the female radical *nü* 女 has been positive, so when we encounter the simple question "doesn't the character for 'good' [*hao* 好] also have a *nü* 女 radical?" we have no comeback! It is obvious that the depth of the dissemination of the "feminist" ideology at the time and the feminine concept of self-protection that it engendered remained quite limited. If we were to introduce the vociferous feminists of today then they no doubt would have immediately offered the following riposte, "On the face of it, there is no doubt that characters such as 'good' 好 or 'clever/wonderful' 妙 are good words, however they all use women as objects of appreciation or amusement. This shows precisely that what is reflected when social questions are viewed from a masculine standpoint is the characteristics of a male dominated society and a male-centric cultural outlook. We only have to contrast such characters as *jian* 奸, traitor, or *ji* 妓, prostitute, to see that they are even more secretive and deceptive!" If those defenders of the *ta* 她 character had been present at the time and had encountered such counterattacks, I am not sure how they would have fashioned a response.

There is no question that the more humorous part of the previously quoted piece from Zhu Ziqing is the adroit analogy of "letting women sit in the second-class carriage and men in the third-class". Mr Zhu himself was uncomfortable with the whole affair, arguing that the "venerable voice" had broken new rhetorical ground, and in fact it was this that had led the attendees, including those feminists who originally opposed it, to eventually apparently all quietly accept the motion regarding the feminine character *ta* 她.

This conveniently segues us into pondering the question of the "privilege" of women in contemporary society and how women themselves ought to confront such privilege. As it turns out, this spurious argument of "privileging" women, and bestowing on them "special rights", this extremely humorous exposé by Zhu Ziqing of patriarchal society's new trick of swindling women, had long since found exquisite expression in this era of the dawning of the concept of gender equality. It

76 *Gender Confusion: Sensitivity Over "Female"-Related Terms*

Figure 5.2 The writer Zhu Ziqing who recorded and evaluated the entertaining early discussion of the character *ta* 她.

goes without saying that given the social psychology of the time, what it was able to practically achieve far exceeded what we today can possibly imagine. During the final years of the Qing Dynasty, it was fashionable across all types of newspapers and magazines for an author to sign off as "Miss So-and-So", which was another kind of evidence: not only were male editors willing to attract readers in this way, but female correspondents were also more than happy to use this to signal their uniqueness.

Nevertheless, it is worth noting that following May Four this type of "Miss So-and-So" contributor, and especially the phenomenon of the personally attributed author, was met with denunciation and criticism. For example, on April 5, 1920, about the same time as the character *ta* 她 came under withering attack, the notoriously "unfilial" Shi Cuntong 施存统 wrote a special article severely attacking the then-strange phenomenon of female correspondents signing themselves as "Miss So-and-So". He asks:

> When we speak of "people" 人 we naturally include both sexes; when we raise the issue of equality, then both men and women should be equal: why then won't women accept that they are "people" and insist on adding the epithet "Miss" 女士? Why don't men add the epithet "Master" 男士, while women alone call themselves "Miss" 女士?

Gender Confusion: Sensitivity Over "Female"-Related Terms 77

Mr Shi moreover sternly asserts that by choosing this epithet, women add not one iota of value to their article but instead disgrace themselves with this "shameless" behavior.[8]

A year later, the debate continued in the pages of *Emancipation Pictorial* 《解放画报》. Attitudes such as Shi Cuntong's 施存统 won the personal endorsement of Zhen Xin 枕薪. In 1921 Zhen Xin 枕薪 pointed out in his essay in the magazine *Miss* 《女士》[9] that there were probably only three psychological reasons why women loved to address themselves as "Miss" 女士: first is their own acceptance

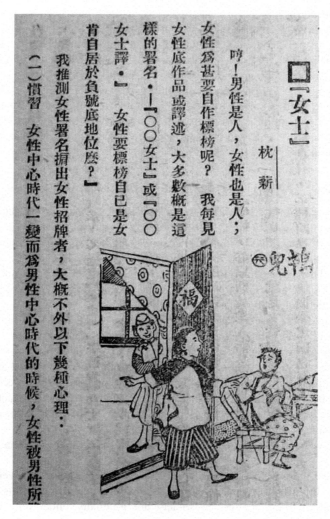

Figure 5.3 A section of Zhen Xin's article *Miss* which opposes women labelling themselves as "Miss".

of their enslaved status in a "male-centric era"; second is a result of their confused and inappropriate emulation of such expressions as "Miss" from the West; third is "the benefit of distinguishing oneself from the crowd and at the same time, highlighting their own ample talent and learning." The editor-in-chief of the magazine, Zhou Jianyun 周剑云, argued that Zhen Xin's 枕薪 view was "incontrovertible", that "it establishes the fact that such appellations as 'Mr' 先生 or 'Miss' 女士 are acceptable if uttered by others, but unnecessary if uttered by oneself," adding "I sincerely hope that my female colleagues meditate calmly on this and not . . . fly into an indignant fit of rage." Zhou Jianyun 周剑云 went on to declare, "This magazine has from its inception never added the epithet 'Miss' to works by its female contributors".[10]

What is intriguing is that, during the criticism of the use of the epithet "Miss" to indicate the special nature of the female sex at a time when the third person pronoun was being discussed, such as the previously mentioned letter of Yi Xuan 忆萱 to Shao Lizi 邵力子, some discussants occasionally and perversely used this as a reason to oppose the use of the feminine *ta* 她 character to distinguish between the masculine and feminine third person singular. The logic of this was that if you oppose the use of the title "Miss" to make a distinction from the masculine, then why must you still create and propagate a special feminine *ta* 她 character? Isn't this just gilding the lily?!

2 "Heroine" 英雌 and "She" 她: Vocabulary, Gender and Politics

The feminine self-awareness that was engendered by the May Fourth gender equality and related tides of thought in fact brought a heightened sensitivity, especially to a cohort of female intellectuals, to vocabulary in the traditional Chinese lexicon relating to "the female", and especially those words which carried a female *nü* 女 radical. Their dissatisfaction with the feminine *ta* 她, though, was not necessarily a result of any association with or extreme aversion to any Chinese characters relating to the lowly status or tragic fate of women.

According to the research of the present author, following May Four, not only did people advocate for the abandonment of such words as *qie* 妾, or concubine, and *ji* 妓, or prostitute, which were seen to be extremely insulting to women,[11] but also some female middle school students penned an article proposing that the character *fu* 婦, married woman or wife, which was ubiquitous at the time, should be substituted by the ancient variant form *fu* 媍. This latter view was in fact identical to that of the proponents of the abandonment of *ta* 她, only that their line of reasoning might have been seen as a little more "elevated".

So here we have some female middle school students making the claim that

> In the past there was no necessity to comment on characters that were used wrongly, but now-a-days we are a little more enlightened and so this should be rectified. Many matters in society are gradually undergoing change because of a change in our language, and people's consciousness must also gradually be reformed in line with society.

This is precisely where the responsibility of educated individuals should lie. As for the *fu* 婦 character, it is obviously a mistake to confine a woman's duty to that of "grasping a broom to serve her parents-in-law and do her husband's bidding". As a married woman, she should at the very least also shoulder some meaningful social responsibilities. The authors were extremely unhappy with the original formation of the characters *fu* 婦, *fu* 媍 and *fu* 夫 in that they already displayed a type of gender inequality. They reproached those in the past who had created the characters, saying: How could they have not considered things when they were developing the relevant character? When they developed the *fu* 媍 (woman) character, they said that it was feminine, and so it belonged to the female *nü* 女 radical; but when they created the *fu* 夫 (husband, man) character they did not add a male *nan* 男 radical, nor do they say that it belonged to the male *nan* 男 radical. It seems that man is an agent and the woman is just an auxiliary. This mirrors the example of humankind as the agent and the myriad of creatures as auxiliaries.

Despite the fact that, as far as the authors are concerned, the *fu* 媍 character remained less than ideal, it can still be said that it is able to demonstrate that "women are not completely worthless, that they bear an equal responsibility to that of men", so therefore it still has some advantage over the *fu* 婦 character and ultimately "its significance is broader", so the female students solemnly argued that the *fu* 婦 character must be replaced by the *fu* 媍 character, and innocently claimed that "everyone today will certainly agree".[12]

If we think about the early years of the Republic, the celebrated conservative Gu Hongming 辜鴻銘 in his universally acclaimed work *The Spirit of the Chinese People* 《中國人的精神》 actually used the architecture of the characters *fu* 婦 and *qie* 妾 as an excuse to publicly defend the traditional Confucian moral code for women[13] and the practice of taking concubines. It is thus not difficult to understand how those early avant-garde female middle school students could conceive of protecting the interests of women by starting with linguistic reform of such words as *fu* 婦 or *qie* 妾.

In fact, this phenomenon of criticism and protest, from the modern viewpoint of feminism and gender equality, over a handful of traditional Chinese characters and expressions which had been handed down over the millennia in order to criticise patriarchal society's articulated oppression of women, had long since made its appearance. It was merely continued and developed further around the time of May Four. For example, in 1907 Liu Shipei's 劉師培 wife He Zhen 何震 published an article entitled "On Restoring the Power of Women" 《女子復權論》 in the magazine *Divine Justice* 《天義》 addressing a group of Chinese characters which contained the feminine *nü* 女 radical and issuing a sharp and critical call for women's rights and thus transparently exposing the spirit and flavor of the new era. The article argued:

> The character *wo* 婐, or maid, belongs to the radical *nü* 女 but is pronounced *guo* 果, perhaps to indicate that it refers to a serving woman or maid. The *er nü wo* 二女婐 in *Mencius* 《孟子》, according to the Zhao 趙 annotation, also explains *wo* 婐 as *shi* 侍 or to serve. This offers ample proof that women in ancient times obeyed the instructions of their men.

The *fu* (妇 or 婦) character is explained as "to serve", and its form takes the appearance of a woman using a brush or broom. The *Qu Rites* 《曲礼》 states, "Allocating a woman to a senior official is said to be for the purpose of watering and sweeping." The reason why slavish tasks were allocated to women is probably because it was the duty of women to serve.

The *pin* (嫔 or 嬪 or imperial concubine) character belongs to the *nü* 女 or female radical and is pronounced *pin* 宾, which in turn belongs to the *bei* 贝 radical. The *Rites of Zhou* 《周礼》 has the expression "to present a concubine" or *bin gong* 嫔贡, which probably refers to the act of gifting a woman to the emperor to serve as his concubine. In other words, women were seen as a good or chattel.

The character *nu* 奴 or slave belongs to the *nü* 女 or female radical, as well as the *you* 又 radical. In classical Chinese it has a curly form, like as if it was manacled – the same as the character *min* 民 or citizen. Women were probably seen in ancient times as something akin to a prisoner.

The character *tang* 帑 is explained as a hoard of gold and coins, and women are also called *tang* 帑, or the variant form *nu* 孥. This is the result of women being seen in ancient times as a symbol of wealth.

The character *fei* 妃 is the word for a particular quantity of coins or silk, and to refer to an imperial concubine as *fei* 妃 is another example of women being seen as a symbol of wealth in the past.

So, from the language we can see that in ancient times women were the lowliest and their duties were the most onerous. Women were the most exploited and they were also seen as the greatest gift that could be offered. The most diligent and competent workers were also women. Men saw women as a means to make money and thus whichever household had the most women was the richest, much like the use of female slaves in the southern United States. Later generations used *pin fei* 嫔妃 or "imperial concubine" as a deferential honorific, so who would think that in ancient times, addressing women in that manner was actually inappropriate? The two characters *fu ren* 妇人 is the common form of address for women, but who would have guessed that the *fu* 妇 character is derived from *zhou* 帚, or broom; is this meant to signify a surrender to slavery? . . . What is more, during the Ancient Dynasties period,[14] ladies of the house called themselves "little child" 小童; and women in subsequent generations even called themselves "concubine" 妾 or "slave". Isn't that an indication that women were willing to consider themselves slaves? Moreover, people commonly refer to "women and children". Isn't it belittling of the female sex to equate a married woman with a child? Further, the *Analects* 《论语》 speak of "Only women and lowly persons", equating women with the lowest of the low. Isn't that denigrating women? While you may be able to stop up women's mouths, it is impossible to erase them completely. These are all indications of autocracy.[15]

What is especially worth noting is that, in a similar fashion, by the end of the Qing and the beginning of the 20th century, this political culture of advocating for these types of Chinese characters to be reformed, and moreover, the courageous execution of this position, was also already a fact. In this process, the creation and utilisation of the expression *yingci* 英雌 or heroine is an extremely apt example. Its target was the term *yingxiong* 英雄 or (masculine) hero, the form of which embodied a patriarchal social and cultural hegemony, and which had, moreover, pervaded the Late Qing, through the entire Republican period and has survived to the present day.

When the expression "heroine" or 英雌 appeared at the end of the Qing, it symbolised the spirit of the era which demanded women's rights to participate in the task of national salvation. In 1903, a new feminist who called herself Heroine of North Chu (Hubei)[16] and who had studied in Japan, published an article entitled "Decrying Women's Rights in China" 《支那女权愤言》 in *Hubei Student's World* 《湖北学生界》 in which she passionately declares:

> The deplorable state of women's rights in this country has continued for thousands of years. We are all descendants of the ancestors, but we treat women as playthings; we all inhabit the same world, but we throw women into the darkest dungeon.... Centuries of Confucian scholars have lauded the great men of history but have remained mute about the great women; they speak of heroes, but never of heroines. Short-sightedness and success have been our only yardstick for man, and this has truly been a stain on our history.[17]

In her pursuit of revolution, the visionary Qiu Jin 秋瑾 not only established a model for female heroism with her utterly fearless spirit of sacrifice, but she was also a pioneer in the practical adoption of the expression *yingci* 英雌 or "heroine" in print. The first chapter of the manuscript of her unfinished epic ballad *Stones of the Jingwei Bird* 《精卫石》 was headed "In the Slumberland Twilight Women are Buried in Dark Prisons, but in the Brightness of an Awakened World Heroines (英雌) Step Together into the Realm of Pearly Clouds". The South Society 南社 poet Liu Yazi 柳亚子 also penned the famous verse "Good housewives and virtuous mothers are petty while heroines (英雌) and women of distinction probe things deeply; ... Their chaste hands shape our nation's soul, and their ruddy beauty ensnares the male libido". The interest shown by members of the revolutionary party in the expression heroine (英雌) led to the expression carrying a certain political flavor of opposition to the prevailing social order.

Nevertheless, from the end of the Qing, as far as the adoption of the term *yingci* 英雌 or heroine is concerned, it appears that it magnified excessively the might (雄), grandeur (豪), and chivalrous (侠) aspects of male-female libation.[18] While the term reflected the distinctive features of a nationalistic language tasked with saving the nation, it simultaneously revealed a proactiveness and an historical impact. However, it was unable to truly free itself from the heroic male *yingxiong* 英雄 paradigm. That female agency which reflected a feminine physiological and psychological foundation was still lacking. It goes without saying that the "Steely Maiden" or *tie guniang* 铁姑娘 of the mid to late 20th century is the ultimate realisation of what the term heroine or *yingci* 英雌 had been attempting to achieve.[19]

82　Gender Confusion: Sensitivity Over "Female"-Related Terms

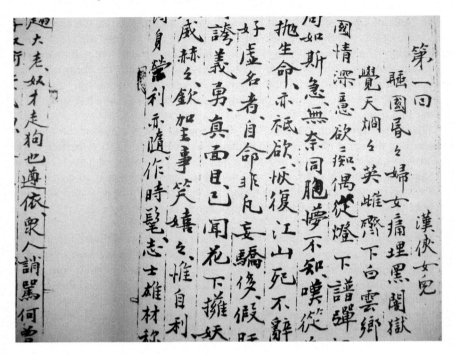

Figure 5.4 Fragments of Qiu Jin's novel *Stones of the Jingwei Bird* employed the term "Heroine" 英雌. Taken from the 1958 *The Exploits of* Qiu Jin 《秋瑾史迹》, Zhonghua Shuju.

On entering the Republican era, the use of heroine or *yingci* 英雌 did not abate, but rather proliferated. When compared to the late Qing, the expression also lost some of its dignity and gained a little humor and "harmoniousness".[20] Nevertheless, it still retained that epochal flavor of resistance to male power. For example, the 9th issue of *The Short Story Magazine* 《小说月报》 in 1916 carried a short story with the title "Heroine's Mirror" 《英雌镜》; in 1924 *Red Magazine* 《红杂志》 carried the article "Heroine of Joffre's Camp" 《霞飞帐下之英雌》; in 1927 the editorial department of the *Social Welfare* newspaper 《益世报》 promoted the six-chaptered work of fiction *Forced Marriage of a Heroine* 《英雌夺婚记》 by Dong Yinhu 董阴狐; between 1928 and 1930 Zeng Pu 曾朴, in the 31st chapter of his serialised *Flower of the Sea of Evil* 《孽海花》 entitled "The Goddess Practices Her Art of War with Roiling Clouds and Beating Rain; Hiding the Luan Bird from the Phoenix, the Heroine Is Goaded to a Deadly Duel" "抟云搓雨弄神女阴符，瞒凤栖鸾惹英雌决斗", used the term heroine 英雌 exclusively;[21] and from the 1930s to the 1940s there were, amongst the names of popular movies, such titles as *Heroine of the Jade Watchtower* 《玉阙英雌》 and *Heroine of Chaos* 《乱世英雌》.

The gradually increasing use of the term *yingci* 英雌 or heroine eventually aroused some antipathy amongst some in society. In 1934, an individual signing themselves Xiang Ru 湘如 publicly expressed their "objection" in the 1115th issue of *The Pei-yang Pictorial News* 《北洋画报》, arguing that *yingci* 英雌 was extremely illogical and that those who used it were all ignorant and rash. To change *nüyingxiong* 女英雄 or "female hero" into *yingci* 英雌 was synonymous with changing "treachery" or *yinxian* 阴险 into a nonsensical *yangxian* 阳险.[22] It was completely meaningless. He thus raged in his article "Down with Yingci!":

> The *Lun Yu* 论语 group of humorists at times delight in playing with words and use such comical terms as "Master" 男士 or "Heroine" 英雌. This naturally is their attempt to attract readers with the most depraved tastes, so I will ignore them. But I have recently noticed several otherwise serious articles which speak of "heroine" 英雌 this or "heroine" that: could it be that this nonsensical term has suddenly been officially accepted into general use? I cannot but object. A heroine [*nüyingxiong* 女英雄] is a heroine. There is no need to cut off her head or lop off her tail and think oneself clever, mincing words and desecrating language, absurdly inventing distinctions just for the sake of it. It is like if we say someone is treacherous or *yinxian* 阴险;[23] if that individual is male, then we don't have to change this and say he is *yangxian* 阳险[24] .... Originally a noun simply represented a certain concept and the individual characters which are used to construct that noun, once combined, no longer maintain their original independent meanings. Otherwise the expression would lose its ability to represent that concept. Take for example, the term "chairperson" or *zhuxi* 主席.[25] We need not change this to say "principal chair" or *zhuyi* 主椅 just because we don't sit on mats anymore. Nor should we use *xuanzu* 选足 or "chosen foot" for a competitor in a foot race just because he uses his legs, rather than the accepted *xuanshou* 选手 (chosen hand).[26] What is more, this is not only true for words composed of multiple characters, but it is the same for single character words.

The author argued powerfully that there were originally six methods of forming characters[27] of which the combined ideogram plus phonetic type forms the overwhelming majority. These ideogram plus phonetic characters "appear at a brief glance to be very reasonable, then as things develop, the sound is retained but the form does not square with it anymore." For example, the character *pao* 砲 or cannon originally incorporated the stone 石 radical, but later with the invention of gun powder, the stone radical was replaced with the fire 火 radical such that the character 砲 finally became 炮. But "today, when firing a canon, there is no longer a visible flame – in fact, they are now making electrically operated canons", so by using the fire 火 radical, its full meaning can no longer be conveyed. Or perhaps another example is the character for bowl, or *wan* 椀: originally this was associated with the wood or *mu* 木 radical, but later, because porcelain resembled stone, the *wood* radical was changed to a *stone* 石 radical and 椀 finally became 碗. But now, with receptacles made from such materials as enamel, Bakelite, or aluminum, how is the idea of wood or stone manifest?

In view of this, the author stressed:

> So you see that the role of radicals in text has its limits whereas objects are capable of infinite change. One character or one word originally represented a complete concept, but if we obstinately focus on the radical part of the character and insist on a separate analysis, and effect change without authorization, then this is inappropriate and highly illegal. The term *yingci* 英雌 or heroine is especially deserving of being banished.[28]

It must be said that from a purely linguistic standpoint, all that Xiang Ru 湘如 says accords with the basic rules of the development of Chinese characters and compounds. It is a valid point of view. We must guarantee the relative stability and authority of the basic Chinese language. However, with the benefit of modern hindsight, although the expression *yingci* 英雌 or heroine did not gain much traction, nevertheless, the fact that neither was it completely unseated is also worth thinking about.

This writer discovered during his research that subsequently, during the mid to late 1930s through the 1940s, the expression *yingci* 英雌 continued to be used,[29] and right up to the 1960s it was still being used by some in Hong Kong and Macau. In the current environment where popular literature and humorous reporting is rife, this expression appears to have even been gradually returning to fashion. In a society where patriarchy maintains a powerful dominance, I believe that it would still be impossible to completely eradicate the expression *yingci* 英雌. Here concepts of ideology and value come into play; no matter how strongly you might oppose it from a purely linguistic point of view, it would be to no avail.

Like *yingci* 英雌, the birth of the feminine third person singular character *ta* 她 shared a similar ideological and cultural context, with questions of gender relations, but the circumstances which it encountered following its creation were even more complex. Its circulation not only met with questioning and opposition from a purely linguistic standpoint, but it was also challenged even more directly by the inherent modern value of gender equality. This challenge was maintained for a relatively long period of time by a certain number of new feminists. We note with interest that, in line with this, right up to the mid-1930s some participants in the movement for women's rights maintained a political objection to the use of the feminine third person singular *ta* 她. For example, the inauguration in 1929 of the extremely influential magazine *Women's Voice* 《妇女共鸣》 steadfastly refused to use the female third person singular character *ta* 她, arguing that to remove the "human" or *ren* 人 radical from the character was not to accept that women were human beings and thus a blatant insult to the integrity of women. They therefore made it clear that they would persist in using the term *yi* 伊 come what may. The May 1934, Issue 5 of volume 3 of *Women's Voice* 《妇女共鸣》 further published an "Announcement" to this specific end:

> Announcement: Ever since Hu Shizhi, Liu Bannong et al. advocated the use of the vernacular, China has split the third person pronoun *ta* 他 character into three, namely *ta* 他, *ta* 她 and *ta* 牠 in order to represent the male, the female and animals or objects. We at this establishment believe that if we take the "human" *ren* 人 radical to represent the male, the female *nü* 女 to represent the female and the beast or *niu* 牛 to represent animals, then we insult women as being non-human. We therefore refuse to use the *ta* 她 character and choose to use *yi* 伊 instead. All contributors please take note!

Using the weight of a magazine to publicly refuse to utilise a certain expression or character is in truth extremely rare in the history of modern Chinese newspapers and magazines and indeed in the culture itself. In fact, it is an extremely significant matter in the history of gendered society and in the women's movement generally. Just one year or so later, in August 1935, *Women's Voice* 《妇女共鸣》 again published an article entitled "Announcement: This Magazine Refuses to Use the Character *ta* 她" 《本刊拒用 "她" 字启事》, publicly proclaiming once again:

> With respect to the feminine third person pronoun, this publication uses the *yi* 伊 character and refuses to use *ta* 她 because if we use *ta* 她 for the third person feminine along with *ta* 他 for the masculine and *ta* 牠 for, let's say, an elephant, then we are saying that men are *human* [*ren* 人], while women are *female* [*nü* 女] and elephants are *bovines* [*niu* 牛]. Is this not inferring somewhat that women are not "human"? The problem is that since May Fourth when the advocates for the new literature created the *ta* 她 character, considerable dispute was created amongst the commentators and as of this moment, probably only the "Free Talk" 自由谈 and "Spring and Autumn" 春秋 sections of *Shen Bao* 《申报》 still occasionally use the *yi* 伊 character. This magazine in its 18-year history of publishing has continued to use the *yi* 伊 character, and we respectfully remind our potential contributors to note this.[30]

From the 1935 re-publication of the "Announcement", *Women's Voice* 《妇女共鸣》 paid close attention to the response from all sectors to their announcements of the previous years, as well as carefully seeking out kindred spirits in the publishing world. The magazine pointedly explained why the structure of the feminine third person *ta* 她 in particular constituted an insult to women and furthermore reminded the general reader to take note: there had always been controversy about the character *ta* 她 ever since its first appearance and its adoption was neither logical nor natural or beyond question, as the general blind follower might assume. This offers a glimpse of its duplicitous intent.

However, from my limited reading on the matter, this resolute "clarion call" to "protect" the rights and dignity of women by *Women's Voice* 《妇女共鸣》

appears not to have attracted much sympathy or response in society – and here the writer is referring specifically to the opposition to the feminine *ta* 她 from the perspective of protecting women's dignity. On the contrary, as revealed by the editors of *Women's Voice* 《妇女共鸣》 themselves: following the publication of their "Announcement", it was in fact subject to numerous bouts of "comprehensive derision, either for its bickering over minutiae or for its stubborn tedium".[31] As far as this author has been able to observe, there are at least two articles which reflect this latter response: the first is the leisure magazine *The Decameron* 《十日谈》 which asserted that it "did not discuss politics" when it published "'*Ta* 她' and the Women's Movement" 《"她"与妇运》;[32] and the second is the article "Refusing to Use the Character *Ta* 她" 《拒用"她"字》, published in *Reading Life* 《读书生活》.[33] From the actual contents of these two articles, it is obvious that both authors are very passionate about the practical sociopolitical movements of the day.

It is not clear who the author "Shu San" 树三 of "'*Ta* 她' and the Women's Movement" 《"她"与妇运》 was. The object of the article is the 1934 announcement by *Women's Voice* 《妇女共鸣》 that it would not be using the feminine *ta* 她. The article responds to the "Announcement" in four respects: first is to point out that this methodology is not uniquely Chinese and that from its intent it is merely imitating the method proposed by the author of the work *The Subjection of Woman*,[34] the famous English philosopher J.S. Mill, of substituting "Person" for "Man" in the British Election Law. Mill argued that since both men and women were human beings, they should have equal voting rights and the right to stand for election. That it was not appropriate to use "Man" to represent "Woman". Instead, if "Person" were used to refer to both men and women then it would be obvious that both men and women were "human". However, even English is unable to remove the difference between male and female. The second aspect of the article's response was to ridicule *Women's Voice* 《妇女共鸣》 for its inability to understand the logic of such individuals as Liu Bannong 刘半农 and others who created the feminine third person singular pronoun *ta* 她; "Did they or did they not see women as 'humans'? This is unclear." Even if the feminine *ta* 她 truly and inadvertently carries an overtone of "disadvantage to the female sex", it is useless to discard this one character because the legendary creator of the Chinese script,

> Cang Jie 仓颉 [legendary inventor of Chinese characters] in one dictionary, under the female *nü* 女 radical, created innumerable characters that are not advantageous to women such as, might we suggest, *jian* 奸（姦）[adultery/rape], *pin* 姘 [mistress], *piao* 嫖 [to visit a prostitute], *jiao* 姣 [cunning], *liao* 嫽 [smart], *xi* 嬉 [amusement], *yao* 妖 [witch], *xie* 媟 [to lust after], *ni* 嫟 [intimate], *chang* 娼 [prostitute], *bi* 嬖 [treat as a favourite], *xian* 嫌 [enmity], *wang* 妄 [rash], *kui* 愧 [ashamed], *nu* 奴 [slave], *du* 妒（妬）[jealous], *ji* 嫉 [jealousy], *tou* 媮 [improper], *lan* 嬾 [lazy], *tuo* 嫷 [beautiful] . . . . Although not all of these are the exclusive domain of women, nevertheless they all employ the female *nü* 女 radical, and isn't this simply "insulting women"? We therefore say that if we merely change one

single *ta* 她 character, how might this make up for all the insults that women have had to bear since time immemorial?

The article's third riposte to the refusal of *Women's Voice* 《妇女共鸣》 to use the *ta* 她 character was to emphasise the absolute necessity of distinguishing between male and female in the written form. It argued that the character *yi* 伊 was too "bookish" and not appropriate for use in the vernacular. At the same time, the article solemnly and empathetically indicated that from the standpoint of gender equality it was not necessary to be picky about the architecture of the character, and that even if one was to use the expression *yi* 伊, then it would not necessarily be able to truly articulate real respect for women, but rather the opposite. The article continues:

> If we are communicating in the written form and do not create some differentiating feature in the character *ta* 他 that we have traditionally used for both men and women, then will not the reader at times be a little confused? But if we were to use the *yi* 伊 character to refer to any aspect of men or women in order to display their difference, then wouldn't that seem "bookish" and not entirely suited to the vernacular style? What is more, women being of a yielding nature choose not to claim the original *ta* 他 for themselves but would rather fight for "dignity" and so replace *ta* 他 with *yi* 伊. So, I think it best for the moment that we not speculate on what effect *yi* 伊 might have on *ta* 他. But what about those that hold women in high esteem? Since they think that women are also "human" [人], then to win their favor we should be frank and allow the women to monopolize this *ta* 他 character and suggest that *the men* go and use the *yi* 伊 character instead. But wouldn't this be even more weird? If we take this logic further, then I say that apart from the *yi* 伊 character, there is also the *bi* 彼 character which is also a third person pronoun, so naturally that can be used as well. What is more, since the *bi* 彼 character has a *double human* 双人 radical, then this would give the sense that both men and women were only half a human and so we can dispense with both the male *ta* 他 and the female *ta* 她 and use this *bi* 彼 character for both men and women. Wouldn't this demonstrate the spirit of cooperation and inter-dependency between men and women even better? But since this cannot escape the odium of "bookishness" either, nor can it display the gender of men or women in text, then we should just not make suggestions or advocate willy-nilly.

Finally, addressing the refusal of *Women's Voice* 《妇女共鸣》 to use the feminine character *ta* 她, the author roundly criticises the magazine editors' intention and the women's movement's aims, denouncing their refusal to use the term *ta* 她 as "not merely 'parting the hairs to discover some blemish' but in fact 'failing to see the wood for the trees'". The article concludes that the editors of *Women's Voice* 《妇女共鸣》

> from start to finish have failed to escape from the trap of the modus operandi of the female elite although occasionally they may make a show. The few articles they have published have merely stated that women would rather die of starvation than prostitute themselves.

88   Gender Confusion: Sensitivity Over "Female"-Related Terms

They argue that since *Women's Voice* 《妇女共鸣》 declares that they are "investigating women's issues" and that their activities are linked to the Women's Committee 妇女会 which was dedicated to the women's liberation movement, therefore their grasp of women's issues and the scope and content of the women's movement should not be so limited. The author therefore issues the following question in denunciation of them:

> Is the task of giving guidance to the women's movement that *Women's Voice* 《妇女共鸣》 has taken upon itself only meant to enable a very few individuals to act as female committee members or female members of staff, or how a good wife or loving mother should perform her duties and manage her maids? Is it that simple? And this "Voice": exactly who is this "Voice" speaking to? And who are they urging to "Speak"? We simply pity those uneducated, illiterate, and destitute women who make up more than eighty or ninety percent of the female population and who continue to endure privation and suffer hardship for years on end and nobody shows an interest in them – especially those intellectual Misses and Ladies who tout their "bureaucratic" and "modern" credentials while they ignore them, turn their back on them, and don't even deign to acknowledge them. So, we once more can see that the whole platform of the women's movement is not only just like the aforementioned announcement about the character *ta* 她, but in fact it is an indication that the women's movement under the leadership of *Women's Voice* 《妇女共鸣》 is trending towards focusing on the minutiae while forgetting the fundamentals.

Not only was this the case, but the author also takes the opportunity to sternly attack the current social and cultural reality which featured a political malaise where all levels of society under the Nationalist Party's suzerainty "neglected the whole in favor of the part" and "busied itself about trivia while ignoring weightier matters". He pointedly continues:

> When the Japanese prey on us they spare no effort, but when our upper echelons stand idle and carefree and constantly declare that recreation will save the nation, chanting the Buddhist classics will save the nation, love will save the nation, dance will save the nation, lotteries will save the nation, or the classics will save the nation, and so on, shouldn't we indeed ask just what kind of a world this is!?

In this way the author undeniably reveals the power of the Left's politico-cultural stance.

And speaking of stances, the debate over the question of the feminine *ta* 她 can be said to have become one initiative which the Leftists consciously used to criticise the prevailing political culture.

In September 1935, in response to the republication by *Women's Voice* 《妇女共鸣》 of a new "Announcement on the Refusal to Use the Character *Ta* 她"

《拒用"她"字启事》 a month earlier, an individual styling themselves Shi Tong 士同 published another article entitled "Refusing to Use the Character *Ta* 她" 《拒用"她"字》 in *Reading Life* 《读书生活》, expressing yet again a critique of the methodology. As far as I have been able to ascertain, Shi Tong's 士同 original name was Liu Shi 柳湜, an individual who at the time was slowly becoming active and who was a prominent figure in Leftist culture at the time because of his promotion of the Mass Culture Movement 大众文化运动. During the early years of the War of Resistance against Japan he published *Culture and National Distress* 《国难与文化》, which was popular for a time.

In the article "Refusing to Use the Character *Ta* 她" 《拒用"她"字》, Liu Shi 柳湜 pointed out that after May Four, the fact that the three characters *ta* 他, *ta* 她, and *ta* 牠 expressed "representative discongruity" was indeed a new phenomenon

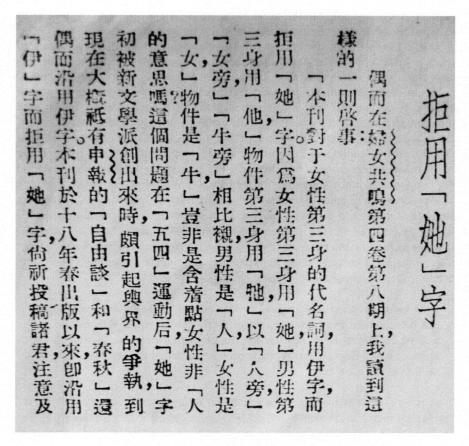

Figure 5.5 A section of "Refusing to Use the Character *Ta* 她". The article castigates as "idly toying with a character" the announcement by *Women's Voice* 《妇女共鸣》 that they refused to use the character *ta* 她.

and that at the time they "incorporated a certain progressiveness". Although its significance was weak at best, nevertheless it demonstrated an effort to "edge the Chinese script, in terms of grammar, closer to precision". "Originally the 'human radical' 人 or 'female radical' 女 did not carry any overtones of privileging the male or slighting the female", and when the feminine *ta* 她 was created there was no talk of any "insult to the female sex". At the same time, the *yi* 伊 character which, in classical Chinese, represented the "third person female pronoun" (and which succumbed to criticism along the lines of Zhu Ziqing 朱自清) was not "widely and commonly used" in the spoken language. Normally "No matter whether 'man', 'woman' or 'object', if it was in the third person then it was always pronounced with a *ta* 他 sound", but now, having created an identically sounding new feminine *ta* 她, there is a slight added difference in terms of form and hence there is no doubt that it must better "fit in with the oral equivalent" in terms of expression. This kind of oral expression – in fact the emphasis on the oral expression of the general public – obviously reflected the trend of the times, namely, the call by the Leftist Cultural Movement for the establishment of a "common language".

While Liu Shi 柳湜 did not believe that the feminine *ta* 她 was insulting to women, he nevertheless acknowledged that there were a great many words in Chinese that *were* insulting to women, like adultery or *jian* 姦, envy or *du* 妒, slave or *nu* 奴, to visit a prostitute or *piao* 嫖, avarice or *lan* 婪, and others. He even went as far as to declare that "characters with a square form themselves are feudal" and therefore stressed that if we want to totally eradicate this type of phenomenon from the language, then we must implement "the Latinization of the Chinese script". "Only then," he continued, "when there is only sound and not form, will genuine script-based gender equality be achieved". The author also declared that the reason why he was making a "call" that differed from that of *Women's Voice* 《妇女共鸣》 was not because he was not a woman or that he was "not sympathetic to the struggle of women to achieve a human status and therefore opposed to women". Rather, he believed that the tactic and concept of "demanding a 'human radical 人' in terms of form in order to elevate one's status is "Not only laughably childish but also represents a move to stand in opposition to linguistic evolution". Finally, he admonishes truly progressive women, saying,

> As a social question, the struggle to win "human" 人 status for women cannot be separated from the question of the liberation of the Chinese people as a whole and requires a combined struggle with their male counterparts. It cannot be an idle play over a single pronoun, wasting energy and scattering the forces of resistance.[35]

It is obvious that this article is somewhat different from the article "'*Ta* 她' and the Women's Movement" 《"她"与妇运》, carried in *The Decameron* 《十日谈》 a year earlier, yet they share many areas of congruence. If the authors of these two articles are not one and the same, then at least they were comrades in arms, with their left-wing colors equally on display. What they were already more concerned with was not the philological import of the feminine *ta* 她 character itself, but over and above the confines of the written word, the situation in which Chinese women found themselves in the present society and the fate of their class – in other words, the actual women's movement and the related people's struggle for liberation.

Confronting Liu Shi's 柳湜 radical proposition with an equally challenging rationale, *Women's Voice* 《妇女共鸣》 magazine specifically published Ji Zhuman's 吉竹蔓 manuscript entitled "On the Refusal to Use the Character *Ta* 她 and a Question for *Reading Life*",[36] offering a powerful rebuttal. The article points out that the original creator of the feminine *ta* 她 may not have had any thought of privileging the male and slighting the female, however "when it is employed as a contrast to the neutral *ta* 牠 character, it imbues the counterpoised *ta* 她 and *ta* 他 characters with a different flavor." In other words, it highlights the discriminatory connotations with respect to women. For this reason, the author makes the judgement that the feminine *ta* 她 is "an abnormal character which, in keeping with its feudal ideological provenance, carries a sense of contempt for women, of denying female dignity." "It is a marker of women being 'less than human' and its use should be completely rejected." The author also goes on to indicate that

> It is still quite urgent . . . that a newly coined and rectified word be endorsed and compared to long-established terms like *jian* 姦, *du* 妒 or *hao* 好. . . . but at the same time, it can also serve as a starting point for correcting these terms which already have a certain historical standing.

This in fact also served to respond to the relevant questions raised in the "'*Ta* 她' and the Women's Movement" 《"她"与妇运》 article.

From the appearance of the name Ji Zhuman 吉竹蔓, this defender of the *Women's Voice* 《妇女共鸣》 viewpoint is probably a woman and she does not shrink from openly demonstrating her approbation of the intent of the editors of *Women's Voice* 《妇女共鸣》 and their refusal to use the feminine *ta* 她:

> I have always enjoyed reading *Women's Voice* 《妇女共鸣》 because its position is correct, and its attitude dignified. They use their full might to heroically do battle with the chains of feudal ideology that bind China's women, never flinching and never holding back. And their refusal to adopt anything which springs from that feudal ideology and denigrates women, including the abnormal character *ta* 她 which denies the dignity of women, especially resonates with my thinking.

Ji Zhuman 吉竹蔓 not only castigates the feminine *ta* 她 as being "rooted in feudal ideology", "denigrating women", and an abnormal character which "denies the dignity of women". She also further pointedly refutes Mr Liu's opinion in four respects: the first is to denounce Liu Shi's 柳湜 basic assertion that "everything that is so-called progressive is proper", saying that to criticise *Women's Voice* 《妇女共鸣》 for refusing to use the feminine *ta* 她 from this premise "is so totally

92 Gender Confusion: Sensitivity Over "Female"-Related Terms

Figure 5.6 A section from "On the Refusal to Use the Character *Ta* 她 and a Question for *Reading Life*". The article supports the position of boycotting the use of the character *ta* 她.

superficial and laughable", and besides, "*Women's Voice* 《妇女共鸣》 does not oppose the appropriate division between male, female, and neuter third person in script. It is just that they oppose the two characters *ta* 她 and *ta* 牠 to fulfil that function, and instead suggest replacing these with *yi* 伊 and *ta* 它 respectively. So how can this be 'reactionary'"? The second was to stress that the three homophonic characters *ta* 他, *ta* 她 and *ta* 牠 "indeed have their advantages", however the character *yi* 伊 is pronounced differently, "so how can that not be seen as an advantage?" The third was to argue that one cannot sweepingly deem "square characters themselves" to be "inherently feudal". Rather, one can only say that "there are a number of characters amongst them that have feudal overtones". Therefore, demands to completely do away with square characters and fully Latinise the language is completely misguided, and moreover "in a semi-colonial China where a national revolutionary consciousness needs to be universally aroused, such a move cannot truly avoid the suspicion of being 'counter revolutionary'." We can see that nationalism also had a role to play in this cognitive process, a role of a different type and direction. Her fourth point was to determine that "The reason why *Women's Voice*'s 《妇女共鸣》 refusal to use the term *ta* 她 and to use *yi* 伊 instead had stirred up the readers so much should be sheeted home to the struggle to regard women as 'human beings'", and she goes on to indicate that *Women's Voice* 《妇女共鸣》 was already leading the calls in this regard. This had nothing whatsoever to do with "idly toying with one specific character". At the same time, the author incidentally stresses the political nature of the use of language, including nouns, which cannot be ignored, and opposes the false generalisation that the question of giving weight to important nouns is somehow "idly toying with language". Not without some irony she retorts, "China's three easternmost provinces of Rehe 热河[37] have already been dubbed 'Manchuria'. Surely this cannot be seen as 'idle toying'!"[38]

I am not aware of any subsequent response by Liu Shi 柳湜.

This debate about the feminine *ta* 她 which occurred in the mid-1930s is obviously a continuation of the May Fourth discussion. By this time the feminine *ta* 她 had almost claimed universal victory in society. Because *Women's Voice* 《妇女共鸣》 took such a stubborn feminist stance, it was truly fighting a lonely battle and presented as a tragic figure of resistance against the world. This solemn protest and the equally solemn countercriticism at the time must remind us today that the reason why *ta* 她 was able to gain the ascendancy over *yi* 伊 and ultimately come out victorious must contain certain linguistic, historical, or epochal cultural factors which transcend the surface phenomena and which are worthy of serious reflection.

Notes

1 Zhuang, Fu 壮甫, "Interrogating the Character *ta* 她" 《"她"字的疑问》. For the full text, see *New Man* 《新人》 magazine, Issue 2.
2 Yi, Xuan 忆萱 and Shao Lizi 邵力子, "Discussion of the Feminine Third Person Pronoun" 《第三身女性代名词底讨论》, *Communications* 通讯 column of *Enlightenment Magazine* 《觉悟》, June 27, 1920. Others expressing a similar opinion at the time included Lu, Yuan 陆元, "It is Not Necessary to Distinguish between Male and Female So Distinctly" 《男女不必分得那么清楚》, *Communications* 通讯 column of *Enlightenment Magazine* 《觉悟》, July 12, 1922; Tian 天, "The Women's Liberation Question Requires the Obliteration of the Boundary between Men and Women" 《解放妇女问题该泯灭男女界限》, *Enlightenment Magazine* 《觉悟》, October 30, 1922.
3 See Da, Tong 大同, "Research on the 'Third Person Pronoun'" 《"第三身代名词"底研究》.
4 See Yi, Xuan 忆萱 and Shao Lizi 邵力子, "Discussion of the Feminine Third Person Pronoun" 《第三身女性代名词底讨论》.
5 This concept was originally outlined by the noted playwright Chen, Dabei 陈大悲. Da Tong argues: "I fear there is no one in the world stupid enough to feel that the idea of annotating the character *ta* 他 with a *nan* 男 character for the male, and a *nü* 女 character for the female, is not bothersome." See Da, Tong 大同, "The Feminine Third Person Pronoun in Drama" 《戏剧里的第三身女性代名词》.

6 You, Luan 友鸾, "'Miss' and 'She'" 《"女士"和"她"》, *Modern Woman* 《现代妇女》, September 16, 1922.
7 Zhu, Ziqing 朱自清, "Random Travel Notes" 《旅行杂记》, carried in the *Literature Weekly* 《文学周报》 supplement to *The China Times* 《时事新报》, Issue 130, July 14, 1924.
8 Shi Cuntong 施存统, "The Two Unsightly Characters for Miss" 《看不惯女士二字》, in the *Random Impressions* 随感录 column of *Enlightenment Magazine* 《觉悟》, April 5, 1920. In fact, at the time it wasn't unheard-of to also find the male equivalent of *Miss* 女士, namely *Master* 男士. From a linguistics point of view, this parallel mobilisation of terms is at times unavoidable – to say nothing of feminists using it deliberately. It is just that in the male dominated Chinese society of the time, it was certainly difficult to identify any male author who would label himself *Master* 男士.
9 Zhen, Xin 枕薪, "Miss" 《女士》, carried in *Emancipation Pictorial* 《解放画报》, Issue 15, September 30, 1921.
10 See Zhen, Xin 枕薪, "Miss" 《女士》 and the magazine's editor in chief Zhou Jianyun's 周剑云 "Postscript".
11 Lu, Qiuxin 陆秋心, "Annihilate the Two Characters *Concubine* 妾 and *Prostitute* 妓" 《消灭"妾"和"妓"两个字》, *New Woman* 《新妇女》, Inaugural Issue, January 1920.
12 Zhou, Huizhuan 周慧专 (Noted as "a third-year student in the Hubei Provincial Girls' Middle School"), "A New Approach to Substituting *fu* 媃 for *fu* 婦" 《婦当作媃新说》 in the *Readers' Forum* 读者论坛 section of *Women's Magazine* 《妇女杂志》, No. 10, Vol. 6, 1920. Zhou Huizhuan's female classmate Fu Shuhua 傅淑华 adopted the same approach, publishing her contribution "How to Awaken the Everyday Chinese Woman" 《如何唤醒一般之中国媃女》 in the same section of the same issue, and in her text, she used the character 媃 for the character 婦.
13 "The three obediences and four virtues" 三从四德 – i.e., obey in turn one's father, husband, and son, plus the four virtues of morality 德, physical charm 容, propriety in speech 言, and efficiency in needlework 功.
14 From the earliest times to approximately 221 B.C.E.
15 He, Zhen 何震, "On Restoring the Power of Women" 《女子复权论》, *Divine Justice* 《天义》, Issue 2, June 25, 1907.
16 Translator's note: *Chu bei ying ci* 楚北英雌. Chu was traditionally the area covered by modern-day Hunan and Hubei.
17 *Chu bei ying ci*, "Decrying Women's Rights in China" 《支那女权愤言》, *Hubei Students' World* 《湖北学生界》, Vol. 2, February 1903, pp. 95–96.
18 See Xia, Xiaohong 夏晓虹, "Heroines and Women of Distinction Probe Things Deeply: The Ideal Late Qing Female Personality" 《"英雌女杰勤揣摩":晚清女性的人格理想》, *Literature and Art Research* 《文艺研究》, Issue 6, 1995. See also Li, Qizhi 李奇志, "Qiu Jin and Lü Bicheng: The Quest for the Spirit of the Heroine in Their Lives and Writing" 《秋瑾、吕碧城其人其文的"英雌"精神追求》, *Hubei Social Sciences* 《湖北社会科学》, Vol. 11, 2008.
19 Some modern feminists perhaps will be unable to accept the writer's emphasis of women's gentle and reserved qualities as being a natural and rational feature of their sex. They may see this as sexist. For them, Simone de Beauvoir's formulation "One is not born, but rather becomes, a woman" (Tao, Tiezhu 陶铁柱 (trans.), Simone de Beauvoir, *The Second Sex* 《第二性》, Beijing: Chinese Book Company, 1998, p. 309) has been accepted as an absolute truth that cannot be questioned. And they may even cite the American anthropologist Margaret Mead's 1935 work *Sex and Temperament in Three Primitive Societies*, pointing to certain primitive societies as a case in point. However, they are still unable to effectively explain the sociocultural foundations of why all major cultures on earth take gentleness and reservation as features of the feminine makeup. I accept the rational basis for the sociocultural construction of gender, but oppose the

biased view that fundamentally neglects, holds in absolute contempt, or even completely disregards the significance of the physiological difference between men and women and its social proliferation.
20 At the end of the Qing, "*yingci* 英雌" was used not without humor, for example the *Interesting Language from the Academic World* 《学界趣语》 section of Issue 2 of *New Fiction*《新小说》, Guangxu 31st year (1905) was attributed to "The playful brush of the heroine [英雌] from Qiannan".
21 The "*ying ci* 英雌" referred to in *Flower of the Sea of Evil*《孽海花》were the two foreign women described by Chen Jidong 陈冀东 (or originally, Chen Jitong 陈季同) in the work *Self-Portrait of a Chinese Citizen*《中国人自画像》, which made a contribution by spreading Chinese culture to the West, and especially to France. They also later participated in the "Democratic Taiwan 台湾民主国" movement to oppose the partitioning off of Taiwan. On this occasion they are described as fighting a duel over Mr Chen. See Chapter 31 of Shanghai Guji Publishing House's 1980 edition of *Flower of the Sea of Evil*《孽海花》.
22 Translator's note: "*yin* 阴" refers to the *feminine* element of the ancient system of dualism in Chinese philosophy while "*yang* 阳" refers to the *male*.
23 When *yin* is the feminine or negative principle of the *Yin/Yang* dualism.
24 i.e., replacing the female *yin* element with the male *yang* in the expression.
25 Literally "leading table or mat".
26 Literally "chosen hand".
27 The Six Methods of forming Chinese characters, first mentioned in the *Rites of Zhou* and formalised by scholars during the Han Dynasty, includes two primary methods: 象形 (pictogram) and 指事 (ideogram); two compound methods: 会意 (combined ideogram) and 形声 (ideogram plus phonetic); and two transfer methods: 假借 (loan) and 转注 (transfer).
28 Xiang, Ru 湘如, "Down with *Yingci*!"《打倒英雌》, carried in *The Pei-yang Pictorial News*《北洋画报》Issue 1115, April 1934.
29 For example, Issues 4 and 26, 1946 of *Shanghai Tan*《上海滩》 separately carried Fang Ru's 方儒 "Fei Mu Perspicaciously Recognizes a Heroine"《费穆慧眼识英雌》, Wu Ke's 舞客 "Heroines in Military Uniform"《穿上军装的英雌们》and others. Before this, in the 1930s, those that I am aware of that used *ying ci* 英雌 also include "Chatting about Heroines of the Silver Screen"《漫谈银国英雌》, which was carried in Issue 1–2 of *Bei Xin*《北新》magazine in 1930. Meanwhile, Issue 5, 1936, of *Modern Youth* 《现代青年》carried Xiang Baolun's 相抱轮 "Eternal Heroine Qin Liangyu"《千古英雌秦良玉》amongst others.
30 See *Women's Voice*《妇女共鸣》Vol. 4, Issue 8, August 1935. Relatively early on, Yu Hualin 余华林 supplied the author with this document, for which I express my gratitude.
31 Ji, Zhuman 吉竹蔓, "On the Refusal to Use the Character *Ta* 她 and a Question for *Reading Life*"《关于拒用 "她"字并质<读书生活>》, *Women's Voice* 《妇女共鸣》Vol. 4, Issue 10, October 1935.
32 Shu, San, "'*Ta* 她' and the Women's Movement"《"她"与妇运》, carried in *The Decameron*《十日谈》, Issue 34, July 10, 1934.
33 Shi, Tong, "Refusing to Use the Character *Ta* 她"《拒用"她"字》, carried in *Reading Life*《读书生活》, Vol. 2, Issue 9, September 1935.
34 Recently some have translated this as *The Compromised Position of Women*《妇女的屈从地位》, see Wang Xi's 汪溪 1996 translation published by Shangwu Yinshuguan.
35 Shi, Tong 士同, "Refusing to Use the Character *Ta* 她"《拒用 "她" 字》, *Reading Life*《读书生活》 Vol. 2, Issue 9, September 1935. Shi Tong 士同 is the *nom de plume* of Liu Shi 柳湜. This writer incidentally learned this whilst thumbing through the *Collected Works of Liu Shi*《柳湜文集》and discovered the included essay "Refusing to Use the Character *Ta* 她"《拒用 "她" 字》.

36 Ji, Zhuman 吉竹蔓, "On the Refusal to Use the Character *Ta* 她 and a Question for *Reading Life*" 《关于拒用 "她"字并质<读书生活>》, *Women's Voice* 《妇女共鸣》, Vol. 4, Issue 10, October 1935.
37 Qing Dynasty province abolished in 1955 and divided among Hebei, Liaoning, and Inner Mongolia.
38 See the aforementioned Ji, Zhuman 吉竹蔓, "On the Refusal to Use the Character *Ta* 她 and a Question for *Reading Life*" 《关于拒用 "她"字并质<读书生活>》, *Women's Voice* 《妇女共鸣》 Vol. 4, Issue 10.

6 *Ta* (她, She), *Ta* (他, He), *Ta* (牠, It) and *Ta* (它, It)

The Formation and Establishment of a New Pronoun Regime

Prior to 1920, the debate around the character *ta* 她 mainly revolved around whether or not the third person pronoun should be differentiated according to gender. The question of whether a pronoun for the "middle" or neuter gender was necessary, and if so, then what form it should take, had largely failed to gain attention or to give rise to debate. It was usually mentioned in passing, raised as a proposal or simply put into practice. For example, in April 1920, Han Bing in his essay "A Detailed Critique of the Question of the Character *Ta* 她" 《关于"她"字问题的申论》 openly declared, "I also suggest that we use the *bi* 彼 character to represent neuter objects; that we assign the three characters *ta* 他, *yi* 伊, and *bi* 彼 the special task of each representing a gender type" (which was in complete agreement with Guo Zansheng's practice in his translation of Allen and Comwell's *English School Grammar* 《文法初阶》 in 1878). Liu Bannong in his "On the Question of the Character *Ta* 她" 《"她"字问题》 parenthetically declared, "I now believe that, apart from the *ta* 她 character, we need to choose another character to represent the neuter or neutral third person pronoun. But this is a different matter, so we will leave it for the moment."

It must be acknowledged that in 1935 when Liu Bannong included this article in his *Essays of [Liu] Bannong* 《半农杂文》, he changed "we need to choose another character" to "we need to choose the *ta* 它 character . . .", consciously adding *ta* 它, which led many later to believe that, like *ta* 她, he was the first to invent *ta* 它 as well. This was Liu Bannong's mistake. Whether or not he had already privately advocated for its use is also uncertain, but we can be sure that at the time he certainly had not yet publicly advocated such a practice.

1 The Introduction and Discussion of Different Proposals for a Third Person Pronoun Schema

It was such contributors and editors of the *The Republican Daily News* 《民国日报》 as Chen Wangdao et al. who, from a linguistics point of view, comprehensively embraced the question of the third person pronoun at a very early stage, brought advocacy for it to the attention of the public, were committed to quickly achieving its wide acceptance and promulgation while daring to use it and to lead society in taking note of and discussing the issue. On May 3, 1920, Chen Wangdao

DOI: 10.4324/9781003359449-7

in his essay "The Female Third Person 'Pronoun'" 《女子性第三身"身次代名词"》 used a chart to demonstrate a systematic recognition of the third person pronoun architecture. His view was that the singular should be divided into three categories: (the masculine) *ta* 他, (the feminine) *yi* 伊 (rather than *ta* 她), and (the neuter) *ta* 他. For the plural, a single expression could be used, namely *tamen* 他们. This view that the third person singular pronoun should be divided but that a plural division was not necessary had already been suggested informally by others such as Da Tong, who agreed that *yi* 伊 should be used for the feminine so as to distinguish it from the masculine *ta* 他, but opposed using *yimen* 伊们 for the feminine plural, believing that

> In written script, even if one were to use the masculine third person plural pronoun or the feminine third person plural pronoun, one would of necessity need to actually name the objects (persons) being referred to anyway, so the common *tamen* 他们 could be used. Look at English, for example . . . it operates in this fashion.[1]

However, at the time Da Tong had obviously not considered the topic fully.

On June 27, 1920, Chen Wangdao, who was focused on the question of establishing a comprehensive plan for the third person pronoun in the Chinese language, once more published the article "Discussion on the Use of Third Person Pronouns" 《第三身次代词用法底讨论》 in the *Enlightenment Magazine* 《觉悟》 supplement to *The Republican Daily News* 《民国日报》 in which he announced a new view which he had formed following deliberations with Shen Xuanlu 沈玄庐 and Li Hanjun 李汉俊. One important change in this view that was worth noting was the fact that he had abandoned his previous advocacy of using *tamen* 他们 to represent the plural form and agreed with a differentiation. Moreover, for the first time, he presented the following comprehensive table for the third person pronoun:

Table 6.1 Comprehensive table of the third person pronoun

Gender Number	Masculine	Feminine	Common (通性)	Neuter
Singular	*ta* 佗	*yi* 伊	*qu* 渠	*bi* 彼
Plural	*tamen* 他们	*yimen* 伊们	*qumen* 渠们	*bideng* 彼等

In the above chart, Chen Wangdao et al. not only created a new common gender pronoun that could be used when the male and female were mixed, employing the corresponding innovative *qu* 渠 and *qumen* 渠们, but they also created the new plural form *bideng* 彼等 for the neuter pronoun. Meanwhile, he pointed out the theoretical basis for this type of distinction:

> It is to be recognized that the more clearly language and script are differentiated, the better and clearer it is, the more convenient it becomes, and for this

reason we are promoting this reform. However, we also recognise that it is possible to consciously change the original meaning of a character and so we also recommend that we do not invent a new character, so with these two provisos in mind we have come up with the above result.

It was precisely based on this type of "the clearer the distinction, the better" mindset that when Li Hanjun suggested that French grammatical conventions be followed such that when a plural common gender pronoun was required then the masculine pronoun be used, or whenever there was a male involved, then *tamen* 他们 be used. However, Chen Wangdao was still unsatisfied, "If you feel you must do it this way, then you don't necessarily have to follow the French practice; you only need to ask how clarity can be achieved." Thus, in the end he endorsed Shen Xuanlu's 沈玄庐 suggestion of using *qumen* 渠们, despite it perhaps initially feeling somewhat amateurish, "But when we recall how awkward the two characters *yimen* 伊们 felt when they were first used only for them now to become so convenient, there should be no objection."

At the end of 1920, seven individuals including Chen Wangdao, Ye Chucang 叶楚伧, Shen Xuanlu 沈玄庐, Shao Lizi 邵力子 and Liu Dabai 刘大白 jointly drafted *New Examples of Assigned Characters* 《用字新例》 and distributed it publicly under the auspices of the "Office of the Republican Daily" in an attempt to accelerate the nationwide discussion and acknowledgement of the issue.[2] *New Examples* included four "Assigned Characters" charts, the first being the "Different iterations of *ta* 他". In this chart, all third person pronouns were basically the same as those that had previously been suggested in the aforementioned article, with the exception of *qu* 渠 and *qumen* 渠们 which had been changed to *qu* 佢 and *qumen* 佢们.[3] This change, apart from the fact that 佢 was a simplified version of 渠, was also undertaken so as to universally incorporate the *ren* 人 (human) radical.

See the table:

Table 6.2 The differentiation of the character *ta* 他 according to *New Examples of Assigned Characters* 《用字新例》[4]

Gender Number	Masculine	Feminine	Common (通性)	Neuter
Singular	*ta* 他	*yi* 伊	*qu* 佢	*bi* 彼
Plural	*tamen* 他们	*yimen* 伊们	*qumen* 佢们	*bideng* 彼等

After *New Examples of Assigned Characters* 《用字新例》 was published, the draughtspersons and their supporters, one after the other, boldly conducted creative experiments in all manner of newspapers and magazines in accordance with the requirement to "always adhere to these principles in your practice whether it be in calligraphy, creative writing, editorial work, translations or preparing teaching materials,"[5] whereupon an assortment of practical applications contended for a period. From October to November 1921, *Light of*

100 *Ta* (她, She), *Ta* (他, He), *Ta* (牠, It) and *Ta* (它, It)

Learning 《学灯》 magazine published many specialist articles on the topic, creating a mini high tide of debate around the question of the "differentiation of the character *ta* 他". Amongst these, Chen Sibai 陈斯白 led the field in voicing his misgivings about *New Examples of Assigned Characters* and proposed a new chart of the third person pronoun which especially attracted a lot of attention. Let us first look at the chart:

Table 6.3 The third person pronoun chart proposed by Chen Sibai 陈斯白

Gender Number	Masculine	Feminine	Common	Neuter (inanimate)	Neuter (animate)
Singular	*ta* 他	*ta* 她	*ta* 侢	*ta* 牠	*shi* 狧
Plural	*tamen* 他们	*tamen* 她们	*tamen* 侢们	*tamen* 牠们	*shimen* 狧们
Creator of the character	Cangjie 仓颉	Liu Bannong 刘半农	Chen Sibai 陈斯白	Guo Moruo 郭沫若	Chen Sibai 陈斯白

The reason why Chen Sibai proposed a schema that differed from Chen Wangdao and his colleagues was mainly because he was dissatisfied with the group's deliberate rendering of the pronunciation of the other third person pronouns in a different manner from that of *ta* 他. This was the exact opposite to the regrets Liu Bannong had expressed about *ta* 她 or the reasons why Han Bing and others had attacked *ta* 她. In Chen Sibai's view, since in the spoken language most regions across the country habitually pronounced the third person singular pronoun as "*ta*", therefore, to allow the "feminine", "neuter" and "shared" gendered third person pronoun to be pronounced differently was completely unnecessary and would also be extremely difficult in practice for the majority of the population to accept because it did not accord with the fundamental principle of "unity of word and script" or "the written word must accord with speech". In any case, *yi* 伊, *qu* 佢, and especially *bi* 彼, along with the plural forms *yimen* 伊们, *qumen* 佢们, and *bideng* 彼等 carried too heavy a classical flavor that it would be difficult for them to avoid producing "the malady of adulterating the vernacular with the classical". Chen Sibai believed that although the third person pronouns that he had developed were numerous, nevertheless, they all comprised the suffix *ye* 也, and "because the sound of the characters were all the same as *ta* 他, there was no conflict with the language at all."[6]

Nevertheless, while the proposals of the two Chens mentioned previously were different, they did in spirit share some ground, namely an excessive belief in the principle that "the more meticulous and precise a language is, the better". And it was precisely for this reason that Chen Sibai admired Chen Wangdao and his colleagues – for moving beyond the English language and creating a universal or shared third person category – arguing that this was where their genius lay. His only disappointment was that their delineation was not fine enough, so he added a further two neuter categories.

The complexity and confusion that this excessively fine delineation created soon irked many. Some were moved to a position of completely rejecting any "subdivision of the character *ta* 他" (such as Sun Xunqun, mentioned previously) while even more tended towards placing a limit on the subdivision. The more active participants in the debate like Gong Dengchao 龚登朝 penned articles that not only opposed the singular shared pronoun, but he also opposed the further division of the neuter category into animate and inanimate, believing that it added unnecessary inconvenience.[7] Qian Xuantong was even more prolific and completely rejected the notion of a common gender subdivision, arguing that it was useless. He gave many specific examples to show that it was "excessively disruptive" and advised that it "can very easily be dispensed with." In his view:

> If a pronoun is required where the gender is unclear or if both genders are present, then the simplest thing to do would be to use *ta* 他 or *tamen* 他们. Specification is a response to a real situation because the new divided character and the original character differ in terms of their meanings and corresponding narrower or broader scopes. Whatever meaning the original character had continues to hold while the character remains undifferentiated. Take *ta* 他 for example. After it has been differentiated, apart from the feminine and neuter meanings, *ta* 他 can continue to be used, including "the remainder/others" (*qita* 其他), "those" (*tazhong* 他种), "that person" (*taren* 他人), "some time in the future" (*tari* 他日) etc. It is not restricted to the single meaning of a masculine pronoun. If one was inclined to feel that using *ta* 他 and *tamen* 他们 in a mixed gender context still carried overtones of masculinity, then perhaps one could use the relevant neuter character.

Viewed from the standpoint of actual current usage, we cannot but admire Qian Xuantong 钱玄同 who, some 90 years ago, was able to possess such outstanding foresight.

The view of Qian Xuantong as described above was outlined in an article entitled "Discussion of the Differentiation between the Two Terms 'He' (*ta*, 他) and 'They' (*tamen*, 他们)" 《"他"和"他们"两个词儿的分化之讨论》, published on November 20, 1922 in *National Language Monthly* 《国语月刊》. Apart from opposing the "common gender", the article expressed many other well-thought-out views, revealing the mature wisdom of a distinguished linguist. For example, on the question of whether neuter words need to be differentiated and separated from masculine words, Zhou Zuoren and others believed that in terms of the actual spoken context, the two were not difficult to differentiate, and since habitually no distinction had been made, both could share the use of the single *ta* 他. In response, Qian Xuantong approached the question from the relationship between "habit" and "clarity" and so raised a comparatively convincing opposite view. He noted:

> Differentiation is fundamentally a means of making improvements to the established national language, so the differentiated terms were never, by definition, "habitual" in the pre-existing language. If we want to create this

"habit", then we must rely entirely on the literature produced hereafter. While in terms of spoken context it may not be difficult to distinguish between masculine and neuter if they both use the *ta* 他 character, nevertheless, there has never been a "habit" in the traditional language of using *ta* 他 for the neuter (it was occasionally used as an object, but never as a subject). Since using either *ta* 他 or a differentiated new character would both be breaking with tradition, if it were differentiated then it would not necessarily cause any more stress, and in the written form would actually be significantly clearer, so I therefore am not in favor of . . . only using two characters to represent the three genders.

As to the question of the plural of the three genders, many also advocated not to make a distinction, like in English. However, Qian Xuantong approached the

Figure 6.1 A snippet of Qian Xuantong's highly original and brilliant essay in which he probes the question of *ta* 她, and advocates, for the first time, for the use of the character *ta* 它 as the neuter third person pronoun.

question from the standpoint of the existing national language and insisted that it would be better to make the distinction. He most insightfully remarked:

> Speaking of plurals, it is probably sufficient to use the one term *tamen* 他们. For example, English only has the single *they*, . . . however, I believe that there are a great many differences between Chinese grammar and the grammar of the European language group. Because Chinese grammar is so exiguous, the semantics are often ambiguous, and misunderstanding is common, so dividing *tamen* 他们 into three according to gender, in line with the singular, would appear to guarantee more clarity. I therefore recommend that it be differentiated.

So, if the masculine, feminine, and neuter genders were to be differentiated, which pronoun would it be appropriate to use for each? Qian Xuantong finally offers his opinion which he condensed into the following chart:

Table 6.4 Qian Xuantong's pronoun table

Gender \ Number	*Singular*	*Plural*
Masculine	*ta* 他	*tamen* 他们
Feminine	A: *yi* 伊 B: *ta* 她	A: *yimen* 伊们 B: *tamen* 她们
Neuter	A: *ta* 它 B: *ta* 牠	A: *tamen* 它们 B: *tamen* 牠们

For Qian Xuantong, both options A and B in the chart could be used. "Either could be used, depending on one's personal preference." Because they were merely "the same character but variant forms". Thus, the pronunciation could also be the same. To this ends he went to great lengths to mobilise his extensive knowledge of traditional linguistics and demonstrated that in the ancient past *ta* 她 could also be pronounced like *yi* 伊, to refute the prevailing view that "the grounds for pronouncing the character *ta* 她 like *yi* 伊 are not fully established." What is more, he found support in the linguist Zhao Yuanren 赵元任's new *Recordings of the National Language Textbook*《国语留声片课本》which had been recently published by the Commercial Press and in which *ta* 她 was pronounced like *yi* 伊. Zhao Yuanren promoted the division of the third person pronoun into *ta* 他, *ta* 她 and *ta* 牠, and Qian Xuantong also thought that this division was "appropriate", although on the choice of character for the feminine and neuter pronouns, he was inclined to favor the characters *yi* 伊 and *ta* 它. This can be deduced from the previous chart where these expressions were listed as his "first choice".

From the various aforementioned proposals it can be seen that while the knowledge of the proponents varied widely, and the resultant influence on the language and literature of the day was also perhaps uneven, nevertheless the third person pronoun structure (*ta* 他, *ta* 她, *ta* 它 and *tamen* 他们, *tamen* 她们, *tamen* 它们)

that was finally settled upon was not an acceptance of the direct product of any single individual's ready-made proposal but rather a product of the guidance of linguists and the practice of litterateurs, with the final imprimatur of common social linguistic and cultural choices.

2 The Reworking of *Ta* 它 (It) and *Ta* 牠 (It) and the Stabilisation of the Position of *Ta* 她 (She)

According to my research, the individual who most clearly led the pack in advocating for the use of *ta* 它 and *tamen* 它们 as the chosen neuter third person pronoun was not Liu Bannong as many would have us believe, but rather it should be Qian Xuantong. This was an important innovation of Mr Qian in his article "Discussion of the Differentiation between the Two Terms 'He' (*ta*, 他) and 'They' (*tamen*, 他们)" 《"他"和"他们"两个词儿的分化之讨论》. Qian Xuantong had already introduced the character *ta* 它 as early as the beginning of 1919 when he and Zhou Zuoren began to discuss the translation of the English word "she". Chen Duxiu 陈独秀 had also informally suggested using *ta* 它 for the feminine pronoun. However, prior to November 1922 it appears that no one had formally advocated for the use of *ta* 它 as the singular neuter third person pronoun. In the article, Qian Xuantong argued that since *ta* 它 was used for *ta* 他 in the classical language, and its pronunciation "*tuo*" in the ancient past was also the ancient pronunciation of the character *ta* 他, to which could be added the fact that in areas that used officialese, there was the lingering phenomenon of the character *ta* 他 still being pronounced as "*tuo*", Mr Qian proposed:

> We should use the current character *ta* 他 and its current pronunciation to represent the masculine, and the ancient character 它 and its ancient pronunciation *tuo* to represent the neuter, . . . the neuter singular should be *tuo* 它, and the plural *tuomen* 它们.

He also argued that "Dividing it this way not only rolls off the tongue more easily than *bi* 彼 and *bideng* 彼等, but it also accords somewhat with general practice." In order to demonstrate the rationality of using *tuo* 它, Qian Xuantong reminded his readers specifically:

> Playing the opportunist for the moment, if for words referring to human beings we are to use the *ren* 人 or "human" radical, like in the two characters *ta* 他 and *yi* 伊, and for words that do not refer to human beings we use *tuo* 它, then I would say that there was some advantage.

This sentence, which he himself acknowledged was "irrelevant to the main thesis", in fact actually revealed some of the advantages of using *tuo* 它 for the neuter third person pronoun.

Qian Xuantong's criticism of Chen Wangdao et al.'s advocacy of *bi* 彼 and *bideng* 彼等 to represent the neuter gender was also insightful. He believed:

> The character *bi* 彼 is not a good choice because if we were to use *bimen* 彼们 for its plural form, then it would be too contrived, and if we were to use *bideng* 彼等 as suggested in *New Examples of Assigned Characters* 《用字新例》 then it would diverge from the practice of using *men* 们 as a plural marker as in *women* 我们 (we) and *tamen* 他们 (they). Even though grammar inevitably has its exceptions, nevertheless this only involves characters that we are familiar with. If we are not familiar with a term and we deliberately construct a new term, then it is always appropriate that we abide by the rules of grammar.

If a new term is constructed and normal grammatical practice is adhered to, then this is precisely the genius of linguist Qian Xuantong's contribution.

The character *ta* 牠 is also worth a special mention in relation to the third person neuter pronoun. While this character (as a glyph) had already appeared in the Tang Dynasty edition of the *Qie Yun* 《切韵》 which had been discovered in Dunhuang, its contemporary use as a neuter pronoun was only developed during the May Fourth period. In 1935, Lu Xun 鲁迅 in his "Remembering Liu Bannong" 《忆刘半农君》 fully credited Liu Bannong with its invention, but I am afraid that this is quite questionable. Previously, we have already described how Chen Sibai 陈斯白 in November 1921 drafted a pronoun chart in which he clearly indicated that this character had been invented by Guo Moruo 郭沫若, but he failed to provide any concrete evidence. Meanwhile, Qian Xuantong in his "Discussion of the Differentiation between the Two Terms 'He' (*ta*, 他) and 'They' (*tamen*, 他们)" 《"他"和"他们"两个词儿的分化之讨论》 advanced another theory, "I am not sure who was the first to propose the use of *ta* 牠 for the neuter gender, but it seems that I first noted it being used in 1919 in *Study Magazine* 《修业杂志》 published by Tsinghua University 清华学校, but I cannot now recall precisely where."[8] I had not originally examined very closely the origins of *ta* 牠, but had discovered that the character was already being utilised by many before 1921 at the very least.[9] Now, having checked the *Study Magazine* 《修业杂志》 to which Qian Xuantong referred, it can truly be shown that Mr Qian's theory does have merit.

Study Magazine 《修业杂志》 was inaugurated in April 1919 by a student organisation belonging to Beijing's Tsinghua University 清华学校 named the Study Group 修业团 (later known as the Truth Association 唯真学会). The magazine's Vol. 1 Issue 2 changed its name to *Study* 《修业》 and was published in December 1919. In this issue, it not only endorsed and employed the character *ta* 她, but it also created a character *ta* 牠 to translate "it" for the first time. For example, in a translation of Tolstoy's *A Grain as Big as a Hen's Egg* 《鸡子那么大的种子》 using the pseudonym Yifan (or Ivan, 伊凡), the translator deliberately uses *ta* 牠 as the neuter third person singular pronoun. In the *Random Thoughts* 杂感 section of the magazine, he specially wrote an article entitled "Invention and the

Nature of Slavishness" 《发明与奴隶的根性》 in which he specifically explained the matter. The article reads:

> I thought that whenever we encountered a part of the script that has survived from the ancients that was no longer fit for purpose that we should innovate – there should be no unwillingness or fear – like the character *ta* 牠, a word that I now frequently use in my translations. It equates to the English word "it" and Chinese doesn't have this word, so I have been so bold as to create it. Because I frequently encounter "he, she, or it" in my translation, all-in-all it makes it hard to translate. "He" can be represented in Chinese with the character *ta* 他; people have recently invented the character *ta* 她 to represent "she" and I don't see anything wrong with that, so I have used it. But for "it", I am yet to find anyone who has invented a word in Chinese that could represent it. And I have not been able to just press on with my translation, so I have presumptively created *ta* 牠 (because the word "it" includes a sense of "matter or object" [*wu* 物], and *wu* 物 is made up of *niu* 牛 and *wu* 勿, therefore my *ta* 牠 also follows the pattern of *wu* 物 in having *niu* 牛 on its left-hand side). Henceforth, whenever I encounter "he, she, or ti [*sic*, i.e., it]", I will have no problem translating it.
>
> I know there will certainly be those who will curse me for "Insulting Lord Cang by creating a character that is neither fish nor fowl";[10] some will definitely curse me, saying, "Hrumph! You little schoolboy, how dare you go inventing script! Only grandees can do that!" But when, pray tell, will the grandees do it? And if the grandees haven't invented it yet, then does that mean that this dumb little student has to go on waiting with no character to use? To go a step further, what if the grandees don't invent it? When those individuals curse me, it just means they are belittling themselves or, to put it another way, they are being irresponsible. As for those who curse me for "disrespecting Lord Cang", they are even more laughable. We create words for our use, and it has nothing to do with "Lord Cang".

Not only did he say this, but the writer also asserted the legitimacy and proactive nature of his creation of *ta* 牠 from the point of view of the incompatibility of invention and creation with the "true nature of slavishness", criticizing the ignorance of those who limited themselves at every turn saying, "What business do we have with creating words?" He believed that they

> Had only two motives: 1. that they were demonstrating their nature as slaves to their ancestors and not willing to innovate; 2. They were self-deprecating (China's so-called "modesty or concealing one's talents") and do not dare to innovate. These two mindsets certainly landed them in a rut, with no hint of invention.

Moreover, "If China wishes to innovate", then it must "Root out the slave mentality as its first order of business", and thereby demonstrate the precious cultural creative spirit of the youth of the new era and their willingness to blaze new trails.[11]

So, who is this "Ivan"? I undertook some investigation and confirmed that he was the renowned representative of the "Strategies of the Warring States Group" 战国策派 during the later War of Resistance against Japan, He Yongji 何永佶.[12] Mr He was from Panyu in Guangdong province and along with Shi Hun 施滉, Ji Chaoding 冀朝鼎, Xu Yonghong 徐永煐 and others was an important early member of the Tsinghua University Study Group 清华学校修业团. In 1924 he left for the United States to study where he won a Doctorate from Harvard University. On his return to China, he successively served as a Professor at Peking University 北京大学, Sun Yatsen University 中山大学, Yunnan University 云南大学 and elsewhere.

Apart from *Study* 《修业》, many of the other newspapers and magazines of the day also employed *ta* 牠. For example, in November 1920, *The Short Story Magazine* 《小说月报》 published Yi Fu's 毅夫 translation of the American author Ben Ames Williams' short story "They Grind Exceeding Small" 《一元纸币》 in which he not only used *ta* 牠 as a neuter third person pronoun, but also skilfully employed *ta* 他, *ta* 她, and *ta* 牠 (in other words, all characters with the *ye* 也 element) to generate a third person gendered distinction in his creative practice.[13]

There have been those who believed that Guo Moruo 郭沫若 was the first "inventor" of *ta* 牠, but this conclusion must be mistaken. Guo Moruo can only be called a relatively early propagator and enthusiastic practitioner of *ta* 牠. The earliest I have seen Guo Moruo use *ta* 牠 is during the summer/fall of 1920. For example, in October of that year he published his poem "Burying the Chicken" 《葬鸡》 in *Light of Learning* 《学灯》 in which he used the character. The poem reads:

Chicken! Daughter of a fowl!
It was we who harmed . . . harmed . . . harmed you!
We plundered the vital forces of all under heaven,
The mouse steals our surplus grain for food,
That is robbery, plain and simple,
And why should we come up with venomous thoughts?
Because we want to poison it (*ta*, 牠),
But we have harmed you instead!
Now I recall those wonderful years together,
And my tears fall uncontrollably like rain, like rain.[14]

Nevertheless, the claim that Guo Moruo invented the character *ta* 牠 is not without basis. There are scholars who have shown that Guo Moruo himself has claimed to have invented the term. On August 24, 1920, in a letter to Chen Jianlei 陈建雷 he writes:

Today I cut out the character *ta* 牠 (this is a new character that I have fabricated in order to express the neuter third person pronoun, using the meaning of "object" but carrying the sound *ta* 他) and pasted it below.

The letter was carried in the October 1, 1920, in Issue 2, Volume 2 of the Taidong Bookstore's *New Fiction* 《新的小说》. On September 11 that same year the

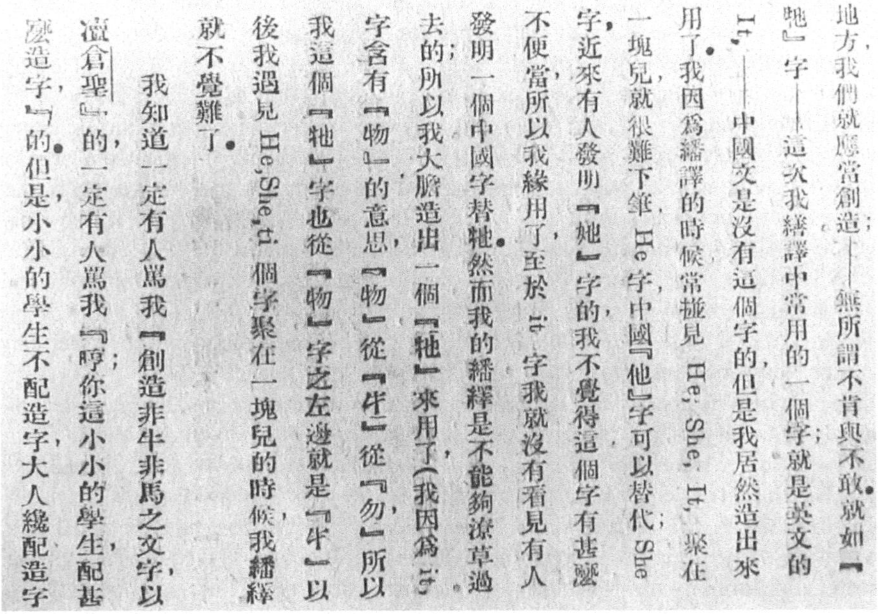
地方，我們就應當創造；——無所謂不肯與不敢。就如『
牠』字——這次我繙譯中常用的一個字；就是英文的
It,——中國文是沒有這個字的，但是我居然造出來
用了。我因爲繙譯的時候常碰見 He, She, It, 聚在
一塊兒，就很難下筆，He 字，中國『他』字可以替代 She
字，近來有人發明『她』字的，我不覺得這個字有甚麼
不便當，所以我緣用了。至於 it 字我就沒有看見有人
發明一個中國字替牠。然而我的繙譯是不能夠潦草過
去的；所以我大膽造出一個『牠』來用了，(我因爲 it
字含有『物』的意思，『物』從『牛』從『勿』，所以
我這個『牠』字也從『物』字之左邊就是『牛』以
後我遇見 He, She, it 個字聚在一塊兒的時候，我繙譯
就不覺難了。
我知道一定有人罵我『創造非牛非馬之文字，以
瀆倉聖』的，一定有人罵我『哼；你這小小的學生，配甚
麼造字，』的。但是，小小的學生不配造字，大人纔配造字

Figure 6.2 Excerpt from Tsinghua University student He Yongji's 何永佶 (Yifan/Ivan 伊凡) article "Invention and the Nature of Slavishness"《发明与奴隶的根性》explaining the process and his reasons for inventing the pronoun *ta* 牠.

Light of Learning 《学灯》 supplement to *The China Times* 《时事新报》 carried a letter from Guo Moruo to Zhang Dongsun 张东荪, Yu Songhua 俞颂华 and Shu Xincheng 舒新城 in which he expresses his view on Zhang Dongsun et al.'s "Letter to the Gentlemen of the *Gongxueshe*" 《致共学社诸君书》. The tenth point in the letter declares:

> In addition, I am about to do the unforgiveable: I intend to use the character *ta* 牠 to act as an *impersonal* third person pronoun. The character *ta* 牠 in the past has referred to a girder (*tuo* 柁), rudder (*duo* 舵), to pull (*tuo* 拖), mackerel (*qing* 角青), tadpole (*ke* 目科), material (*liao* 料), and polled oxen (*wujiaoniu* 无角牛). The character has long passed from use, so if we follow the precedent set by the ancients where "same-sounding characters can be used interchangeably", then it would be convenient to use *ta* 牠 when referring to objects. We could say that it is pronounced like *ta* 他 but uses the "ox" (*niu* 牛) radical to indicate an "object" (*wu* 物). The *wu* 物 character meaning "object" contains the *niu* 牛 radical anyway. According to *Shuo Wen* 说文 [An Explication of Written Characters], "an ox (牛) is a large object . . . and therefore [wu 物 or 'object'] contains the radical niu 牛". . . . So, we can see that the ancients took the ox to represent all objects.[15]

It is obvious that Guo Moruo, who was brimming with creativity, first used the construct *ta* 牠 while apparently remaining unaware that Tsinghua University's He Yongji 何永佶 had already used the character at the end of 1919 in *Study* 《修业》, nor was he aware that the character already had other uses. There were also quite a few other scholars at the time similarly unaware of the situation. It is precisely for this reason that Chen Sibai 陈斯白, who we have mentioned above as having enthusiastically discussed the delineation of *ta* 他 in the pages of *Light of Learning* 《学灯》, in 1921 saw Guo Moruo as the "inventor" of *ta* 牠.

There is yet another reason why Guo Moruo was mistakenly seen by society at large as the earliest creator of the *ta* 牠 character, namely that in his early years he did indeed employ the characters *ta* 她 and *ta* 牠 quite actively in his literary practice. In July 1921, Mr Guo and Qian Junxu 钱君胥 jointly translated and published the German author Theodor Storm's poetic novella *Immensee* 《茵梦湖》.[16] Published, then re-published, the work was a best-seller, and it became one of the earliest major, and comparatively influential, works to deliberately employ the character *ta* 她. In August 1921 Guo Moruo's famous poetry collection *Goddess* 《女神》 was published and in it he employed *ta* 她 reasonably frequently. This was a relatively early influential poetry collection that used the character *ta* 她 and was crucial to the early dissemination of the term. After 1922, the work *Immensee* 《茵梦湖》 used the pronouns *ta* 他, *ta* 她, and *ta* 牠, and was extremely influential in popularising the use of the two characters *ta* 她 and *ta* 牠.[17] Right up until 1932 when people spoke of these two new characters, there were those who continued to credit Guo Moruo and Qian Junxu with their invention:

> Following the popularization of the vernacular language, in terms of personal pronouns, the two characters *ta* 她 and *ta* 牠 were developed and used. The first to use these terms were Qian Junxu and Guo Moruo in their jointly translated *Immensee* 《茵梦湖》. The character *ta* 她, as well as *ta* 牠, referring to an object, gained notability and formed a three-way equilibrium with the pre-existing term *ta* 他.[18]

What is worth noting is that from *The Short Story Magazine* 《小说月报》 it can be seen that by 1923 *ta* 牠 was already in common usage in the pages of the magazine and that it continued to be both active and persistent over a relatively long period of time. Up until at least the start of the 1940s *ta* 牠 was indeed much more popular than *ta* 它 – to the extent that it could be said to have been totally dominant.[19]

Qian Xuantong was obviously not as enthusiastic about *ta* 牠 as he was about *ta* 它, nevertheless he adopted an attitude of active acceptance and specifically alerted people to be mindful of the fact that:

> The *ta* 牠 character uses *niu* (牛, ox) as an indicator of meaning, but it does not refer to an "ox"; it is indeed taken from, and represents, the character 物 or "object". And the other part of the character, *ye* 也, is not used in the affirmative sense of the word, i.e., *is*, but is taken from a half of the *ta* (他, he) character.[20]

110 *Ta* (她, She), *Ta* (他, He), *Ta* (牠, It) and *Ta* (它, It)

Figure 6.3 Cover of the third edition of *Immensee* 《茵梦湖》, translated by Guo Moruo et al.

Maybe, to a certain extent, he meant to dissuade people from interpreting the characters as: *renye* 人也 [i.e., this is a human being], *nüye* 女也 [i.e., this is a woman], and *niuye* 牛也 [i.e., this is an ox] and overthinking the logic behind the creation of the three personal pronouns "*ta* 他, *ta* 她, *ta* 牠"?

The *ta* 他, *ta* 她, *ta* 它 pronoun regime in general use today began to ferment in around 1922 and gradually achieved broader acknowledgement after the mid-1930s.[21] However the competition between *ta* 牠 and *ta* 它 continued for much longer and, during their deployment, some minute differences appeared between them. In 1939, someone published the article "How to Use *Ta* (他), *Ta* (她), *Ta* (牠), and *Ta* (它)" 《"他"、"她"、"牠"、"它"的用法》 in which they made the following pointed explanation of how to use *ta* 牠 and *ta* 它:

> The radical of the *ta* 牠 character is *niu* 牛, and that is of course appropriate for representing all animals. Nowadays people regularly also use *ta* 牠 to refer to inanimate objects and events. We cannot be critical of this . . . . Finally, we speak of the character *ta* 它. It is possible to use *ta* 它 for any event or inanimate object. Nowadays people also use *ta* 它 to refer to everything that is not "human", and we will not pursue the matter further.
> Apart from this, the character *ta* 它 also has one peculiar use and that is to refer to a fetus. Because the gender of the fetus is not established, nor is it obvious, whenever we speak of it there is truly no means of working out whether it is male or female and so we can only use *ta* 它 to represent it. Admittedly we could use *ta* 他, but, if we were to use *ta* 牠, then we would unavoidably convey a sense of insult.[22]

From this we can also see that in contrast to *ta* 牠 and *tamen* 牠们, *ta* 它 and *tamen* 它们 were in fact already gradually displaying a certain latent competitive advantage.

However, as *ta* 牠 and *tamen* 牠们 proceeded towards their demise only to be finally eclipsed by *ta* 它 and *tamen* 它们, this only became a reality after the political implications of the equality of the sexes gained strength and New China was established. Just as *yi* 伊 and *yimen* 伊们 were eventually cast aside, so too did the victorious conclusion of *ta* 它 and *tamen* 它们 equally give people food for thought.

In conclusion, the gradual popularisation of the neuter pronouns *ta* 牠 and *ta* 它 to form a type of mutually complementary third person pronoun regime undoubtedly strengthened and consolidated the legitimacy of terms of gender differentiation. Apart from the influence of other factors, the eventual victory of *ta* 她 over *yi* 伊 was, to a certain extent, also the result of a relative selection and positioning process similar to the interplay between *ta* 牠 and *ta* 它. This point will be discussed further in Chapter 8 of this work.

Notes

1 Da, Tong 大同, "Research on the 'Third Person Pronoun'" 《"第三身代名词"底研究》, carried in *New Man* 《新人》, Issue 2, April 1920.
2 It was included in the *Collected Works of Chen Wangdao* 《陈望道文集》, however the footnote claiming that it had been published in *Enlightenment Magazine* 《觉悟》 on October 22, 1922, is incorrect. In fact, *New Examples of Assigned Characters* 《用字新例》 was completed around October to November 1920. In 1921 when Chen Sibai

陈斯白 and others were discussing the question of the "division of the character *ta* 他", they mentioned it and stated that it had been completed in "the previous year". Chen, Wangdao 陈望道 also included it as an "Appendix" to his *Handout on Composition* 《作文法讲义》 which was known as "The first systematic work on vernacular essay writing" and was published in its first edition by the Minzhi Bookstore in March 1922.

3 The *qu* 佢 character acting as the third person singular pronoun was used in many places in a similar manner to *ta* 他. For example, in the *Chinese and English Phrase Book* 《华英通语》, which was compiled in 1855, it was used regularly. The English-Chinese sample sentences corresponding to "he", "she" and "it" all use this word. Nor was it created by Chen Wangdao and others. On October 22, 1921, *Light of Learning* 《学灯》 especially carried Gong Dengchao's 龚登朝 discursive article "The Discussion of '*Qu* 佢' (he/she/it) and 'Mr.' (xiansheng 先生)" 《"佢"和"先生"的讨论》.

4 The rule of the division of the character *ta* 他 which was proposed by *New Examples of Assigned Characters* 《用字新例》 was soon formally adopted by works on grammar. For example, *Lectures on Chinese Grammar* 《中国语法讲义》 edited by Sun Lianggong 孙俍工 adopted it completely (East Asian Library 1922 edition, p. 36). Mr Sun was also a long-term user of the *yi* 伊 character.

5 For example, Shen Xuanlu 沈玄庐 implemented the "*ta* 他 (*tamen* 他们), *yi* 伊 (*yimen* 伊们), *qu* 佢 (*qumen* 佢们)" directive in his February 13, 1921, publication "The Principle Behind the Publication of the *Labor and Women* Magazine" 《劳动与妇女发刊大意》. See the inaugural edition of *Labor and Women* 《劳动与妇女》 magazine.

6 Chen, Sibai 陈斯白, "Opinions on the Differentiation of the Character *Ta* 他 (he)" 《"他"字分化的意见》, carried in *Light of Learning* 《学灯》 October 8, 1921.

7 To Gong's 龚 mind, since the common gender "通性" is used collectively for the masculine and feminine, then before the term is employed, we are already aware that both male and female are involved, or at least that it includes at least two people, so therefore it should only require a plural form and no singular form. See Gong, Dengchao 龚登朝, "Discussion of 'The Division of *Ta* 他'" 《"他的分化"的讨论》, carried in *Light of Learning* 《学灯》 on October 13, 1921. On this issue, Chen Wangdao 陈望道 represented his fellows in explaining that a singular expression for the common gender "通性" was still necessary because it described a situation where it was unclear whether males or females were involved, and so *qu* 佢 could be used. The plural form *qumen* 佢们 represented a situation where "a number of both genders are present" or where "a number are present, but the gender is unclear." See "Reply to Mr Gong Dengchao's Doubts over '*New Examples of Assigned Characters*'" 《答龚登朝先生对于<用字新例>"怀疑的所在"》, carried in *Enlightenment Magazine* 《觉悟》 on October 16, 1921 and signed "Contributors to *New Examples of Assigned Characters*" ("用字新例一同人") and included in the *Collected Works of Chen Wangdao* 《陈望道文集》, Shanghai: People's Publishing House, Vol. 3, 1981.

8 Qian, Xuantong 钱玄同, "Discussion of the Differentiation between the Two Terms 'He' (*ta*, 他) and 'They' (*tamen*, 他们)" 《"他"和"他们"两个词儿的分化之讨论》, carried in the *National Language Monthly* 《国语月刊》, Vol. 1, No. 10, November 20, 1922.

9 Huang, Xingtao 黄兴涛, "The Story of the Character *Ta* 她: Invention, Debate and Early Circulation" 《"她"字的故事：女性新代词符号的发明、论争与早期流播》, see Yang, Nianqun 杨念群 (ed.), *New History* 《新史学》, Vol. 1, Beijing: Zhonghua Bookstore, 2007, p. 153.

10 A reference to Cangjie 仓颉, the legendary inventor of Chinese characters [Translator].

11 Yi, Fan (Ivan) 伊凡, "Invention and the Nature of Slavishness" 《发明与奴隶的根性》, carried in *Study* 《修业》, Vol. 1, No. 2, December 1919. It should be noted that the cover of this magazine is incorrectly labelled as Volume 2, No. 2.

12 "Record of Interview with Comrade Ji Chaoding" 《冀朝鼎同志访问记录》 [a restricted document, not for distribution], a mimeographed document arranged by

Mr Liu Guisheng 刘桂生, and printed by the Editorial Board of the History of Tsinghua University on November 26, 1959, notes: "An article by He Yongji [ji] 何永吉[佶] where he advocates the use of the term *ta* 牠 (i.e., apart from *ta* 他 and *ta* 她, we should add a neuter *ta* 牠) is published above. And he has also in the past translated articles by Tolstoy." This writer subsequently determined that He Yongji was "Ivan/Yi Fan (伊凡)". The relevant information from "Record of Interview with Comrade Ji Chaoding" 《冀朝鼎同志访问记录》 was gleaned from "Xu Suizhi's 徐绥之 Blog".

13 Yi, Fu 毅夫 (trans.), "They Grind Exceeding Small" 《一元纸币》, carried in *The Short Story Magazine* 《小说月报》 Vol. 11, No. 11, November 1920.

14 See Deng, Niudun 邓牛顿 (comp.), "Missing Items from Guo Moruo's *Goddess* Collection" 《郭沫若<女神>集外佚文》 (1919–1921), carried in the *Nankai University Journal* 《南开大学学报》, 1978 (3).

15 See Zhu, Jinshun 朱金顺, "Regarding the Character '*Ta* (牠, it)'" 《说"牠"字》, carried in *Lu Xun Research Monthly* 《鲁迅研究月刊》, 1996 (2); Chen Fukang 陈福康, "Also Regarding the Character '*Ta* (牠, it)'" 《也说"牠"字》, carried in *Lu Xun Research Monthly* 《鲁迅研究月刊》, 1996 (6).

16 Guo, Moruo 郭沫若 et al. (trans.), *Immensee* 《茵梦湖》, first published in July 1921 by the Taidong Bookstore, and republished the following month.

17 I have viewed, in the library of the Renmin University of China, the Taidong Bookstore third edition, published on March 20, 1922, of Guo Moruo and Qian Junxu 钱君胥's jointly translated *Immensee* 《茵梦湖》 which was still not using *ta* 牠 as a third person pronoun but rather uses the character *ta* 他. See the work referred to, pages 57 and 69.

18 Li, Xiaotong 厉筱通, "The Question of the Vulgar Scripted 她 and 牠" 《"她"和"牠"的俗书问题》, carried in *Current Opinion* 《时代公论》, No. 114.

19 This point was reflected in its application in teaching materials, newspapers, and magazines etc. and in the relevant explanations in dictionaries. Let us just take the dictionary explanations as an example. As the entry for the term *ta* 牠 reads in the *Dictionary of the Chinese Language* 《国语普通词典》 co-edited by Ma Junru 马俊如 and Hou Jue 后觉: "Apart from human beings, everything else in the third person is referred to by using *ta* 牠". This dictionary even uses *ta* 牠 to explain *ta* 它. For example, the dictionary entry for *ta* 它 reads: "*ta* 它 : *ta* 牠"; "*tamen* 它们 : *tamen* 牠们". See p. 111 of the First section and p. 91 of the Second section of the late 1923 Zhonghua Bookstore edition of the dictionary. Or alternatively, see the entry for *ta* 牠 in Zhang, Wenzhi 张文治 et al. (eds), *Standard Student Dictionary of the Sounds of the National Language* 《标准国音学生字典》, which reads: "Pronoun for the third person neuter gender"; the entry for *ta* 它 reads: "The same as *ta* 牠". See Zhonghua Bookstore 11th edition (1947; first published in 1935), *Yin* Volume, Part 2. The Commercial Press 1935 edition reprinted in 1936: *Grand Standard Dictionary* 《标准语大词典》 carries an entry for *ta* 牠, but not for *ta* 它. The explanation for *ta* 牠 reads: "Term for the neuter third person". See p. 355 of the dictionary.

20 Qian, Xuantong 钱玄同, "Discussion of the Differentiation between the Two Terms 'He' (*ta*, 他) and 'They' (*tamen*, 他们)" 《"他"和"他们"两个词儿的分化之讨论》, carried in *National Language Monthly* 《国语月刊》, Vol. 1, No. 10.

21 For example, the 1935 edition of the widely circulated Zhonghua Bookstore publication *A National Language Reader* 《国文读本》 (New curriculum standards for teachers), edited by Song Wenhan 宋文翰, when discussing the content of the grammar of "third person terminology" uses the "*ta* 他, *ta* 她, *ta* 它", "*tamen* 他们, *tamen* 她们, *tamen* 它们" sequence. See p. 266 of the 1935 edition of this work.

22 Wei, Hua 韦华, "How to Use *Ta* 他, *Ta* 她, *Ta* 牠, and *Ta* 它" 《"他""她""牠""它"的用法》, carried in *Self-Study* 《自修》, Issue 53, 1939.

7 The Socialisation of the Character *Ta* 她 after April 1920

An Examination of Its Deepening Acceptance and Popularisation

In the preceding chapters we spoke of events prior to April 1920 which cover the question of the earliest written experience of the character *ta* 她 before the heated public debate. What then of the state of its social dissemination in the period following that date?

We can take the relevant contents of such popular media as *The Short Story Magazine* 《小说月报》 as well as middle school Chinese language and literature textbooks, children's magazines, and Chinese language dictionaries as evidence and from the point of view of literature, education and more, recognise and get a handle on the process of the social popularisation of the character *ta* 她. This process was intimately linked to the movement for a national language which was instigated by the proponents of the New Culture. Apart from the primacy of the vernacular language, the standardisation of pronunciation around the Peking dialect and the introduction of modern punctuation into the written script, within the national language movement the tri-gendered division of the character *ta* 他 and the differentiation and use of *de* 的, *di* 地 and *de* 得 are also components worth mentioning. It is only that the initial divergence of opinion amongst the members of the national language movement over the latter was much greater.

1 The Socialised Recognition of the Character *Ta* 她 in *The Short Story Magazine* 《小说月报》, Middle School Chinese Language Textbooks, and More

The Short Story Magazine 《小说月报》 was a literary magazine that was inaugurated in 1910 by Commercial Press and could be said to be the most important, most influential, and also the largest publication medium for contemporary fiction in China in the 1920s. What is more, fiction was one of the leading forms of New Literature and therefore the written practice of the character *ta* 她 in the pages of *The Short Story Magazine* 《小说月报》 was unquestionably symbolic and trailblazing.

In August 1920 *The Short Story Magazine* 《小说月报》 carried in its Volume 11 Issue 8 the translated short story "Fate and Faith" 《命与信》 in which the character *ta* 她 was already beginning to be used to represent the female third person singular. Issues 10, 11, and 12 also employed *ta* 她. Not only was this the case with translated literature, but the original fiction and dramatic scripts carried in the magazine also used the term. Nevertheless, there were still some who did not make a gendered distinction in the third person amongst those who published their work in *The Short Story Magazine* 《小说月报》 (for example, Zhou Shoujuan 周瘦鹃 who has been recognised as the representative of the "Mandarin Ducks and Butterflies School" 鸳鸯蝴蝶派). What is more, of those who *did* make a gendered distinction, the number who used the character *yi* 伊 were considerable. Overall, it could even be said that the *ta* 她 and *yi* 伊 camps were evenly matched in the pages of *The Short Story Magazine* 《小说月报》 at this time.

In January 1921, under the management of Zheng Zhenduo 郑振铎, *The Short Story Magazine* 《小说月报》 instituted a reform and the situation subsequently experienced a clear transformation. The employment of the two characters *ta* 她 and *yi* 伊 became increasingly common and the frequency of the character *ta* 她 increased dramatically. Taking a broad view across the year 1921 as a whole, when compared with *yi* 伊, the character *ta* 她 commanded an absolute dominance and accounted for more than 90% of the occurrences of the two terms.

Beginning with Volume 12, Issues 1 and 2 of *The Short Story Magazine* 《小说月报》 in January and February 1921, many distinguished writers began using *ta* 她 (the vast majority of whom had previously used *yi* 伊). These authors included Bing Xin 冰心, Xu Dishan 许地山, Qu Shiying 瞿世英, Shen Zemin 沈泽民, Zheng Zhenduo 郑振铎, Shen Yanbing 沈雁冰 (Mao Dun 茅盾),[1] Wang Tongzhao 王统照, Geng Jizhi 耿济之, Lu Yin 庐隐 and others, among whom Bing Xin, Lu Yin, Xu Dishan, Wang Tongzhao and others used it more frequently. Apart from a few individuals like Shen Zemin who tended to waver somewhat, the remainder henceforth all largely adhered to this practice, and it became a habit. Across the year 1921 a mere handful of famous writers like Lu Xun 鲁迅, Zhou Zuoren 周作人, Ye Shaojun 叶绍钧（Ye Shengtao 圣陶）, Zhu Ziqing 朱自清, Zhou Shoujuan 周瘦鹃, Wang Jingzhi 汪静之, and Liang Zongdai 梁宗岱 et al. continued to persevere in using *yi* 伊.

From *The Short Story Magazine* 《小说月报》 it appears that Zhu Ziqing abandoned *yi* 伊 and adopted the *ta* 她 character beginning in April 1922 with his second poem "Lamplight" 《灯光》 in the series "Random Poems from Taizhou" 《台州杂诗》.[2] In the poem Zhu Ziqing writes:

> Glistening in that vast darkness,
> A golden lamplight beam;
> And in the brilliance of those rays,
> I gaze into her (她) beautiful eyes.

Zhu Ziqing had also previously used the *ta* 她 character in other circumstances occasionally.

It was July 1922 when Ye Shengtao abandoned *yi* 伊 in *The Short Story Magazine* 《小说月报》 and adopted *ta* 她 with the publication of his short story "Grandma's Heart" 《祖母的心》.[3] Apart from these, in April 1922 such figures as Li Jieren 李劼人 and Wang Renshu 王任叔 joined the ranks of those who were adopting the character *ta* 她. In May 1923 when Xu Zhimo began to publish his poetry in the magazine, he was already using *ta* 她. And towards the end of that year and in 1924, Liang Shiqiu 梁实秋, Zhang Wentian 张闻天, Fu Donghua 傅东华 and others also separately used *ta* 她 in the same magazine.

It was the end of 1923 and the beginning of 1924 when the brothers Lu Xun and Zhou Zuoren finally converted to using *ta* 她. Of the two, it would appear that Zhou Zuoren was slightly earlier. When in November 1923 Zhou Zuoren published his translation of Saneatsu Mushanokōji's "A Certain Woman" 《某夫妇》 in *The Short Story Magazine* 《小说月报》 (originally carried in Volume 14, Issue 11 of the magazine), he had already replaced *yi* 伊 with *ta* 她. The "Translation Postscript" is dated July 17, 1923, and in that he also uses *ta* 她. On December 26, 1923, Lu Xun delivered his famous lecture "What Happens after Nora Walks Out?" 《娜拉走后怎样》 to the Women's Higher Normal School 北京女子高等师范学校 in Beijing, the text of which was published at the beginning of the following year in Issue 6 of the *Journal of the Women's Higher Normal School Literature and Art Society* 《女子高等师范学校文艺会刊》 (the specific publication date of this magazine is not clear[4]) and in this he already employs the character *ta* 她. In this document, which revealed, with such iconic perceptiveness and symbolism, the fate of the modern "New" woman, Lu Xun's decision to change to *ta* 她 was a warning to his contemporaries that if the social and economic system was not changed fundamentally and the desire for women's freedom and liberation was not acted upon, then there was no way forward. Thus, we can see that Lu Xun's first use of the word *ta* 她 was indeed profound. In the past the academic community broadly believed that Lu Xun's abandonment of *yi* 伊 in favour of *ta* 她 began in March 1924 with his publication of "New Year's Sacrifice" 《祝福》 in *The Eastern Miscellany* 《东方杂志》[5] (the author of the story himself notes that it was written on February 7, 1924) . In "New Year's Sacrifice" Lu Xun uses *ta* 她 some 153 times to successfully create the image of Aunt Xianglin 祥林嫂, a woman who was deeply influenced by the traditional Confucian code of ethics and who had been persecuted by the secular social culture. This was also his first successful construction of a feminine figure in literature. In May 1924, in Volume 15, Issue 5 of *The Short Story Magazine* 《小说月报》 Lu Xun published his short story "In the Wine Shop" 《在酒楼上》 in which he used the character *ta* 她 more than 20 times. The author credits his writing of this short story as February 16, 1924. So, we should say that Lu Xun started first officially using the character *ta* 她 at the end of 1923 to the beginning of 1924, a judgement which would largely be correct.

There is another interesting "clash of the pens" regarding Lu Xun's early use of the character *ta* 她 that is worth mentioning here. On February 4, 1925, a gentleman who went by the pseudonym of Qian Yuan 潜源 (or "Hidden Source") was unhappy with Lu Xun's satirizing of several "shortcomings" in the world of translation as expressed in his article "On Chewing Words" 《咬文嚼字》 which was published in the *Literary Supplement to the Peking Press* 《京报副刊》. He felt that Lu Xun had made too much of a fuss by criticizing those who specially

Figure 7.1 Lu Xun begins to use the *ta* 她 character from the end of 1923 to the beginning of 1924.

"add a few flowery radicals, feminine or silken affixes" when they encounter the name of a foreign woman in the process of translating from western languages. He argued that this was not a case of "being shackled by traditional ideology" as Lu Xun chose to call it, but simply a way to "determine his (他) or her (她) gender". The article was entitled "The Blandness of Chewing Words" 《咬嚼之乏味》. In the article he argues:

> To use "flowery" vocabulary to translate the name of a foreign woman is not to advocate for the inequality of the sexes, and it is therefore not shackled by traditional ideology. Where I went wrong was that I should not have added "often" when I said that "I often think about the character's gender" to which Mr Lu Xun responds, "To think *often* is to be shackled." Does thinking about something frequently really mean that one is shackled? Is this really "being shackled by traditional ideology"? He is just trying to be too funny; I can't follow him . . . . If, according to Mr Lu Xun's logic, we compare the creation some years ago by the advocates of the New Culture movement of the character *ta* 她 to represent the female sex with "dreaming up" "flowery" terminology to translate the name of a woman, isn't this even more shackled by traditional ideology and more problematic? Yet, Mr Lu Xun has never satirized the *ta* 她 character.

118 *The Socialisation of the Character Ta 她 after April 1920*

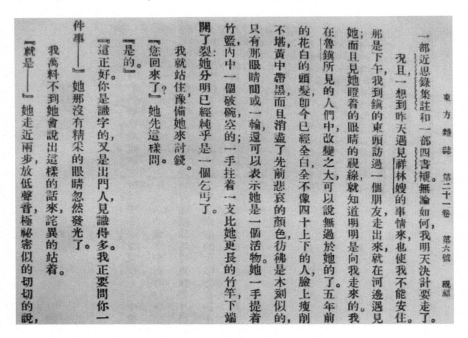

Figure 7.2 A section from the original publication in *Eastern Miscellany* of Lu Xun's short story "New Year's Sacrifice" 《祝福》 at the beginning of 1924 in which he officially used the character *ta* 她 to create the immortal female literary image of Aunt Xianglin 祥林嫂.

Nor was the author happy with Sun Fuyuan 孙伏园, convenor of the *Literary Supplement to the Peking Press* 《京报副刊》, for calling him a "neophile". Sensing the mockery in Sun's tone, the author responded satirically:

> If I really were so *avant garde*, then I would definitely say that using *ta* 她 to represent the feminine gender was the most depraved thing that the Chinese New Literature world has done and be sardonic about it because the character is not sufficient to show "advocacy for gender equality", nor is it sufficient to demonstrate that it has "thrown off the shackles of traditional ideology."[6]

Within a week, the deft Lu Xun had written the rejoinder "Chewing Words Is Not So 'Bland'" 《咬嚼未始"乏味"》 in which he humorously and incisively responded:

1. The original text [by Qian Yuan] reads: to wish to know the gender does not mean that one supports the inequality of the sexes. In response I say: true. However, it is another matter when a small but arbitrary distinction is introduced when such differentiation is unnecessary. In the past, binding women's feet or

piercing their ears can also be said to be nothing but creating a simple distinction; and nowadays, the ban on women cutting their hair is also simply an attempt to differentiate. The same goes for forcefully adding the silk or grass radical to a character [to make a gendered distinction].
2. The original text reads: [Mr Lu Xun] has never satirized the *ta* 她 character. To which I say: This is a translation of "she"; it is not without reason. And even if this wasn't the case, it is not my responsibility to ridicule everything. Nor do I have to satirize the character *ta* 她 in order to ridicule the use of flowery characters in translation.
3. The original text reads: Is "frequently thinking" really "being shackled by traditional ideology"? In response I say: it is, because it contains a strong "gender consciousness". This is a natural phenomenon in a country where men and women are strictly divided. For now, it is hard to free oneself from one's natural constraints, so it is indeed the shackles of traditional ideology.[7]

From the above "clash of the pens" between Lu Xun and Qian Yuan, apart from being able to observe clearly his personal attitude toward the character *ta* 她, we can also get a snapshot of the complex and tortured relationship between the birth of *ta* 她 and traditional "gender awareness" on the one hand, and gender equality on the other.[8]

As far as *The Short Story Magazine* 《小说月报》 is concerned, after 1924 the number of writers who continued to use the *yi* 伊 character for the feminine third person singular pronoun was already rare, and during 1925 Liang Zongdai 梁宗岱 also finally changed from using *yi* 伊 to using *ta* 她.[9]

Apart from the important modern authors and men of culture mentioned previously, we should mention the attitude of Hu Shi 胡适 who largely did not publish his work in *The Short Story Magazine* 《小说月报》 at the time. Probably beginning in 1922, Hu Shi had already begun to use the character *ta* 她,[10] and in the following two or three years, while he occasionally used *yi* 伊, nevertheless his use of *ta* 她 visibly increased, and after the end of 1924 *ta* 她 was all but victorious over *yi* 伊 in his work. This transformation occurred largely at the same time as it did with Lu Xun and others.

In addition, it is also worth giving a special mention to the attitudes of the prominent female authors. Bing Xin 冰心 and Lu Yin 庐隐 were undoubtedly the most influential female authors at the time. They published a great many pieces of fiction in the pages of *The Short Story Magazine* 《小说月报》 and as I have already indicated, beginning at the start of 1921 they generously employed the newly created female pronouns *ta* 她 and *tamen* 她们. Not only that, but other female writers for the magazine (at the time they were normally referred to as "Miss So-and-so") were also mostly happy to use these new feminine pronouns. They were completely devoid of that small-minded and sensitive attitude of the members of the women's movement who published in the *Women's Voice* 《妇女共鸣》 magazine mentioned previously and who believed that the *ta* 她 character implied that "women were not human". Such female authors as Shi Pingmei 石评梅 and Feng Yuanjun 冯沅君 who rose to fame slightly later than Bing Xin 冰心 and Lu Yin 庐隐 were also enthusiastic adopters of *ta* 她 in their creative writing. In the autumn of 1923 when Feng Yuanjun 冯沅君 had just embarked on her writing career, she habitually used *ta* 她; at the beginning of 1922 Shi Pingmei 石评梅 was already generously using *ta* 她, and in the two years following it was common to see it in the titles of her poems.[11] Chen Hengzhe 陈衡哲 also used *ta* 她 relatively frequently around 1924.[12] Through these works which employed the new age pronouns and in order to freely give vent to their distinctive thoughts and emotions as well as their social engagement, these female writers gave voice to the new feminine consciousness that was flourishing at the time.

If we say that the attitude of *The Short Story Magazine* 《小说月报》 and similar new-style literary and art magazines and newspapers as well as that of distinguished authors towards its use reflected a move towards a new reality, then the use of *ta* 她 in general social newspapers and magazines and the relevant provisions in the educational sphere as well as its use in middle school Chinese language textbooks and entries in associated dictionaries and so on revealed even more clearly the degree to which it was socially accepted and recognised.

In the summer of 1923, China's "father of popular music" Li Jinhui 黎锦晖 made a unique and extremely valuable contribution to the social popularisation of *ta* 她. In the magazine *Little Friend* 《小朋友》 which he himself edited and which was extremely influential in the world of Chinese child education, he published the popular children's song "*Ta* 他, *Ta* 她, *Ta* 牠" which he had specifically written for children to broadcast and popularise linguistic knowledge of the third person singular pronoun. The song became an extremely proactive strategy in promoting the social recognition of the character *ta* 她.

The song was in the key of G and the lyrics were as follows:

a. There once was an old man from Zhang Village called Ma Dama, Ma Dama, Ma Dama, Ma Dama, Ma Dama, he (*ta* 他).
b. And in the Li family there was Aunty Thirteen; her (*ta* 她) name was Small Jasmine, she (*ta* 她), Small Jasmine, Small Jasmine, her (*ta* 她) name was Small Jasmine, she (*ta* 她).
c. My family has an old camel, and it (*ta* 牠) is called Brother Bing, it (*ta* 牠), Brother Bing, Brother Bing, called Brother Bing, it (*ta* 牠).

The rhyming of the lyrics was very mindful of the stipulation at the time that 他, 她, and 牠 were separately pronounced as *ta*, *yi*, and *tuo*, and through repetitive singing it would assist in strengthening memory. What is more, Li Jinhui 黎锦晖 clearly and succinctly illustrated the different pronunciations of the three characters and what they represented on the right-hand side of the lyrics, plus the reason why it was important to divide them into three:

他 should be pronounced ㄊㄚ, and refers to male persons.
她 should be pronounced ㄧ, and refers to female persons.
牠 should be pronounced ㄊㄛ, and refers to all things.

The Socialisation of the Character Ta 她 *after April 1920* 121

So why exactly should this distinction be made? "An old camel runs hither and yon, Thirteenth Aunt Li plays with it (*ta*, 他), Ma Dama's son always loved it (*ta*, 他), and he unconsciously stands there laughing loudly. Later she (*ta*, 他) gave it (*ta*, 他) to him (*ta*, 他)."

No matter whether in speech or in a book, this statement will always be a little confusing; but if you, my dear young friends, were to make a distinction between *ta* 他, *ta* 她, and *ta* 牠, then it would be abundantly clear.[13]

Regarding the popularisation and social recognition of *ta* 她, it can be said that this effort of Li Jinhui 黎锦晖 was extremely timely. He is most worthy of being seen as the younger brother of the famous linguist and major leader of the National Language Movement, Li Jinxi 黎锦熙. His grasp of the import of the *ta* 他, *ta* 她, *ta* 牠 pronoun schema was not only so incisive, but his explanation of its meaning was also extremely down-to-earth and accurate. The song spurred the rapid socialisation of the two characters *ta* 她 and *ta* 牠 and its efficacy is clear to see.

It can be said that the social recognition and acceptance of the character *ta* 她 around 1924 strengthened visibly. If we take the most influential *Shen Bao* 《申报》 as an example, the newspaper employed the character *ta* 她 very rarely prior to 1923, but after 1923 the incidence gradually increased and by 1924 it began to be used generously. Or if we take another extremely influential newspaper, reflective of the new society, and publishing its inaugural issue on August 3, 1924, the *Guowen Weekly* 《国闻周报》 as an example, its Literature and Art columns from September and October of that year not only employed the character *ta* 她 in most of its articles but several pieces of fiction carrying *ta* 她 in the title also appeared, such as Mr Ma Er's 马二先生 translated short stories "Why He Married

Figure 7.3 Li Jinhui 黎锦晖's song "*Ta* 他 [he], *Ta* 她 [she], and *Ta* 牠 [it]" carried in Issue 69, 1923 of *Little Friend* 《小朋友》.

Her" 《他为什么娶她》 or "The Girl of His Dreams" 《理想中之她》, or Ling Xiaofang 凌晓肪's "Her Ideal Man" 《她的理想中之他》, to name a few.[14]

Regarding propagation through dictionaries, at the end of 1923 the Zhonghua Shuju 中华书局 published the general *Dictionary of the Chinese Language* 《国语普通词典》 in which the *nü* 女 section listed the character *ta* 她. It was a move that cannot be ignored in the process of the socialisation of *ta* 她. The entry reads, "*Ta* 她: *ta* 他 but used when referring to a female"; "*tamen* 她们: the plural of *ta* 她". At the same time, the entry for the character *yi* 伊 surprisingly uses the character *ta* 她 to explain it – "*yi* 伊: *ta* 她"; "*yimen* 伊们： *tamen* 她们".[15] This is of hugely iconic significance for the history of the social popularisation and recognition of the character *ta* 她.

In education circles a major incident relating to the popularisation of *ta* 她 occurred during this period, namely from July 3 to 9, 1924 when the nation's largest and most influential education organisation, the China Education Improvment Institute 中华教育改进社, convened its third annual conference at Southeast University in Nanjing. The National Language Teaching Group 国语教学组 at this conference discussed and finally adopted Cai Xiaozhou's 蔡晓舟[16] proposal that "Such pronouns and adjectives as *ta* 她, *ta* 牠, *na* 哪, etc. be adopted and that their pronunciation be formulated so as to reform the national language". The resolution to accept and implement this proposal was couched in the following terms:

> It is resolved that the character *ta* 她 is equivalent to the English word "she" and the German word "sie" and equates to the third person feminine pronoun with the national pronunciation of ㄧ, different from the *ta* 他 character which is equivalent to the English "he" and represents the third person masculine pronoun. *Ta* 他 in the national language is pronounced "ㄊㄚ". The character *ta* 牠 is equivalent to the English "it" and the German "es" and is a pronoun that is used to refer to a broad range of third person items and is pronounced "ㄊㄜ" in the level tone in the national language . . . . The foregoing can all take Dr Zhao Yuanren's 赵元任 *Chinese National Language Records* 国语留声机片 as the standard pronunciation. Our Society has forwarded this information to the Education Department's National Language Unification Preparatory Committee asking that they enter it into the *National Language Pronunciation Dictionary* to promote and popularise it. Moreover, we have asked Mr Zhu Jingnong 朱经农 and Mr Tao Zhixing 陶知行 from our Society to ask the Commercial Press when they reprint the *Everyman's One Thousand Basic Characters* 平民千字课 if they would use these characters.[17]

People now-a-days are no longer very familiar with Mr Cai Xiaozhou 蔡晓舟, but he featured prominently in the newspaper publishing industry, education, and National Language circles during the early Republican period. The first collection of materials on the May Fourth movement entitled *May Fourth* 《五四》, which was published just two months after the movement itself, was edited by Cai Xiaozhou and Yang Lianggong 杨亮功. His wife Deng Chunlan 邓春兰 was an even more notable figure in the May Fourth period, being hailed as "the first person to break through the prohibition on women entering universities". At the time she initiated many articles regarding equal gender rights to education, etc., such as "Chunlan's Letter to University President Cai" 《春兰上蔡校长书》, "Letter to All Female Graduates from Middle and Primary Schools" 《全国女子中小学毕业生同志书》 and more, all of which were passed on to various newspapers and magazines. At the same time, Cai Xiaozhou also promoted writing in the vernacular language and became one of the earliest pioneers of research into the grammar of the National Language, publishing such works as *Organisational Principles of the National Language* 《国语组织法》 and *Research Methods of Vernacular Writing* 《白话文研究法》. It is therefore not surprising that he was extremely passionate about the promotion and popularisation of *ta* 她 and *ta* 牠 in the realm of education.

Zhu Ziqing termed the aforementioned strategy of Cai Xiaozhou the "Use *Ta* 他, *Ta* 她, *Ta* 牠 Plan". According to his memoirs following the conference, this proposal "was debated for a full two and a half hours before the matter was settled by leaving it unsettled." He wrote an interesting and teasing account of this:

> Indeed, I must first admire the person who proposed this course of action! At a time when everyone was already using *ta* 他, *ta* 她, and *ta* 牠, he calmly proposed the motion. How very experienced and steady! "Not daring to be the first", he was certainly following philosopher Laozi's teachings. In our nation which values rituals and ceremonies, no matter where, Father Time must always beckon us onward. So, this plan of action must not be neglected for its tardiness but must instead be revered for its calmness. This is what the ancients mean by "Yielding to the Virtuous". Just looking at the situation that day, who could not be excited and enthusiastic? The power of the proposal is plain to see. Originally, the third person pronoun in the "new literature" was too divided! *Ta* 她 and *yi* 伊 were used interchangeably, and *ta* 她 and *ta* 它 were different. And then along comes *qu* 佢 and *bi* 彼 jumping in between them, muddying the waters, and creating a mess! The proposer was only attempting to distinguish gender, but the three characters that he was assigning all belonged to the *ye* 也 schema, which certainly set the matter straight. If in the future the *ye* 也 schema really becomes orthodox, then all the praise for the initial invention will accrue to the proposer. The proposer has the strength of beryllium; how could we not admire him?[18]

From the adoption of the relevant education resolution and Zhu Ziqing's above quoted light-hearted missive, we can assume that the move to accept *ta* 她 and abandon *yi* 伊 as the feminine third person singular pronoun in the new National Language education system seems to have already gradually begun to assume a commanding position. However, if we scan a few middle school national language textbooks from before 1930, the conclusion we draw might not be so optimistic. This may be because the setting of textbooks is invariably several steps behind forward-leading practice. Apart from this, while the "*ye* 也 schema" successfully dominated the field for a relatively long period of time, it was eventually not such a complete success as the figures of the day predicted; its defeat was snatched from the jaws of victory and *ta* 牠 was eventually abandoned.

In reality, at the beginning of the Republican era, middle school Chinese language education textbooks were all comparatively behind the times with regards the question of *yi* 伊 and *ta* 她 and were not completely in sync with the nationally sponsored rapid introduction of the vernacular into the middle school curriculum or the enthusiastic adoption of the modern punctuation regime. Generally speaking, prior to the mid-1920s, it was rare to see a work in the middle school Chinese language textbooks that introduced the modern *ta* 她 or *yi* 伊 characters because at the time the new intellectual world was yet to reach a consensus on the issue, and especially on the choice between *ta* 她 or *yi* 伊, even though a clear trend had already emerged towards a common consensus.

As far as I am aware, one of the earliest and more influential middle school Chinese language textbooks to adopt *ta* 她 was the 5th edition of the *National Language Textbook for the New Education System* 《新学制国语教科书》 which appeared in 1925 following its inaugural edition in 1923. This work was edited by Gu Jiegang 顾颉刚, Fan Xiangshan 范祥善, Ye Shaojun 叶绍钧 et al., and revised by Hu Shi 胡适 and Wang Xiulu 王岫庐 et al., and was aimed at early middle school students of the Chinese language.[19] Despite the fact that the work used *ta* 她 as the third person feminine pronoun, it also inconsistently employed *yi* 伊 in the same context, as well as separately using *ta* 牠 and *ta* 他 for the neuter, a situation that continued to varying degrees in the middle school Chinese language textbooks from the late 1920s through to the early 1930s.

I'm not currently in a position to acquaint myself with all of the middle school Chinese language textbooks from the mid-1920s to the mid-1930s and can only use the relatively rich holdings of the Peking Normal University library on the topic to construct a rough outline of the situation regarding the propagation of *ta* 她 and *yi* 伊 during this period. In Peking Normal University library's *Complete Library of Textbooks of Normal, Middle and Primary Schools from Before Liberation Held by this Library* 《馆藏解放前师范学校及中小学教科书全文库》 some 151 different types of middle school Chinese language textbooks are collated, and if we dispense with works published before 1925 and after 1935 and further remove those works of annotated classics or specialist Chinese language grammars which are not really relevant to the question of the use of the modern *ta* 她 or *yi* 伊, we are left with a total of 92 titles of readers, selections or textbooks on the Chinese language. Of these, only 9 titles use *yi* 伊 for the feminine third person pronoun; some 11 titles use both *ta* 她 and *yi* 伊 interchangeably and without distinction; and some 26 titles use *ta* 她 exclusively to represent the feminine singular pronoun. These three categories when added together total 46 titles which constitutes half of the total, and those that employ the *ta* 她 character account for 40% of the total. If we take into account other factors which might influence the compilation or selection process, then this proportion could already be said to be considerable. And as for the relationship between *ta* 她 and *yi* 伊, while there remains a certain degree of competition, still the superiority of *ta* 她 had already been comprehensively

The Socialisation of the Character Ta 她 after April 1920   125

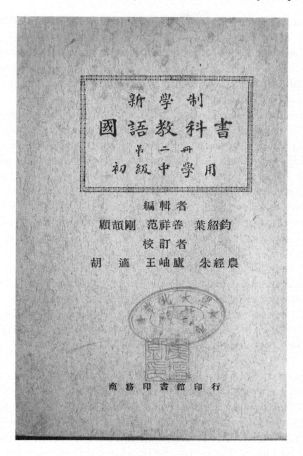

Figure 7.4 Cover of Volume II of the *National Language Textbook for the New Education System* 《新学制国语教科书》.

established. Nevertheless, it should be noted that the period between 1925 and 1930 only included 4 titles and so what they reflect was basically the situation prior to the 1930s.[20]

Naturally, compared to the "selective" treatment of the terms in the middle school Chinese language textbooks, the broad popularised use of the character *ta* 她 in the newspapers and magazines of the 1930s is able to reflect more fully its social recognition and epochal features. At the same time, the propagation of several relevant dictionary entries also became symbols of this social recognition while propelling forward and deepening this recognition. Apart from the *Dictionary of the Chinese Language* 《国语普通词典》 mentioned above, an even more representative dictionary was the *Pronunciation Dictionary of Common National Language Terms* 《国音常用字汇》 published in 1932 by the Education Department and distributed nationwide, as well as the proliferation of other dictionaries which it engendered. These dictionaries were largely the product of the Republican-era modern "National Language" movement. In some sense, the National Language movement, in which Liu Bannong was a major figure, never abandoned its partiality for *ta* 她, and its merit in the social propagation and recognition of the *ta* 她 character cannot be denied.

The *Pronunciation Dictionary of Common National Language Terms* 《国音常用字汇》 was a dictionary based on the Education Department's original 1920 publication, the *National Language Pronunciation Dictionary* 《国音字典》 following continuous revision and expansion. A major emendation was undertaken in 1923, and later, primarily under the direction of Qian Xuantong and others, the work was completed and in May 1932 the whole nation was exhorted to follow it, leading to significant repercussions. The relevant sections concerning the character *ta* 她 clearly reflected the dissemination of Qian Xuantong's early views. In the "About this book" section, the editors specifically stress and highlight:

> The character *ta* 他 has been split into the three characters *ta* 他, *ta* 她, and *ta* 牠, but the pronunciation is yet to be determined – perhaps they will all be pronounced ㄊㄚ (i.e., *ta*); the form of the character is differentiated but the sound is not. Script is the symbol of language, so if the script diverges but the language does not, then this is unreasonable.

In Zhao Yuanren's *Chinese National Language Records* 《国语留声机片》 which Commercial Press published for him in 1921, *yi* 伊 and *ta* 它 were added in addition to the two characters *ta* 她 and *ta* 牠; and in order to distinguish them in terms of pronunciation from the character *ta* 他, Zhao Yuanren gave specific instructions that the two characters *ta* 她 and *ta* 牠 should be pronounced the same as *yi* 伊 and *ta* 它. The editors believed that this pronunciation schema of Zhao Yuanren's was "great" and so adopted it. In other words, they stipulated that "*ta* 她 and *yi* 伊, *ta* 牠 and *ta* 它 embodied the theory of the same character taking two different forms," and that *ta* 她 should be pronounced "*yi*", and *ta* 牠 pronounced either "*tuo*" or "*te*". Not only that, but the editors also went on to argue that in ancient China *ta* 她 and *ta* 牠 were indeed pronounced in this manner:

> *Ta* 她 already appears in the sixth century Chinese dictionary, the *Yu Pian* 《玉篇》 and *ta* 牠 appears in the *Qie Yun* 《切韵》 (the edition of Tang Dynasty manuscript discovered in the Dunhuang caves). *Ta* 她 is a variant form of *jie* 姐. Zhang Binglin's 章炳麟 *New Dialects* 《新方言》 has shown that it was pronounced like *yi* 姐 (the *Yu Pian* 《玉篇》 has it as a variant of *jie* 姐, meaning sister, but this is not the case). And 牠 is a variant of *ta* 牠, pronounced *te*. If we were to say that the pronunciation has undergone some change, then "It just changed from the second (rising) tone 阳平 to the first (level) tone 阴平."[21]

The Socialisation of the Character Ta 她 *after April 1920* 127

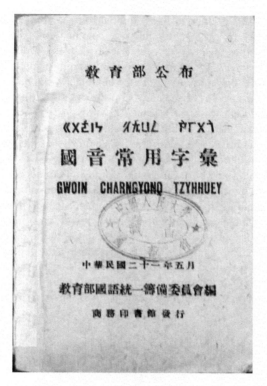

Figure 7.5 Cover of the 1932 edition of *Pronunciation Dictionary of Common National Language Terms* 《国音常用字汇》.

Later, when the *Pronunciation Dictionary of Common National Language Terms* 《国音常用字汇》 was published in a revised and annotated version, *ta* 她 was clearly described as "the feminine third person" and that *yi* 伊 was the equivalent of *ta* 她, but it continued to hold that the favoured pronunciation of *ta* 她 was *yi* 伊.[22]

In August 1935, Zhonghua Shuju published the *Standard Student Dictionary of the Sounds of the National Language* 《标准国音学生字典》 which was edited and compiled by Zhang Wenzhi 张文治 et al. and circulated widely. In it, the character *ta* 她 was introduced thus, "Pronounced *yi* 伊; in the spoken and written language it constitutes the third person feminine pronoun". In introducing the character *ta* 牠, it states that it is pronounced *tuo* or *te*, and that it was the "neuter third person pronoun". It also lists *ta* 它 as being the equivalent of *ta* 牠.[23] By February 1947 this dictionary was already in its 11th edition and so it is obvious that its social impact had been considerable. Around about the same time or perhaps a little later, the *Standard Dictionary of Common National Language Sounds* 《标准国音常用字典》 describes *ta* 她 as, "Commonly used for *ta* 他 and refers to the feminine."[24]

128 *The Socialisation of the Character Ta* 她 *after April 1920*

In December 1935 Commercial Press published its *Grand Dictionary of Standard Chinese* 《标准语大辞典》 which was another comparatively influential dictionary at that time. In it, *ta* 她 was described in the following manner, "*yi*, 他, the feminine", and *ta* 牠 was described as, "*te*, the neuter third person pronoun." In other words, at the time, while the character *ta* 她 had already achieved broad social recognition,[25] nevertheless, the pronunciation stipulated by a number of authoritative dictionaries mostly leaned towards *yi* 伊. So how was this new character *ta* 她 pronounced in reality? How many people actually conformed to the directive of these linguists who, with the full authority of the state behind them, declared in the dictionaries that it be pronounced *yi* 伊? I was most interested in this question and so I made a special visit to some eight historians in my acquaintance who were around the age of 80 years. These eight historians hailed from a range of places including Jiangsu, Shanghai, Fujian, Sichuan, Hubei, Yunnan, and elsewhere. I asked them whether, when they were studying in their native areas during the late 1930s and 1940s, the teaching material in the primary and secondary schools included the character *ta* 她, representing the feminine third person pronoun? And how was it pronounced? The eight historians confirmed to me that the teaching materials at the time already included the character and that it carried its current meaning. Seven of the eight historians also recalled that it was

Figure 7.6 Cover of the *Standard Student Dictionary of the Sounds of the National Language* 《标准国音学生字典》.

pronounced *ta*, identical to the character *ta* 他. Only one individual clearly stated that at the time *ta* 她 was pronounced *yi* 伊. This broadly accords with the facts as I understand them as they are outlined by a number of participants in the debates at the time.[26] Perhaps it is for this reason that by the late 1930s or the early 1940s there were linguists who had no choice but to face up to this societal linguistic reality. For example, in 1939 the China Dictionary Editing and Compilation Office 中国辞典编纂处 completed their revision and expansion of the *Dictionary of the National Language* 《国语辞典》 and in 1943 openly published the work, which included: *ta* 她, pronounced *ta*, but may also be pronounced *yi*; *ta* 牠, pronounced *ta*, but may also be pronounced *tuo* or *te*; *ta* 它, the same as *ta* 牠 and pronounced *ta*, but may also be pronounced *tuo*.[27] Despite still being unwilling to abandon the phonetic design of Qian Xuantong and others, nevertheless they had no choice but to acknowledge the socially widespread pronunciation "*ta*".

We may say that the question of the pronunciation of the character *ta* 她 was in fact an important interlude in the process of the character's social acceptance that cannot be ignored.

At the same time, the specialist works on language and grammar of the day could not but pay close attention to the division of *ta* 他 into *ta* 她 and *ta* 牠, and so on, and respond to it definitively. For example, when Yang Bojun's 杨伯峻 1936 publication *An Explanation of the Grammar of the Chinese Language* 《中国语文文法通释》 discusses "pronouns", it declares:

> In the spoken vernacular, the common pronoun *ta* 他 is only represented by a single *ta* 他. Recently, under the influence of Western languages, the character *ta* 他 has been divided into three characters, namely *ta* 他, *ta* 她, and *ta* 牠. *Ta* 牠 is the pronoun referring to things or objects . . . and *ta* 她 is equivalent to the English "she" and refers to the feminine. Besides the two characters *ta* 他 and *ta* 牠, people from Guangdong like to use the character *qu* 佢 and people from Jiangsu love to use *yi* 伊.[28]

This demonstrates that the late 1920s to the mid to late 1930s was probably the period when *ta* 她 had already spread widely to represent the feminine third person singular pronoun and that it had achieved a relatively broad-ranging recognition in society.[29]

2   Chen Yinke 陈寅恪 et al.'s Valedictory Defiance and Zhou Shoujuan 周瘦鹃's Final Capitulation

The path to recognition is invariably accompanied by murmurs of doubt and resistance, and the more passionate and closer to victory the trend towards recognition is, the more intense those sounds of doubt and resistance can become. This was the case with the recognition of *ta* 她.

It was precisely in the mid-1920s and following that the character *ta* 她 was spreading throughout the nation and by the beginning to the mid-1930s when it had already become an unstoppable force, the sounds of confused doubt and determined opposition surfaced. In 1928 someone by the name of "Qia 恰" published an article "*Ta* 他 [he], *Ta* 她 [she], and *Ta* 牠 [it]" 《他、她、牠》 in *Society Reports* 《会报》, adopting the form of a conversation and expressing confusion as to the reasons why people at the time insisted on such precision in dividing *ta* 他 into *ta* 他, *ta* 她, and *ta* 牠. The article was brief, so I will quote it in full:

A says to B:	Flipping through newspapers and fiction I find that there are three types of *ta* 他 character – sometimes they use *ta* 他 while at other times they use *ta* 她, and still other times, they use *ta* 牠. So, what is the point of this, I ask you?
B replies:	That is easy to understand. It is because the male is different to the female which is in turn different to the neuter. [Using the same character] jumbles everything up and leads to confusion. They use the three elements *ren* 人, *nü* 女, and *niu* 牛 in order to make a distinction. So, for the masculine they use *ta* 他, and for the feminine they use *ta* 她. The neuter follows the *Shuo wen jie zi* 《说文》 which notes that an ox is a large object and therefore the character for "things" should take the ox radical, and so is represented as *ta* 牠 with an ox (牛) radical. In forming the three characters *ta* 他, *ta* 她, and *ta* 牠, they have distinguished between the male, female, and neuter.
A says:	But there are so many other characters like this, such as *yi* 伊, *ni* 你, *bi* 彼, *wo* 我 and more, so why don't we add one of the three elements *ren* 人, *nü* 女, or *niu* 牛 to these as well to distinguish them? Why do those who clamor to differentiate between male, female and neuter only concentrate on the single *ta* 他 character. Do none of the remaining characters not require differentiation?!
B says:	This is not the case. The progress of civilization moves gradually higher just as the tide rises higher over time. But it is not the time for that yet. The people of this country are hell-bent on Europeanisation and spare no pains to emulate it. When the time comes, this is not the only type of character that will be divided along gender lines. For example, nouns, verbs, and adjectives, etc., if we were to follow the practice of the countries on the European mainland then the task of applying gender and other distinctions would be huge. If you don't believe me, note it down and remember what I have told you today.
A says:	I believe you. So, in the future all words, no matter what type, will need to be accompanied by one of the three elements *ren* 人, *nü* 女, or *niu* 牛 in order to distinguish their gender? To make it easy to understand: Say, for example, schools – they fundamentally belong to the neuter gender. If we wish to show that they belong to the neuter gender, then they must all be allocated to the *niu* 牛 (ox) category? But what if they were a boys' school? Or a

girls' school? Apart from the *niu* 牛, should we also add a *ren* 人 (human) radical? Or if it is a school with both boys and girls, then what should we do? If it is a co-ed school, should we add all three elements *ren* 人, *nü* 女, and *niu* 牛? How confusing would that be just because we had to reflect its actual composition accurately? Of all the affairs in the world, if they are performed by men, then they are lauded, but if they are executed by women, then they are seen as the work of prostitutes?!

Whereupon B mutters to A: Indeed! How can that be! I am unlearned, so I leave this question to the real scholars.

(Sent from Hulan 呼兰 on November 15, 1927.[30])

The author of the piece calls those people who advocate for and approve of the adoption of *ta* 他 [he], *ta* 她 [she], and *ta* 牠 [it] to distinguish gender "ignoramuses" – in other words, people who do not understand linguistics – and his scepticism is obvious. But compared to previous arguments throughout the debate, his view does not contribute anything new, nor does he appear to fully comprehend the specific view expressed by Liu Bannong, Gong Dengchao 龚登朝 and others regarding the three-way division into *ta* 他, *ta* 她, and *ta* 牠 for gender differentiation.

What is also worth mentioning is that, around 1933 to 1934, the opposition to the two characters *ta* 她 and *ta* 牠 formed a small crest. We have already touched previously on the fact that in 1934 the magazine *Women's Voice* 《妇女共鸣》 began to publicly refuse to use the character *ta* 她. This principally stemmed from the standpoint of equality of the sexes, and it undeniably constituted an integral part of this crest. In addition, scholars who approached the question from a linguistics point of view, and comparative linguistics especially, opposed the use of *ta* 她, including Chen Yinke 陈寅恪, Li Xiaotong 厉筱通, Zhu Xin 诛心 and others who on the whole were scholars who had a broad understanding of language beyond Chinese culture. In fact, this group of people came to the same conclusion independently and expressed their views, forming what might be seen as the final push in the history of Republican China to publicly resist the character *ta* 她.

In 1933, not long after the Education Department had released its *Pronunciation Dictionary of Common National Language Terms* 《国音常用字汇》 and called on the nation as a whole to comply, Chen Yinke 陈寅恪 openly opposed the formal adoption of the two characters *ta* 她 and *ta* 牠 in an article in the pages of the magazine *The Critical Review* 《学衡》, arguing that the grammars of Western languages were all different, that none were perfect, and that they need not be blindly imitated. He writes:

The foreign language grammar that our countrymen are used to seeing today is only English grammar from a recent era. Its pronouns include the masculine, feminine and neuter and our countrymen have managed to create the two terms "she" (她) and "it" (牠) to distinguish these, and they boast that this is a convenient and timely innovation. However, if we take this reasoning and follow it to its logical conclusion, then we will discover that languages like Arabic and Hebrew divide their verbs by gender and number, and their grammatical variations all have their own distinct manifestations. For example, if a single man is sleeping, then you use the singular masculine identifier, but if two men are sleeping then you use the plural masculine identifier. And if a single woman is sleeping, then you use the singular feminine identifier, but if two women are sleeping then you use the plural feminine identifier. But if a man and a woman are sleeping together, you use the neuter plural. So, if we were to follow the new style of creating characters, then the resultant character would be "儂". Nouns in ancient Sanskrit take 24 forms and verbs 18, so should our scholars imitate them all one by one so as to achieve perfection? Among the world's languages, type A has type A's peculiarities, and so it follows type A's grammar, while type B has type B's peculiarities, and it follows type B's grammar. But in the same modern Western European language group English has three different types of nouns while German has four. French nouns are divided into masculine or feminine and German nouns have the three: masculine, feminine or neuter. So, if contemporary languages exhibit these types of unique differences, they must of necessity develop their own peculiar rules, and whoever fails to abide by these rules has no way of being understood. It is not the case that when Germans created their own grammar, they wanted to be complicated; or that when the English developed their grammar, they preferred simplicity.[31]

Figure 7.7 Chen Yinke 陈寅恪 who was opposed to the character *ta* 她.

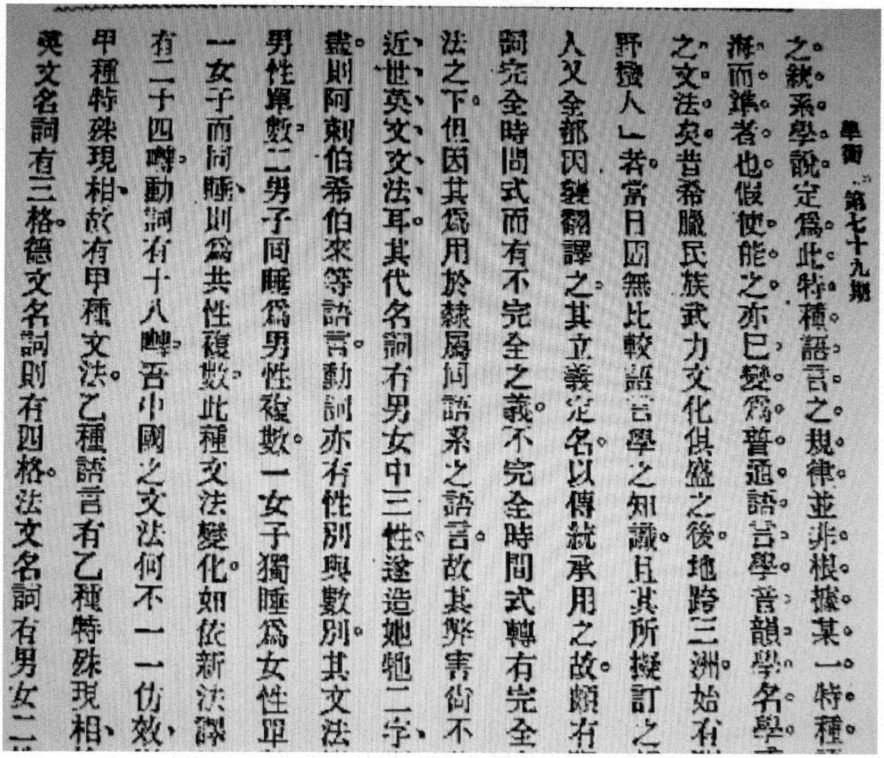

Figure 7.8 A section from Chen Yinke's 陈寅恪 essay "Discussing National Language Examination Topics with Professor Liu Wendian" 《与刘文典教授论国文试题书》.

On the first of June 1934, *Current Opinion* 《时代公论》 published Li Xiaotong 厉筱通 (Ding Huang 鼎煌, 1907–1959)'s article "The Question of the Vulgar Scripted 她 and 牠" 《"她"和"牠"的俗书问题》 in which he specifically employed Chen Yinke's above-cited argument to assert that "from the standpoint of comparative linguistics" or "grammatology" "there is absolutely no use for the newly coined pronouns *ta* 她 and *ta* 牠", and praised Mr Chen's statement for having "destroyed the absurd fantasies of those neophiles." The article also clearly targeted the content of the *Pronunciation Dictionary of Common National Language Terms* 《国音常用字汇》, which the Education Department had distributed, where it attempted to standardise the two characters *ta* 她 and *ta* 牠, reflecting the persistence of the opposing views at the time.

134 *The Socialisation of the Character Ta* 她 *after April 1920*

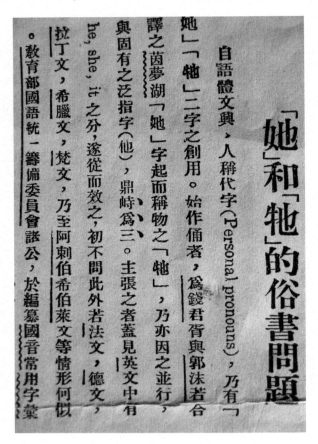

Figure 7.9 A section of Li Xiaotong 厉筱通's article "The Question of the Vulgar Scripted 她 and 牠" 《"她"和"牠"的俗书问题》.

Li Xiaotong was a linguist who later made valuable contributions to the study of the Khitan script. Li's article summarised the views of those opposing the character *ta* 她 in society at the time courtesy of the following three points:

A: (The character *ta* 她) has not been used in the Classics and is not included in the *Shuo Wen* 《说文》; it is however included in the *Yu Pian: Qie Yun* 《玉篇·切韵》. The dictionary prefers diversity and has included this vulgar variant for record purposes only. And since its real meaning has not yet been settled, why should we rush to use it? (As the philosopher Zhang Taiyan 章太炎 noted in his argument against ancient text from thousands of years ago, one should not simply believe what the ancients said and brook no change).

B: There are questions about the *Pronunciation Dictionary of Common National Language Terms* 《国音常用字汇》 itself. While it has been released by the Education Department, nevertheless, there should be protracted deliberations over whether these two characters should be adopted or not, and that debate is still pending.

C: This is an imitation of English grammar and lacks a comprehensive view of different languages. It obliterates the unique qualities of our own language and is therefore totally unacceptable.

These arguments were nothing new when compared to the opinions that had circulated earlier. However, in this article, the author decided that the two characters *ta* 她 and *ta* 牠 "will always be vulgar script and never standard". Moreover, he assumed an elitist attitude of resisting the vulgar tide and pointedly declared "It is up to our generation to turn the tide. We must not ignore or blindly accept, and not state our case just because it is becoming popular", therefore

> During this transition phase where there are advocates and practitioners [of the two characters in question] which we are unable to stop, the only thing we can do is to see it as a vulgar practice and to abhor and reject it![32]

In April 1934, someone published the article "*Ta* (他), *Ta* (她), *Ta* (牠), and *Ta* (它)" 《"他"、"她"、"牠"、"它"》 in the *The Pei-yang Pictorial News* 《北洋画报》 which echoed Chen Yinke's thinking but took it further, grasping the reality of the confused situation at the time surrounding the use of a number of characters and continuing to express opposition to *ta* 她 and *ta* 牠, both ridiculing and berating with an equally clear determination:

> From the time that the so-called "New Literature" was born, a single *ta* 他 spawned three new similar terms – *ta* 她, *ta* 牠, and *ta* 它 – out of thin air. But how these three characters were to be used was not definitively stated. As a result, they are used indiscriminately in the new literature, which is a result of the lack of certainty. Add to this the frequent mistakes of the typesetters and people are even more mystified. The most laughable are those works of translation which foolishly follow the rules of the original language where people use "she" to represent a bunch of flowers, a nation or a chair and the clueless translator will also use the "*ta* 她" word in the Chinese text. Little do they know that in one country a certain object is feminine while if you move to another country, it is often the opposite! In Chinese we do not classify things apart from animals. Since you are translating into Chinese, you must use the Chinese language; you are translating into Chinese for the benefit of the Chinese people, so you must follow the rules of the Chinese language. You should not be so inflexible. For example, in German, French, Spanish and Italian, all nouns are divided into male or female; much clearer than English, and with many more neuter items (neither male nor female). If you want to brag about the fact that your translation is genuinely transcribed

from a Western language (and this is what they really want), and depending on the masculinity, femininity, or neuter quality of the subject you add a character like *ta* 他, *ta* 她, or *ta* 它, then how laughable is that?! It is fortunate that most translators can only translate from English, otherwise I am afraid it would be much more laughable! I therefore propose: 1. Translations should be rendered according to the Chinese practice; and 2. All these weird, clumsy characters should be removed completely.[33]

From the arguments presented previously we can see that the author of the article "*Ta* (他), *Ta* (她), *Ta* (牠), and *Ta* (它)" 《"他"、"她"、"牠"、"它"》's understanding of Western languages remained limited. Perhaps he had not yet read Chen Yinke's aforementioned opus or, at least, had not read it carefully because Chen Yinke clearly stressed that English had three genders, masculine, feminine and neuter, while French only had the two, namely masculine and feminine. However, the main objective of the article is the same as the two articles quoted previously by Mr Chen 陈 and Mr Li 厉, namely that they all believe that Chinese people should hold to their own unique linguistic culture and write Chinese according to "Chinese rules" and "Chinese customs" and not bend willy-nilly to foreign influences and arbitrarily change oneself. This cannot be divorced from the powerful backdrop of rising nationalism that followed September 18, 1931, namely the Mukden Incident, which marked the beginning of the Japanese invasion of China and the cultural nationalist mentality in particular.

What is worth noting is that around 1934 when a cascade of articles opposing *ta* 她 appeared, it coincided with the "China National Culture Construction Movement" 中国本位文化建设运动 directed by the Nationalist Government and the "Classical Revival" movement which was launched by Wang Maozu 汪懋祖 and others. This was not pure coincidence. As Wang Maozu stressed, middle school textbooks removed the classical language and replaced it with the vernacular, "thinking that this would of necessity enhance the popularization of education and advance society, but unexpectedly, national consciousness took a dive." The works that encapsulate Wang's advocacy for the "Classical Revival" include, "Banning the Study of the Classical Language and Ordering the Study of the Classics" 《禁习文言与强令读经》 and "Movement for the Study of the Classical Language in Primary and Middle Schools" 《中小学文言运动》. These works were published in several issues of *Current Opinion* 《时代公论》 along with Li Xiaotong's 厉筱通 article "The Question of the Vulgar Scripted 她 and 牠" 《"她"和"牠"的俗书问题》 in which he opposed *ta* 她 and scorned it as a "vulgar script". Among these, "Movement for the Study of the Classical Language in Primary and Middle Schools" and Li's article were both published in the same issue, a relationship that is worth investigating. If we cast our minds to *Current Opinion* 《时代公论》, which was published in Nanjing, and if we take into account the political and cultural context of the Chiang Kai-shek government, the connection becomes even clearer. It becomes clear that the social recognition and survival of the character *ta* 她, which should have been an issue confined to the field of language alone, had by then become intertwined with the nationalist sociocultural mindset and, in particular, with the cultural nationalism that was being orchestrated by the Chiang government.

I recently read Wang Xinming's 王新命 memoir *Forty Years in Journalism* 《新闻圈里四十年》 and was surprised to discover that the Wang Xinming 王新命 who was listed as one of the "ten professors" who were signatories to the "Declaration on the Construction of Standard Chinese Culture" 《中国本位文化建设宣言》, which was published on January 10, 1935, turned out to be Wang Wuwei 王无为, editor-in-chief of *New Man* 《新人》 monthly at the time. He and Sun Hanbing 孙寒冰, who opposed the character *ta* 她, were both key figures in launching the "Movement for the Construction of Standard Chinese Culture". Wang Wuwei was the draftsman of the Declaration and Sun Hanbing 孙寒冰 invited eight others to join them in signing. The text of the "Declaration" was revised and finalised in Sun Hanbing's home.[34]

As far as principle is concerned, Chen Yinke et al. stressed that we should not lightly "abandon our principles and follow others". Their warning against the blind adoption of Western linguistic conventions was certainly valid and necessary. However, on the specific subject of the limited division of *ta* 他 into *ta* 她 and a neuter third person pronoun, we cannot conflate this but rather analyse it concretely from the point of view of the contemporary requirements of the Chinese language and the modern nature of the mutual interaction of cultural exchange. The final section of this work will offer a concentrated summary of this question from a reflective modernist perspective, so we will not go into detail here.

While we have dubbed the 1934 protest of Chen Yinke and others the final opposition to the character *ta* 她 during the Republican era, in reality the number of individuals opposed to the character at the time was already quite limited. What is more, their own faith in the results of their words of opposition was weak, so that is why they invariably expressed a type of personal, virtue-signaling, lofty attitude and were already bereft of ideas on what could be done in the face of the widespread social dissemination of *ta* 她.

By the beginning of the 1940s, with the widespread popularisation of the character *ta* 她, the previous representative of the Mandarin Ducks and Butterflies School, Zhou Shoujuan 周瘦鹃 and others, who had consistently opposed the character *ta* 她 and whose opposition was fundamentally in accord with Han Bing, finally had no choice but to change his mind. In 1943 when Mr Zhou edited the magazine *Violets* 《紫罗兰》, he resolutely decided to abandon *yi* 伊 and embrace *ta* 她, and moreover advised and even "coerced" his fellow-travelling friends, renowned writers who had stubbornly insisted on using the *yi* 伊 character in their work, like Cheng Xiaoqing 程小青 and Gu Mingdao 顾明道, to capitulate and use *ta* 她. The process and reasons for this transformation were quite typical. Zhou Shoujuan himself experienced a self-congratulatory moment in the process which is worth reflecting on, and savouring. Not only was this the case, but in my estimation, because of Zhou Shoujuan's special position in the modern Chinese literary world and his prolonged aversion to *ta* 她,[35] in some sense this personal account is also representative of the literary world's announcement of the final defeat of *yi* 伊 and the symbolic social significance of the resounding victory of *ta* 她. Since this is the case, we will quote it in full, despite its length:

> Brother Liu Bannong, my departed friend, was a colleague more than twenty years ago in the editorial department of Zhonghua Book Company. We became inseparable and understood each other well. We invariably borrowed each other's books and shared what we were reading. I always admired his tireless appetite for study. Later he left the Zhonghua Book Company because he was a frequent contributor to *New Youth* 《新青年》 and met Chen Duxiu 陈独秀 when Mr Duxiu took up the position of head of the Literature Department at Peking University. He took Liu along with him . . . . Liu created the character *ta* 她 to represent the third person feminine in the new literature movement and the character continues to be used right up to the present. But I have always disagreed with him because *ta* 她 is the classical form of *jie* 姐 (sister), so its meaning is different, and it is also pronounced differently. So, in the past twenty years, in the articles I have written and in the magazines I have edited, the character *ta* 她 has never appeared and I have consistently used *yi* 伊 instead. Last year, brother Xie Tihong 谢啼红 in his *Letters from the Yinfeng Pavillion* 《因风阁小简》 mentioned this and praised my spirit of not bending to the common will, and that the *yi* 伊 character contains a certain charm. However, he did object to my changing the *ta* 她 in other people's works to *yi* 伊, believing that the individuality of every work should be preserved and that I should not bend others to my will. Naturally, I agree with this, but for some reason, the *ta* 她 character has never sat comfortably with me, so as soon as others' works came into my possession, I just had to alter them. I truly do apologize for this! This time as I turn my hand to edit *Violets* 《紫罗兰》, our literary friends have graced us with their "pearls and jades", and apart from brother Cheng Xiaoqing's 程小青 "Battle of the Dragons and Tigers" 《龙虎斗》 and brother Gu Mingdao's 顾明道 "Kunlun Slave" 《昆仑奴》 which continue to use the *yi* 伊 character, all of the other contributions, without exception, use *ta* 她. My old affliction was threatening to leap into action when I remembered brother [Xie] Tihong's 啼红 words and I found that I no longer had the courage. I do think that one should heed good advice. Should I really continue to be my old obstinate self? What is more, all of my children objected and told me that everyone was using *ta* 她, so father, why be so obstinate? Hadn't you noticed that old Mr Bao Tianxiao 包天笑, who is approaching seventy, has long since been using *ta* 她? These days, you can never go wrong if you follow the crowd. So, old man, why not follow the crowd and try using *ta* 她 in your own writing? It is hard to go against the "crowd", and perhaps also because of my affection for my children, I bit the bullet and stopped changing people's *ta* 她 characters. On top of that, I have broken my own rules and used *ta* 她 for the first time. If brother Liu Bannong's soul still lingered on this earth, he would certainly stroke his beard and laugh (when I worked with him, he didn't have a beard, only a tash. I assume he has a full-grown beard by now! hee, hee!)

> and declare, "My friend, from this day forward, you will never again quarrel with me!" Here, I must shout out to Brother Cheng Xiaoqing 程小青, champion of Sherlock Holmes, and Brother Gu Mingdao 顾明道, devotee of the Kunlun slave, "My apologies, dear Cheng and Gu, please for the sake of your old friend, use *ta* 她 where a *ta* 她 is required!"[36]

This entertaining account of the acceptance of the character *ta* 她 reflects the sociocultural environment in which the character finally took this last group of "diehard opponents" prisoner and the changing mental states of those who were forced to accept it; satisfying indeed for historians who thrive on the minutiae.

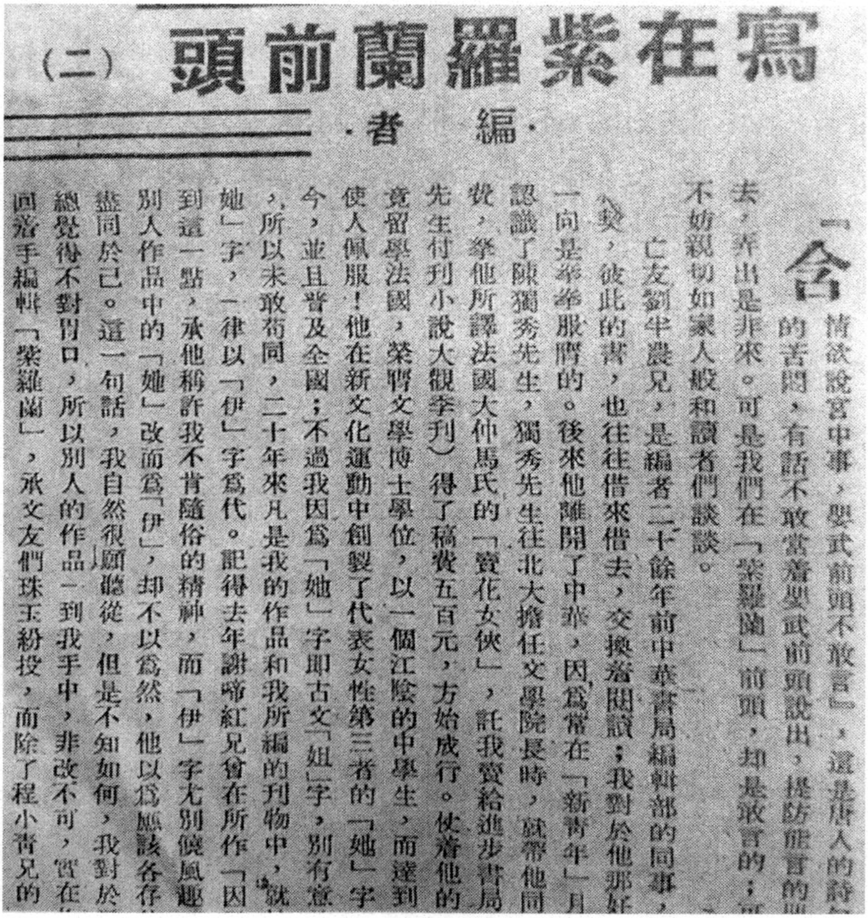

寫在紫羅蘭前頭（二）

·編者·

「含情欲說宮中事，鸚鵡前頭不敢言」，這是唐人的詩
的苦悶，有話不敢當着鸚鵡前頭說出，提防能言的鸚
去，弄出是非來。可是我們在「紫羅蘭」前頭，却是敢言的；可
不妨親切如家人般和讀者們談談。
亡友劉半農兄，是編者二十餘年前中華書局編輯部的同事，
髮，彼此的書，也往往借來借去，交換着閱讀；我對於他那好
一向是拳拳服膺的。後來他離開了中華，因爲常在「新青年」月
認識了陳獨秀先生，獨秀先生往北大擔任文學院長時，就帶他同
敎，拏他所譯法國大仲馬氏的「寶花女俠」，託我賣給進步書局
先生付刊小說大觀季刊）得了稿費五百元，方始成行。使着他的
竟留學法國，榮膺文學博士學位，以一個江陰的中學生，而達到
使人佩服！他在新文化運動中創製了代表女性第三者的「她」字
今，並且普及全國；不過我因爲「她」字即古文「姐」字，別有意
，所以未敢苟同，二十年來凡是我的作品和我所編的刊物中，就
她」字，一律以「伊」字爲代。記得去年謝啼紅兄曾在所作「因
到這一點，承他稱許我不肯隨俗的精神，而「伊」字尤別饒風趣
別人作品中的「她」改而爲「伊」，却不以爲然，他以爲應該各存
盡同於己。這一句話，我自然很願聽從，但是不知如何，我對於
總覺得不對胃口，所以別人的作品一到我手中，非改不可，實在
回溶手編輯「紫羅蘭」，承文友們珠玉紛投，而除了程小青兄的

Figure 7.10 A section from Zhou 周瘦鹃's "Foreword to Violets" 《写在紫罗兰前头》.

140 *The Socialisation of the Character Ta* 她 *after April 1920*

Notes

1 Apart from *The Short Story Magazine* 《小说月报》, at this time Mao Dun 茅盾 had already commenced using the *ta* 她 character in *New Youth* 《新青年》 and other magazines. For example, in May and August 1921, his translations "Simon's Father" 《西门的爸爸》 (carried in *New Youth* 《新青年》 Vol. 9, No. 1) and "A Team of Horsemen" 《一队骑马的人》 (carried in *New Youth* 《新青年》 Vol. 9, No. 4) both employed the character.
2 Zhu, Ziqing 朱自清, "Random Poems from Taizhou: Lamplight" 《台州杂诗·灯光》, carried in *The Short Story Magazine* 《小说月报》 Vol. 13, No. 4.
3 Ye, Shengtao 叶圣陶, "Grandma's Heart" 《祖母的心》, carried in *The Short Story Magazine* 《小说月报》 Vol. 13, No. 7. Ye Shengtao's collection *Separation* 《隔膜》 which was published in 1922 included works which he had published in 1919–1921 and in which he frequently used *yi* 伊 to represent the feminine third person singular. However, in his work *Fire* 《火灾》 which was published for the first time in 1923, and which included works which he had published in 1921–1923, now used *ta* 她 wherever he had previously used *yi* 伊.
4 The two previous issues of this magazine were both published in April of the respective year. It was also announced on May 1, 1924, that the Beijing Women's Advanced Normal School 北京女子高等师范学校 would henceforth be called Beijing Women's Normal University 北京女子师范大学 but the magazine continued to use the old name, so it can be assumed that the 6th issue of the magazine was probably published around April 1924 or slightly earlier. I know that Lu Xun retained a manuscript version of the article and I have put this question directly to Professor Sun Yu 孙郁, a specialist in research on Lu Xun, and he informs me that the manuscript has been taken by the son of Mr Tai Jingnong 台静农 to America. I finally managed to see his earliest handwritten *ta* 她 character in the People's Publishing House 2014 publication *Lu Xun Manuscript Series* 《鲁迅手稿丛编》.
5 Lu, Xun 鲁迅, "New Year's Sacrifice" 《祝福》, *Eastern Miscellany* 《东方杂志》 Vol. 21, No. 6.
6 Qian, Yuan 潜源, "The Blandness of Chewing Words" 《咬嚼之乏味》 carried in the *Literary Supplement to the Peking Press* 《京报副刊》, February 4, 1925.
7 Lu, Xun 鲁迅, "Chewing Words Is Not So 'Bland'" 《咬嚼未始"乏味"》, carried in the *Supplement to the Peking Press* 《京报副刊》, February 10, 1925.
8 Speaking of Lu Xun's relationship with *ta* 她, Tian Zhongmin 田仲民 in his "*Yi* 伊 and *Ta* 她 in Lu Xun's Fiction" 《鲁迅小说中的"伊"与"她"》 [carried in *On Chewing Words* 《咬文嚼字》, 1999 (5)] has recorded the fact that the reason why Lu Xun in the period between July 1920 and April 1924 chose not to use the term *ta* 她 and instead used *yi* 伊 was because he was influenced by Li Yitao 李毅韬 (1897–1939). Ms. Li was from Yanshan 盐山 in Hebei. During the May Fourth period she joined the Tianjin Enlightenment Society and advocated for gender equality. Moreover, she served as the vice president of the Tianjin Women's Patriotic Association 天津女界爱国同志会 and along with Liu Qingyang 刘清扬, Deng Yingchao 邓颖超 and others, produced the *Women's Daily* 《妇女日报》 where she acted as Editor-in-Chief. Li Yitao tried her utmost to oppose *ta* 她 and advocated the use of *yi* 伊 to represent the feminine third person singular. She believed that "*Ta* 他 is a combination of 'human' plus *ye* 也 while *ta* 她 is a combination of 'female' plus *ye* 也. If we use *ta* 他 for men and *ta* 她 for women, then it seems to indicate that men are human while women are not." On the other hand, if *yi* 伊 were to be used, then it would be perfect, "not only because *yi* 伊 includes the 'human' radical, but the *yin* 尹 portion approximates *yi* 亦 in terms of pronunciation, and it carries both the feminine and human meanings." She subsequently rushed around Tianjin, Beijing and other places vigorously promoting the proposal. Lu Xun also took her opinion on board for a time, using *yi* 伊 for a number of years until such time that *ta* 她 gradually gained popularity, when he himself made the change. Unfortunately,

Mr Tian Zhongmin 田仲民 fails to reference in his article from whence this view arises and so this point requires further investigation.

9 See Liang, Zongdai's 梁宗岱 short story "Travelling Companion" 《游伴》 which already uses *ta* 她. Carried in *The Short Story Magazine* 《小说月报》 Vol. 16, Number 3, 1925.

10 Hu Shi 胡适 published "Chinese Teaching in Middle School" 《中学的国文教学》 in the *Morning Post Supplement* 《晨报副刊》, August 27–28, 1922, in which he wrote:

> Does the poem from the *Book of Odes* beginning with "*Guan Guan Jujiu*" refer to "the virtue of the King's wife" in general? Or does it refer to a particular queen, the wife of King Meiwen 美文王? Or is it making fun of her (她) great granddaughter-in-law, Queen Kang 康王后? Or is it just a conventional poem about lovesickness?

He may have used the term *ta* 她 in his poetry a little earlier.

11 For example, items such as "Tell Her (她) to Come Back" 《叫她回来吧》 (April 22, 1924) and "Tell Her (她)" 《你告她》 (June 20, 1924) which Shi Pingmei 石评梅 published in *Morning Post Supplement* 《晨报副刊》.

12 For example, the short story "West Wind" 《西风》 which Chen Hengzhe 陈衡哲 published in the *Eastern Miscellany* 《东方杂志》, Vol. 21, No. 17, employs the character *ta* 她.

13 Li, Jinhui 黎锦晖, "*Ta* 他 [he], *Ta* 她 [she], and *Ta* 牠 [it]" 《他、她、牠》, carried in *Little Friend* 《小朋友》 Magazine, Issue 69 (1923), pp. 23–24.

14 Mr Ma Er 马二先生 (trans.), "Why He Married Her" 《他为什么娶她》, and "The Girl of His Dreams" 《理想中之她》; Ling, Xiaofang 凌晓肪, "Her Ideal Man" 《她的理想中之他》, separately carried in Issues 8 and 11, Vol. 1, 1924 of the *Guowen Weekly* 《国闻周报》.

15 See the aforementioned *Dictionary of the Chinese Language* 《国语普通词典》, Shanghai: Zhonghua Bookstore, 1923, Section A, pages 104 and 19.

16 Cai, Xiaozhou 蔡晓舟 (1886–1933) was from Hefei in Anhui Province. In his early years he had participated in the anti-Qing revolution, then threw himself into the patriotic May Fourth movement, as well as raising funds to establish Anhui University which nurtured many a famous newspaper editor, political activist, and educator of modern China. He was an early organiser of the Anhui Socialist Youth League and was later killed by KMT agents. According to some, he died of illness. This is yet to be investigated.

17 See China Education Improving Institute's 中华教育改进社 Third Annual Conference: "Group Meeting Minutes: 18th National Language Teaching Group: Record of Proposal C" "分组会议记录：第十八、国语教学组：（丙）议决案汇录", carried in *New Education* 《新教育》 Vol. 9, Issue 3, 1920.

18 Zhu, Ziqing 朱自清, "Random Travel Notes" 《旅行杂记》, carried in *Literature Weekly* 《文学周报》, supplement to *The China Times* 《时事新报》, Issue 130, July 14, 1924.

19 This book includes Ye, Shaojun's 叶绍钧 article "Han Xiao's Song for the Qin" 《寒晓的琴歌》 in which he uses *tamen* 她们 to refer to females and *tamen* 牠们 to refer to tree branches or in other words, the neuter gender; Zhou, Zuoren's 周作人 two items "Little Match Girl" 《卖火柴的女儿》 and "The Swallow and the Butterfly" 《燕子与蝴蝶》 are also included, with the former using *yi* 伊 to refer to females and the latter also using *yi* 伊 for females along with *ta* 他 for the neuter gender. See Gu, Xiegang 顾颉刚, Fan, Xiangshan 范祥善 and Ye, Shaojun 叶绍钧 (eds.), Hu, Shi 胡适, Wang, Xiulu 王岫庐 and Zhu, Jingnong 朱经农 (rev.), *National Language Textbook for the New Education System* 《新学制国语教科书》, Vol. 2, Shanghai: Commercial Press, 1924.

20 See the "Junior Middle School" National Language and National Language Textbook section of the Beijing Normal University library's "Special Collections" feature *Complete Library of Textbooks of Normal, Middle and Primary Schools from Before Liberation Held by this Library* 《馆藏解放前师范学校及中小学教科书全文库》.

Whilst checking these textbooks, I was fortunate to have the valuable assistance of Han Qiuhong 韩秋红 for which I am eternally grateful. For the situation regarding the propagation of *ta* 她 and *yi* 伊 in textbooks, please see the list of major referenced materials at the back of this work.

21 See *Pronunciation Dictionary of Common National Language Terms* 《国音常用字汇》, Shanghai: Commercial Press, 1932, pages 172 and 244.
22 See *Expanded and Annotated Pronunciation Dictionary of Common National Language Terms* 《增订注解国音常用字汇》, Shanghai: Commercial Press, 1949, pp. 84–85, 375.
23 See Zhang, Wenzhi 张文治 et al. (eds.), printed and distributed by the Zhonghua Bookstore, August 1935; 11th edition, 1947, "Chou 丑" Volume, p. 29 and "Yin 寅" Volume, p. 2.
24 See *Standard Dictionary of Common National Language Sounds* 《标准国音常用词典》 held in the library of the Renmin University of China, p. 66. The compiler, place of publication and specific time of publication of this work is not known, but it would appear to be a product of the 1930s or 1940s in the Republican period.
25 Apart from the common dictionaries already mentioned, there were also a number of specialist dictionaries published during the late 1920s and early 1930s which typically used the *ta* 她 character. For example, in *New Dictionary of Literary Description* 《新文艺描写辞典》 and *Sequel to the New Dictionary of Literary Description* 《新文艺描写辞典续编》 which were edited by Qian Qianwu 钱谦吾, the great number of sections that include feminine examples all use *ta* 她. See the Shanghai: Nanqiang Bookstore, 1931 edition, pp. 283–303; and the *Sequel* 《续编》, pp. 557–572.
26 The eight historians who separately consented to my visits were Mr Dai Yi 戴逸, Mr Li Wenhai 李文海, Mr Wang Sizhi 王思治, Mr Shi Song 史松, and Mr Wang Daocheng 王道成, all members of the Renmin University of China Department of Qing History, as well as Mr Wang Rufeng 王汝丰 and Mr Li Peifen 李佩芬 of the History Department, along with my old teacher from the Beijing Normal University, Mr Gong Shuduo 龚书铎. Of these, Mr Gong informed me that when he was studying in Fujian and in the early 1950s when he went to Taiwan to study, the character 她 was always pronounced with the sound *yi* 伊 (Meanwhile, as far as I am aware, in Fujian dialect the character 他 is pronounced *yi* 伊, and it does not necessarily follow the dictionary pronunciation). Mr Shi Song 史松 told me that when he was studying at the Hubei No. 3 Primary School, while 她 and 他 were both pronounced "*ta*", 牠 was pronounced "*tuo*". It is therefore obvious that the pronunciation mandated by the linguists was not without impact.
27 See the relevant sections of China Dictionary Editing and Compilation Office 中国辞典编纂处, (ed.), *Dictionary of the National Language* 《国语辞典》, Vol. 2, Shanghai: Commercial Press, 1943.
28 Yang, Bojun 杨伯峻, *An Explanation of the Grammar of the Chinese Language* 《中国语文文法通释》, 1st edition, Shanghai: Commercial Press, 1936, pp. 47–48.
29 In the 1940s, a number of Japanese who had come to China specially documented the clear change in the representation in Chinese of the third person singular. See Shintaro Katsutsugu 挾間新太郎, "Discussion on Chinese: He, She, It 《華語漫談（其の二）・"他と她と牠"》", *Cooperation in North China* 《華北合作》, Vol. 9, Issue 5, 1943.
30 Qia 恰 (Quechou 却酬), "*Ta* 他 [he], *Ta* 她 [she], and *Ta* 牠 [it]" 《他、她、牠》, carried in *Society Reports* 《会报》, Vol. 33, 1928.
31 See Chen, Yinke 陈寅恪, "Discussing National Language Examination Topics with Professor Liu Wendian" 《与刘文典教授论国文试题书》, carried in *The Critical Review* 《学衡》 magazine, Vol. 79, published by the Zhonghua Bookstore, 1933.
32 Li, Xiaotong 厉筱通, "The Question of the Vulgar Scripted 她 and 牠" 《"她"和"牠"的俗书问题》, carried in *Current Opinion* 《时代公论》, Issue 114, June 1, 1934.
33 Zhu, Xin 诛心, "*Ta* (他), *ta* (她), *ta* (牠), and *ta* (它)" 《"他"、"她"、"牠"、"它"》, carried in *The Pei-yang Pictorial News* 《北洋画报》, Issue 1080, 1934. I was fortunate to have the assistance of Professor Xia Mingfang 夏明方 in accessing this material.

From the name of the author, i.e., Zhu Xin 诛心 or "Duplicitous", it appears that he/she is unhappy with the motivation of the inventors and practitioners of *ta* 她, believing that they had "ulterior motives".

34 See Wang, Xinming 王新命, *Forty Years in Journalism* 《新闻圈里四十年》, Vol. 2, Taibei: Longwen Publishing Co., Ltd, 1993, p. 453. I benefited from Professor Yuan Yidan's 袁一丹 tips, inspiration, and assistance in determining the true identity of Han Bing 寒冰, his relationship with Wang Wuwei 王无为, and this work by Wang Xinming 王新命. See Yuan, Yidan 袁一丹, "The New Culture as a Movement" 《作为运动的新文化》, carried in *Modern China* 《现代中国》, Issue 12, 2009.

35 See Zhou, Shoujuan 周瘦鹃, "Nonsense" 《一片胡言》, carried in *Shen Bao* 《申报》, July 7, 1922. The article satirises the courting of the leader of the New Culture Movement, Hu Shi 胡适, by the abdicating Xuantong 宣统 emperor Puyi 溥仪. The article satirically reads: "Go ahead and be friends; exchange ideas and compare notes. Mr Puyi might get to play with a few new signs. If it is still necessary to issue edicts from the Qing palace, then perhaps we can add a few new words like *ta* 她 (she), *di* 底 (the possessive article), or *ta* 牠 (it), Ha! Ha!" Some of his short items published in 1921 and 1923 in *Shen Bao: Free Talk* 《申报·自由谈》 also indicate his aversion to *ta* 她.

36 Zhou, Shoujuan 周瘦鹃, "Foreword to Violets" 《写在紫罗兰前头》, carried in *Violets* 《紫罗兰》 magazine, Issue 2, May 1943. This item was kindly provided by Professor Chen Jianhua 陈建华 from the Department of Humanities, Hong Kong University of Science and Technology. During the May Fourth period, the attitude of the Mandarin Ducks and Butterflies School generally appeared negative. Apart from Zhou Shoujuan, another leading representative of the group, Li, Dingyi 李定夷, was originally of the same mind. However, in *New Fiction Magazine* 《小说新报》 which he edited, he was able to tolerate the use of *ta* 她 by other people. For example, in the piece of "fiction for awakening" entitled "Your Happiness" 《你的幸福》 published in Vol. 8, Issue 4, 1923 of *New Fiction Magazine* 《小说新报》, the character *ta* 她 was used copiously.

8 The Quest for Modernity and the Interaction Between Foreign Language Factors and Chinese Language Traditions

The Roots of *Ta* 她's Victory and Its Historical and Cultural Impact

As previously mentioned, it was largely following the mid-1920s that the third person singular female pronoun *ta* 她 eventually spread throughout China. Of these, 1923 to 1924 constituted a relatively crucial turning point. Around this time several important writers, educators, academics, and cultural figures actively chose the term and used it in their writing. The degree of consciousness with which they chose to use *ta* 她 varied and their circumstances perhaps differed, but there is no doubt that they all performed a profound demonstrative and orientating function in the gradual social popularisation of the term.

Nevertheless, in hindsight, the fact that these important cultural and literary figures abandoned *yi* 伊 and embraced *ta* 她 following May Fourth cannot be taken to be mere coincidence. As to *ta* 她 eventually finding social acceptance, this came much later, and the early to mid-1930s were a pivotal juncture when a certain number of historico-linguistic and even politico-cultural factors which operated independently of human consciousness came into play.

1 Identical in Sound With *Ta* 他 But Slightly Different in Form: The Main Reason Why *Ta* 她 Won Against *Yi* 伊

There is very little research being conducted at the moment on why the character *ta* 她 was able to eventually be victorious. Occasionally there is a response, but each time the victory is credited to the three reasons that Liu Bannong elucidated in his 1920 article "On the Question of the Character *Ta* 她" 《"她"字问题》.[1] I believe that what Liu Bannong stated does definitely have merit, however if we take into consideration the full history of the debate around the character *ta* 她 as outlined above, then Mr Liu's decidedly unconvincing arguments at the time are far from adequate; in fact it is possible that he may not have even grasped the crux of the question. If we only address the question of *ta* 她 gaining the ascendancy over *yi* 伊, then I am afraid that it is not because of the fact that *ta* 她 possessed a precise structure with a similar form to *ta* 他 while maintaining its difference, or that it "revealed the feminine aspect more clearly" and so on. Rather, it is possible the more important factor was that it was pronounced in the same manner as *ta* 他. What is interesting is that this later point was precisely

DOI: 10.4324/9781003359449-9

an important reason why some (like Han Bing et al.) at the time opposed *ta* 她 and the reason why Liu Bannong himself was also not completely comfortable with the character. It was this misgiving that motivated Liu and many supporters of *ta* 她 to suggest that it be pronounced *tuo, te*, or *yi*, so as to distinguish it from the pronunciation of *ta* 他. The view described above of those advocates in the journal *Women's Voice* 《妇女共鸣》 who argued that it "may indeed be an advantage" that the character *yi* 伊 differed in terms of pronunciation with *ta*, fully echoed this position.

However, facts later revealed Liu Bannong's recommendation that it be pronounced differently – a rule that occupied the primary position in linguistics circles in the Republican period and that was finally adopted and repeatedly reaffirmed by the state – in hindsight not only appears to be "superfluous", but possibly also "erroneous", which is more than a little ironic. As for the third person singular pronoun, which is used so frequently in vernacular Chinese, "sounding identical but with a slightly different form" was the likely outcome brought about by the linguistic features of the Chinese language with its historical emphasis on precision, on the character conveying the meaning of the word, and the existence of multiple characters with the same sound. It was also a result of the interaction between the modernist quest for precision and differentiation which had been aroused during the late Qing and early Republican period along with the vernacular principle of "the spoken and written word being one", and other factors. What could not be ignored, especially, was the restriction that the existing pronunciation of the third person singular pronoun *ta* 他 imposed, having enjoyed a long and entrenched existence and being resistant to change itself because it had had such wide currency in the social lives of everyday people. In fact, the reason why *yi* 伊, along with *bi* 彼, *qu* 渠, and other third person singular pronouns appeared so "bookish" was because in the vast majority of Chinese dialects the established pronunciation of *ta* 他, representing the third person, was truly so widespread, so common, and so powerful that it seemed that it could not offer any opportunity or space at all to any other term representing the third person with an alternative pronunciation to exist within the modern vernacular language.

In other words, the reason why *yi* 伊 was eventually defeated in its battle with *ta* 她 was, in the main, probably not because of its form (both could be distinguished in form from *ta* 他 and their forms were similarly uncomplicated) but precisely because it differed in terms of pronunciation with *ta* 他 and was unable to adopt *ta* as its pronunciation. In this regard, for a long time it was difficult to see which of the two characters *ta* 它 and *ta* 牠 would be victorious in representing the neuter third person (since both were pronounced *ta*), and the fact that the proposed alternatives, namely *qu* 渠, *qu* 佢, *bi* 彼 and other characters with different pronunciations had been abandoned by the beginning of the 1920s cannot be said not to constitute comparatively powerful supporting evidence for this thesis.

On this point, Chen Sibai 陈斯白 and Liu Shi 柳湜 et al. mentioned above in fact all had something to say, although the earliest to realise this and, moreover, the first to comprehensively and clearly articulate the relevant position from the point of view of the "literary revolution" was an individual by the name of Jin Fushen 金福申. On March 18, 1921, Jin Fushen published his article "The Pronouns *Ta* (他, he) and *Ta* (她, she)" 《代名词他(He)同她(She)》 in *The Morning Post Supplement* 《晨报副刊》 where he specifically addressed the point. Unfortunately, this work appears to have escaped people's attention and deliberations at the time. In the article, he emphasises that those engaged in the revolution in literature ought to be aware that:

> "Language and script must be unified", "script must fit in with language and language must not be altered to fit in with script". Also "the national language must be broadly propagated and unified". These three matters ... are precisely the reason why Classical Chinese gave way to the vernacular — in other words, this is the basis of the literary revolution. Presently, the character *yi* 伊 is the pronoun used by a section of people from the two provinces Jiangsu and Zhejiang, but it not only refers to women; it is used to refer to both male and female. So, does this not conflict with the third requirement above? If we were to use *yi* 伊 in our writing, would it not then be out of step with the pronunciation of *ta* 他 which is in common use within the current national language? This, then, conflicts with the first principle outlined above. If we were to have people refer to the masculine third person by saying *ta* 他 and refer to the feminine third person by saying *yi* 伊, like in the written form, then I am afraid it would be unworkable. It would conflict with our second principle — that language must not be altered to fit in with script.

Based on this logic, Jin Fushen 金福申 argued:

> We should use the *ta* 他 sound for the feminine third person pronoun but link it to the character *ta* 她. It is sufficient to use the single sound of the *ta* 他 character to represent the third person pronoun; if we then add a *ta* 她 character to our written script, it will be much more convenient. The proponents of *yi* 伊 are of the opinion that *ta* 他 translates the sound of the English "she"; but the *ta* 她 character is a phono-semantic compound character with the *nü* (女, female) part constituting the form and the *ye* 也 part forming the sound. People understand it instantly the minute they see it, and moreover it is currently popular in the written language and quite a number of people are using it. This is indeed a more convenient reform.[2]

Having the same sound but different forms represents a "moderate reform", which in fact was a response to the demands of the new age for clear gender delineation while at the same time conforming to the convenient feature of the Chinese language whereby a single sound can be represented by a number of different characters. This statement is almost "prophetic" given the choice society has since gone with. The only slightly regrettable feature being that for Jin Fushen, the neuter pronoun *ta* 它 was yet to extricate itself from *ta* 他.

The Quest for Modernity 147

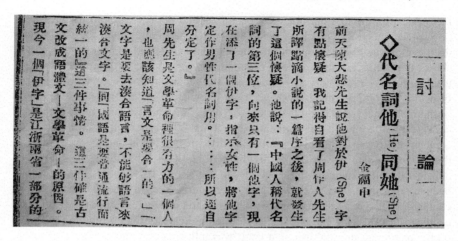

Figure 8.1 A section from Jin Fushen 金福申's neglected article "The Pronoun *Ta* (他, he) and *Ta* (她, she)" 《代名词他(He)同她(She)》. The article indeed displays much brilliance.

Nevertheless, I do not believe that it was a natural and "foregone" conclusion that *ta* 她's similarity in pronunciation to the character *ta* 他 was the main factor in its eventual vanquishment of *yi* 伊. To be frank, even though things may conform to the modern linguistic principle of the unity of language and script, that does not guarantee that there are no exceptions. What needs to be stressed here is that the *ta* 他 pronunciation of the common third person pronoun in everyday speech has a strong and clear-cut "mass" element, and that mass literature, language, and so on were primary pursuits of the leftist cultural movement of the day. The late 1920s and early 1930s also witnessed the unprecedented social acceptance of *ta* 她 which coincided with the leftist cultural movement and the burgeoning rise of the vernacular literature and language movements in particular. This was a period when the surrounding social language and culture was trending towards expansion and this created a type of "common language" whereby the broad masses could "express themselves, understand what is being said, commit to the page, and read what is being written" (as Chen Wangdao 陈望道 put it in his 1934 publication *Popular Language Theory* 《大众语论》[3]). This soon became an unstoppable trend of the age which motivated the agency and consciousness of the intellectuals of the day. No matter what the overall cultural outcome of this movement might have been, there is no doubt that its pursuit and emphasis on achieving "unity of language and script" had created a linguistico-cultural environment which favoured strongly the social recognition of *ta* 她 over *yi* 伊. This is a sociocultural factor which performed a major "selecting" function behind the move for identical pronunciation of *ta* 她 and *ta* 他.

Naturally, as far as the full establishment of a singular third person pronoun regime is concerned, identical pronunciation was in fact still not the only deciding factor, despite the fact that identical pronunciation perhaps formed the precondition for its survival. The character *ta* 牠, which had represented the non-human third person singular pronoun during the May Fourth period and shortly thereafter, shows that while it had also been pronounced "*ta*" and for a time had also been used frequently, eventually met its demise. The success of the character *ta* 它, apart from the important consideration of its pronunciation as "*ta*", lies in its evasion of the ideational association that a *niu* (牛 or ox, in other words, the animal kingdom) element conjured up when compared to *nü* 女 or *ren* 人. It also offered *ta* 她 some space to transcend the connotations that surrounded it, and thereby softened the element which was so easily highlighted, and which had been the subject of debate for a time, namely the inequality of the sexes. This would appear to have been another important factor that cannot be overlooked. In other words, the *ta* 它 character that Qian Xuantong 钱玄同 "designed" was certainly not an irrelevant or insignificant factor, but rather it performed quite a significant function whereby on the one hand, its establishment itself was influenced by the existence of *ta* 她, while on the other, the establishment of *ta* 它 performed an actively complementary role in the legitimate propagation and consolidation of *ta* 她. This point can be glimpsed from *Women's Voice* 《妇女共鸣》's 1935 declared refusal to employ *ta* 她 and the associated debate. This is also the reason why I have specifically sought to address the establishment of *ta* 她 in the third person pronoun schema. It can be deduced from this that the reason why *ta* 她 was successful was originally because of its close similarity to the simple architecture of *ta* 他. That this architecture was also able to readily highlight the distinctive characteristics of the female sex should also not be discounted.

Hence, in sum, we can say that having a pronunciation similar to *ta* 他 and *to* 它 was not the only reason why *ta* 她 was able to defeat *yi* 伊. Other socio-historico-cultural factors such as the vernacular language movement and the tide of cultural popularisation, as well as the character's simplistic construction and its visible feminine characteristics played a role in determining the linguistic choice made by the modern Chinese population.

2 The Perspective of Modernity: A Multi-Dimensional Analysis That Still Awaits Exploration[4]

The question as to how *ta* 她 was able to be separated from *ta* 他 and become a widely used character in China cannot be answered fully if we were to only look at the competition between the two characters. To explore the deeper reasons, we need situate it in the matrix of the complex relations between China and the West, between tradition and modernity, even the mutual relationships between the different factors of modernity itself, and comprehensively locate it within the active choice of the modern Chinese people before undertaking a closer analysis.

Liu He 刘禾 has, from the point of view of the unequal relationship between the Chinese and Western cultures, already grasped the essence of the move by the Chinese people to create *ta* 她. In her view, it is better to say that the lack of a third person feminine pronoun in Chinese to match those occurring in European languages is a reflection of "the inequality between languages" rather than saying that it is "a flaw in the Chinese language itself" and thus devising a variety of strategies to make up for this deficiency. "The proof can be found in, for example, when you translate the feminine plural *elles* from French into English. *They* carries no gender delineation yet people do not feel that there is any inconvenience caused."[5] Of course, there is logic in Liu He's view. However, based on all the narratives outlined above, I have a slightly different take on the question.

Speaking of the emergence of the question of *ta* 她, it is indeed directly related to the contact between Chinese and Western languages, but that is only the direct link. Its final dovetailing with *ta* 他, *ta* 它, *tamen* 他们, *tamen* 她们, and *tamen* 它们, when it finally became an authentic Chinese third person pronoun regime, still fundamentally hinged on the requirements of the modernisation which the new era demanded of the Chinese language itself. To be more precise, it depended on the demands and choices of the individuals actually using the language. In other words, the true essence of the *ta* 她 character, which had been the subject of all manner of debates and choices, and which was eventually successful, was not dependent on any direct "Westernising" factor. It was not a product of any hegemonic pressure by Western culture, but rather a crystallisation of the demands of an intensifying modernisation of the Chinese language in the modern age, even though factors of inequality between the Chinese and Western languages undoubtedly did hasten the process. To put it more clearly: the legitimation of the *ta* 她 character in the Chinese language is not a result of any hegemonic attitude of the West, i.e., because it existed in Western languages and therefore was a necessity in the Chinese language. It was embraced by the Chinese language because on a fundamental level it became associated with the modernist demands of the Chinese language that were kindled by the new age – in other words, the demands of modernisation. Here the congress of the Western and modern natures of the *ta* 她 character is coincidental. Because the character *ta* 她 was initially designed to represent the feminine third person singular, it differed in several important respects from that which emerged from the academic debates and the real sociocultural choices as well as its ultimate popularisation. At the time, the Chinese language did not simply absorb all Western linguistic peculiarities. For example, in Western languages, plural personal pronouns generally do not distinguish between genders, while modern Chinese distinguishes between the male (*tamen* 他们), female (*tamen* 她们), and neuter (*tamen* 它们). That is the first point. The second point is that in Western languages, and especially English, the feminine third person pronoun was not the product of the modernisation of the language, but rather constituted an integral part of the language from its early formation. Its formation and existence bears no direct relationship to modernisation; it simply accompanied the development of other modern Western phenomena. It was therefore simply absorbed by China along with other objects of modernisation and was thus incidentally imbued with a modernist significance.

The import of modernity is rich, multidimensional, and contradictory. It carries within it a specific historical content, including modern values such as "science", "democracy", "equality", "freedom", "human rights", and "rule of law", which differentiate it from earlier traditions. It can also be a general principle that is grasped and understood from the broader perspective of "reason" as well. The former demonstrates its historical nature and constitutes something that historians are able to master, while the latter invariably encompasses a certain type of continuity and openness which philosophers who care about universal values delight in addressing. As to the latter, it also displays obvious relativities. Modernism has its ambiguities, its unknowns, and its eternally unsatisfactory features. These features may bring challenges as it faces the future and is forced to embrace the requirements of human existence, and man's search for meaning. It is therefore foreordained that its latent features and well-springs must be continually critiqued, renewed and reformed. The profound meaning of Jürgen Habermas' "Modernity is a work in progress" is displayed here – it is the process of mankind's reflection on on-going modernisation; it makes possible the continued enhancement of human beings' indispensable capacity for "reflection". As we presently struggle to grasp the meaning of modernity, we ought at least to embrace the solicitude of both Max Weber and Jürgen Habermas,[6] and if we are able to mobilise and adopt certain postmodern concepts, then that would be a good start.

Modernity demands accuracy and precision. In modern China, this accuracy and precision was associated with the powerful stamp of the scientific spirit. During the process of *ta* 他 being successfully differentiated into *ta* 她, *ta* 它, etc. and with *tamen* 他们 being made more precise through the use of such terms as *tamen* 她们 and *tamen* 它们, this modernist principle of seeking accuracy and precision played a direct guiding role for those who were consciously designing the language. From the innumerable debates outlined in the previous chapters, it is not difficult to establish this fact. However, modernity does not negate man's preference for conciseness and brevity either. There is no certainty that anything that is more accurate and precise will be seen as "reasonable", but in everyday life, it is invariably true that what is both accurate and precise as well as being concise and brief is commonly seen as "reasonable". If the differentiation of the third person pronoun is excessively precise to the point of being tedious or superfluous, then it is in our nature to resist it, which highlights the internal contradictions and conflicts of modernity. Those excessively complex and fine differentiation proposals for the third person pronoun in the early 1920s, such as designing common gender and neuter terms, at the time not only attracted very few advocates, but it was also very quickly abandoned by society, a fate that was not entirely unrelated to this concept of "reasonableness". On this point, the expression of the Chinese language and certain concise traditions in its grammar happened to resonate with this requirement, and so served a naturally supportive function. It can thus be seen that, traditionally, the Chinese language was not always at odds with the demands of modernity.

However, the effect of these demands for precision and simplicity cannot be viewed in a vacuum. Even when viewed from within the demands of modernity, these, and the influence of such other factors as gender equality, mutually stimulated and constrained one other.

But as far as the demands which modernity makes on the "accuracy and precision – simplicity and brevity" architecture is concerned, if we were to put it in layman's terms then if we care to make a distinction in the third person pronouns along gender lines in order to demonstrate gender difference, then gender distinction of the singular is directly related to the independent, individual subject. Compared to the plural term, the singular would also appear to require delineation even more urgently. As Liu He 刘禾 pointed out, recently, "when you translate the feminine plural *elles* from French into English, *they* carries no gender delineation yet people do not feel that there is any inconvenience caused", so perhaps some kind of resolution might be found if approached from this perspective of relative "reasonableness".

There is no doubt that people from differing eras will perceive and hold to standards regarding this "accuracy and precision" and "simplicity and brevity" differently. Even people of the same era may differ, which can be easily glimpsed from the debate over the question of *ta* 他 as discussed above. But it cannot be denied that the driving force behind the propagation and eventual recognition of the feminine third person singular and plural pronouns in modern China came from the "overall demands of modernity" which was created when these two contradictory demands (both bathed in the modern scientific spirit) met with the demand for gender equality. Of course, this does not indicate that the ultimate success of the character *ta* 她 and its regime of third person pronouns lay in the fact that they conformed completely to the mainstream values of modernity and its inherent contradictions. Because all the third person pronouns in modern Chinese shared a common "*ta*" pronunciation, it is difficult to make a direct connection between the so-called "accuracy and precision – simplicity and brevity" architecture and the demands of modernity. We can only conclude that it was a product of the interaction between the combined effect of the persistence of the Chinese language tradition of "multiple characters being able to share the same pronunciation" and other modern factors.

It needs to be stressed that the installation of a feminine third person singular pronoun (like "she" or "*elle*") or even the existence of a pronoun system that differentiates between the masculine, feminine and neuter, can itself never be said to be an inherent measure of the modernity of a language. In the West, this can be evidenced by the fact that the various languages had already produced this type of linguistic phenomenon well before the commencement of their modernisation. However, in Western languages those terms and concepts which originally did not necessarily indicate any "modern" value, when transmuted into an element in the Chinese language, still did not necessarily imply that it must carry elements or functions of "modernity" or that it could not be tied to the immediate quest of the Chinese people for "modernity". Here, an anachronism has occurred and Liu He's 刘禾 theory of "Translingual Practice"[7] might provide some explanation. Because the societies of China and the West were at different stages of development, as a people with a new culture whose nation was experiencing a "late" modernisation, during the "translingual practice" where China was adapting to the feminine third person pronouns of languages of countries that had experienced an "earlier" modernisation, to consciously imbue this gendered pronoun with various types of modernising missions and significances, even the quest for modernisation itself, is completely natural. At the same time, what also needs to be stressed is that these gendered pronouns of the Western languages were able themselves to offer the Chinese people the space to incorporate more accuracy and precision as well as more value concepts such as the equality of the sexes, which provided the preconditions for the unfolding of this "translingual practice".

In fact, even if we put aside the question of any relationship between the differentiation of a feminine third person pronoun and any modernist factors in the culture of Western languages and view it solely as one of the many phenomena in the matrix of Western linguistic culture that require a concise and effective response from the Chinese language, a certain logic remains. At the time, the process of globalisation which accompanied modernism satisfied or adapted to the needs of the times, or to the challenge of the intense linguistic engagement and the capacity for inter-cultural exchange, which could never be said not to be an expression of linguistic modernity or the demands of modernisation. During this process, did not Western languages also absorb some features from the East? Liu Bannong has already pointed out while discussing the logic of the character *ta* 她 that even if this character could not ultimately be popularised as part of the Chinese language and remained exclusively as a term to be used in the translation of Western linguistic culture, then it would still have its uses. Thus, it can be seen that he already had some understanding of this concept.

Fundamentally, different languages within a civilization perhaps cannot be divided into better or worse, and whether or not they display a gendered division in their third person pronouns does not determine whether that language is internally "deficient", "flawed" or "superior". On this point, I agree with Liu He 刘禾 because the formations of different languages undoubtedly have their own individual historical and sociocultural contexts.[8] However, if we examine any specific language, then each language has its own undeniable unique and rich development and has experienced its own baptism of modernity. Not previously having a *ta* 她 admittedly cannot be said to be a "flaw" of the Chinese language, but the inclusion of that character indeed enriched and developed the inner qualities of the culture of the Chinese language itself (which we will further discuss below). This is one of the benefits that cross-cultural exchange brought during the process of global modernisation. Why then must these newly added "charms" be seen as having been flaws or shortcomings when compared with other civilizations in the past?[9]

Because the society, politics, and culture of such Western countries as England, America, France, or Germany experienced an earlier modernisation, their languages also in many ways displayed the hallmarks of modernity at a relatively early stage. When these Western countries, through their colonizing invasion, arrived in the East, the power of their language and even the oppression of their culture naturally also included some of these elements. Both the pain and the enlightenment that the reality of this cultural "inequality" brought coexisted. Looking back on the modern era, rational Chinese people cannot deny that the importation and creation of the vast volume of new scientific terminology during the late Qing and early Republican period, along with the conscious exploration and realistic demands of the formal Chinese grammar and the selection and adoption of the new Western punctuation system, no doubt all formed an important component of the modernisation of the Chinese language. Although the character *ta* 她 cannot be said to be a modern element that was directly introduced into China from Western languages, nevertheless it was undoubtedly an inspired product of the Chinese people's quest for modernity which had been created through contact and collision with Western linguistic culture.

Apart from this, if we examine the question from the standpoint of the historical import of "modernity", then the creation and successful socialised recognition of the character *ta* 她 was not unrelated to the modern value principles of gender equity and feminine self-determination as well as the complex multidirectional function which the participation of the democratic imagination with its privileging of the masses engendered.

Regarding the effect of the democratic imagination with its privileging of the masses, we can discern from our analysis in previous chapters the influence that the mass vernacular pronunciation push and the movements for a national language had on the selection of the character *ta* 她. However, the role that the principle of gender equality played was tortuous and complex and did not always assume a uniform direction – in fact at times it operated in a contrary direction. As we have revealed in our previous pages, the true effect of the principle of gender equality in the final analysis depended on the cooperation of other factors acting at the same time. On the one hand, it was not only used by those who were totally opposed to the differentiation of the *ta* 他 character, but it also for a time constituted an important ideological element for those who defended *yi* 伊 and rejected *ta* 她. On the other hand, it also resonated with the principle of accurate and precise differentiation. Gender equality, or in other words the call for an end to the delineation between the sexes and the celebration of a shared standard humanity, was at the same time an appeal for a clear gendered division of the sexes and for their mutual independence. To put it more precisely, if you want "equality", then you must first have "delineation". Only when mutual "differences" are grasped can true "equality" be finally found. This profound contradiction of modernity can be said to have been fully manifested in the question of the diminutive character *ta* 她. Speaking of which, the character *ta* 他 which made no gendered distinction in traditional Chinese also failed to indicate a respect for women or the equality of the sexes – in fact, rather than say that it was a symbol in script of gender equality in ancient times, as some previously mentioned did declare at the time, it should be said that it ignored women and that it was a linguistic indicator that debased the independence and individuality of women because this was an era when women were commonly discriminated against and where the consciousness of female independence had yet to be awakened.[10] Naturally, an even more balanced view might be that the use of the undifferentiated character *ta* 他 in traditional Chinese is merely a unique feature of Eastern language practice which has no direct link to the equality or otherwise of the sexes.

Nevertheless, the May Fourth period which gave birth to the *ta* 她 character, gave rise to a new environment. Despite the fact that I, during my review of the debate over the term, have been unable to identify anyone who has used "gender equality" as a direct prompt to demand that women should have a third person singular marker in parallel with men, however, who can completely deny that in the hearts of the multitude of those who either acknowledged or utilised the term, that this equality may have formed a latent motivating consideration? In truth, the character *ta* 她 was born in an era where such intellectual movements as social equality, co-education, equal pay for equal work, and female suffrage were burgeoning. The testimony of the earliest utilisation of the character by such individuals as Kang Baiqing 康白情 as well as the defense and promotion of *yi* 伊 from a standpoint of "gender equality" by many, all either directly or indirectly speak to this point.

When speaking of the process of the ultimate establishment of *ta* 她 in the "*ta* 他, *ta* 她, *ta* 它" matrix, then the path of the involvement and effect of this principle of "gender equality" is even more subtle: although it was not capable of fundamentally posing a challenge to the position of *ta* 她, nevertheless it helped to inhibit *ta* 牠 (at a minimum, in the process of maintaining the traditions of the Leftist cultural movement and the political culture of enhancing the equality of the sexes on the mainland, *ta* 牠 was eventually discarded), and thus guaranteeing the emergence of *ta* 它. In contradistinction to this, it undoubtedly also aided the consolidation of the position of *ta* 她. Today, with the passage of time, as people enjoy using this convenient feminine pronoun marker at will, from the form of the character it is already difficult to imagine how it had at one time been a sensitive issue. Because habit is a natural language attribute, it has helped people forget this fact.

In sum, I would like to stress once again that the emergence and success of *ta* 她 as the singular feminine third person pronoun in Chinese, while initially springing from contact with Western culture, was also influenced by traditional linguistic factors. However, in the final analysis it was a product of the leading role of the contradictions and tensions within China's quest for modernity. It was the crystallisation of the interaction between these demands and needs, between Western languages and the traditions of the Chinese language, even though its final result and the pattern that it eventually settled on might not have been totally in accord with the core values of "modernity". In other words, there may have been a direct relationship between the existence of Western languages as represented by English and the Chinese tradition of using the *nü* 女 or the female radical to create feminine characters in the process of the emergence and eventual recognition of the character *ta* 她, despite it not being the ultimate deciding factor. The most compelling and deciding factor remained the modernist needs and demands of the primary agents, the Chinese people themselves, and their choices.[11] And because of this, it is not surprising that when *ta* 她 first emerged and when it was first employed in the written script, it came imbued with a vital and uninhibited modernity.

3   An Historical Explanation of the Cultural Effect of the Linguistic Symbol *ta* 她

If we wish to respond to the question as to what new modifications and effects the appearance of the character *ta* 她 brought to our culture, then we must first clarify the actual conditions in which it was used in modern Chinese.

In general, the character *ta* 她 was initially used in two ways following its appearance. The first was to represent the feminine third person, and the second was to act as a symbolic marker of femininity, to represent those abstract things that in people's minds had values of beauty or were worth holding dear, such as the motherland, freedom, science, literature, and so on.[12]

In the previous chapters we outlined in comparative detail the circumstances in which *ta* 她 was used prior to the period from 1919 to April 1920, and we mentioned in passing how it was used in the early 1920s. These can all corroborate its aforementioned application. If we look only from the point of view of the early history of the character's entry into the realm of poetry and the humanities, then it clearly participated in the quest to expose the oppression of women and the calls by the women's liberation movement for women's rights while at the same time participating in the vernacular language and new literature movements via the reform of grammar and the theme of women's liberation. Because it was mainly individuals in the literary camp who first used the character after it had been designed and pressed into service, we can therefore in some sense say that it also constituted an organic element in the history of the May Fourth New Culture movement, or even one of the special symbols of that movement.

Let us here consider the first use of the character *ta* 她 in an illustration, in 1921, in *Emancipation Pictorial* 《解放画报》 – this was also the earliest series of illustrations known to have specifically used *ta* 她 in China – as an example to visually supplement this point. *Emancipation Pictorial* 《解放画报》 was inaugurated in May 1920 and it strove to perform the work of "liberation" and "reform", advocating for reform of the old society and bringing forth a New China because it believed that "the question of women was more important than any other question, and if we wish to speak of liberation, then we must naturally begin with women." The magazine therefore became a popular forum for the discussion of questions concerning women.[13] Among the new style women's magazines of the later May Fourth period, *Emancipation Pictorial* 《解放画报》 was one which clearly differentiated between the third person pronouns for men and women at a relatively early stage and, moreover, it used the character *ta* 她 quite copiously.[14] In August 1921, in its 14th issue, it specifically published a "Correction" announcement which was rather eye-catching, "Correction: our 13th issue published Mr Bu Zhuo's 不浊 short story "Neighbor" 《邻人》 in which '*ta* 他', which represents men, was used mistakenly in the illustration to represent women. This is hereby corrected."[15] It can be seen how seriously the magazine took the differentiation

156 *The Quest for Modernity*

between masculine and feminine in the third person pronoun. While *Emancipation Pictorial* 《解放画报》 is an illustrated journal in name, its number of illustrations were in fact limited. It mainly consisted of written pieces which made any illustrations that it included all the more noticeable.

The first use of *ta* 她 as the feminine third person pronoun in an illustration in *Emancipation Pictorial* 《解放画报》 occurred in Issue 13 in July 1921 in the illustration entitled "Whose Fault? Why Did She Commit Suicide?!" 《谁的罪，她为甚么要自杀？！》 (See Figure 0.10). This is also the earliest work of art that I have seen which uses *ta* 她. In using this brand-new feminine gender defining marker it highlighted the tragic fate of the victim of suicide depicted in the illustration along with the feminine cohort which she represented and denounced the banal feudal concept of being "Faithful to one's husband unto death" which, like an evil apparition, was poisoning and devastating the women of China. We could say that it was a new attempt to denounce the rotten culture ravaging the women of China. The author of this work's given name was Linxin 麟心 (Literally "Precious Heart") and her full name Xi Linxin 席麟心. Her biography is unknown. There are four other works which were published in this illustrated journal at the same time or slightly thereafter (see Figures 8.2–8.5). The works either criticise

Figure 8.2 Drawn by Linxin 麟心. In the sketch the text reads, "She (她) is also the husband's flesh and blood, so why hate her (她) so?" By using *ta* 她, the aim is to criticise society's discrimination against women and especially women's self-deprecating behavior. Originally carried in *Emancipation Pictorial* 《解放画报》 Vol. 14 (August 1921).

The Quest for Modernity 157

Figure 8.3 Drawn by Linxin 麟心. In the sketch the text reads, "The weapon lies beside her (她) but she (她) chooses not to use it. Could it be that she (她) does not wish to be free of these fetters?!" The two *ta* 她 characters are laden with the cry for "women's liberation" and express a lamentation for the subject's misfortune or resentment at her failure to struggle, calling on women to save themselves. Originally carried in *Emancipation Pictorial* 《解放画报》 Vol. 15 (September 1921).

the self-debasement or self-harm of women, with their numb, submissive behaviour, perhaps appealing to women or encouraging them to begin by resisting the traditional teaching that they are subjected to within the family and gradually enter society and save themselves. Overall, the works consistently focus on the liberation of women, encouraging them to become self-aware and resilient.

Ying Xia's 映霞 two items that employ the character *ta* 她 (Figures 8.6 and 8.7) are similar. They especially highlight women's sense of introspection, self-esteem, and independence. These seven works are the sum of what I have been able to identify in *Emancipation Pictorial* 《解放画报》 where the character *ta* 她 has been used and specifically refers to women. There is another work which includes the *ta* 她 character, but it refers to the nation, which we will refer to later.

It is clear from the seven sketches (including one which is partly coloured), that the artists contributing to *Emancipation Pictorial* 《解放画报》 were using the new gender marker *ta* 她 to promote women's self-respect, self-love, self-improvement, and self-awareness. This not only represented their artistic and cultural pursuits but also captured the spirit of the May Fourth movement in its advocacy for cultural change.

If we are to examine the cultural effect that *ta* 她 had after it had been incorporated into the Chinese language, we must explore more broadly the question of the significance of the character in modern Chinese literature. Of course, this can

158 *The Quest for Modernity*

Figure 8.4 Drawn by Linxin 麟心. Responding to the old lady who is lecturing the young girl, "Young girls are not allowed to question matters of societal or national affairs." The author comments, "Is she (她) willing to continue to submit herself to this type of discourse which shackles women?!" Originally carried in *Emancipation Pictorial* 《解放画报》 Vol. 16 (October 1921).

only be a case of "the benefit of hindsight". At the beginning of 2007, after I had presented a paper on the question of *ta* 她 at an international conference in Kyoto, Japan, Professor Chen Jianhua 陈建华 who was sitting beside me, asked: Do you think that *ta* 她 is a keyword in modern Chinese literature? Through our simple conversation, we both came to the conclusion that it was,[16] however at the time we

The Quest for Modernity 159

Figure 8.5 Drawn by Linxin 麟心. In the sketch the text reads, "This mother and daughter-in-law interplay illustrates the evil practices of the autocratic household. To me, she (她) is merely torturing her own sex. Why is this not reformed immediately?!" Originally carried in *Emancipation Pictorial* 《解放画报》 Vol. 16 (October 1921).

did not have the opportunity to explore the question more deeply. I think that if we are to reply to this question, then we may need to approach it from the following angles: the first would be what narrative function does the third person pronoun regime *ta* 他, *ta* 她, and *ta* 它 etc. play in modern vernacular literature? The second would be what do the changes in, and strengthening of, female gender consciousness mean for modern literature? Also, how important a topic is female liberation and the concept of promoting women's rights as a topic in modern Chinese literature? And thirdly, how is the character *ta* 她 and its associated terms expressed as a literary symbol?

I'm afraid it is beyond my capacity to comprehensively address this question. I can only offer a brief interpretation based on my own reflections. Recently, there have been academics who have stressed that the state of gender consciousness "must be incorporated into studies of the modernisation of modern Chinese literature."[17] Some scholars even point out that the salient characteristics of the gender consciousness of modern Chinese literature are "the mutual coexistence of a state of positive modernist values, a state of modernist alienation, and a state of pre-modern values."[18] I feel that this view is relatively objective. In other words, as an increasingly common phenomenon in modern Chinese, the character *ta* 她, which has become one of the most widespread symbols of the female sex, is a

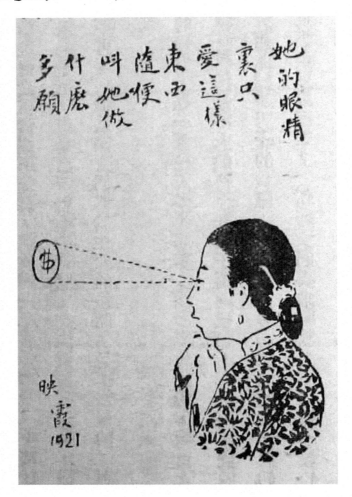

Figure 8.6 Drawn by Ying Xia 映霞. The text in the sketch reads, "The only thing that her (她) heart desires (indicating US$), she (她) will do anything you ask." Originally carried in *Emancipation Pictorial* 《解放画报》 Vol. 14 (August 1921). The author uses this to lament her protagonist's misfortune and her failure to put up a fight.

character that is at once able to represent the individual woman and at the same time transcend her. With the increasingly socialised status of the character, the female subjectivity that it functionally represents in literature might become both a medium for the positive value of modernity and a medium for modernist alienation and pre-modern values – or perhaps even more frequently a complex vehicle for the carriage of all of these values acting in inalienable "mutual coexistence". Even so, because of the integration of the modernist value of gender equality and the

The Quest for Modernity 161

Figure 8.7 Drawn by Ying Xia 映霞. The text in the sketch is headed "In the Boudoir" 《深闺》, "Why does she sit here all day and not go and do something worthwhile. She appears to be locked in a prison. Of what use is such a person?" Originally carried in *Emancipation Pictorial* 《解放画报》 Vol. 14 (August 1921).

modernist principle of the accurate and precise differentiation of the sexes (or as has been discussed above, gender equality with the precondition of an independent and clear delineation of the sexes), we are still able, within the scope of the positive values dominated by modernity, to discuss the significance of the character *ta* 她 to modern Chinese literature.

If we take Lu Xun's modern literary practice, for example, the three immortal modern female literary figures which he so successfully created, namely Aunt Xianglin 祥林嫂 from "New Year's Sacrifice" 《祝福》, Zijun 子君 from "Regret for the Past" 《伤逝》 and Aigu 爱姑 from "Divorce" 《离婚》, all appeared after he began using *ta* 她. Although this should mainly be seen as a product of Lu Xun's skills of literary creation and intellectual maturity, nevertheless if he had disassociated himself from his frequent use of the gender differentiating *ta* 她 to help realise the creation of his female subjects, then would these female literary images still be as clear, striking, vivid, natural, and archetypal? Would Lu Xun's critique of patriarchy and his portrayal of women's fate be as recognizable? I believe these questions are worth asking and the answer is yes, Lu Xun's prowess would be somewhat diminished. In other words, the success of the female literary images that Lu Xun created basically paralleled the process of his formal adoption of *ta* 她. And this is certainly not coincidental. The pertinent practice of other writers might also be able to confirm this view.

In discussing the significance of the character *ta* 她 in modern Chinese literature, we should not simply juxtapose the traditional and the modern because that will obscure the deeper linkages and content. In China, the cultural tradition of seeing things as either male or female (or *yin* and *yang*) has always existed. For example, flowers and grasses, water or the moon have invariably been described by litterateurs as objects replete with a *yin* or feminine quality; it is just that they have not been delineated in terms of a third person pronoun. But now if we were to distinguish them and to use the clearly feminine marker *ta* 她 to identify them, then the original cultural connotations that they carried not only would not be stifled by our action, but on the contrary, would be enhanced. It would enable the creation and communication of an image of unbridled feminine beauty which would be different from that of the West. This point can be glimpsed from the text of the poem quoted previously regarding the character *ta* 她 from before April 1920. Is this not an excellent inheritance and full utilisation of tradition? Creation and tradition, the relationship between modernity and the Chinese national character, at times is precisely realised in this way. Might this not constitute a lesson to those who are always willing to take a cursive view of the relationship between tradition and modernity or between China and the West?

What is worth stressing is that the birth of the character *ta* 她 and its practice undoubtedly created more literary and cultural space for the penetration of feminine gender consciousness. When femininity is assigned to all manner of beautiful objects, it delivers such a richness along with both ideological and emotional associations. How this ideology and emotion differed from that of the past is a question that is worthy of close attention and reflection. Take for example the character *ta* 她 being used to represent the motherland: on the one hand, it would obviously aid in arousing sentiments of beauty and adoration towards the landscape of the motherland while concurrently transmitting new value concepts of a modern nation and embracing the traditional filial consciousness, thus strengthening the nationalism of the modern Chinese people and expanding the reservoir of new rationalism and emotional motivation. For this reason, as far as research into modern Chinese nationalism is concerned, the advent and popularisation of the character *ta* 她 is not irrelevant. On this point the charm of Liu Bannong's widely distributed "How Could I Not Think of Her" 《教我如何不想她》 can stand as proof. The feelings of longing for the motherland of a traveler who ventures abroad that are expressed in this poem lingers in the heart to this very day.

(1)

Wispy clouds float in the heavens,
And the earth is caressed by a gentle breeze.
Ah! The breeze has ruffled my hair,
How Could I Not Think of Her (她)?

(2)

The moonlight kisses the ocean,
And the ocean caresses the moonlight.
Ah! This silvery evening, sweet as honey,
How Could I Not Think of Her (她)?

(3)

Fallen petals gently ride the stream,
As fish swim idly below.
Ah! Sweet swallow, what do I hear you say?
How Could I Not Think of Her (她)?

(4)

The wizened tree sways in the chill wind,
And the wildfire burns in the twilight.
Ah! Some lingering clouds cling to the Western sky,
How Could I Not Think of Her (她)?

If people wish to experience for themselves the different impressions that are gained from either *ta* 她 or the non-gendered *ta* 他 character when referring to the motherland, then we might do a comparative reading of this poem by Liu Bannong along with Yu Pingbo's 俞平伯 poem "Bidding Her Farewell" 《别她》 which was mentioned earlier, and Hu Shi's 胡适 1916 poem "*Ta*" 《他》 in which similar emotions are expressed.[19] What is interesting is that after the feminine *ta* 她 and the neuter *ta* 牠 or *ta* 它 became widely established, looking back and reading Hu Shi's new vernacular poem "*Ta*" 《他》 will confirm that there have been some subtle changes – that the *ta* 他 character may arouse poetic feeling in its gender duality, but it can no longer transcend gender and convey a sense of poeticism.

Figure 8.8 This sketch drawn by Jing Rong 镜蓉 is the earliest Chinese illustration that I have seen that uses the female figure to represent the motherland while at the same time using the character *ta* 她 in the description. Originally carried in Issue 17 of *Emancipation Pictorial* 《解放画报》 on November 30, 1921, the text in the sketch reads, "She (*ta* 她) has been fettered for more than four thousand years and is already half paralysed. Now she (*ta* 她) is aided to walk, and will eventually become mobile." Here not only is the motherland represented by the female form, but a female is supporting "her" (*ta* 她) to rise up and move, thus establishing the feminine form in the context of the construction of the modern nation state through a conceit of symbolism and agency.

While in ancient China, one's native country was often referred to as "the country of one's parents", generally speaking, it is associated with the figure of the patriarch. The proliferation of the use of "mother" as a metaphor for "the motherland" was one of the consequences of modernity. It was a result of the influence of the relevant practice in such Western nations as the United Kingdom, America, France, and Russia, and was intrinsically tied to the emotional response that was triggered by the fate of China as it suffered the bullying and humiliation of foreign peoples.[20] In March 1925, the poet Wen Yiduo 闻一多, who was studying in America, passionately penned the versed poem "Song of the Seven Sons" 《七子之歌》 in which he compared some seven regions such as Macao, Hong Kong, and Taiwan to seven "sons" of the motherland who, through a series of moving and passionate appeals to their "mother", conveyed a profound and heart-rending emotion for the motherland which can be said to be the acme of this type of literary expression.

Regarding the relationship between femininity and nationalism, Đurđa Knežević has pointed out in her *Affective Nationalism* 《情感的民族主义》:

There are many examples in history that prove that nationalism has always had a gendered component . . . . It is clear that rape is a strategy meant to symbolize humiliation and debasement of a nation. It is also very clear that the nation is the female body or that it is indeed a woman. People believe that a woman is "not just a woman", but the personified symbol of the nation . . . . In male parlance, women are presented as a group which is full of (certain imagined traits), and these traits are quite similar to those of the nation. For example, we frequently say "the motherland" or "mother country" which are two examples of this point of view.[21]

This phenomenon was similarly present in modern China,[22] and it created the conditions for mobilising *ta* 她 to give expression to a unique passion for the motherland or to one's hometown, and to use calamity and distress as a metaphor for its tragic fate. In May 1934, when the poet Ai Qing 艾青 used *ta* 她 copiously in this manner in his poem "My Nanny, the Great Yan River" 《大堰河 – 我的保姆》, it was impossible not to evoke a strongly resonant emotion in the suffering citizens. The "Great Yan River" in the poem is the poet Ai Qing's nanny, and is it not at the same time a metaphor and symbol of the fate of the afflicted nation and homeland? In fact, in Ai Qing's heart of hearts, the "Great Yan River" is a mothering entity composed of an amalgam of nurturing grace, profound love, and ethnic passion.

It can be said that the formation of the practice of using a woman and the signature mark *ta* 她 to represent and symbolise the modern nation state – the motherland – is a product of the transformation of the traditional Chinese view of women and gender, while at the same time aiding in the consolidation and development of respect for women, the new gender value orientation of a new age.

In modern China, the creation and employment of the character *ta* 她 also for a time mobilised and triggered in citizens a type of new imagination and awareness of the relationship between the individual and the state, between gender and the state, and even between the nature of the state and the fate of its citizenry. It is worth reflecting that in the early years of the Republic, Yan Fu 严复, Gu Hongming 辜鸿铭 and others made a big fuss over the use of the feminine third person pronoun which had been in fact, their rather solemn and yet playful way of opposing the new republic and advocating for the continuation of monarchic rule. This is also a unique episode in the application of the word "she" or the character *ta* 她 in the history of Chinese political ideology.

As Liu Chengyu 刘成禺 records in his "Annotations of Chronicle Poems of Yuan Shikai's Reign (Hong Xian)" 《洪宪纪事诗本事簿注》, Yan Fu disliked the republican system and declared that the monarchical system was a masculine (*yang*) system, while the republican system was feminine (*yin*).

> The French god of liberty was a woman with a golden crown and a long dress. The American Stars and Stripes is sewn for a resplendent female body or to be draped around the shoulders like a shawl. The emblems of ancient Rome were Mars and Apollo; there is no veneration of Diana. At the Olympian assembly, Jupiter was venerated, which goes to show that imperial authority is masculine, and therefore has the authority to rule all under the heavens. What is more, in English, the nation is female, and they use the word "she" to represent it. The land is feminine in nature, but all under heaven and all who populate the earth are ruled by men.

At the same time, Yan Fu deliberately quotes the *Book of Han: The Empresses and Imperial Affines* 《汉书·外戚传》 to show that "*gonghe* 共和" (which equates to the modern "Republic") was the lowest rank in the imperial harem. "In the language of the ancients, the two characters *gonghe* (共和) represented the lowest of the female kind, which is why it was relegated to the 14th rank." In this way he inferred that the republican system was also the "most lowly and feminine". In response to this type of argument from Yan Fu, the conservative Gu Hongming 辜鸿铭 enthusiastically agreed, and went on to declare "Mr Yan identifies republican states as feminine, daring to state that which others have failed to, in order to establish a narrative for an abiding nation." He declares that he has perused many Western books and surveyed the ancient Chinese texts intensively and concluded that "I have always suspected that the republican system lacked vigor, and now I realize that it is excessively feminine and that this puts it at a disadvantage."[23]

For Yan and Gu, using the word "she" to refer to the nation became the reason for opposing the overly "feminine" modern republican states in Europe and America. Naturally, they opposed the creation of a corresponding new character for "she" in Chinese. In contrast to this, the creation of *ta* 她 to represent the third person singular was achieved by the New Culture Movement stalwart Liu Bannong. Initially, the New Culture youth enthusiasts like Kang Baiqing led the field in its use, which was not simply a chance outcome of the contact between China and the West, but in fact was an active choice by the members of the New Culture Movement.

Liu He 刘禾 has, from the perspective of the application of the character *ta* 她 in literature, and in reference to the aftermath of the appearance of this new gender

Figure 8.9 Yan Fu 严复 (left) and Gu Hongming 辜鸿铭 (right), both well versed in Western knowledge and the English language but opposed to republicanism and thus indirectly opposed to the use of the character *ta* 她.

marker, offered a simple suggestive analysis of the question of "the ability to create social power relations within a new language". She notes that *ta* 她, representing a symbol which is a "directional gender marker", "both reflects and participates in an even greater gendering process which had already commenced implementation at the beginning of the 20th century. And during this process, China's men, women and the state itself all independently yet at the same time discovered this question of vital interest, namely how should gender difference be constructed and what kind of political capacity should or could be released by gender difference in the process of China's quest for modernity?"[24] Because I am yet to investigate whether or not the so-called "even greater gendering process which had already commenced implementation at the beginning of the 20th century" was a fact, or indeed what the real situation was, I have no means of determining what the precise function of *ta* 她 might have been. But I have observed that since the beginning of the 20th century the gender consciousness of the Chinese people has certainly witnessed a new strengthening. And in this process, many new terms that have incorporated the feminine *nü* 女 element, such as women's circles 女界, women's rights 女权, women's studies 女学, female citizens 女国民, Ms 女士, women's magazines 女报, the female sex 女性, or women 妇女 (i.e., the re-use of an old term), have undoubtedly had an impact that cannot be underestimated. And of these new characters and terms that signify the female experience, the ones that have the greatest propensity for everyday social utility are the two terms "woman (*funü* 妇女)" and "she (*ta* 她)". Scholars who study the question of the history of gender in China since the beginning of the Republican period cannot truly avoid addressing the question of the implementation of the raft of new terms to describe the female sex, including the character *ta* 她, and their function;[25] nor can the social effect of the sequential insertion of a "gender" element into all kinds of registration forms (those that have an administrative function) be ignored either.

In China, the awakening of consciousness that the gendered differentiation of the third person pronoun as typified by the distinction between *ta* 她 and *ta* 他 represented also led to a consideration of differentiating the divine from the human by followers of various religions. This led, to a certain extent, to its insertion into the realm of religion. When representing male or female gods, people typically would use *ta* 他 and *ta* 她. However, there were some who believed that this practice was inappropriate, and especially some of the Christian faith who were especially aware and sensitive, whereupon the special third person pronoun *ta* 祂 was born to represent God or Jesus. I have not determined when exactly this term appeared, but the practice persists among figures in the church in Hong Kong and Taiwan and within Christian organisations, and it is relatively common in the Christian hymnal and articles in the newspapers and magazines in their street stalls. It even led to a debate over whether the third person pronoun used in a new translation of the Bible for Jesus should be *ta* 祂 or *ta* 他. The Taiwanese priest Zhou Lianhua 周联华 (who presided over the memorial service for Chiang Kai-shek and his wife) has written an article "*Ta* 祂 and *Ta* 他 in the Holy Bible" 《圣经中的"祂"和"他"》 in which he discussed this question specifically. He accepted that under normal circumstances it was reasonable to use *ta* 祂 when referring to God or Jesus but opposed it for translations of the Bible, arguing that this had been the practice historically.[26]

I have not researched the period following the popularisation of the character *ta* 她, so I am unsure whether the translation and propagation of Christian, Buddhist and other classics and literature have been affected. For example, since the Republican period, when the Buddhist world mentions the Bodhisattva Guanyin, do they use *ta* 他, *ta* 她, or some other term to refer to her in the third person? I think questions like these also deserve attention and investigation.

Apart from this, I would also like to say a few words about the question of whether the character *ta* 她 was "borrowed" or "invented". As outlined previously, during the May Fourth period when the question of *ta* 她 had just raised its head, Han Bing had complained that the character was not a new creation of Liu Bannong's, but that it had been "dug up from a thousand-year-old tomb". In 2005, in a short article by myself supplementing Liu He's 刘禾 work on the history of the character *ta* 她 – because, like Liu He, I employed the term "invented" – I was similarly the subject of Mr Zhang Juling 张巨龄's questioning, arguing that the character *ta* 她 already existed in ancient Chinese and rigorously asserting that Liu Bannong could only be said to have "borrowed" it; he cannot be said to have "invented" it.[27] The evidence that Mr Zhang relied on was basically the same as that of Han Bing.

Indeed, in such ancient texts as the *Yu Pian* 《玉篇》, a dictionary from the Liang of the Southern Dynasties (502–557), we can find the written symbol *ta* 她. But this character is either a variant form of the character *jie* 姐 or *jie* 毑 (mother).

While the former interpretation is widely supported, *jie* 姐 does not mean "older sister", but rather is another word for mother; it is also not a pronoun, but a noun. The only features the ancient character 她 share with the character denoting "she" are their form and the fact that they both represent the female sex. They are as different as they could be in terms of pronunciation, meaning, and lexical category. Not only that, but this character had long since fallen from use and perhaps was not used at all. When Liu Bannong first created the character, he was unaware that it had been used in ancient Chinese because he had clearly stated in "On the Question of the Character *Ta* 她"《"她"字问题》, "If it has never existed, then let us just say that we created it; and if it has existed in the past but is not much used now-a-days and has become superfluous, then just say that we have borrowed it." If we simply based our argument on the form of the character, then we could take this statement by Liu Bannong as evidence that his action amounted to "borrowing". But we also know that when he first created the term, not only was he not aware of the earlier existence of a character with this exact form – in fact, Qian Xuantong 钱玄同 and Zhou Zuoren 周作人 and many, many more individuals who addressed the issue also held the same view. Han Bing was the only person to delight in repeatedly stressing the point that *ta* 她 had been borrowed. The author believes that there is merit in pointing out that the physical form of *ta* 她 indeed existed in ancient Chinese and that it did function as representing the female sex, and we could even say that its present-day status represents a continuation of the Chinese language tradition of lexical creation, but if we are basing our conclusion on the overall situation, including the meaning, pronunciation or lexical category of the item, or the term's original applicant Liu Bannong's actual "non-borrowing" of the term, then it would appear that to term this action one of "creating" or "inventing" is not far off the mark, and compared to "borrowing", is more able to convey the sense of the act of creation of a new linguistic culture. This is the reason why Hu Shi 胡适, Lu Xun 鲁迅, Lin Yutang 林语堂, Zhou Yang 周扬 and many historians of language after Liu Bannong's passing all believed that the character *ta* 她 was created and invented by Liu Bannong.

To put it more precisely: the singular third person pronoun *ta* 她 (if we are not simply looking at the character's outward appearance but at the internal logic of both its form and meaning) remains as having been created and invented by Liu Bannong.

In a memorial article written in the 1930s, Lu Xun mandated Liu Bannong's right to the invention of the character *ta* 她 with its modern meaning. Speaking as an authoritative witness to the occasion, he praised Liu Bannong's actions highly:

> He was high-spirited and bold, and fought a number of great battles. For instance, the answer to Wang Jingxuan's factitious letter and the creation of the Chinese characters for "she" (她) and "it" (它) were his work. Naturally, these things seem trivial today; but that was over ten years ago, when if you so much as advocated the new punctuation, many people behaved "as if their parents had died" and longed "to eat your flesh and sleep on your skin." So, these were in fact great battles.[28]

This type of reasonable commendation from Lu Xun is clearly of value to the understanding and comprehension of present-day individuals of the ideological and cultural history of the creation and implementation of *ta* 她 by Liu Bannong and others. However, his allocation of the rights of invention of the *ta* 牠 character to Liu Bannong is not accurate.

Strictly speaking, as far as the form, pronunciation, and meaning is concerned, to bestow the rights of invention of *ta* 她 on Liu Bannong is not entirely appropriate; it should be seen as a crystallisation and result of the clash of intellect between many individuals including Liu Bannong, Kang Baiqing et al. through debate and practice, because Liu Bannong rejected the pronunciation of *ta* 她 as "*ta*", right until his passing. In his opinion "*ta*" should *not* be the first pronunciation of the character. At the time there were many who were advocating for the character to be pronounced "*ta*", so it should be said that this pronunciation was a result of a choice made between the traditions of the Chinese language and the sociocultural practices of the 1920s and 1930s.

It has now been more than 90 years since the birth of *ta* 她. As people employ this new gendered pronoun regularly, naturally, even profusely, there are already few who really care about its past. I believe that if people did understand the colorful and tortuous history of *ta* 她, or if they hear or witness the stirring and real stories of its recent past, then their cultural self-awareness would unquestionably increase whenever they used the term. Their recognition and understanding of the cultural history of the blending and interaction that occurred between China and the West during this period would also be immeasurably enriched and deepened.

Finally, I would like to point out that *ta* 她 has now long since become an extremely common "keyword" in the modern Chinese language. However, it seems that the debate over the character cannot be said to have ended completely during the Republican period. Even today, as ever, there still exist critics of the character and even of the gendered division of the third person pronoun. For example, from the 1990s onwards, there have been those in the world of linguistics who have continued to declare, "there is no need for" the *ta* 她 character, that it "shouldn't be used" or that it is "superfluous".[29] However, apart from the old reasoning, the vast majority of these critics employ so-called "pragmatics" to evaluate it and stress such new formulations as claiming that it does not conform to the traditional "rules of the Chinese language or Chinese script", and so on. At the same time, some who are concerned with women's rights most naturally continue to express dissatisfaction with any continued use of "*ta* 他 (*men* 们)" and not "*ta* 她 (*men* 们)" because it blends or confuses the distinction between the genders in the third person, arguing that this is continuing discrimination against women.[30] Perhaps at some time in the future, similar debates will take advantage of new opportunities, assume new forms, and persist. But what we can be certain of is that the position of *ta* 她 will, come what may, never be shaken.

Notes

1 Work by Liu, He 刘禾, translated by Song Weijie 宋伟杰 et al., *Translingual Practice* 《跨语际实践》, Beijing: Sanlian Bookstore, 2002, p. 51.

2 I am indebted for the assistance of Dr Wei Wanlei 魏万磊 of Tsinghua University in reviewing this article by Jin Fushen 金福申.
3 In the summer of 1934, the popular language movement initiated by Chen Wangdao 陈望道, and other leaders specifically targeted the "Classical Revival" movement promoted by Wang Maozu 汪懋祖 and others, and the emotions aroused by the "Classical Revival" movement were obviously not conducive to the popularisation of the character *ta* 她 as mentioned earlier.
4 I do not have a "modernisation" or "modernity" complex; however, I do think the two concepts continue to be effective tools for analysing the specific history of late Qing and Republican China. As an analytical method, they still have the space and the requirement for improvement and development. In any case, did not the term "modern" become popular as early as the early 1920s, and by the mid-1930s, the concept of "modernisation" was understood by intellectuals and cultural figures, and became an important concept that affected the political and cultural life of the actual society at the time? The open and developing new cultural history research certainly may place an emphasis on "narrative", but it should not reject "analysis" out of hand, let alone restrict analytical tools. The author believes that the fundamental intent of the new cultural history is a more diverse and vivid narrative method, represents a more extensive and flexible use of materials, a more conscious spirit of searching for meaning and reflection, and a stronger interest in language . . . it also places an emphasis on revealing, from an elevated position, the "process", and attempts to demonstrate as far as possible the various possibilities that once existed, and so on. In the final analysis, the new cultural history is founded on nothing more than an acute emphasis on the role of cultural "proactiveness", and an unprecedented consciousness which perceives, grasps, and reflects on the history of various domains from the perspective of cultural and social interaction. Since the beginning of the new century, there have been many introductions and studies on the "new cultural history" of the West on both sides of the Taiwan Strait, and it has gradually attracted more attention. [See Chen, Heng 陈恒 and Geng, Xiangxin 耿相新 (eds.), *New History* 《新史学》, Vol. 4: *New Cultural History* 《新文化史》, Zhengzhou: Daxiang Publishing Co., 2005; Zhou, Bing 周兵, "The Rise and Direction of Western New Cultural History" 《西方新文化史的兴起与走向》, carried in the *Hebei Journal* 《河北学刊》, 2004 (6). In addition, Zhou has written a PhD dissertation, *Research on New Western Cultural History* 《西方新文化史研究》; Zhang, Zhongmin 张仲民, "New Cultural History and Chinese Research" 《新文化史与中国研究》, carried in the *Fudan Journal: Social Science Edition* 《复旦学报》社会科学版, 2008 (1), etc.] In reality, we should adopt a dual attitude of reference and reflection toward the current "new cultural history" of the West, and not blindly sing its praises.
5 See the previously referenced Chinese translation of Liu, He's 刘禾, *Translingual Practice* 《跨语际实践》, p. 50.
6 The import of modernity can be grasped from the two dimensions of historicity and openness. In other words, we can gain some insight from the dual perspectives of history and philosophy. See Huang, Xingtao 黄兴涛, "The Question of 'Modernity', a New Term and a New Concept in the Late Qing and Early Republican Period: Revisiting China's Recognition of the Concepts of 'Ideological Modernity' and Modern 'Society'" 《清末民初新名词新概念的"现代性"问题 – 兼谈"思想现代性"与现代性"社会"概念的中国认同》, carried in *Tianjin Social Sciences* 《天津社会科学》2005 (4).
7 See the previously referenced book by Liu, He 刘禾, *Translingual Practice* 《跨语际实践》.
8 In this respect, the observation of the British new cultural historian (Ulick) Peter Burke might perhaps be more insightful. His theories about culture also apply to language. He writes:

> A hard relativist, as I would define the term, is someone who assumes that all cultures are equal, as good as one another. My position is more sceptical. I am a soft

172　*The Quest for Modernity*

cultural relativist. I don't think that we can know whether cultures are equal or not, so it might be wise to proceed as if every culture had something to teach every other culture! . . . . From this position it appears to me that some cultures are strong in some domains, others in others.

(Peter Burke, in Maria Lúcia Pallares-Burke (ed.), *The New History: Confessions and Conversations,* **Cambridge: Polity Press, 2002, p. 139.)**

9　I presented a paper on this topic in March 2007 at "The On-Going Development of Comprehensive Research on Science and Art in East Asia" "东亚科学与艺术综合研究的继续发展" International Conference convened by the International Japanese Culture Research Center, and moreover, had a lively discussion with Sun Jiang 孙江, Liu Jianhui 刘建辉, Chen Liwei 陈力卫, Feng Tianyu 冯天瑜, Fang Weigui 方维规, Arakawa Kiyohide 荒川清秀, Suzuki Masami 铃木贞美, Yoshizawa Seiichiro 吉泽诚一郎, Kawajiri Fumiko 川尻文彦, Yang Nianqun 杨念群, Wang Qisheng 王奇生, Chen Jianhua 陈建华, Zhang Shouan 张寿安, Iwazuki Junichi 岩月纯一 and other scholars concerning this topic which benefited me tremendously and also helped to strengthen my views.

10　Professor Xia Mingfang 夏明方 has offered me great inspirational insights into this issue as well as on the point that the Chinese language was hugely inspired by the appeal of "modernisation" at the end of the Qing and the beginning of the Republican period.

11　For a further analysis of this question please see Appendix II of this work.

12　For example, Liu Bannong 刘半农 wrote in his letter to Zhou Zuoren 周作人 in January 1925, "Speaking of literature, I really must apologize profusely to her (她); she (她) was my darling! . . . She (她) is like a lover that I have abandoned far, far away." See *Essays of [Liu] Bannong* 《半农杂文》, Beiping: Xingyuntang Bookstore, 1934, Vol. 1, p. 199.

13　See *Emancipation Pictorial* 《解放画报》, *Introduction to Periodicals of the May Fourth Era* 《五四时期刊介绍》, Sanlian Bookstore, 1959. Series 2, Part 2, p. 196. However, *Introduction to Periodicals of the May Fourth Era* 《五四时期期刊介绍》 notes that *Emancipation Pictorial* 《解放画报》 only saw the publication of 16 issues, which is incorrect. I personally have viewed Issue 17.

14　The short story "Why She Regretted the Marriage" 《她悔婚的理由》, the title of which includes the character *ta* 她, already appeared in *Emancipation Pictorial* 《解放画报》, Issue 7 (January 26, 1921).

15　See *Emancipation Pictorial* 《解放画报》, Issue 14, p. 22.

16　Chen, Jianhua 陈建华 is also a woke individual when it comes to discussing the issue of literary modernity from the perspective of gender-conscious keywords. His "City of Breasts and the Revolutionary Utopian Imagination" 《"乳房"的都市与革命乌托邦想象》 is an attempt in this regard. See Chen, Jianhua 陈建华, *Form and the Revolution: The Development of Modernity in Mao Dun's Early Novels* 《革命与形式 – 茅盾早期小说的现代性展开》, Shanghai: Fudan University Publishing House, 2007, pp. 220–259.

17　Li, Ling 李玲, "Gender Consciousness and the Modernity of Modern Chinese Literature" 《性别意识与中国现代文学的现代性》, carried in *Research on Chinese Culture* 《中国文化研究》, 2005 (2). See also Li, Ling 李玲, *Gender Consciousness in Modern Chinese Literature* 《中国现代文学的性别意识》, Beijing: People's Literature Publishing House, 2002.

18　Li, Ling 李玲, *Gender Consciousness and the Modernity of Modern Chinese Literature* 《性别意识与中国现代文学的现代性》.

19　Hu Shi's 胡适 poem "*Ta*" 《他》 was written in September 1916 and was a vernacular five-character poem. The poem reads: In your heart you love *ta* (他), do not say that you do not love *ta* (他)/To show that you love *ta* (他), wait until someone harms *ta* (他)./ And if someone harms *ta* (他), how will you treat *ta* (他)?/And if someone loves *ta*

(他), how should *ta* (他) be treated? "*Ta*" 《他》 was first published in February 1917 in Volume 2, No. 6 of *New Youth* 《新青年》. In 1920 it was included by Hu Shi in his *A Collection of Experiments* 《尝试集》. In 1922, Zhao Yuanren 赵元任 included it in *A Collection of New Poems* 《新诗歌集》 by Commercial Press in 1928, after he had set it to music. Zhao also set Liu Bannong's 刘半农 1926 work "How Could I Not Think of Her" 《教我如何不想她》 to music and similarly included it in his *A Collection of New Poems* 《新诗歌集》, however, Zhao changed the *ta* 她 characters into *ta* 他. According to Zhao's explanation in his later years, after changing it to *ta* 他, the meaning became broader, and it contributed to the exercise of various imaginations. There are more interesting stories about "How Could I Not Think of Her" 《教我如何不想她》. For example, according to Zhao Yuanren's wife's account, carried in *Random Notes on the Zhao Family* 《杂记赵家》, around 1930 the students at the school at which she taught thought Liu Bannong was quite a distinguished and elegant talent, but one day they saw Liu Bannong and discovered that he was an ugly old man and were bitterly disappointed. On learning of this, Liu Bannong wrote a self-deprecating limerick: "How could I not think of him? I invited him for a cup of tea, and he turns out to be an old codger. How could I ever think of him again?!"

In 1934, after Liu Bannong had passed away prematurely, Zhao Yuanren wrote an elegiac couplet which ran: "For decades together we sang, now without him, there will be no lyrics to my song; when a member departs from the throng, how can I not but think of him?"

20 The German experience would appear to be an exception among European nations. Li Hongyan 李洪岩 points out: "Germans use father rather than mother to refer to their nation and the Rhine is their 'Father River'. This is the exact opposite of our practice of referring to our nation or the Yellow River as 'mother'." See his work: "The Joy of Reading" 《读书逢喜事》, carried in *China Reading Weekly* 《中华读书报》, December 19, 2007.

21 See Đurđa Knežević, *Affective Nationalism* 《情感的民族主义》, referenced in Dai, Jinhua 戴锦华 (Selected and Edited), *Women, Nation and Feminism* 《妇女、民族与女性主义》, Beijing: Central Compilation and Translation Press, 2004, p. 143. See also the paper presented by Yang, Hui 杨慧, "Interrogating the Highest Poetic Sentiment Shared by the Chinese Nation: 'Our Mother, the Motherland'" 《中华民族共有的最高诗情 – "祖国母亲" 考辨》 (unpublished, 2007).

22 Guo Moruo's 郭沫若 famous work "Coal in the Furnace – Nostalgia for the Motherland" 《炉中煤 – 眷念祖国的情绪》 (published in *Light of Learning* 《学灯》 on February 3, 1920) started comparing China to a "young woman" who is missed infinitely, singing the passionate love song of overseas wanderers for their homeland.

23 Liu, Chengyu 刘成禺 and Zhang, Boju 张伯驹, *Three Hong Xian Chronicle Poems* 《洪宪纪事诗三种》, Shanghai: Shanghai Classics Publishing House, 1983, pp. 266–269.

24 Liu, He 刘禾, *Translingual Practice* 《跨语际实践》, Chinese translated edition, Beijing: San Lian Bookstore, 2002, pp. 52–53.

25 Current academic circles have not paid sufficient attention nor conducted sufficient research into the relationship between the awakening of the consciousness of modern women and the new gender terminology. For example, the term "women/female" has become extremely popular as a group symbol in the modern era, however the fact that a two-character male equivalent is yet to be constructed is a phenomenon that demands an explanation. To a certain extent this illustrates the fact that as a vulnerable group, women cannot be ignored and must be regularly discussed as a bloc as a "problem/question" or as a "discursive topic". Only those objects not requiring special attention or special treatment do not require a definitive and popular appellation.

26 Zhou, Lianhua 周联华, "*Ta* 祂 and *ta* 他 in the Holy Bible" 《圣经中的 "祂" 和 "他"》, carried in *Bible Quarterly* 《圣经季刊》, 2007 (21). I am grateful to Zhang

Shouan 张寿安 from the Institute of Modern History, Academia Sinica, Taiwan for his assistance in providing this information.

27 See Zhang, Juling 张巨龄, "The Character '*Ta* 她' Is Not an Invention, But Rather Another Picto-Phonetic Character Taken from It" 《"她"字不是发明，而是借用成的另一形声字》 (carried in *Guangming Daily* 《光明日报》, August 9, 2005) and Huang, Xingtao 黄兴涛, "Also Discussing the Invention of the '*Ta* 她' and '*Yi* 伊' Characters" 《也谈"她"字的发明与"伊"字》, carried in *Guangming Daily* 《光明日报》, July 26, 2005. The former is in part a response to the latter article. I would like to take this opportunity to respond again to Mr Zhang's article. In fact, apart from those instances already mentioned in this book, opinions similar to that of Mr Zhang were common in the Republican period (for example, this type of argument appears in Xu Ke's 徐柯 "Daily Jottings" 《闻见日抄》 which appears in *Collected Jottings from the Kang Residence* 《康居笔记汇函》). Similar opinions also surfaced during the 1980s and 1990s, for example Liu, Youxin 刘又辛 and Bao, Yanyi 鲍延毅, "The Discussion over the Character '*Ta* 她'" 《关于"她"字的商榷》, carried in *Language Research and Teaching* 《语言研究与教学》, 1984 (3); Liu, Zhaoji 刘兆吉, "A Brief Study on the Character '*Ta* 她'" 《"她"字略考》, carried in *Garden of the Chinese Language* 《语文园地》, 1985 (11); He, Xiang 贺祥, "The Character '*Ta* 她' Was Not Created by Liu Bannong" 《"她"字并非刘半农所造》, carried in *On Chewing Words* 《咬文嚼字》, 1997 (5) and other works.

28 Lu, Xun 鲁迅, "Remembering Liu Bannong" 《忆刘半农君》, included in *Essays from Qiejie Pavillion* 《且介亭杂文》, *The Complete Works of Lu Xun* 《鲁迅全集》, Vol. 6, Beijing: People's Publishing House, 1981, pp. 71–72. Translation taken from Yang, Xianyi and Yang, Gladys (trans.), *Lu Xun: Selected Works*, 3rd edition, Beijing: Foreign Languages Press, 1980, Vol. 3, pp. 76–77.

29 See Zhang, Zhixiang 张质相, "'*Ta* 她' and '*ni* 妳' Should Not Be Used" 《不该用"她"和"妳"》, carried in *The Culture of Chinese Characters* 《汉字文化》, 1994 (2); Li, Dongchen 李栋臣, "The Superfluous '*Ta* 她'" 《没有必要的"她"》, carried in *Building the Chinese Language* 《语文建设》, 1995 (4); Wang, Yuanyuan 王媛媛, "Looking at '*Ta* 他' and '*Ta* 她' from the Standpoint of '*Ta*'" 《从"ta"看"他"与"她"》, carried in *Popular Literature* 《大众文艺》, 2010 (6). For example, Wang Yuanyuan believes that

> The character "*ta* 她" is in fact superfluous; from its creation to its employment, it does not conform to the rules of the Chinese language or its characters, and its value to the functionality of language can be entirely replaced by "*ta* 他". If we did not have "*ta* 她", then we would completely avoid such instances of irregular grammar as "*ta* 他／*ta* 她", "*ta* 他 (*ta* 她)", and "*ta* 他 (*ta* 她) men 们" etc., or even do away with "*ta*" altogether.

30 See Chen, Congyun 陈丛耘 and Li, Tong 李彤, "On the Language Gender Difference between '*Ta* 他' and '*Ta* 她'" 《谈"他"与"她"的语言性别差异》, carried in *Modern Chinese* 《现代语文》 (Language Research Edition), 2011 (8). One of the more important reasons why Mr Zhang Zhixiang 张质相 opposed the use of the character "*ta* 她" in the 1990s continued to be because he insisted that the character carried a sense of discrimination against women. See his previously mentioned article "'*Ta* 她' and '*Ni* 妳' Should Not Be Used" 《不该用"她"和"妳"》.

Appendix I
Some Reflections on Cultural History Research

When we speak of "research on cultural history" we must first touch on the question of how to understand "cultural history". Since the 1980s, research on China's cultural history, and especially on recent Chinese cultural history, has continued to advance to the point of it in some sense being seen as booming, however, the theoretical reflections on cultural history by researchers in this field have always been lacking and, even when compared to the theoretical investigations of social history in this country, it falls far short. At the beginning of the 1980s, a member of the senior generation, Zhou Gucheng 周谷城, championed the phrase, "There is no pattern to straw shoes; we just get on with making them until they look right", suggesting that scholars of cultural history should first just put their head down and write according to their individual understanding, and for the moment avoid getting bogged down in theoretical discussions. This type of approach does have a certain kind of urgency at this point in time. However, the neglect and the cognitive limitations on the theory of cultural history that this brings is a major factor in the increasing constraint on the progressive deepening of research on the subject.

1

In recent years, the number of works by Chinese scholars specifically probing the theory of cultural history has been extremely low. Of the limited number of specialist works that I have sighted, Mr Chang Jincang's 常金仓 book *Change and Continuity: The Theory and Practice of Cultural History* 《穷变通久 – 文化史学的理论与实践》 is worth mentioning. The author of this work is not satisfied with the fact that much research in this country halts at a description of cultural figures and events, and at the standard of criticism. He is also dissatisfied with the current situation where different classes of culture are subdivided and randomly combined and strongly emphasises the unified and holistic nature of culture itself, and its research. This cannot be but a critique of the current research on cultural history. In this, he is mainly carrying on from and developing certain points made by the Japanese cultural historian Ichirō Ishida 石田一良.

Ichirō Ishida 石田一良 points out:

> The greatest misreading of cultural history is to see "culture" as a counterpart to politics and economics, and narrowly as a cultural phenomenon related to religion, learning, art, etc., and thus see "cultural history" as a type of special history that is partly or wholly confined to the narration of this type of history.[1]

Chang Jincang 常金仓 expands on this, saying:

> The reason why historians adopt the strategy of research into cultural history is precisely so that they can see the sum of human history as a study of culture which has been synthesized, and it is this synthesis that is able to overcome the old exceptionalism and uniqueness of narrative history and thus discover the general principles of cultural development. Politics, economics, religion, philosophy, customs, ethics and morality, literature and art, and academic thought are all forms of cultural expression, and if we separate them and study them in isolation, it is like studying a person's physiological behaviors following their dismemberment.[2]

Based on this understanding, Mr Chang goes on to explain that the task of cultural history is to transcend "the most superficial and crude history of events and individuals" and to "concentrate all our attention on the various cultural phenomena manifest by those events and individuals"; "the first task of cultural historians is to capture, discover, and confirm cultural phenomena from a broad range of facts" and then to unravel and analyse them. As to which research method it is feasible to adopt, he railed against the so-called strategy of "explaining culture through culture", i.e., to "break a cultural phenomenon into a certain number of opposing simple key cultural ingredients" and then strive to reveal the "compilation methodology" of those key ingredients. To his mind, "Only when culture relies on itself can it achieve a satisfactory interpretation" and it is of no avail to draw on any elements external to culture, like the natural environment etc., to explain culture.[3] This style of thinking has been influenced by some of the passages in White's work *The Science of Culture: A Study of Man and Civilization*. White has stated, "To explain culture in terms of culture is merely to say that cultural elements act and react upon one another, form new syntheses, . . ."[4] At the same time, it also finds resonance with the view of the French *École des Annales*. In France, the representative figures of the *École des Annales* believe that "It is not possible to use experience which is external to a culture to draw inferences or to interpret the practice of that culture."[5] The work *Telling the Truth About History* by Joyce Appleby et al. even argues that the new post-modern research on the history of culture also exhibits similar features, and points out:

> But postmodern theories of interpretation invariably go further than simply insisting on the integrity of the cultural artifact. They challenge all endeavors

to relate culture (or discourse or text) to something outside or beneath it, either to nature or material circumstances, and in so doing they undermine the traditional foundations of knowledge claims in both the natural and the human sciences.[6]

Clearly, this view is quite influential and therefore worthy of serious consideration.

I largely endorse Chang Jincang et al.'s emphasis on coming to grips with the holistic nature of cultural factors, and wholeheartedly approve of Chang's suggestion that the key point in deepening our understanding of cultural history is to see "cultural phenomena" as an amalgam of multiple cultural elements. Nonetheless, his understanding of what constitutes culture can be too all-encompassing. As a result, he overemphasises its holistic and unified nature, and doggedly uses the strategy of "explaining culture through culture" to the exclusion of other strategies.

In fact, culture still exists within its own constraints and political, economic, and other phenomena, when they are present, can, to a certain extent and within a certain range, be seen as culture. However, as far as their basic nature is concerned, they continue to carry "unique connotations" which differ from those of culture. Therefore, to me, the study of cultural history has two implications which it actually incorporates, or perhaps we could say that it is actually constructed from two different attributes: firstly it signifies a type of comparative discursive space created for research convenience which demands that any cultural development in history that is separate from politics and economics is seen as a holistic object of specialist research; and secondly, it is a type of methodology, a perspective that requires that questions of social history be discovered, analysed, and recognised from a cultural angle. However, this does not mean that it sees all social history phenomena as purely cultural phenomena, but rather maintains that all phenomena in social history to a greater or lesser extent contain cultural elements (like social psychology, political attitudes, and economic ideology, etc.). Revealing the unique form of existence and modus operandi of these cultural elements, their innate interactive morphology, their overall architecture, and the function they serve in society, I believe is the mission of cultural history research. The two connotations outlined here are often seen as mutually contradictory, but this is not so: fundamentally they are unified. The argument that culture is all-encompassing is undoubtedly absurd. Similarly, no matter what form of "cultural determinism", as Qin Hui 秦晖 has said, it may be bankrupt after all. However, the widespread presence and penetration of cultural factors and their functions can neither be denied nor ignored. This is also the fundamental reason why the discipline of cultural history is required and is able to exist.

2

In my opinion, the import of "cultural history" determines the fact that research on cultural history can broadly be composed of the following three aspects: One is research on the general state of cultural figures, events, various branches or classes of culture themselves, which is relatively straightforward and at a level of comparatively low integration, but is the foundation for pursuing deeper research; the second is, as Chang Jincang describes, the discovery and interpretation of "cultural phenomena" which are a composite of many cultural elements. That is, to identify, question, and analyse certain meaningful interlinked and relevant shared cultural traits from the vantage point of the interplay between the various cultural elements and branches. Its main role is to reveal the true relationship between the different elements of a specific culture. Because of the range that they involve, the time periods they span, and the differing depth and importance of the elements they embrace, "cultural phenomena" themselves embody different aspects. If researchers are not equipped with a broad reserve of knowledge or an ability to grasp the culture as a whole, then, apart from analysis, even discovering or identifying cultural phenomena of value or questions will be difficult. The third is that research which addresses the interactive relationship between social politics, economics, and more. This normally goes to the analysis of specific cultural phenomena and questions, but its highest realm is invariably manifest in an ability to reveal the spirit of the cultural era and the social function of culture. Methodologically, it fundamentally breaks through the limitations of "using culture to explain culture". But this type of research all too easily stoops to vulgarisation and simplification of all in its purview. This is the stiff, disjointed politico-economic narration of many earlier cultural histories as mentioned previously. This is precisely what it means to be so-called "lonely in one's Ivory Tower".

On the third point, we can take on board the current prominent European representative of the "new cultural history", Oxford professor of cultural history Peter Burke's admonition on the subject when he emphasises:

Rather than simply replacing the social history of culture by the cultural history of society we need to work with the two ideas together and simultaneously, however difficult this may be. In other words, it is most useful to see the relation between culture and society in dialectical terms, with both partners at once active and passive, determining and determined.[7]

Burke does not see cultural history as simply a second-tier matter that is determined, nor does he mention the "counterproductivity" of culture. Rather, he argues that culture can determine social politics and economics, and that to decide ultimately which determines which, we must look at the concrete situation. This differs from the materialist view of history. However, his insistence that research on the new cultural history cannot ignore the historical relationship of the reciprocal interaction of culture and society is not lost on us. Speaking of which, the practice of calling the new cultural history "society's cultural history" directly is also possibly one-sided and not very accurate because it overlooks another important orientation, namely the "social history of culture" which it encompasses. If we speak of the orientation of the "cultural history of society" then the stress is even more strongly on the interpretation of social factors in the formation of culture; so, the orientation of the "social history of culture" concentrates more on explaining ideological concepts, the degree of socialisation of cultural values and their permeation and influence on society. In this way, the "social history of culture" orientation not only cannot be substituted, rather, on the contrary, it is quite possible that it will reflect even more strongly the distinguishing features of research into cultural history. However, its difficulty is obviously much greater. We can perhaps take as representatives of the concrete practice of the two types of research orientation mentioned previously the oft-quoted American sinologist Benjamin A. Elman's research on the economics of the Qing Dynasty, along with the "cultural network of power" which Prasenjit Duara strove to reveal during his investigation into the rural villages of North China.

In 2001 I participated in a "Sociocultural History" conference convened by Liu Zhiqin 刘志琴, Li Changli 李长莉, Zuo Yuhe 左玉河, and others. In this conference, I gave a talk entitled "Also Addressing the Subject of 'Sociocultural History'" in which I pointed out:

> While society and culture cannot be separated, history is even more a synthetic whole. Culture has its social aspect and society also carries a cultural quality . . . . This type of methodology, if I were asked to summarize it, perhaps could be done using two expressions, the first of which would be: the social observation and investigation of cultural phenomena; and the second: the cultural refinement or abstraction of social life.

I would also stress that this type of new research methodology "Is not the same as the formerly popular 'old cultural history'" (this may not be entirely accurate, but for the moment that is how we will label it) which is made up of fixed blocs like academia, education, customs, morality, literature etc. and overlaid with a layer that is elitist, fractured, dry, uninteresting, one-sided, and simplistic. I also maintained that from my research experience to date,

> No matter whether it be from a concern for its innate qualities or from its fundamental logic and the way it is enunciated, it should all contribute towards truly and effectively overcoming the abovementioned systemic problems of the "old cultural history".

I therefore expressed my enthusiastic endorsement for the research direction of "sociocultural history". However, at the time, I still had not clearly realised nor stressed the important direction of the "social history of culture". Nor was my attitude to the so-called traditional "old cultural history" entirely perfect.[8]

Naturally, the aforementioned three aspects are differentiated relatively, and their relationship is one of interpenetration in which the latter two aspects invariably combine to deepen the quest for cultural history research. In other words, to me, to realise the depth and unique content of research on cultural history requires the revelation of the real state of two historical "relationships": one being the form of the interactive relationship between the various categories and factors within a culture such as language, religion, literature and the arts, ethics, and scholarship or the historical relationship between such categories as elite and popular culture, or between local culture and the holistic culture; and the second being the form of the interactive relationship between culture and external social political and economic elements. In other words, the relationship between cultural "passivity" and "agency" in which the relationship between the utility of cultural research and its "agency" should perhaps be taken as central. (Social history must also resolve these two types of relationships, but its emphasis should be the direct opposite of this.) The organic shape of the makeup of these two types of "relationship histories" forms the subject and the heart of common cultural history.

As a historian, the more you incorporate the various elements of the culture and the relationship between the culture and political and economic elements external to it, the more insightful and subtle your revelation of these relationship patterns are. The richer in flavour and coloration will your research in cultural history be, and the more it will be able to reflect the unique aspirations of the study of cultural history.

3

Since the aforementioned three aspects of differentiation in cultural history research embody a relative, mutually permeating, and intersecting relationship, there is no hierarchy in terms of their intrinsic qualities. In other words, every avenue of research can realise its different academic standard by revealing the pattern of the quantum and depth of the historical relationship of various cultural factors. For example, in researching the individual Liang Qichao 梁启超, it is possible to analyse his words and deeds from a multi-disciplinary and multi-angled perspective and delve deep into the higher realm of his cultural import and influence. Who says that only the interaction between the Hunan-Hubei, Guangdong, and Jiangsu-Zhejiang communities can be counted as cultural phenomena and that the unique emergence of Liang Qichao and the tremendous cultural influence that his appearance generated cannot? Who says that only the "May Fourth New Culture Movement" can be counted as a cultural event and that the development of the character *ta* 她, the debate around it, and its sociocultural recognition is not? In truth, the crucial point is that the research route you employ determines your research goal.

Recently, I have been quite inspired by an article entitled "What Is an Event in the History of Thought?" 《什么是思想史事件》 [9] that Professor Chen Shaoming 陈少明 has published. In fact, we might suggest a corresponding concept, namely an "Event in Cultural History". Those events which have had a profound influence on cultural history are naturally "Events in Cultural History", and those events that at the time were not so influential, or whose influence was yet to emerge – or were not easily revealed yet in essence still carried a "cultural significance", and where this significance appears and is clarified with the passage of time and in a new sociocultural context – cannot *not* be termed an "Event in Cultural History".

In a series of lectures on a New History that was recently convened by the Renmin University of China, I termed the invention of the character *ta* 她, the debate surrounding it and its early propagation, as one of modern China's "Events in the History of Culture". Because its birth and propagation was not only a linguistic reform relating to grammar and vocabulary, but it also involved questions of societal gender consciousness and became a significant vehicle for new modern gender concepts. At the same time, it also influenced new literary keywords in the themes of modern Chinese literature. Its propagation and early socialisation not only constituted an organic component of the May Fourth New Culture Movement, but it also awakened the Chinese people to a new imagination and awareness of the relationship between the individual and the state, even the nature of the state itself, and while commonly being used to represent the motherland through a mutual integration of the traditional filial consciousness, provided a new rational resource and emotional motivation to strengthen the modern nationalism of the Chinese people. Amassed within it are profound questions of modernity and mutual cross-cultural interaction and exchange, giving it a rich "cultural significance", and thus making it a new object of cultural history research which focused on "relationship patterns between multiple cultural factors and between these and society."[10]

Revealing the history of the interaction between culture and society is certainly a major avenue for deepening the current research into cultural and social history. It leads researchers of social history to concentrate more closely on the dimension of ideological culture and to avoid simplistic and rigid politico-economic analysis and a dearth of intelligent structural analysis, enhancing ideological penetration and spiritual sensibility.[11] At the same time, it is able to help cultural history scholars avoid vacuousness and superficiality. For example, research on the concept of the "native place (*tongxiang* 同乡)" in modern China is an important topic in cultural history that is eminently worth exploring from the angle of the interaction between culture and society. It is both uniquely Chinese while also being a creature of its time. In my "Research on the History of China's Modern Ideological Culture" class this has already been discussed for many years. Several years ago, under the guidance of the research scholar Li Changli 李长莉, Tang Shichun 唐仕春 successfully completed the master's thesis "Back Door Deals among Native Place Associations in Beijing During the Beiyang Period: A Study of the Guangdong Native Guild" 《北洋时期在京同乡会馆的请托与受托 – 以广东会馆为中心》. Although this thesis approaches the topic from the point of view of social history, however its vivid exposé of the social function of the Beijing Guangdong Guild Hall in the new environment of the Beiyang period still revealed clearly the new channels and patterns the role the concept of "native place" played in society. It was an inspirational piece of work. But if we were to research the whole concept of "native place" in modern China and its evolution from the point of view of cultural history, then the connotations that it would evoke would naturally remain incomplete. Apart from the Guild, "native place" has other manifestations, and its dissemination also has other channels. Its function and style are also manifest in other ways. Apart from this, such questions as how it was itself configured and its relationship with other concepts at the time also require thorough probing. I continue to look forward to seeing high quality research results emerge along these lines.

In the process of undertaking research into cultural history, paying close attention to the history of the mutual linkages and flow between the upper and lower echelons should attract more serious attention. If, as some would stress, in essence "sociocultural history" should mainly incline towards research into the so-called lower stratum or mass culture for it to have definite merit, then the "social history of culture" ought to concentrate on the upper echelon elite consciousness and elite culture. But to this writer's mind, no matter whether our research orientation is the "cultural history of society" or the "social history of culture", both in fact should entail a holistic study of the culture of all levels of society. If you want to insist on stressing the significance of researching the lower stratum, then you must clearly realise that this is only a provisional strategy in the present environment where research on the lower echelons of society and culture remains decidedly inadequate. If we wish to undertake research on cultural history which includes both orientations, then from a strategic point of view, the most pressing or the most methodologically meaningful thing is for us to aim our research practice directly at linking both the upper and lower cultural strata. Take the example of my current research into "The acceptance of the concept of 'the modern Chinese people'", which looks at how the Chinese national identity has become transformed from an archetypal elitist concept into a sociocultural consciousness of the ordinary citizen. This question is extremely important and I to date still lack the capacity to answer it successfully.

As for the relationship between the history of local culture and that of intralocal culture, we should emphasise research on the interplay between the fluidity of regionality and the permeation of the composite entity, and here we can take a similar approach.[2]

(Originally carried in Issue 3, 2007 of the *Journal of Historiograhpy* 《史学史研究》)

Notes

1 Wang, Yong 王勇 (trans.), Ichirō Ishida 石田一良, *Cultural History: Theory and Method* 《文化史学：理论和方法》, Hangzhou: Zhejiang People's Publishing House, 1989, p. 144.
2 Chang, Jincang 常金仓, *Change and Continuity: The Theory and Practice of Cultural History* 《穷变通久：文化史学的理论与实践》, Shenyang: Liaoning People's Publishing House, 1998, p. 39.
3 Ibid., pp. 43–48: "Strategies in Cultural History – Explaining Culture with Culture" "文化史的策略 – 用文化解释文化".
4 White, Leslie A., *The Science of Culture: A Study of Man and Civilization* (*Foundations of Anthropology*), New York: Farrar, Straus and Company, 1949, p. 201.
5 See Chartier, Roger, "Intellectual History or Sociocultural History? The French Trajectories", in Liu, Beicheng 刘北成 and Xue, Xuan 薛绚 (trans.), Appleby, Joyce et al., *Telling the Truth About History* 《历史的真相》, the section "The Rise of Cultural History" in Chapter 6, Beijing: Central Compilation and Translation Press, 1999, p. 202.
6 Oldham, Joyce, *Telling the Truth about History*, New York: Norton, 1994, p. 225.
7 Burke, Peter, *History and Social Theory*, New York: Cornell University Press, 1992, p. 123.
8 Widely known as a renowned expert in "New cultural history", Peter Burke does not reject "Old cultural history" completely. He stresses: The research path of new cultural history is

> Not just a new fashion; it is simply a response to an earlier model which had obvious shortcomings. Nor does it mean that all cultural historians should follow where the

wind blows. We can be certain that a diversity of historic styles can coexist, and that this is better than one strain occupying a monopoly position.

See Burke, Peter, *Varieties of Cultural History*, Ithaca, NY: Cornell University Press, 1997, p. 198.
9 Chen, Shaoming 陈少明, "What Is an Event in the History of Thought?" 《什么是思想史事件》, carried in the *Jiangsu Social Sciences* 《江苏社会科学》, 2007 (1).
10 Huang, Xingtao 黄兴涛, "The Story of the Character *Ta* 她: Invention, Debate and Early Circulation" 《"她"字的故事：女性新代词符号的发明、论争与早期流播》, see Yang, Nianqun 杨念群 (ed.), *New History* 《新史学》 Vol. 1, Beijing: Zhonghua Bookstore, 2007, pp. 115–164.
11 The text of this sentence has been somewhat adjusted compared to when it was originally published in *Journal of Historiography* 《史学史研究》.
12 This last section was omitted when it was published in *Journal of Historiography* 《史学史研究》.

Appendix II
Revisiting the Question of the Character
Ta 她 and Understanding "Modernity":
A Response to Dr Yang Jianli 杨剑利

Recently I read the book review "Modernity and the Recognition of the Character '*Ta* 她'" 《现代性与"她"字的认同》 by the young scholar Dr Yang Jianli, published in the First Issue, 2015 of *Modern Chinese History Studies* 《近代史研究》. The review offered some praise for my humble work *A Cultural History of the Chinese Character "Ta* (她, She)" *– Research on the Invention and Adoption of a New Feminine Pronoun* 《"她"字的文化史：女性新代词的发明与认同研究》 (Fujian Education Publishing Company, 2009 edition, hereinafter referred to as "the original work"), however she had some issues with questions around the Western and modern nature of *ta* 她, and with gender equality, which, upon reading, I was quite inspired. Nevertheless, amongst Dr Yang's criticism some misunderstanding exists regarding the points presented in my work and some sections that this writer finds it difficult to blindly accept. I would therefore like to take this opportunity to offer a brief explanation and description which might also complement the contents of my work, and I hope might also be of some benefit to readers in understanding the history of *ta* 她 as well as the question of "modernity".

I

The main thrust of Dr Yang's issue with my work can perhaps be summarised in three points: one is that she suspects my work of engineering the mutual isolation of "modernity" and "Westernness (西方性)"; the second is that my work overemphasises, on a theoretical level, the "difference" between men and women in realizing the true meaning of the equality of the sexes, and that my apparent neglect of the historical context of modern China in turn affects the objective evaluation of the historical status and importance of the absolute equality of men and women in modern China; and third, that my grasp of "modernity" continues inevitably to fall into the trap of "Weberianism", and that my historical analysis of the question of the character *ta* 她 ultimately fails to resist the temptation of "modernity" and the fetters of "teleology". I will respond individually to these points:

> First, I would like to address the question regarding my understanding and handling of the relationship between "modernity" and "Westernness".

In my work, I never denied the Western factors which directly influenced the creation of the character *ta* 她. This is indeed a straightforward linguistic and cultural phenomenon. At the same time, I did not, as Dr Yang accuses me of doing, simply "divide and juxtapose" the two spheres of modernity and "Westernness", and from a perspective of so-called "internal and external factors", affirm the deciding role of the "internal factors". What is more, I never saw the need, quest, and choices of the Chinese people for modernity as "something that is capable of transcending the West and which was dependent on China itself" or that it thoroughly "rejected Westernness and remained entirely separate from it" and took it as "purely embodying the Chinese factor or something that is inherently 'Chinese'" (*Modern Chinese History Studies* 《近代史研究》 2015 (1) p. 142; hereinafter the direct page number only will be cited). These points are merely speculative statements, executed in an exaggerated manner by Dr Yang in her quest to establish her theory. Anyone who has conscientiously read my work and who is able to holistically grasp its objective would have no difficulty at all in realising this. In fact, what I have emphasised is simply the leading role that the modern Chinese people play as the creative and utilising agents in their modern choice of vocabulary. In my book, I did not specifically divide "modernity" into "Western" and "Chinese" camps or even at any stage clearly employ the concept of "Chineseness" in contradistinction with "Westernness" within the "theoretical framework of modernity" because for any scholar who is engaged in research on modern Chinese intellectual history, the permeation and profound influence of the modernity that quickly emerged in the West following the Renaissance on China is common knowledge. The expression "choice of social history and culture" used in my work in the final analysis remains nothing more than a reference to the choices made by the modern Chinese people who were the agents at the time, and this is the natural result of the writer choosing the perspective of "modernity" to analyse the question of the character *ta* 她.

To stress the function of the individual as an agent is precisely one of the basic principles and distinctive features of "modernist" thinking. Despite the international standing of modern China being so lowly, nevertheless, in my mind, the Chinese people as agents were still not reduced to a state like India which was a colony of the United Kingdom and completely forfeited their autonomy *vis à vis* their own language and script. In this process, the comprehensive advantage of the West in having first entered the era of modernisation, and the "cultural hegemony" that accompanied its invasion, naturally had repercussions to the point of generating major influences that could not be ignored. However, actual reform to language and script can only be realised after it has been chosen, tried, and filtered by the Chinese people themselves, and after they, as conscious agents, have negotiated directly with the "demands of modernity". When it comes to the third person pronoun especially, its semiotic meaning is a far cry from "modernity" – and it is even more apparent that in the West it was not something that was directly related to the modernisation process. Irrespective of whether the reader agrees with these views or not, they remain firmly those of this writer.

At the same time, I did not in any way simplify, separate, or isolate "Westernness" from "modernity" but simply refused to treat them as the same and see them as a single entity. Because after all, they are two different concepts: the two are both linked, but there are also differences. For example: speaking of modernity as a whole, despite having first surfaced in the West, nevertheless, in the West as far as the linguistic differentiation between male and female in the third person itself is concerned, it was not a direct product of the modernisation process or of modernity, but a linguistic construct that had existed internally from early times. Meanwhile, in China, the *ta* 她 character was simply assigned a "modern" significance in the Republican period by many Chinese individuals in the process of its creation and social acceptance. That is to say, not everything that is "Western" necessarily equates to being "modern"; and things originating in the West which have nothing to do with modernity would never be considered "modern" by the Chinese people in their quest for modernity. The important thing is the "quest for modernity and the choices made" by the Chinese people at the time. (See the original work, pp. 156–158)

To take English as an example, while modern Chinese adopted its practice of differentiating between male, female, and neuter in terms of third person singular pronouns, however, in the case of the third person plural, it did not adopt the English convention of not differentiating and using the pronoun "they". Instead, based on the perceived and imagined idea of "modernity" and its inherent demands for clarity and accuracy, the reformers of modern Chinese continued to create and differentiate by using *tamen* 她们 and *tamen* 它 (牠) 们. When I discussed the creation and recognition of the character *ta* 她 and associated terms, I specifically emphasised:

> It was not because it existed in Western languages that it was a necessity in the Chinese language (or vice versa), but it was fundamentally the demands of modernity on the Chinese language that were kindled by the new age, or that the need for modernisation initiated an association which was embraced by the Chinese language. Here the congress of the Western and modern natures of the character *ta* 她 is coincidental because there are substantial differences between the character *ta* 她 that was initially designed to represent the feminine third person singular and the widely accepted *ta* 她 which emerged from the academic debates, and which was subsequently adopted by the society and its culture. This is a valid and indirect proof that not every Western linguistic peculiarity was absorbed by the Chinese language at the time.

(Refer to the original work pp. 154–155; the parenthesis have been newly added on this occasion.) It should be noted that what I was clearly explaining here was the Western nature of the term *ta* 她 (she), and in a broader sense, certain "Western linguistic features", and not a wholesale "Westernness". At the same time, I was revealing the historical function of that kind of "real sociocultural choice" which at the time embodied the agency of the Chinese people (including such factors as the "movement for a national language"). Elsewhere I further indicated that in the process of the emergence and eventual (socialised) recognition of the character *ta* 她, the existence of such Western languages as represented by English is only a direct factor but not the deciding factor. The ultimate deciding factor remains the demands and quest of the Chinese people themselves (as agents) for modernity. (See the original work, p. 160; parentheses have on this occasion been newly added.) Or to put it more clearly:

> While the *ta* 她 character cannot be said to be a modern element that had been directly introduced into China from Western languages, nevertheless it was undoubtedly an inspired product of the Chinese people's quest for modernity which had been created through contact and collisions with Western linguistic culture.

(See p. 158 of the original work.) While my articulations might have been slightly different, nevertheless, the inherent meaning is largely the same.

There are different levels of "Westernness" as well as specific features. In her criticism, Dr Yang has not only intentionally or otherwise taken what I specifically defined and spoke of as "the Western nature of the *ta* 她 character" or the "Western nature" of language in my work and blown it up to become fully or totally "Western", but she has also clearly taken the quest of the Chinese people for linguistic "autonomy" which was part of their "modernity consciousness", a point which I highlighted, and misrepresented it as a deliberate pursuit of some "inner motivation of Chinese modernity". This does not accord with my intent. To be honest, I have never, nor would I wish to take this type of question and breezily elevate it to, and grasp it from, some kind of boundless discursive "West-centric" or "Sinocentric" exalted plane. To my mind, the needs, quests and imaginings of "modernity" by the Chinese people in recent times (and these three things each have their own connotations, and are not, contrary to what Dr Yang would have us believe, all the same thing) in essence modern products which have been "inspired by the times" in the course of the interaction between China and the West from time immemorial. (I have repeatedly expressed this idea, either using the phrase "the modernity which was aroused during the late Qing and early Republican period" or calling it "the modernisation needs triggered by the (new) era". My aim was to stress the effect that the "immediacy" of the interplay between China and the West had on the Chinese people's "quest for modernity" at the time. Readers can be the judge of this.) Their relationship to the spread of Western modernity following the Western Renaissance as well as to the West's colonial expansion remains common knowledge. However, when it comes to the linguistic question of the character *ta* 她, it behooves us to analyse it in greater detail. In other words, our modern countrymen, as the creating and affirming agents of the character *ta* 她, actually managed to implement it via the interaction of a multitude of complex factors between China and the West and between the ancient and the modern. This unquestionably included Western elements and Chinese elements as well as historical and pragmatic elements and certainly was not restricted to any single "external push from the West" and even less from any pre-existing internal Chinese stimulus. It can be said that this is in fact where the crux of the work's argument lies and that fundamentally, there is no difference between this book and Dr Yang's overall view of the question.

If I was genuinely attempting to isolate "modernity" and "Westernness" from each other, then I would certainly not have titled the last chapter of my book "The Quest for Modernity and Its Interaction with the Traditions of the Chinese Language". I point this out lest Dr Yang attack me and accuse me of understanding "modernity" as being somehow "Western".

Naturally, the cause for Dr Yang's misunderstanding could, in all probability, be that my articulations were not sufficiently precise or clear. For example, on several occasions, I mention "the modernist demands of the Chinese people themselves", which appears to have been misread in some way by Dr Yang. What I meant by "the Chinese people themselves" is nothing more than the Chinese people at the time, in other words, the modern Chinese people as agents themselves. Following on from this, "the demand for modernity by the Chinese people themselves" in no way refers to any "innate" modern impetus within the Chinese tradition. As a result of such misunderstanding, Dr Yang's "detailed exegesis" on the inseparability of "modernity" and "the West" is like shooting arrows in the dark. As to the degree of autonomy that modern Chinese people have as the subjects of their language, while being closely related, this is, nevertheless, a separate question, so we will put it aside for the moment.

Next, I would like to address the recognition of the concept of absolute gender equality in modern China.

I recognised the complex structures of "modernity" and its demands and focused on the internal tensions and contradictions of "modernity". Thus, when discussing "clarity and preciseness" I also looked at "simplicity and brevity". When it comes to the question of the "equality of the sexes", my focus is on the physiological and psychological "differences" and their inherent relationship with real social "equality". The reader would realise without much difficulty that my theoretical analysis of the concept of "gender equality" is mainly from the vantage point of the inherent contradictions within modernity. Regarding the mode of existence and influence of the concept of "gender equality" during the late Qing and early Republican periods, my main aim was also to demonstrate it, through an exposure of the concrete, multidimensional and complex relationship between this concept and the development and recognition of the character *ta* 她. In modern China, both supporters and opponents of the creation of a singular feminine third person pronoun were able to use gender equality as their justification. Even among the supporters, the concept of the equality of the sexes was used to justify their opposition to the character *ta* 她 and their preference for *yi* 伊. This struck me quite deeply. The existence of this contradiction led me to realise that the concept of "gender equality" itself could indeed harbor internal tension and contradiction. Might we possibly see it this way: the reason why the issue of gender equality exists in the first place is because of the difference and distinction that is present between the two sexes as subjects, and if we want to ultimately institute genuine gender equality, then do we have any choice but to rely on a scientific determination as well as a respect for the unique characteristics of each? In other words, the modernist value of gender equality and the modern principle of the clear and precise distinction between men and women is in itself an internally contradictory "whole" which is difficult to dissect.

Because the "social acceptance of the issue" lies elsewhere, my work did not fully present all aspects of the gender equality *Zeitgeist*, nor did it bother to directly affirm the historical rationality and positive value of those calls to not make any distinction between the sexes and to call for absolute equality. But this does not mean that I was not willing to accept the historical rationality and objective historical status this *Zeitgeist* had already possessed. To be honest, to objectively and comprehensively demonstrate and evaluate the modern movement for gender equality was not a task that this small work was capable of, and in any case, the research achievements of our colleagues is already quite impressive.

It is because of the aforementioned concerns that, while describing the calls in early modern China for women to be seen as equals with men, I could not avoid accusing it of being unable to "cast off" the "shortcomings" of the concept of the absolute equality of the sexes. Nonetheless, this still attracted Dr Yang's special criticism. She says that at the time "women's liberation" and "gender equality" was only in its infancy, and so how could its shortcomings be "cast off"?! And how could this "casting off" be accomplished?! "The so-called casting off is probably a wish that the author unintentionally imposed on the historical parties based on his own observations" (page 145). Little does Dr Yang realise that in modern China, like everywhere else in the world, when the idea of the "equality of the sexes" first emerged, the "historical parties" who advocated for equality between men and women were quite complex and diverse. And not all of them believed that women should strive for the "male standard" and be fully manlike. Instead, there were numerous people, perhaps more than people might imagine, who realised to a certain extent that there is no "absolute" equality between the two sexes and that some attention should be paid to their physiological differences and social malleabilities. And for the entire Republican period, the existence and spread of this way of thinking was even more prevalent. Here, this writer would like to offer a few examples from the late Qing as evidence. For example, in 1903 Gong Yuanchang 龚圆常, who was an early advocate of "equal rights for men and women", stressed:

> Among our compatriots, there are some high-minded individuals who have been enraged by the injustice of our social norms and by the simplistic division of the inner and outer quarters. As a result, they have advocated for the equality of men and women. They claim that since the two sexes co-exist and co-habit, their relationship should be one of equality. In theory, this ought to be the case. But men and women are endowed with different skills and responsibilities. Their interests vary and their talents are distinct. In politics and military affairs, men have more advantages than women. In education and art, women have more advantages than men. The two sexes complement one another; they cannot be treated as equal in every respect. In my humble opinion, equal rights are like the equal distribution of wealth. This can only

be achieved when each follows his/her own path and fulfills his/her duties as they support one another and combine their efforts to elevate Chinese civilization to its zenith.[1]

In 1907, when another individual penned an article in *New Women's World of China Magazine* 《中国新女界杂志》 in which they introduced the latest views on gender equality from around the world, they clearly pointed out that from the point of view of production and consumption,

> Men and women can have equal rights without having the same rights. Same rights mean that their rights are exactly the same while equal rights acknowledge that the nature of their rights can be different but are nonetheless equal. Even though there are inner and outer differences between the two sexes, there is no differentiation of upper and lower statuses.

From a physiological perspective, "The physiological differences between men and women are undeniable. However, men's advantages are women's disadvantages and women's advantages are men's disadvantages. Men and women complement each other; this constitutes equal rights",[2] and this was by no means an isolated case.

Not only was this so, but at the end of the Qing there were also those who fully recognised that if gender equality was to be genuinely achieved, the relevant characteristics of the two sexes must be scientifically analysed to clarify where the differences between the two lay and the true relationship between them, and that this should be taken as a precondition. In 1905, the author of the article "The Question of Men and Women" 《男女问题》 which was published in the magazine *Mainland* 《大陆》 can be taken as representative. The article opposed those who made no distinction between men and women and insisted on absolute equality, declaring:

> Some say that women can take on all the work performed by men and shoulder the same responsibilities and be active members of society. This is ludicrous. Even though we advocate for equal rights, there are real differences between the two sexes. It is not enough to argue, those who wish to know where these differences lie must engage in scientific study.

The author also stressed:

> The characteristic differences between men and women are there for all to see. Still, it is hard for a scholar to accept the statement that women are delicate and therefore weak in comparison to men. On what basis can women be considered "delicate"? Even if this is a shortcoming, men also have shortcomings that women do not have and vice versa. In sum, each has different strengths and weaknesses. To be able to explicate the different characteristics of men and women, and allow them to utilize their strengths, we must first

investigate the differences between the two and the nature of their relationship. If one only looks at their outer advantages and disadvantages, and fails to note their inner natures, then that is just narrow-mindedness, and not worthy of our attention.[3]

What is most striking is that in order to encourage his compatriots to investigate the topic "within a scientific framework", the author of the article also earnestly recommended some 20 different relevant titles by scholars from Euro-America and Japan at the time such as *The Evolution of Gender* 《性之进化》, *The Female Sex* 《女性》, *On Male and Female* 《男女论》 and other works on anthropology, biology, and evolution as specialist reference works which he listed at the end of the article. It is obvious that the author was not one of those shallow, uneducated fellows who had no contact with the new knowledge or new thinking of the time.

I have encountered quite a number of points of view similar to those mentioned above amongst the late Qing materials.[4] Their insights may vary in terms of perception or novelty; however, it is obvious that they all approve of or at the least are not opposed to advocating for gender equality. They all oppose any refusal to differentiate between male and female or the concept of the absolute equality of the sexes. To be frank, if we are completely unable to see the rising ideology of gender equality during the late Qing, then we perhaps might overlook the depth of the influence of the interplay between China and the West in this matter, and so, to a certain extent, easily underestimate the level of ideological awareness of gender equality by the people at the time.

I believe that contemporary researchers should not deny the historical rationality, and the importance, of the concept of the absolute equality of the sexes in modern China just because it was imperfect at the time but should examine the questions that exist within the concept itself, which is necessary and beneficial to us in the present day. In any case, just as has been pointed out previously, I approached the complex structure of the physiological "difference" and social "equality" of the sexes from the profound angle of the "innate contradictions within modernity", in order to demonstrate the theoretical deficiencies and deep inherent roots of that absolute equality thinking which ignores the "difference" between the sexes. This is hardly a profound insight. Nonetheless, it does contain some sort of honest historical reflection. But for Dr Yang to mix it up, intentionally or unintentionally, with a discussion of the traditional Chinese saying that "men and women are different" (this can be seen from Dr Yang's assertions such as "What Professor Huang is proposing has here been rejected by that traditional emphasis on the 'difference between men and women' and the 'softness of the female sex'" (p. 144)), which took me by surprise.

In this revised and enlarged edition, in an attempt to reduce the chance of any unnecessary misunderstanding, in places where I discuss the shortcomings of the concept of absolute equality, I have specifically added the phrase "even though this concept did have historical rationality and played an active role at the time." For this, I would seek the reader's indulgence. I would also like to mention that a similar modification has been made when analysing the question of the pronunciation of the *ta* 她 character as "*yi*". Originally, to strengthen the contrast between the suggestion and rule of pronouncing the 她 character as "*yi*" as well as its opposite social outcome, I have declared that from later facts it can be seen that this suggestion and rule seems to be "not only superfluous, but also possibly mistaken – which is certainly rather ironic." Because of this, some scholars criticise me for having made this kind of "wise after the fact" determination. It should be said that if one were to seriously contemplate the narrative language and combine that with the context of my work, then perhaps it might have been more appropriate not to enunciate it in this manner. For this reason, while I have been revising and expanding the work, in order to clarify and highlight my true intent and to avoid any associated misunderstanding, I have solemnly added quotation marks around the two terms "superfluous" and "incorrect", and before it I have added the phrase "in the light of historical hindsight". As to whether or not we are able to use "hindsight" in historical research, opinions can differ, and I have already stated my opinion in the post-script to my original work, so I will not repeat it here.

II

Continuing on, I would like to respond to Dr Yang's third point of criticism regarding the question of the relationship between knowledge of "modernity" and the character *ta* 她. This question would appear to be much more complex than the previous two.

As far as I'm concerned, this work sees "modernity" as a tool to be used in explaining a historical concept, a practice which I employ relatively consciously whilst fully acknowledging its limitations in effecting that explanation. I have included a lengthy endnote on page 171 stressing this fact to which the reader can readily refer. The footnote reads:

> I do not have a "modernisation" or "modernity" complex; however, I do think the two concepts continue to be effective tools for analyzing the specific history of late Qing and Republican China. As an analytical method, they still have the space and the need for improvement and development. In any case, the term "modern" became popular as early as the early 1920s, and by the mid-1930s, the concept of "modernisation" was understood by intellectuals and cultural figures and became an important concept that affected the political and cultural life of the actual society at the time. The open and developing new cultural history research certainly may place an emphasis on "narrative", but it should not reject "analysis" out of hand, let alone restrict analytical tools. . . . In reality, we should adopt a dual attitude of reference and reflection toward the current "new cultural history" of the West, and not blindly sing its praises.

It appears from Dr Yang's criticism that she was not sufficiently attentive to the conscious intent of my dual attitude. Of course, the crux of the question could also be that some sections of my work are still not quite accurate.

In fact, in the last chapter of the work, I principally approached the topic from the standpoint of "modernity" or, to be more precise, I adopted "the demands of modernity" as my theme to survey questions relevant to the process of the creation, socialised recognition and ultimate victory of *ta* 她 over *yi* 伊 and did not, as Dr Yang has accused me, simplistically characterise the victory of *ta* 她 as a result of a complete conformity to "modernity". As my work attests, in the process of the creation and recognition of *ta* 她, some phenomena are unable to be sufficiently explained from the perspective of the contradictory structure of modernity or from the interaction between the multiple factors of modernity. For example, the point about the pronunciation of *ta* 她 ultimately remaining the same as *ta* 他 simply cannot be explained from a narrow perspective of the Chinese people's demand for "modernity". The major role tradition played should also be taken into account. Thus, I remain convinced that in essence the creation and socialised acceptance of *ta* 她 can only properly be attributed to the modernist demands of the Chinese people – including social realities like "the movement for a national language" that reflect such demands – the historical crystallisation and cultural product of the mutual interaction between such factors as Western languages and the traditions of the Chinese language. To put it another way, the "modernist demands and choices" of the modern Chinese people had indeed influenced the beginning and conclusion of the story of *ta* 她. This could be seen as the most active deciding factor, but it was not the only important factor to function single-handedly. As far as the opening scenes of the drama surrounding the character are concerned, they cannot be divorced from the direct stimulus and inspiration of Western languages; and as to the conclusion to the drama, it was even less possible to avoid the peculiar restrictions and subtle influence of tradition.

In addition, in my analysis surrounding the "modernist demands", I did not drift towards one-sidedness or partiality. For example, in my discussion of the influence of the concept of gender equality on character *ta* 她, I not only paid close attention to canvassing those social opinions which opposed *ta* 她 on this basis, but also did not ignore the other aspect of how this concept had a hidden background impetus on the differentiation of *ta* 他. So how could this method of exposing and recognising the positive and negative as well as the multidimensional "impact orientation" of modernity encompass the "resultant conformity with 'modernity'" that Dr Yang criticises?! My strenuous efforts to avoid the modernist "teleology" in my work is plain for all to see.

Is it truly impossible, as Dr Yang believes, to adopt the useful "narrative" methodology of "new cultural history" on the one hand, and retain some traditional elements of historical causal analysis on the other?

Dr Yang's perception of "modernity" is different from mine, but there is no disagreement regarding our analysis of the character *ta* 她 from the perspective of "modernity". Can this be called "unable to resist the temptations of modernity?" To parrot Dr Yang's criticism of my treatment of the idea of absolute gender equality: at a time that is crying out for modernity and where the demand for modernity is just emerging, and when the heads of the Chinese people are filled with "demands of modernity", why should this temptation be resisted? And how might this "resisting" be accomplished? It must be assumed that Dr Yang herself could not be completely satisfied with this type of critique either. Looking through her article as a whole, Dr Yang in fact makes demands of my work according to her own understanding of "modernity" and while I can largely understand her concerns, nevertheless I feel that I am fundamentally unable to agree with her views.

To Dr Yang's mind, I actually employ the concept of "modernity" in two different ways. One is Weberian, i.e., seeing it as a process or general principle of "rationality"; the other resembles that of Leo Ou-fan Lee 李欧梵, i.e., seeing it as "demands of modernity" or "need for modernity".[5] She believes that the latter's understanding of the concept of "modernity" is merely a type of "imagining" by the people of a "modern era", and that it "does not have a set meaning and is riddled with conflicting views"; "as far as historical interpretation is concerned, the former perhaps slips into 'teleology', while the latter would appear to be the better choice." Perhaps because I am fond of using the phrase "modernist demands" in my work, Dr Yang feels that the second style of approach might "more closely" accord with the "real intent" of my work. (p. 142, p. 147). However, this writer's understanding of "modernist demands" does indeed differ from that of Dr Yang. It includes a blend of the relevant connotations of Weber's unique "rational" approach, so it is not surprising why Dr Yang believes that my work ultimately falls into that "teleological" quagmire which it is at such pains to avoid.

In Dr Yang's eyes, my confused application of the Weberian and Leo Ou-fan Lee readings of "modernity" in my work must result in contradiction. Needless to say, I have sought to reconcile these readings to a certain degree. I believe that the abovementioned approaches to the unique characteristics of "modernity" are inevitably static and easily slip into essentialism; meanwhile, a "modernist demands" type approach which takes into account the special dynamic applications of the agents would appear to reveal the tensions even more readily, but one must not proceed from this to the extreme of totally imagining its content. Because after all, it must unavoidably be based on those unique connotations of "modernity" and is certainly not some boundless, random impulse or desire.

In her understanding of "modernity", Dr Yang was probably heavily influenced by post-modernism because she would rather adopt Arif Dirlik's "associating modernity with an epoch", while failing to acknowledge the fixed meaning of the term, as if she were giving people the impression that any age has its own "modernity". This could easily result in "extreme relativism". On the surface, this understanding also pays special attention to the specific historicity of the "modernity" of past eras which is in fact epochal, but it fundamentally ignores the fact that concepts of modernity and modernisation themselves have not always existed and are products that occur at a specific stage of historical development. It also fails to see or is not willing to confront the specific value parameters and historical connotations which the Western post-Renaissance modernist demands relied on and which underpins present-day individuals' understanding of "modernity".[6] Just imagine if there had been no market economy and civil society that took the lead in the West after the Renaissance, no process of industrialisation, no relatively established structural constructs such as the rise of the modern spirit of rationalism with science and democracy as the core value categories. Would "modernisation or modernity" still be concepts that historians could use?

The value of modernity cannot be generated out of thin air. It is a product of historical development and naturally carries its own specific historical connotations. These connotations are not only partly comprised of historical continuity, but they also bear epochal characteristics which transcend those of times past. At the same time, modernity does not automatically play a role; it can only be realised through the sovereign people's "modernist demands and choices". The book *A Cultural History of the Chinese Character "Ta* (她, She)" 《"她"字的文化史》 does not contain a systematic explication of the theory of "modernity", but when it comes to the relevant issues, it consciously follows a middle path of reconciliation. This is why I write:

> The scope of modernity is rich, multidimensional, and contradictory. It carries both a specific historical content like such (epochal) values that are included within the concepts of "science", "democracy", "equality", "freedom", "human rights", "rule of law" etc., and it can also be a general principle that is grasped and understood from the broader perspective of "reason" as well. As far as the latter is concerned, it often has a significance (a continuity) for mankind that transcends historical time and space.

Here, what I originally meant to say was that while modernity contains both "temporal characteristics" and "historical continuity", its specific composition is not necessarily the same. Sometimes its scope is relatively broad and expresses general categories of "reasonableness" (such as "precision", "simplicity" and other Weberian so-called categories of "instrumental rationality"), and it tends to have more historical continuity across the ages (of course, it will inevitably be marked with the stamp of the times and with the new standards of those times). However, I could have been more rigorous and precise in the statement quoted above. For example, the expression "often has a meaning that transcends historical time and space" which was turned into "supra-historical"[7] by Dr Yang in her book review. This led to a bevy of unnecessary discussions, which is most regrettable.

It is worth pointing out that there are two reasons why I am willing to take "precision" along with "simplicity" and "effectiveness" as examples, apart from the inherent contradictory tension within "modernity" which I deeply care about. One is that these categories of "instrumental rationality" are more closely related to the spirit of modern "science". This is especially true of the demand for "precision"; it is also a common understanding of the traditional definition of "modernity". In any era, people will never be completely indifferent to "precision", and people's standards for accuracy or otherwise are not exactly the same in different eras either. What is important is that following the baptism of the modern scientific spirit, people's social attitude towards "precision" and the characteristics of the *zeitgeist* have undergone a fundamental change. This is why Hu Shi and other Chinese Enlightenment thinkers repeatedly criticised the "near enough" (差不多) tradition. Compared to "precision", "simplicity" obviously occupies a relatively secondary and marginal position in the architecture of the demand for modernity, but it does not violate the general principles of modernity. I originally did not want to address this specifically, because it might be distracting. Why not simply take the conclusion that "those overly complex differentiated proposals, such as the bi-divisional 'common gender' and 'neuter' pronouns, will eventually be cast aside by society" and see it as the demands of modernity, as represented by "precision", having "struck the wall" of Chinese tradition? This would simplify matters to no purpose! And intuitively, this is more in line with my macro-concept of seeing it as the fruits of "the interaction between the 'appeal of modernity' and the Chinese tradition". But if we were really to treat it like that, then the question would be unavoidably simplified on another level.

The second reason why I use "precision", "simplicity" and "effectiveness" as examples is that: they were not only the "rational" grounds that those who were concerned about the differentiation of the character *ta* 他 ("he") in modern China most liked to express when they participated in discussions, but they were also the most appealing and convincing categories for Chinese people when they discussed the overall issue of the modernisation and reform of the Chinese language at the time. At the same time, it was inevitable that their demands for "rationality" also contradicted one another.

Of course, I'm not so conceited as to claim that my understanding of the connotations of "modernity" is self-evident. They are merely my comprehension and reflection of mainstream ideas since the late Qing and Republican periods and my overall understanding and imperfect grasp of the demands for "modernity" of the Chinese people at the time. But from this, we can see that Dr Yang's critique of my work for "simplifying the complex modernity into a model that includes 'rationality' (precision, simplicity, and effectiveness)" (page 146), and for thinking that my emphasis on "precision" and so on continues to focus on "the aspect of modernity transcending Westernness" (page 146) is overly "simplistic", even bordering on conjecture. For she fails to understand and accurately grasp my real intentions.

Not only is this the case, but my analysis of the relationship between the character *ta* 她 ("she") and the demands of modernity is primarily based on the historically factual opinions held by those who advocated for and endorsed *ta* 她 as described in previous chapters of the book, and is not simply a logical inference. Objectively speaking, my relevant analysis is restrained. For example, when talking about the role of the "demand for precision", I simply point out that it "had a direct induction effect on those who were engaged in consciously designing the language". That is, it played an inductive role, nothing more. When talking about the impact of the demand for "simplicity", it is inevitable that some mixing of the causes and demands of the results of "social choices" would occur, and that a slight gap would remain. However, a positive correlation also exists at the same time between the factors governing the quest (for modernity) and the results.

The crux of the problem lies in the fact that when discussing the influence of the "demands of modernity" on the differentiation of the character *ta* 他, I did not focus on the sole effect of what I termed the demand for "precision" and "simplicity", but also paid close attention to "the value principle of gender equality and of women's autonomy, and the role played by the popular imagination for democracy." In other words, I merely regarded the demand for "precision" as just one facet of the general "demand for modernity." Moreover, I did not take "the demands of modernity" as the sole reason for the successful popularisation of the character *ta* 她. Instead, to avoid any prejudice or one-sidedness, I gained an integrated grasp of the situation by actively approaching it from the various elements of modernity, and their dynamic interactions with actual social movements, Western languages, and the traditional Chinese language. Thus, viewed independently, Dr Yang's criticism of my "precision" and "simplicity" is not without merit. However, it is fractionalising to single out the relevant analysis of "precision" and "simplicity" in my work and criticise it, whilst ignoring my holistic and dynamic approach to the question of *ta* 她.

The question of "modernity" is extremely complex. One cannot approach it without historical vision or philosophical insight. Like any grand abstract concept, it not only has specific internals which have been shaped by history, but it also has a certain vagueness and unknown connotations; it not only includes some historical "continuity", but also encompasses and embodies a "transcendence" of a specific era and an "openness" towards the future; it is both part of the historical reality that has been presented and even more an "ideal to be realised" (approaching what Habermas calls the "unfinished plan"). What is more, it started organically in the West following the Renaissance, and it bears the characteristics of interminable expansion across the globe. In the dual embrace of history and philosophy, the former undoubtedly occupies a fundamental position,[8] while the latter is inseparable from humanity's deep understanding of its own "rationality" as well as from humanity's reliance on "rationality" to continuously reflect on the enhanced wisdom of their place in the universe.

I believe that with such a dynamic grasp of "modernity" from an overall historical starting point, the future of this endeavor might avoid falling into the trap of a linear historical view of human society and of so-called "teleology".

At this point, I am afraid I have a small confession to make, namely that for a "modernity" that may never be ultimately complete, while I personally have no particular "complex" that I cherish, nevertheless some anticipation remains; as to mankind's unlimited possibilities for "rational" advancement (and here I by no means am restricting myself to Weber or Habermas' understanding of "rational"), I also harbor some unavoidable expectation. Because, apart from this, I really cannot see what else human beings can hope for. If this misty "rational" expectation of "modernity", which has been improved through continuous reflection, is also to be deemed to be the work of the "teleology" of modernity, then I will have no choice but to accept it calmly, even gladly.

The above are some of my responses to Dr Yang's discussion. If any part is deemed inaccurate, I am happy to be corrected.

(Originally carried in 2015 Issue 3 of *Modern Chinese History Studies* 《近代史研究》. Slightly abridged)

Notes

1 Gong, Yuanchang 龚圆常, "On Equal Rights for Men and Women"《男女平权说》, carried in *Jiangsu*《江苏》, Tokyo, 1903, Issue 4, p. 145.
2 Chan, Bi 忏碧, "Traditional Views on Women's Issues and Modern Theories"《妇人问题之古来观念及最近学说》, originally carried in *New Women's World of China Magazine*《中国新女界杂志》1907, Issue 5. See Li, Youning 李又宁 and Zhang, Yufa 张玉法 (eds.), *Historical Materials on the Feminist Movement in Modern China*《近代中国女权运动史料》, Vol. 1, Taibei: Longwen Publishing Co., Ltd., 1995, pp. 247–248.
3 Anon. 佚名, "The Question of Men and Women"《男女问题》, carried in *Mainland*《大陆》, Shanghai, Vol. 3, No. 6, 1905, p. 5.
4 For example, those who advanced similar opinions from the point of view of education included the article "On the Advantages and Disadvantages of Male-female Co-education"《论男女共学之利害》, see *Education World*《教育世界》1904, Issue 3 (Cum. Issue 71), p. 7.
5 Whether or not Dr Yang's summary of Mr Leo Ou-fan Lee's 李欧梵 view is accurate perhaps requires further analysis. For the moment, I simply pass it on.
6 To Dr Yang's mind, "Modern China" and "modernity" are therefore constructed of various actual "relationships" that exist within this period and that it should only be regarded as "a definition of the Sino-Western relationship or the relationship between tradition and modernity in a particular era" (p. 147), and that it is not appropriate to make an essential overall summary.
7 See the so-called "If modernity has a supra-historical dimension" statement. I would also like to point out that Dr Yang's discussion of this question in her paper takes a number of leaps of logic and personal assumptions with regard to my narrative, many of which I myself am not willing to make, like her claim that "'rationality' transcends historical time and space" (p. 146), which readers may wish to take a look at.
8 See Huang, Xingtao 黄兴涛, "The Question of 'Modernity', a New Term and a New Concept in the Late Qing and Early Republican Period: Revisiting China's Recognition of the Concepts of 'Ideological Modernity' and Modern 'Society'"《清末民初新名词新概念的"现代性"问题 – 兼谈"思想现代性"与现代"社会"概念的中国认同》, carried in *Tianjin Social Sciences*《天津社会科学》, 2005 (4).

Appendix III
Illustrations and Figures

0.1   A section of Zhen Xin's 枕薪 article "Miss" which opposes women labelling themselves as "Miss".   vii

0.2   In 1878, Guo Zansheng 郭赞生 translated the book *English School Grammar* 《文法初阶》, in which he first used the Chinese "他, 伊, 彼" to translate "he, she, it".   viii

0.3   In 1917, Liu Bannong 刘半农 is the first editor of *New Youth* 《新青年》 magazine to propose the use of the word "*Ta* 她" but he is not the first practitioner. He elucidated the question systematically in his 1920 article "On the Question of the Character *Ta* 她" 《"她" 字问题》.   viii

0.4   In 1918, Zhou Zuoren 周作人 was the first person to discuss the question of "*Ta* 她" publicly in *New Youth* 《新青年》 magazine. He also advocated imitating the Japanese translation of *Kanojo* 彼女 by using the two Chinese characters *ta'nü* 他女. Later Ye Shengtao 叶圣陶 et al. followed his creation and used *ta'nü* 他女.   ix

0.5   The article "The Discussion over the Translation of the English 'She'" 《英文"she"字译法之商榷》 published in *New Youth* 《新青年》 in April, 1919. Qian Xuantong 钱玄同 proposed creating a character *Ta/To* 她 but Zhou Zuoren 周作人 argued that both "*Ta* 她" and "*To* 她" shared the same pronunciation and so preferred to use *Yi* 伊. This idea had an enormous impact. Later *Ta* 她 and *Yi* 伊 began to compete in discussions and practice, resulting in *Yi* 伊 at one stage gaining the upper hand.   ix

0.6   Two of the earliest formal uses of the *Ta* 她 word in Kang Baiqing 康白情's article "A Harbinger of Male-Female Relations in Peking's Student World" 《北京学生界男女交际之先声》, carried in *The Morning Post* 《晨报》, May 20, 1919.   x

0.7   The poem "Bidding Her Farewell" 《别她》 is the first poem to refer to the nation as *Ta* 她 and was carried in *The Renaissance* 《新潮》, February 1920.   x

0.8   "She?" 《她么》 is the first new poem to use "*Ta* 她" in its title, written by Jin Dezhang 金德章 and carried in *The Republican Daily News* 《民国日报》, March 12, 1920.   xi

200 *Appendix III*

0.9 Qian Xingcun 钱杏邨 published the poem "The Dahlia" 《大丽花》 (carried in *Emancipation Pictorial* 《解放画报》 Issue 13, July 30, 1921), and is an example of how the character *yi* 伊 was used in verse to represent the feminine third person. xi

0.10 "Whose Fault? Why Did She Commit Suicide?!" 《谁的罪，她为甚么要自杀？！》, drawn by Lin Xin 麟心, *Emancipation Pictorial* 《解放画报》 Issue 13, July 1921. This is probably the earliest work of art to use *ta* 她. The author denounces the banal feudal concept of being "faithful to one's husband unto death" which, like an evil apparition, was poisoning and devastating the women of China. xii

0.11 In 1921, *Emancipation Pictorial* 《解放画报》 used *ta* 她 as part of Women's Liberation Movement to fight against the oppression and constraint of the old society. xii

0.12 *Emancipation Pictorial* 《解放画报》 is the first magazine to use the character *ta* 她 in an illustration. This contributed greatly to the artistic practice of using the word *ta* 她. xiii

0.13 Such New Culture Movement magazines as *The Renaissance* 《新潮》, *The Journal of the Young China Association* 《少年中国》 and *The Short Story Magazine* 《小说月报》 were the largest contributors to the use of the word *ta* 她 in writing practice. xiv

0.14 Female writers used *ta* 她 in their works before 1924: Lu Yin 庐隐 (top-left), Bing Xin 冰心 (top-middle), Chen Hengzhe 陈衡哲 (top-right), Feng Yuanjun 冯沅君 (bottom-left), Shi Pingmei 石评梅 (bottom-right). xiv

0.15 Section of "Down with '*Yingci*'!" 《打倒"英雌"》, carried in *The Pei-yang Pictorial News* 《北洋画报》, Issue 1115, 1934. xv

0.16 "*Ta* (他), *Ta* (她), *Ta* (牠), and *Ta* (它)" 《"他"、"她"、"牠"、"它"》, carried in *The Pei-yang Pictorial News* 《北洋画报》, Issue 1080, 1934. xvi

0.17 "Announcement: This Magazine Refuses to Use the Character *ta* 她" 《本刊拒用"她"字启事》, *Women's Voice* 《妇女共鸣》, 1934. xvii

0.18 Cover of *Women's Voice* 《妇女共鸣》. xvii

0.19 "'*Ta* 她' and the Women's Movement" 《"她"与妇运》, carried in *The Decameron* 《十日谈》, Issue 34, 1934, criticizing *Women's Voice* 《妇女共鸣》's refusal to use *ta* 她, arguing that this was grasping at shadows and abandoning the substantive. xviii

0.20 Yang Gang 杨刚, "*Tiao* (frivolous) – Mei Lanfang" 《亻她–梅兰芳》, *True Words* 《真话》, Issue 1, 1946. The writer satirically uses 亻她 to refer in the third-person singular to a female character in Chinese opera. xviii

0.21	Historian Chen Yinke's 陈寅恪, "Discussing National Language Examination Topics with Professor Liu Wendian" 《与刘文典教授论国文试题书》, carried in *The Critical Review* 《学衡》, Issue 79, in which he publicly opposes the use of *ta* 她 and states that he has never used the word *ta* 她 in his life.	xix
0.22	Zhou Shoujuan 周瘦鹃, representative of the Mandarin Ducks and Butterflies School 鸳鸯蝴蝶派. He long opposed the use of *ta* 她 and advocated using *yi* 伊, only to surrender in 1943 and publicly use the word *ta* 她. See "Foreword to Violets" 《写在紫罗兰前头》, carried in *Violets* 《紫罗兰》 magazine, Issue 2, May 1943.	xix
0.23	A section from Zhou Shoujuan's "Foreword to Violets" 《写在紫罗兰前头》, carried in *Violets* 《紫罗兰》 magazine, Issue 2, May 1943.	xx
1.1	The Chinese translation of the word "she", Robert Morrison, *A Dictionary of the Chinese Language*, 1822 edition, reprint from the 1996 Japanese version, Vol. 6, p. 388.	8
1.2	Morrison and his assistants.	8
1.3	Wilhelm Lobscheid's translation of "she", "he", and "it" in his *Chinese-English Grammar* 《英话文法小引》. See the 1864 Hong Kong edition of this work, Section 2, p. 7.	9
1.4	*English School Grammar* 《文法初阶》 clearly translates "she", "he" and "it" as *ta* 他, *yi* 伊, and *bi* 彼 in order to address gender distinction. But he reverses the terms when he applies them to animals. From the context, it appears that this is but a slip of the pen.	12
2.1	Cover of *New Youth*, Vol. 5, No. 2, 1918.	16
2.2	Zhou Zuoren's relatively early use of *ta'nü* 他女 as published in his translation of *The Little Match Girl* in January-February 1919.	18
2.3	Responding to Zhou Zuoren's suggestion, the New Literature writer Ye Shaojun (Ye Shengtao) is the first to employ the term *ta'nü* 他女 in a work of fiction.	19
2.4	A section of Ye Shaojun's "Spring Excursion" 《春游》 where he employs the term "*ta'nü*" 他女.	21
2.5	The linguist Qian Xuantong who was the first to engage in the discussion of the question of the character *ta* 她.	23
3.1	A portrait of some members of the Young China Association. Fifth from the right is Kang Baiqing, the earliest and most comprehensive adopter of the character *ta* 她.	29
3.2	A section from the earliest short story to use the character *ta* 她 in the creative process – Kang Baiqing's "Society" 《社会》.	32
3.3	Yu Pingbo 俞平伯, who was a relatively early adopter of the character *ta* 她 in literary creation.	34
3.4	The novelist Wang Tongzhao 王统照, a relatively early experimenter in the use of the character *ta* 她 in creative writing.	36

3.5	Liu Fu (Liu Bannong)'s "Love Song" 《情歌》 carried in *The Morning Post Supplement* 《晨报副刊》, 1923.	38
3.6	An extract from Zhou Zuoren's relatively early translated work "Three Dreams in the Desert" 《沙漠间的三个梦》 in which he used *yi* 伊 as the feminine third person pronoun.	44
4.1	Compilation of previous articles discussing the character *ta* 她, *New Man* 《新人》 magazine, Vol. 2.	50
4.2	A section of Han Bing's article "Further Discussion on 'the Question of the Character *Ta* 她'" 《续论"她字问题"》 in which he rejected the use of *ta* 她.	55
4.3	Magazine cartoons continue to use the character *ta* 他 *to* refer to women. Taken from Issue 5, September 1920 of *Emancipation Pictorial* 《解放画报》.	59
4.4	The *yi* 伊 character is used to specifically refer to the feminine and to illustrate the plight of women. Originally carried in the May 1921 Issue 11 of *Emancipation Pictorial* 《解放画报》.	63
5.1	You Luan 友鸾 uses the character "男也" and the word "男士" in the work "'Miss [女士]' and 'She [她]'".	73
5.2	The writer Zhu Ziqing who recorded and evaluated the entertaining early discussion of the character *ta* 她.	76
5.3	A section of Zhen Xin's article *Miss* which opposes women labelling themselves as "Miss".	77
5.4	Fragments of Qiu Jin's novel *Stones of the Jingwei Bird* employed the term "Heroine" 英雌. Taken from the 1958 *The Exploits of* Qiu Jin 《秋瑾史迹》, Zhonghua Shuju.	82
5.5	A section of "Refusing to Use the Character *Ta* 她". The article castigates as "idly toying with a character" the announcement by *Women's Voice* 《妇女共鸣》 that they refused to use the character *ta* 她.	89
5.6	A section from "On the Refusal to Use the Character *Ta* 她 and a Question for *Reading Life*". The article supports the position of boycotting the use of the character *ta* 她.	92
6.1	A snippet of Qian Xuantong's highly original and brilliant essay in which he probes the question of *ta* 她, and advocates, for the first time, for the use of the character *ta* 它 as the neuter third person pronoun.	102
6.2	Excerpt from Tsinghua University student He Yongji's 何永佶 (Yifan/Ivan 伊凡) article "Invention and the Nature of Slavishness" 《发明与奴隶的根性》 explaining the process and his reasons for inventing the pronoun *ta* 牠.	108
6.3	Cover of the third edition of *Immensee* 《茵梦湖》, translated by Guo Moruo et al.	110
7.1	Lu Xun begins to use the *ta* 她 character from the end of 1923 to the beginning of 1924.	117

7.2	A section from the original publication in *Eastern Miscellany* of Lu Xun's short story "New Year's Sacrifice" 《祝福》 at the beginning of 1924 in which he officially used the character *ta* 她 to create the immortal female literary image of Aunt Xianglin 祥林嫂.	118
7.3	Li Jinhui 黎锦晖's song "*Ta* 他 [he], *Ta* 她 [she], and *Ta* 牠 [it]" carried in Issue 69, 1923 of *Little Friend* 《小朋友》.	121
7.4	Cover of Volume II of the *National Language Textbook for the New Education System* 《新学制国语教科书》.	125
7.5	Cover of the 1932 edition of *Pronunciation Dictionary of Common National Language Terms* 《国音常用字汇》.	127
7.6	Cover of the *Standard Student Dictionary of the Sounds of the National Language* 《标准国音学生字典》.	128
7.7	Chen Yinke 陈寅恪 who was opposed to the character *ta* 她.	132
7.8	A section from Chen Yinke's 陈寅恪 essay "Discussing National Language Examination Topics with Professor Liu Wendian" 《与刘文典教授论国文试题书》.	133
7.9	A section of Li Xiaotong 厉筱通's article "The Question of the Vulgar Scripted 她 and 牠" 《"她"和"牠"的俗书问题》.	134
7.10	A section from Zhou 周瘦鹃's "Foreword to Violets" 《写在紫罗兰前头》.	139
8.1	A section from Jin Fushen 金福申's neglected article "The Pronoun *Ta* (他, he) and *Ta* (她, she)" 《代名词他(He)同她(She)》. The article indeed displays much brilliance.	147
8.2	Drawn by Linxin 麟心. In the sketch the text reads, "She (她) is also the husband's flesh and blood, so why hate her (她) so?" By using *ta* 她, the aim is to criticise society's discrimination against women and especially women's self-deprecating behavior. Originally carried in *Emancipation Pictorial* 《解放画报》 Vol. 14 (August 1921).	156
8.3	Drawn by Linxin 麟心. In the sketch the text reads, "The weapon lies beside her (她) but she (她) chooses not to use it. Could it be that she (她) does not wish to be free of these fetters?!" The two *ta* 她 characters are laden with the cry for "women's liberation" and express a lamentation for the subject's misfortune or resentment at her failure to struggle, calling on women to save themselves. Originally carried in *Emancipation Pictorial* 《解放画报》 Vol. 15 (September 1921).	157
8.4	Drawn by Linxin 麟心. Responding to the old lady who is lecturing the young girl, "Young girls are not allowed to question matters of societal or national affairs." The author comments, "Is she (她) willing to continue to submit herself to this type of discourse which shackles women?!" Originally carried in *Emancipation Pictorial* 《解放画报》 Vol. 16 (October 1921).	158

204 *Appendix III*

8.5 Drawn by Linxin 麟心. In the sketch the text reads, "This mother and daughter-in-law interplay illustrates the evil practices of the autocratic household. To me, she (她) is merely torturing her own sex. Why is this not reformed immediately?!" Originally carried in *Emancipation Pictorial* 《解放画报》 Vol. 16 (October 1921). 159

8.6 Drawn by Ying Xia 映霞. The text in the sketch reads, "The only thing that her (她) heart desires (indicating US$), she (她) will do anything you ask." Originally carried in *Emancipation Pictorial* 《解放画报》 Vol. 14 (August 1921). The author uses this to lament her protagonist's misfortune and her failure to put up a fight. 160

8.7 Drawn by Ying Xia 映霞. The text in the sketch is headed "In the Boudoir" 《深闺》, "Why does she sit here all day and not go and do something worthwhile. She appears to be locked in a prison. Of what use is such a person?" Originally carried in *Emancipation Pictorial* 《解放画报》 Vol. 14 (August 1921). 161

8.8 This sketch drawn by Jing Rong 镜蓉 is the earliest Chinese illustration that I have seen that uses the female figure to represent the motherland while at the same time using the character *ta* 她 in the description. Originally carried in Issue 17 of *Emancipation Pictorial* 《解放画报》 on November 30, 1921, the text in the sketch reads, "She (*ta* 她) has been fettered for more than four thousand years and is already half paralysed. Now she (*ta* 她) is aided to walk, and will eventually become mobile." Here not only is the motherland represented by the female form, but a female is supporting "her" (*ta* 她) to rise up and move, thus establishing the feminine form in the context of the construction of the modern nation state through a conceit of symbolism and agency. 164

8.9 Yan Fu 严复 (left) and Gu Hongming 辜鸿铭 (right), both well versed in Western knowledge and the English language but opposed to republicanism and thus indirectly opposed to the use of the character *ta* 她. 167

Afterword

Some may question why I have expended so much effort on the history of such a small term "she" and whether such an effort was worth it. My response would be: Indeed, it has been worth it! Events in history certainly must be divided into large and small, but the criteria for division differ. For modern and "post" modern people whose hearts and minds are increasingly refined and whose thirst for "wisdom" remains unabated, it is vital to gain from the clever insights and wise mastery of historians as they present their various "histories"; so as to experience the vastness of humanistic reflection and attain meaningful appreciation. And from this perspective, can the question of "she" be said to be small?!

Hu Shi wrote during the May Fourth period, "All learning is equal. Working out the ancient meaning of a word and discovering a star are both great feats" ("On National History – Responding to Mao Zishui" 《论国故学 – 答毛子水》). I do appreciate the meaning and weight of this statement. Compared to those illustrious platitudes that people mouth about how the national academic policies on the humanities, social sciences and natural sciences are the "two wheels of a car or two wings of a bird", Hu Shi's statement is obviously more down to earth, perceptive, and inspired, and at the same time, much more brilliant. While the history of *ta* 她 is by no means "ancient", for the people of today it has long been "both clear and obscure," especially since I do not limit myself to a traditional linguistic study of the history of the character, but instead have committed to a multi-faceted excavation of the connotations of its cultural history. If Chen Yinke's sentence "Every explanation of an individual character is a work of cultural history" which I have mentioned in my "Introduction" is a methodological pointer to my research, then Hu Shi's remarks represent my own aspirations and motivations in writing this small book – or perhaps they serve as some measure of self-assurance.

I officially embarked on my research of the history of the word "she" from 2003 to 2004. As a visiting scholar at the Harvard-Yenching Institute at that time, the research topic I proposed was not a new project, but rather it was a continuation of the National Social Science Fund project which I had been funded to undertake in 2000, namely "The Formation and Dissemination of New Terms in Modern China and the Modern Transformation of Academic Culture"《近代中国新名词的形成、传播与学术文化的现代转型》. The question of *ta* 她 is merely a newly established part of that project. On July 26, 2005, *Guangming Daily* 《光明日报》 published my clumsy piece "Also Discussing the Invention of the '*Ta* 她' and '*Yi* 伊' Characters" 《也谈"她"字的发明与"伊"字》 which led to some discussion, and it aroused my interest in gathering a more comprehensive collection of relevant materials and undertaking a systematic study. At the end of 2006 I completed the document "The Story of the Character *Ta* 她: Invention, Debate and Early Circulation" 《"她"字的故事：女性新代词符号的发明、论争与早期流播》 which basically achieved my initial goal. The article was published in April of the following year in the inaugural issue of *New History* 《新史学》 (also initiated by colleagues). Before the article appeared, I was invited to take part in "The Continuing Development of Comprehensive Research on Science and Art in East Asia" "东亚科学与艺术综合研究的继续发展" international conference in Japan to which I submitted and presented the article. The article and my presentation gave rise to lively debate and at the same time, resulted in much positive input from various Chinese and Japanese scholars from different academic disciplines (which I have mentioned in Chapter 8 of this work). Unfortunately, at the time I did not have the opportunity to make any further revisions to the paper. Not long afterwards the article appeared publicly in *New History* 《新史学》 where it received even more attention and encouragement. Sun Jiang 孙江 in particular constantly pushed me to expand and improve the paper, and also partially translated it into Japanese for class discussion, which moved me tremendously. In the two years since, with the constant urging of my colleague Sun Jiang, along with generous assistance from such friends as Zhang Shouan 张寿安, Chen Jianhua 陈建华, Yang Nianqun 杨念群, Xia Mingfang 夏明方, Wang Qisheng 王奇生, Shen Guowei 沈国威, and Zhu Jingwei 朱京伟, as well as my wife Liu Hui 刘辉, I have continued to add and revise the content substantially so as to further enrich and perfect the original research.

Whilst completing this small work, I made four demands of myself. One was to present as many "stories" about the character *ta* 她 as possible. That is, the origins of the character, the disputes over different design schemes, the earliest written practice of the character, and the cultural intent as well as the specific and moving historical process of the different questions of recognition that appeared during its practice, taking great pains to combine "narrative" with "textual verification". Second, using the form of illustrations, to try to present the original form of the carrier texts when the character "she" and its sister characters were first used or debated in the early days, as well as the individual style of the user, hoping to give readers a sense of the historical context. Third, on the basis of the first two, to reveal as many relevant historical connections as possible whilst undertaking some modest analysis and comment and trying to avoid over-interpretation. Fourth: not just to concentrate on the words, but to remember the people as well. After all, words are used by people. Lexical research without reference to "people", "environment" or "historical connotations" should not be the main pursuit of historians. As for the extent to which I fulfilled the abovementioned demands of myself, I will leave it to the readers to comment. In addition, in order to help readers understand my research intent, I have specifically attached my 2007 article "Some Reflections on Research into Cultural History" 《文化史研究的省思》 to this work for reference.

Research on the word "she" (*ta* 她) is only one result of my long-term research into new Chinese terms in the modern era. Originally, I did not intend to publish it as a monograph, but later changed my mind at the suggestion of friends. What I need to make clear is that although the cultural connotations of the word "she" (*ta* 她) are rich, as a concept its inherent ideological tension is still limited and does not fully reflect my pursuit of research on the history of modern Chinese neologisms. This is the single unavoidable regret that I have in publishing this work.

The research and writing of this book to a certain extent has been influenced by the Western "New Cultural History", however I have also tried not to be constrained by some of the more extreme inclinations of post-modernism and am willing to "seek the truth" through traditional historiography and to pursue an appropriate search for cause and effect (and do my best to avoid the temptation of "teleology") along with persevering in the belief of "learning from the past". To my mind, the view that "New Cultural History" should only focus on micro-issues is also just a superficial view. The purpose of new cultural history is not to reveal micro-phenomena, but rather the overall significance of these. Only if its purpose is thus, is it more worthy of our enterprise.

In fact, there are many similarities between the "New Cultural History" and the "old" tradition of studying history during the Republican era. Take Mr Chen Yinke for example. His strong interest in "proving history with poetry" and his special emphasis on the historical connotations of language and script, his unique efforts to integrate intellect, psyche, language, and literature, as well as gender history in the one forge in his later years all coincide with many manifestations of "new cultural history", except that his expression is more "old style". All these days while proofreading the manuscript for this book, I have been constantly reading the 800,000-character masterpiece of Mr Chen's senior years, the *Unofficial Biography of Liu Rushi* 《柳如是別傳》. Apart from constantly experiencing the "spirit of independence and free thought" that flickers between the lines of his work, I also strongly sense the boldness and novelty of his philosophy of curating history. At the same time, all through the text we encounter the "Gentleman from East of the River"[1] yet no trace of the word "she" (*ta* 她), so it seems I may have discovered the answer to the question that I pose myself in the "Introduction" to this book. I seem to hear the old man, faced with the "rampantly proliferating" word "she" (*ta* 她), crying stubbornly from deep within his soul: I have good reason not to use the word "she" (*ta* 她), and have the freedom not use it! This has nothing to do with my historical research method.

Of course, due to the limitation of my own knowledge structure and cognitive ability, there will unavoidably still be many defects and even errors in this work which need to be augmented or corrected by colleagues. The breadth and depth of the world of the humanities always makes researchers feel "inadequate" and filled with awe. What is more, gaining "hindsight" is the social responsibility of historians, a fact that has continuously inspired countless of its practitioners to pursue it with difficulty. This kind of "precarious existence" has long been the fate that sober historians have found it hard to extricate themselves from, and in the course of writing this book, I have constantly maintained this sense of sobriety.

Finally, I would like to express my heartfelt gratitude to those fellow scholars, friends, teachers, and students who have provided selfless help to me in completing this small work. I have mentioned most of them in various comments, so I will not repeat them here. I would like to especially mention Professor Fang Weigui 方维规, however. Professor Fang is a colleague and friend of many years. On this occasion he kindly supplied the preface and offered encouragement for which I am most grateful. In addition, Lin Guanzhen 林冠珍 and Chen Yiming 陈一鸣 of Fujian Education Publishing House worked extraordinarily hard to see the publication of this book. Not only did they put forward many helpful suggestions, but they also helped me reproduce those unique photos, and for this I would like to express my appreciation.

Huang Xingtao 黄兴涛
The Institute of Qing History, Renmin University of China
July 25, 2009

Note

1 Here he is being ironic since the "Gentleman from East of the River" 河东君 was in fact a woman.

Afterword to the Revised Edition

It is already five years since my humble work *A Cultural History of the Chinese Character "Ta* (她, She)*" – Research on the Invention and Adoption of a New Feminine Pronoun* 《"她"字的文化史：女性新代词的发明与认同研究》 first saw the light of day. In these five years, it has met with the encouragement of many scholars, some whom I have met and others that I have not, and it has also received many unexpected awards. That such a small "biography" of a single word "she" (*ta* 她) could have such an impact, to be honest, has long since exceeded my expectations. What is particularly gratifying is that this kind of research, which is rather like detective work and inevitably considered "micro", has not only attracted the attention, and even praise of friends in language and literature circles and gender studies, but it has also quickly gained the approval of many fellow historians, which demonstrates the inclusiveness of this ancient, far-reaching, and profound discipline. For me, in this cacophonous era, to be able to settle down and make a real effort towards the accumulation of knowledge, no matter how small, gives one a real sense of fulfillment.

At the beginning of 2015, Beijing Normal University Press hoped to update and republish *A Cultural History of the Chinese Character "Ta* (她, She)*"* 《"她"字的文化史》, and I readily agreed. The present update has mainly accomplished the following tasks: One is to take the opportunity to add some valuable new materials, such as the relationship between Guo Moruo 郭沫若 and the word "it" (*ta* 牠); Lu Xun's 鲁迅 textual battle over the character *ta* 她 ("she"); the song "*Ta* 他 [he], *Ta* 她 [she], and *Ta* 牠 [it]" 《他、她、牠》 published by Li Jinhui 黎锦晖, the "Father of Popular Music" in 1923 to promote the correct understanding and usage of third-person singular pronouns; Cai Xiaozhou's 蔡晓舟 proposal to the China Education Society on the word "she" (*ta* 她) in 1924 and the content of the resolution passed at that meeting; a number of distinctive new relevant illustrations, and so on. At the same time, I have also added some previous research done by other scholars that I originally omitted. The second was to modify some parts of the text. For example, in order to avoid misunderstanding, the title of Chapter 8 has been changed to "The Quest for Modernity and the Interaction between Foreign Language Factors and Chinese Language Traditions", with the addition of the words "Foreign Language Factors" in particular. In the first section of the chapter, the original title was changed to "Identical in Sound with *ta* 他 but Slightly Different in

Form: the Main Reason Why *Ta* 她 Won Against *Yi* 伊". The phrase "Slightly different in form" was added, but the basic point of view remained the same. Also, in order to standardise the titles of the chapters in the book, subtitles have been added to the third, fourth, and seventh chapters respectively. Additionally, the sections on "Events in the history of culture" and its narrative methods, along with theoretical thinking on the issue of "modernity" and its relationship to the generation of the term "she" (*ta*, 她) and its social acceptance have been augmented somewhat in order to further clarify the original point.

In this update, so as to make up for omissions and to make improvements wherever possible, I also found the time to read some 20 or so relevant reviews of my work that appeared both at home and abroad following its publication. While the authors of the book reviews mostly have encouragement for the work, some do also offer criticisms or suggestions. Unfortunately, due to time constraints, data limitations or differences in understanding, this update can only be adjusted for certain individual expressions and cannot be revised more fully. It is especially worth noting that in the process of revising the book, I was fortunate in being able to view Dr Yang Jianli's review "Modernity and the Recognition of the Character '*Ta* 她'", which was quite enlightening and at the same time, thought provoking. Because I have responded to the criticisms raised in the article and I have included it as an appendix to this updated edition, I hope it will be of some assistance in helping readers understand the views and inferences of my work.

Finally, I would like to take the opportunity presented by this present update to express my sincere thanks to Liang Wendao 梁文道, Zhao Gang 赵刚, Zhang Zhongmin 张仲民, Hu Qizhu 胡其柱, Shen Jie 沈洁, Yue Xiukun 岳秀坤, Jia Yongmei 贾永梅, Hu Chuanji 胡传吉, Bi Xinwei 毕新伟, Hu Wenhui 胡文辉, Zhang Junfeng 张俊峰, Wang Fei 王飞, Cao Jing 曹静, Ni Xuejun 倪雪君, Li Qian 李倩, Li Yue Jing 栗月静, Wang Tiangen 王天根, Yang Jianli 杨剑利 and all other scholars who have written reviews of my book. Their comments will certainly assist me in undertaking further reflection. In the process of writing and updating the original book, Dai Yi 戴逸, Li Wenhai 李文海, Gong Shuduo 龚书铎, Wang Sizhi 王思治, Wang Rufeng 王汝丰, Wang Daocheng 王道成, Shi Song 史松, Li Peifen 李佩芬, and other senior scholars kindly agreed to my interviews, and the three gentlemen Li Wenhai 李文海, Gong Shuduo 龚书铎, and Wang Sizhi 王思治 especially, whom, while they have all passed away, still their instruction and encouragement will be imprinted on my heart forever. After the book was published, Mr Li Wenhai took the initiative to propose an academic seminar, which not only surprised me, but also filled me with warmth. My colleagues and I will not forget this esteemed scholar's expectations for academic innovation. In addition, Yu Hualin 余华林, Shen Jie 沈洁, Han Qiuhong 韩秋红, Chen Peng 陈鹏, and others assisted in access to other materials and Zhang Zhongmin 张仲民, Qu Jun 瞿骏, and others provided reference suggestions, for which I would also like to thank them. At the same time, I would like to thank editor Wang Ning 王宁 of Beijing Normal University Press for her hard work in publishing the updated edition of this book and for changing the illustrations.

Huang Xingtao
Beijing, March 2015

References

1. Relevant Qing and Republican period newspaper and magazine articles, works by various figures, poetry collections (including those edited by contemporaries), interviews (including memoirs of Republican figures who have been interviewed recently) and different types of dictionaries.

    1. Chen, Hengzhe 陈衡哲, "West Wind" 《西风》, *The Eastern Miscellany* 《东方杂志》, Vol. 21, No. 17.
    2. Chen, Meiyan 陈美延 ed., *Chen Yinke's Collection of Letters* 《陈寅恪集·书信集》, Beijing: SDX Joint Publishing Company, 2001.
    3. Chen, Sibai 陈斯白, "Opinions on the Differentiation of the Character *Ta* 他 (he)" 《"他"字分化的意见》, carried in *Light of Learning* 《学灯》, October 8, 1921.
    4. Chen, Wangdao 陈望道, "Reply to Mr. Gong Dengchao's Doubts over '*New Examples of Assigned Characters*'" 《答龚登朝先生对于〈用字新例〉"怀疑的所在"》, carried in *Enlightenment Magazine* 《觉悟》, October 16, 1921.
    5. Chen, Wangdao 陈望道, "The Female Third Person 'Pronoun'" 《女子性第三身"身次代名词"》, *Enlightenment Magazine* 《觉悟》, May 3, 1920.
    6. Chen, Wangdao 陈望道, *Handout on Composition* 《作文法讲义》, Minzhi Bookstore in March 1922.
    7. Chen, Wangdao 陈望道, Ye Chucang 叶楚伧, Chu Xuanlu 沈玄庐, Shao Lizi 邵力子, Liu Dabai 刘大白 and etc., *New Examples of Assigned Characters* 《用字新例》, *The Republican Daily News*, 1920.
    8. Chen, Yaoming 陈耀明, "*She* 她: *The Most Important Character in 21st Century*" 《她：21世纪最重要的一个字》, *Golden Time*, No. 4, 2000.
    9. Chen, Yinke 陈寅恪, "Discussing National Language Examination Topics with Professor Liu Wendian" 《与刘文典教授论国文试题书》, *The Critical Review* 《学衡》 magazine, Vol. 79, published by the Zhonghua Bookstore, 1933.
    10. Chu bei ying ci 楚北英雌, "Decrying Women's Rights in China" 《支那女权愤言》, *Hubei Student's World* 《湖北学生界》, Vol. 2, February 1903, pp. 95–96.
    11. [Shi] Cuntong [施]存统, "The Two Unsightly Characters for Miss" 《看不惯女士二字》, *Random Impressions* column of *Enlightenment Magazine* 《觉悟》, April 5, 1920.
    12. Da, Tong 大同, "Research on the 'Third Person Pronoun'" 《"第三身代名词"底研究》, carried in *New Man* 《新人》, Issue 2, April 1920.
    13. Da, Tong 大同, "The Third Person Feminine Pronoun in Drama" 《戏剧里第三身女性代名词》, *Communication* column of *Enlightenment Magazine* 《觉悟》, June 7, 1921.

14. Deng, Niudun 邓牛顿 (comp.), "Missing Items from Guo Moruo's *Goddess* Collection" 《郭沫若（女神）集外佚文》 (1919–1921)", *Nankai University Journal* 《南开大学学报》, No. 3, 1978.
15. Dong, Yinhu 董阴狐, *Forced Marriage of a Heroine* 《英雌夺婚记》 (6-chaptered fiction), Social Welfare Newspaper Press, 1927.
16. Fang, Ru 方儒, "Fei Mu Perspicaciously Recognizes a Heroine" 《费穆慧眼识英雌》, *Shanghai Tan* 《上海滩》 Issue 4, 1946.
17. *Women's Voice* 《妇女共鸣》 magazine, "Announcement: Steadfastly Refused to Use the Female Third Person Singular Character *Ta* 她" 《本刊拒用"她"字启事》, *Women's Voice* 《妇女共鸣》 magazine, Vol. 4, No. 8, August 1935.
18. *Women's Voice* 《妇女共鸣》 magazine, "Announcement" 《启事》, *Women's Voice* 《妇女共鸣》 magazine, Vol. 3, No. 5, May 1934.
19. Language Research Center of Fudan University ed., *Vol. 3 of Collected Works of Chen Wangdao* 《陈望道文集》, Shanghai: Shanghai Renmin Press, 1981.
20. Fu, Shuhua 傅淑华, "How to Awaken the Everyday Chinese Woman" 《如何唤醒一般之中国妇女》, *Readers' Forum* section of *Women's Magazine* 《妇女杂志》 "读者论坛", Vol. 6, No. 10, 1920.
21. Gong, Dengchao 龚登朝, "The Discussion of '*Qu* 佢' (he/she/it) and 'Mr.' (xiansheng 先生)" 《"佢"和"先生"的讨论》, *Light of Learning* 《学灯》, October 22, 1921.
22. Gong, Dengchao 龚登朝, "Discussion of 'The Division of *Ta* 他'" 《"他的分化"的讨论》, carried in *Light of Learning* 《学灯》, October 13, 1921.
23. Gong, Dengchao 龚登朝, "Reading on 'Discussion of He 他'" 《读"他的讨论"》, *Light of Learning* 《学灯》, November 2, 1921.
24. Guo, Luogui 郭罗贵 (Guo Zansheng), *Postscript to Trade Essentials* 《通商须知》, typeset using movable type, Hong Kong: Wenyutang Bookstore 文裕堂书局, 1899.
25. Guo, Moruo 郭沫若, "Taking One's Leave" 《别离》, "At the Performance" 《演奏会上》 and etc., *Light of Learning* 《学灯》, January 8 and 9, 1920.
26. Guo, Moruo 郭沫若, *Goddess* 《女神》, Shanghai: Taidong Press, 1921.
27. Guo, Moruo 郭沫若, "Mouse Plague" 《鼠灾》, *Light of Learning* 《学灯》, January 26, 1920.
28. Guo, Moruo 郭沫若, "The Lure of Death" 《死的诱惑》, *Light of Learning* 《学灯》, September 29, 1919.
29. Guo, Zansheng 郭赞生 trans., *English School Grammar* 《文法初阶》 (Both Chinese and English), Hong Kong: Fourth Year of the Guangxu Era, 1878.
30. Han, Bing 寒冰, "Refuting the Research on the Character *Ta* 她: If Liu Bannong Is Not Wrong Then Who Is?" 《驳"她"字的研究 – 刘半农不错是谁错？》, carried in *Light of Learning* 《学灯》, April 20, 1920, and reprinted in *New Man* 《新人》, Vol. 1, No. 2, 1920.
31. Han, Bing 寒冰, "A Detailed Critique of the Question of the Character *Ta* 她" 《关于"她"字问题的申论》, carried in *Light of Learning* 《学灯》, April 27, 1920, and reprinted in *New Man* 《新人》, Vol. 1, No. 2, 1920.
32. Han, Bing 寒冰, "Further Discussion on 'the Question of the Character *Ta* 她'" 《续论"她字问题"》, published on August 12 in *Light of Learning* 《学灯》 and later reprinted in Issue 6 of *New Man* 《新人》.
33. Han, Bing 寒冰, "Refuting Again the Research on the Character *Ta* 她" 《再驳"她"字的研究》, *Light of Learning* 《学灯》, April 27, 1920.
34. Han, Bing 寒冰, "This is Liu Bannong's Error" 《这是刘半农的错》, *New Man* 《新人》, Vol. 1, No. 1, April 1920.

35. He, Zhen 何震, "On Restoring the Power of Women"《女子复权论》, *Divine Justice*《天义》, Issue 2, June 25, 1907.
36. Hu, Shi 胡适, *A Collection of Experiments*《尝试集》, Shanghai: Taidong Press, 1920.
37. Hu, Shi 胡适, "Story of Li Chao"《李超传》, *The Renaissance*《新潮》, Vol. 2, No. 2.
38. Hu, Shi 胡适, "Him"《他》, *New Youth*《新青年》, Vol. 2, No. 6, February 1917.
39. Hu, Shi 胡适, "Chinese Teaching in Middle School"《中学的国文教学》, *The Morning Post Supplement*《晨报副刊》, August 27–28, 1922.
40. Yuan, Yidan 袁一丹, "The New Culture as a Movement"《作为运动的新文化》, carried in *Modern China*《现代中国》, Issue 12, 2009.
41. Hu, Shi 胡适 ed., *Short Stories*, Vol. 1《短篇小说（第一集）》, Shanghai: The Oriental Book Company, 1919.
42. Ji, Zhuman 吉竹蔓, "On the Refusal to Use the Character *Ta* 她 and a Question for *Reading Life*"《关于拒用"她"字并质<读书生活>》, *Women's Voice*《妇女共鸣》Vol. 4, No. 10, October 1935.
43. Jin, Dezhang 金德章, "She?"《她么》, *Enlightenment Magazine*《觉悟》, March 12, 1920.
44. Jin, Fushen 金福申, "The Pronoun *Ta* (他, he) and *Ta* (她, she)"《代名词他(he)同她(she)》, carried in the *Discussion* 讨论 column of *The Morning Post Supplement*《晨报副刊》, March 18, 1921.
45. Kang, Baiqing 康白情, "A Harbinger of Male-Female Relations in Peking's Student World"《北京学生界男女交际之先声》, *The Morning Post*《晨报》, May 20, 1919.
46. Kang, Baiqing 康白情, "Universities Should Take the Lead in Lifting the Ban on Female Students"《大学宜首开女禁论》, *The Morning Post*《晨报》, May 6 to 10, 1919.
47. Kang, Baiqing 康白情, "Kang Baiqing Notice"《康白情启事》, carried in *The Renaissance*《新潮》, Vol. 2, No. 1, October 1919.
48. Kang, Baiqing 康白情, "Society"《社会》, *The Journal of the Young China Association*《少年中国》, Vol. 1, No. 3, September 1919.
49. Kang, Baiqing 康白情, "The Question"《疑问》, *The Renaissance*《新潮》, Vol. 2, No. 1.
50. Kuang, Qizhao 邝其照, *Integrated Dictionary*《字典集成》, Hongkong, 1875.
51. Li, Jinghui 黎锦晖, "*Ta* 他, *Ta* 她, *Ta* 牠"《他、她、牠》, *Little Friend*《小朋友》, No. 69, 1923.
52. Li, Dingyi 李定夷, "Your Happiness"《你的幸福》, *New Fiction Magazine*《小说新报》, Vol. 8, No. 4, 1923.
53. Li, Xiaotong 厉筱通, "The Question of the Vulgar Scripted 她 and 牠"《"她"和"牠"的俗书问题》, *Current Opinion*《时代公论》, No. 114, June 1934.
54. Liang, Zongdai 梁宗岱, "Travelling Companion"《游伴》, *The Short Story Magazine*《小说月报》, Vol. 16, No. 3, 1925.
55. Liaozuobuyi 辽左布衣, "Brilliant Sister of Mine"《慧姐》, carried in the *Fiction* column of *The Morning Post*《晨报》"小说"栏, June 5, 1919.
56. Ling, Xiaofang 凌晓肪, "Her Ideal Man"《她的理想中之他》, *Guowen Weekly*《国闻周报》, Vol. 1, No. 11, 1924.
57. Liu, Fu (Bannong) 刘复(半农), "On the Question of the Character *Ta* 她"《"她"字问题》, originally carried in *Light of Learning*《学灯》, Issue 8, 1920 and reprinted in *New Man*《新人》, No. 6.
58. Liu, Fu 刘复, *Essays of [Liu] Bannong*, Vol. 1《半农杂文》, Beijing: Xingyuntang Bookstore, June 1934.

214 *References*

59. Liu, Fu 刘复, "Love Song" 《情歌》, *The Morning Post Supplement* 《晨报副刊》, September 16, 1923.
60. Liu, Fu 刘复, *Raising the Whip* 《扬鞭集》, Beijing: Beixin Bookstore, 1926.
61. Liu, Fu 刘复, "Evening in a Small Peasant Household" 《一个小农家的暮》, *New Youth*, No. 4, Issue 9, August 1, 1921.
62. Liu, Guisheng 刘桂生 (collected), "Record of Interview with Comrade Ji Chaoding" 《冀朝鼎同志访问记录》, Editorial Board of the History of Tsinghua University, November 26, 1959.
63. Lu, Xun 鲁迅, "What Happens after Nora Walks Out?" 《娜拉走后怎样》, *Journal of the Women's Higher Normal School Literature and Art Society* 《女子高等师范学校文艺会刊》, Issue 6.
64. Lu, Xun 鲁迅, "Chewing Words Is Not So 'Bland'" 《咬嚼未始"乏味"》, *Literary Supplement to the Peking Press* 《京报副刊》, February 10, 1925.
65. Lu, Xun 鲁迅, "New Year's Sacrifice" 《祝福》, *The Eastern Miscellany* 《东方杂志》, Vol. 21, No. 6.
66. Lu, Xun 鲁迅, *The Complete Works of Lu Xun* 《鲁迅全集》, Vol. 6, Beijing: People's Publishing House, 1981.
67. Lu, Bohong 陆伯鸿 and etc. ed., *Dictionnaire Francais-Chinois* 《法华新字典》, Shanghai: Commercial Press, 1914.
68. Lu, Qiuxin 陆秋心, "Annihilate the Two Characters *Concubine* 妾 and *Prostitute* 妓" 《消灭"妾"和"妓"两个字》, *New Woman* 《新妇女》, Inaugural Issue, January 1920.
69. Lu, Yuan 陆元, "It Is Not Necessary to Distinguish between Male and Female So Distinctly" 《男女不必分得那么清楚》, *Communication* column of *Enlightenment Magazine* 《觉悟》, July 12, 1922.
70. Mr. Ma Er 马二先生 trans., "Why He Married Her" 《他为什么娶她》, "Her Ideal Man" 《她的理想中之他》, separately carried in *Guowen Weekly* 《国闻周报》, Vol. 1, No. 8, 1924.
71. Ma, Junru 马俊如 and Hou, Jue 后觉 eds., *Dictionary of the Chinese Language* 《国语普通词典》, Shanghai: Zhonghua Bookstore, 1923.
72. Mao, Dun 茅盾 trans., "Simon's Father" 《西门的爸爸》, *New Youth* 《新青年》, Vol. 9, No. 1, May 1921.
73. Mao, Dun 茅盾 trans., "A Team of Horsemen" 《一队骑马的人》, *New Youth* 《新青年》, Vol. 9, No. 4.
74. Meng, Shen 梦沈, "Refuting the Research on the Character *Ta* 她: Could It Be That Liu Bannong Is Wrong?" 《驳"她"字的研究：难道是刘半农错么？》, *Light of Learning* 《学灯》, April 25, 1920.
75. Ming, Xi 鸣希, "The Past and the Present of the Truth Association" 《唯真学会的过去与现在》, carried in the inaugural issue of *Truth* 《唯真》, May 1920.
76. Ouyang, Zhesheng 欧阳哲生 ed., *Complete Works of Fu Sinian* 《傅斯年全集》, Hunan: Hunan Education Publishing House, 2003.
77. Qia 恰 (Quechou 却酬), "*Ta* 他 [he], *Ta* 她 [she], and *Ta* 牠 [it]" 《他、她、牠》, carried in *Society Reports* 《会报》, Vol. 33, 1928.
78. Qian, Qianwu 钱谦吾 ed., *New Dictionary of Literary Description* 《新文艺描写辞典》 and *Sequel to the New Dictionary of Literary Description* 《新文艺描写辞典续编》, Shanghai: Nanqiang Bookstore, 1931.
79. Qian, Xingcun 钱杏邨, "The Dahlia" 《大丽花》, carried in *Emancipation Pictorial* 《解放画报》 Issue 13, July 30, 1921.
80. Qian, Xuantong 钱玄同, "Discussion of the Differentiation between the Two Terms 'He' (*ta*, 他) and 'They' (*tamen*, 他们)" 《"他"和"他们"两个词儿的分化之讨论》, carried in *National Language Monthly* 《国语月刊》, Vol. 1, No. 10, November 20, 1922.

81. Qian, Xuantong 钱玄同, Wang Pu 王璞, Zhao Yuanren 赵元任 and etc., *Pronunciation Dictionary of Common National Language Terms* 《国音常用字汇》, Shanghai: Commercial Press, 1932.
82. Qian, Xuantong 钱玄同 and Zhou, Zuoren 周作人, "The Discussion over the Translation of the English 'She'" 《英文 "she"字译法之商榷》, carried in *New Youth* 《新青年》, February 1919, Vol. 6, No. 2.
83. Qian, Yuan 潜源, "The Blandness of Chewing Words" 《咬嚼之乏味》, *Literary Supplement to the Peking Press* 《京报》文学副刊, February 4, 1925.
84. Qiangnan Yingci Xicao 黔南英雌戏草, *Interesting Language from the Academic World* 《学界趣语》 section of Issue 2 of *New Fiction* 《新小说》, Guangxu year 31 (1905).
85. The Word Committee of National Chinese Education 全国国语教育促进会审词委员会编 ed., *Grand Standard Dictionary* 《标准语大词典》, Shanghai: Commercial Press, 1935.
86. Shen, Jianshi 沈兼士, "The Original Meaning of 'Gui 鬼'" 《"鬼"字原始意义之试探》, 载 *Journal of Sinological Studies* 《国学季刊》, Vol. 5, No. 3, 1935.
87. Shi, Pingmei 石评梅, "Tell Her (她) to Come Back" 《叫她回来吧》, *The Morning Post Supplement* 《晨报副刊》, April 22, 1924.
88. Shi, Pingmei 石评梅, "Tell Her (她)" 《你告她》, *The Morning Post Supplement* 《晨报副刊》, June 20, 1924.
89. Shi, Tong 士同 (柳湜), "Refusing to Use the Character *Ta* 她" 《拒用"她"字》 in *Reading Life* 《读书生活》, Vol. 2, No. 9, September 1935.
90. Shusan 树三, "'Ta 她' and the Women's Movement" 《"她"与妇运》, *The Decameron* 《十日谈》, No. 34, July, 1934.
91. Sun, Lianggong 孙俍工 ed., *Lectures on Chinese Grammar* 《中国语法讲义》, Shanghai: East Asian Library, 1922.
92. Sun, Xunqun 孙逊群, "A Discussion of '*Ta*, 他'" 《"他"的讨论》, carried in the *Youth Club* "青年俱乐部" column of *Light of Learning* 《学灯》, October 27, 1921.
93. Sun, Zuji 孙祖基, "Research on the Character *Ta* 她: Is Liu Bannong Really Wrong?" 《"她"字的研究 – 刘半农果真是错吗？》, *Light of Learning* 《学灯》, April 18, 1920.
94. Sun, Zuji 孙祖基, "Against 'Refuting the Research on the Character *Ta* 她'" 《非"驳'她'字的研究"》, *Light of Learning* 《学灯》, April 24, 1920, later in *Newman*, No. 2.
95. Tian 天, "The Women's Liberation Question Requires the Obliteration of the Boundary between Men and Women" 《解放妇女问题该泯灭男女界限》, *Enlightenment Magazine* 《觉悟》, October 30, 1922.
96. Tian, Han 田汉, "Ideology in Goethe's Poetry" 《歌德诗中所表现的思想》, *The Journal of the Young China Association* 《少年中国》, Vol. 1, No. 9, 1920.
97. Tian, Han 田汉, "The Three Works' Poets and Labor" 《诗人与劳动问题》, *The Journal of the Young China Association* 《少年中国》, Vol. 1, No. 8–9, 1920.
98. Tian, Han 田汉, "New Romanticism and Other Things" 《新罗曼主义及其他》, *The Journal of the Young China Association* 《少年中国》, Vol. 1, No. 12, 1920.
99. Wang, Tongzhao 王统照, "Remorse" 《忏悔》, *The Dawn* 《曙光》, Vol. 1, No. 4, February 1920.
100. Wang, Tongzhao 王统照, "The Voice of the 20th Century" 《二十世纪的声》, *The Morning Post* 《晨报》, February 5, 1920.
101. Wang, Tongzhao 王统照, "Why She Died" 《她为什么死》, *The Dawn* 《曙光》, Vol. 1, No. 2, December 1, 1919.
102. Wang, Xinming 王新命, *Forty Years in Journalism* 《新闻圈里四十年》, Taibei: Longwen Press, 1993.

103. Wei, Hua 韦华, "How to Use *Ta* 他, *Ta* 她, *Ta* 牠, and *Ta* 它" 《"他""她""牠""它"的用法》, carried in *Self-Study* 《自修》, Issue 53, 1939.
104. Wu, Ke 舞客, "Heroines in Military Uniform" 《穿上军装的英雌们》, *Shanghaitan*, No. 26, 1946.
105. Xiang, Baolun 相抱轮, "Eternal Heroine Qin Liangyu" 《千古英雌秦良玉》, *Modern Youth* 《现代青年》, Issue 5, 1936.
106. Xiang, Ru 湘如, "Down with *Yingci*!" 《打倒英雌》, carried in *The Pei-yang Pictorial News* 《北洋画报》 Issue 1115, April 1934.
107. Xiao, Ziqin 萧子琴 et al. eds., *Model French-Chinese Dictionary* 《模范法华辞典》, Shanghai: Commercial Press, 1922.
108. Yang, Baosan 杨宝三, "Seeking the Moon" 《找月亮》, *The Morning Post* 《晨报》, May 8, 1920.
109. Yang, Gang 杨刚, "*Tiao* (frivolous): Mei Lanfang" 《佻 – 梅兰芳》, *True Words* 《真话》, Issue 1, 1946.
110. Yang, Shaoping 杨少坪, *A Guide to the English Language* 《英字指南》, Vol. 6, Shanghai: Fifth year of the Guangxu era, 1879.
111. Ye, Shaojun 叶绍钧 (圣陶), "Is This a Person Too?" 《这也是一个人？》, carried in *The Renaissance* 《新潮》 Vol. 1, No. 3, March 1, 1919.
112. Ye, Shaojun 叶绍钧, "Spring Excursion" 《春游》, carried in *The Renaissance* 《新潮》, Vol. 1, No. 5, May 1, 1919.
113. Ye, Shaojun 叶绍钧, *Separation* 《隔膜》, Shanghai: Commercial Press, 1922.
114. Ye, Shaojun 叶绍钧, *Fire* 《火灾》, Shanghai: Commercial Press, 1923.
115. Ye, Shengtao 叶圣陶, "The Question of Women's Personality" 《女子人格问题》, *The Renaissance* 《新潮》, Vol. 1, No. 2, February 1, 1919.
116. Ye, Shengtao 叶圣陶, "Grandma's Heart" 《祖母的心》, *The Short Story Magazine* 《小说月报》, Vol. 13, No. 7, 1922.
117. Yifan 伊凡 (何永佶) trans., "A Grain as Big as a Hen's Egg" 《鸡子那么大的种子》, *Study* 《修业》 Vol. 1, No. 2, December 1919, Tsinghua University Study Group 清华学校修业团 (later known as the Truth Association 唯真学会). It should be noted that the cover of this magazine is incorrectly labelled as Vol. 2, No. 2.
118. Yifan 伊凡, "Invention and the Nature of Slavishness" 《发明与奴隶的根性》, *Random Thoughts* column of *Study* 《修业》 Vol. 1, No. 2.
119. Yi, Xuan 忆萱 and [Shao] Lizi [邵]力子, "Discussion of the Feminine Third Person Pronoun" 《第三身女性代名词底讨论》, *Communications* column of *Enlightenment Magazine* 《觉悟》, June 27, 1920.
120. You, Luan 友鸾, "'Miss' and 'She'" 《"女士"和"她"》, *Modern Woman* 《现代妇女》, September 16, 1922.
121. You, Luan 友鸾, "Why Not Start the Male Ban?" 《为什么不开男禁?》, *Modern Woman* 《现代妇女》, Issue 2.
122. Yu, Pingbo 俞平伯, "Bidding Her Farewell" 《别她》, *The Renaissance* 《新潮》, Vol. 2, No. 3, February 1920.
123. Yu, Pingbo 俞平伯, "Dogs and Badges of Honor" 《狗和褒章》, *The Renaissance* 《新潮》, Vol. 2, No. 3, February 1920.
124. Yu, Pingbo 俞平伯, "Chrysanthemum" 《菊》, *The Renaissance* 《新潮》, Vol. 2, No. 2, 1919.
125. Yu, Pingbo 俞平伯, "Around the Stove" 《炉景》, *The Renaissance* 《新潮》, Vol. 2, No. 1, 1919.
126. Yu, Pingbo 俞平伯, "Inscription on a Photograph Taken at Keyan in Shaoxing" 《题在绍兴柯严照的相片》, carried in *New Youth* 《新青年》, Vol. 8, No. 3.

127. Yu, Pingbo 俞平伯, "Reflections on a Week in Shanghai" 《一星期在上海的感想》, *The Renaissance* 《新潮》, Vol. 2, No. 3, February 1920.
128. Zeng, Pu 曾朴, *Flower of the Sea of Evil* 《孽海花》, Shanghai: Guji Publishing House.
129. Zhang, Wenzhi 张文治 et al. eds., *Standard Student Dictionary of the Sounds of the National Language*, Eleventh Edition 《标准国音学生字典》, Shanghai: Zhonghua Bookstore, 1947, first published in 1935.
130. Zhao, Yuanren 赵元任, *A Collection of New Poems* 《新诗歌集》, Shanghai: Commercial Press, 1928.
131. Zhen, Xin 枕薪, "Miss" 《女士》, *Emancipation Pictorial* 《解放画报》, Issue 15, September 30, 1921.
132. Zhen 箴, "Regarding *ta* 她" 《说她》, carried in *Shen Bao* 《申报》, February 27, 1922.
133. China Dictionary Editing and Compilation Office 中国辞典编纂处 ed., *Dictionary of the National Language* 《国语辞典》 Vol. 2, Shanghai: Commercial Press, 1943.
134. China Dictionary Editing and Compilation Office 中国辞典编纂处 ed., *Expanded and Annotated Pronunciation Dictionary of Common National Language Terms* 《增订注解国音常用字汇》, Shanghai: Commercial Press, 1949.
135. China Education Reform Society's 中华教育改进社 Third Annual Conference, "Group Meeting Minutes: 18th National Language Teaching Group: Record of Proposal C" "分组会议记录：第十八、国语教学组：（丙）议决案汇录", carried in *New Education* 《新教育》, Vol. 9, No. 3, 1920.
136. Zhonghua Shuju Shanghai Editing Office 中华书局上海编辑所编 ed., *The Exploits of Qiu Jin* 《秋瑾史迹》, Shanghai: Zhonghua Shuju, 1958.
137. Zhou, Huizhuan 周慧专, "A New Approach to Substituting *Fu* 媭 for *Fu* 婦" 《婦当作媭新说》, *Readers' Forum* section of *Women's Magazine* 《妇女杂志》, Vol. 6, No. 10, 1920.
138. Zhou, Shoujuan 周瘦鹃, "Foreword to Violets" 《写在紫罗兰前头》, carried in *Violets* 《紫罗兰》 magazine, Issue 2, May 1943.
139. Zhou, Shoujuan 周瘦鹃, "Nonsense" 《一片胡言》, carried in *Shen Bao* 《申报》, July 7, 1922.
140. Zhou, Wu 周无 trans., "Happiness" 《幸福》 published in *The Journal of the Young China Association* 《少年中国》, Vol. 1, No. 3, September 1919.
141. Zhou, Zuoren 周作人 trans., *Fragments* 《点滴》, Beijing: The Renaissance Press, August 1920.
142. Zhou, Zuoren 周作人 trans., "Reform" 《改革》, *New Youth* 《新青年》, Vol. 5, No. 2, 1918.
143. Zhou, Zuoren 周作人 trans., "The Darling" 《可爱的人》, *New Youth* 《新青年》, Vol. 6, No. 2, 1919.
144. Zhou, Zuoren 周作人 trans., "Little Match Girl" 《卖火柴的女儿》, *New Youth* 《新青年》, Vol. 6, No. 1, 1919.
145. Zhou, Zuoren 周作人 trans., "A Certain Woman" 《某夫妇》, *The Short Story Magazine* 《小说月报》, Vol. 14, No. 11, 1923.
146. Zhou, Zuoren 周作人 trans., "Three Dreams in the Desert" 《沙漠间的三个梦》, *New Youth* 《新青年》, Vol. 6, No. 6, 1919.
147. Zhu, Ziqing 朱自清, "Random Travel Notes" 《旅行杂记》, carried in the *Literature Weekly* 《文学周报》 supplement to *The China Times* 《时事新报》, Issue 130, July 14, 1924.
148. Zhu, Ziqing 朱自清, "Random Poems from Taizhou" 《台州杂诗》, carried in *The Short Story Magazine* 《小说月报》, Vol. 13, No. 4, 1922.

149. Zhu, Xin 诛心, "*Ta* (他), *Ta* (她), *Ta* (牠), and *Ta* (它)" 《"他"、"她"、"牠"、"它"》, carried in *The Pei-yang Pictorial News* 《北洋画报》, Issue 1080, 1934.
150. Zhuang, Fu 壮甫, "Interrogating the Character *Ta* 她" 《"她"字的疑问》, for the full text see *New Man* 《新人》 magazine, Issue 2.
151. Zhuo, Ru 卓如 ed., *Complete Works of Bingxin* 《冰心全集》, Hongkong: Haixia Wenyi Publishing House, 1994.
152. Zou, Zhengjian 邹政坚, "The Debate over 'Refuting the Research on the Character *Ta* 她'" 《"驳她字的研究"的讨论》, carried in *Light of Learning* 《学灯》, April 24, 1920.
153. Wilhelm, Lobscheid, *Chinese-English Grammar*, Hongkong: Printed at Noronha's Office, 1864.
154. Chekhov, Lujiangfengsheng 庐江凤生 trans., "Old Age" 《暮年》, *Shen Bao* 《申报》, February 15, 1920, p. 15.
155. Morrison, Robert, *A Grammar of the English Language*, Macau, 1823.
156. T T, "Light of the Full Moon" 《满月的光》, *The Morning Post* 《晨报》, February 5, 1920.
157. Unknown, *Standard Dictionary of Common National Language Sounds* 《标准国音常用字典》, collected by Renmin University. No indication of specific publication date, but definitely published in the 1930s to 40s in Republican China.

2. Catalogue of middle school Chinese language textbooks (1919–1935) listed in Peking Normal School Library's *Complete Library of Textbooks of Normal School and Middle and Primary Schools from Before Liberation Held by this Library* 《馆藏解放前师范学校及中小学教科书全文库》 which use the characters *ta* 她 or *yi* 伊.

a. Textbooks that use both *ta* 她 and *yi* 伊:
   1. Peiping Cultural Society 北平文化学社ed., *Chinese Readings for the First Grade of Junior High School* 《初中一年级国文读本》, Peiping: Peiping Cultural Society, 1932.
   2. Peiping Cultural Society 北平文化学社ed., *Chinese Readings for the Third Grade of Junior High School* 《初中三年级国文读本》, Peiping: Peiping Cultural Society, 1932.
   3. Compiled by Chen Chunnian 陈椿年, *New Asia Chinese Language Teaching Book* 《新亚教本初中国文》, Shanghai: New Asia Bookstore, 1932–1933.
   4. Fan, Xiangshan 范祥善 et al. eds., proof read by Wang, Xiulu 王岫庐 et al., *Chinese Textbook under the New Academic System* 《新学制国语教科书》, Shanghai: Commercial Press, 1923–1925. The second volume is edited by Gu Jiegang 顾颉刚, Fan Xiangshan 范祥善, Ye Shaojun 叶绍钧 and proof read by Hu Shi 胡适, Wang Xiulu 王岫庐, Zhu Jingnong 朱经农, Shanghai: Commercial Press, January 1924.
   5. Fu, Donghua 傅东华 and Chen, Wangdao 陈望道 eds., *Basic Chinese Textbook* 《基本教科书国文》, Shanghai: Commercial Press, 1931–1933.
   6. Compiled by Luo, Genze 罗根泽 and Gao, Yuangong 高远公, edited by Li, Jinxi 黎锦熙, *Selected Works of Early Chinese Literature* 《初中国文选本》, Peiping: Lida Book Company, 1933.
   7. Ma, Wenhou 马厚文 ed., proof read by Liu, Yazi 柳亚子 and Lǚ, Simian 吕思勉, *Collection of Standard Chinese* 《标准国文选》, Shanghai: Daguang Bookstore, 1935.
   8. Shen, Ronglin 沈荣龄 et al. eds., proof read by Wang, Maozu 汪懋祖 et al., *Experimental Chinese Readings of Junior High School* 《试验初中国文读本》, Shanghai: Dahua Bookstore, 1934–1935.
   9. Wang, Kanru 王侃如, Chinese Conference of Yangzhou Middle School and et al., ed., proof read by Chinese Literature Conference Federation of Jiangsu Provincial Middle School, *Chinese Language Textbooks for Junior High Schools under New Academic*

Structure 《新学制中学国文教科书初中国文》, Nanjing: Nanjing Bookstore, 1931–1932.
10. Zhao, Jingshen 赵景深 ed., *Mixed Chinese of Junior High School* 《初中混合国语》, Shanghai: Qingguang Bookstore, 1932–1934.
11. Zhu, Jianmang 朱剑芒 ed., proof read by Wei, Bingxin 魏冰心 and Lu, Xiang 陆翔, *Junior High School Chinese* 《初中国文》, Shanghai: World Bookstore, 1932.

b. Junior middle school textbooks that use the character *yi* 伊:
  1. Peiping Cultural Society 北平文化学社 ed., *Chinese Readings for the Second Grade of Junior High School* 《初中二年级国文读本》, Beiping: Beiping Cultural Society, 1931–1932.
  2. Selected and edited by The High School Affiliated to Beijing Normal University 北师大附中, *Chinese Readings of Junior High Middle School* 《初中国文读本》, Beiping: Beiping Cultural Society 北平文化学社, 1931.
  3. Compiled by Committee of Middle School Chinese Liberal Arts Teaching Schedule of Jiangsu Provincial Department of Education, Wang, Delin 王德林 et al. noted, *Standard Chinese of Junior High School* 《初中标准国文》, Shanghai: Shanghai Middle School Students' Bookstore, 1934–1935.
  4. Shen, Xingyi 沈星一 ed., proof read by Li, Jinxi 黎锦熙 and Shen, Yi 沈颐, *New Elementary Chinese Readings of Middle School Textbook* 《新中学教科书初级国语读本》, Shanghai: Zhonghua Bookstore, 1925–1929. Among them, the first and third volumes are 1929 editions, and the second volume is the 1925 edition.
  5. Sun, Lianggong 孙俍工 and Shen, Zhongjiu 沈仲九 eds., *Chinese Readings of Junior Middle School* 《初级中学国语文读本》, Shanghai: Minzhi Bookstore, 1923–1926.
  6. Ye, Chucang 叶楚伧 ed., proof read by Wang, Maozu 汪懋祖 and Meng, Xiancheng 孟宪承, *Chinese Readings of Junior Middle School* 《初级中学国文》, Nanjing: Zhengzhong Bookstore, 1934–1936.
  7. Zhang, Gong 张弓 ed., proof read by Cai, Yuanpei 蔡元培 and Jiang, Hengyuan 江恒源, *Chinese Textbook of Junior Middle School* 《初中国文教本》, Shanghai: Dadong Bookstore, 1933.
  8. Zhengzhong Junior Middle School Chinese Textbook Editorial Committee ed., *Chinese Textbook of Junior Middle School* 《初级中学教科书国文》, Nanjing: Zhengzhong Bookstore, 1935.
  9. Zhou, Yifu 周颐甫 ed., proof read by Cai, Yuanpei 蔡元培, *Guidance of Basic Chinese Textbook* 《基本教科书国文教本》, Shanghai: Commercial Press, 1932.

c. Junior middle school textbooks that use the character *ta* 她:
  1. Dai, Shuqing 戴叔清 ed., *Chinese Textbook for Junior Middle Schools* 《初级中学国语教科书》, Shanghai: Wenyi Book Company, 1933.
  2. Du, Tianwei 杜天縻 ed., *Chinese Language and Grammar* 《国语与国文》, Shanghai: Dahua Book Company, 1933.
  3. Du, Tianyu 杜天縻 and Han, Chuyuan 韩楚原 eds., *Senior High Chinese Language by Du and Han* 《杜韩两氏高中国文》, Shanghai: World Book Company, 1933–1934 edition.
  4. Hu, Shi 胡适, *Classical Chinese Ci Poetry* 《词选》, Shanghai: Commercial Press, 1928.
  5. Selected and Noted by Jiang, Liangfu 姜亮夫 and Zhao, Jingshen 赵景深, *Selected Works of Beixin for Junior Middle School Students* 《初级中学北新文选》, Shanghai: Beixin Bookstore, 1931–1933 edition.
  6. Selected and Noted by Jiang, Liangfu 姜亮夫, *Selected Chinese Works of Senior High School* 《高中国文选》, Shanghai: Beixin Bookstore, 1934 edition.

7. Nankai Middle School 南开中学 ed., *Chinese Textbook of Grade 3 of Nankai Middle School* 《南开中学初三国文教本》, Tianjin: Self-published, 1930–1931.
8. Nankai Middle School 南开中学 ed., *Chinese Textbook of Grade 1 of Nankai Middle School* 《南开中学初一国文教本》, Tianjin: Self-published, 1935.
9. Nankai Middle School 南开中学 ed., *Chinese Textbook of Grade 2 of Nankai Middle School* 《南开中学初二国文教本》, Tianjin: Self-published, 1935.
10. Annotated by Shi, Zhecun 施蛰存, et al., ed. by Liu, Yazi 柳亚子 et al., *Contemporary Chinese of Junior High School* 《初中当代国文》, Shanghai: Middle School Student Book Company, 1934.
11. Song, Wenhan 宋文翰 ed., *Chinese Readings* 《国文读本》(New curriculum, applicable for normal universities), Shanghai: Zhonghua Book Company, 1935–1936.
12. Sun, Lianggong 孙俍工 ed., *Chinese Textbook* 《国文教科书》, Shanghai: Shenzhou Guoguang Press, 1932.
13. Sun, Nuchao 孙怒潮 ed., *Chinese Textbook for Junior High School Students* 《初级中学国文教科书》, Shanghai: Zhonghua Book Company, 1934–1935.
14. Wang, Boxiang 王伯祥 ed., *Kaiming's Edition of Chinese Readings* 《开明国文读本》, Shanghai: Kaiming Bookstore, 1932–1933.
15. Wang, Yunwu 王云五 and Fu, Donghua 傅东华 eds., *Renaissance of Chinese Textbook for Junior High School Students* 《复兴初级中学教科书国文》, Shanghai: Commercial Press, 1933–1935.
16. Xia, Mianzun 夏丏尊 et al., eds., *Kaiming's Edition of Chinese Handouts* 《开明国文讲义》, Shanghai: Kaiming Bookstore, 1934.
17. Xu, Gongmei 徐公美 et al., eds., by Chinese Literature Conference of Yangzhou Middle Schools of Jiangsu Province 江苏省立扬州中学国文科会议, proof ready by Jiangsu Provincial Middle School Chinese Literature Conferences 江苏省立中学国文学科会议联合会校订, *Chinese Textbooks for Middle Schools in the New Academic Structure High Chinese Language* 《新学制中学国文教科书高中国文》, Nanjing: Nanjing Bookstore, 1931–1933.
18. Xu, Weinan 徐蔚南 ed., *Creating Chinese Readings* 《创造国文读本》, Shanghai: World Bookstore, 1932–1934.
19. Xue, Wujin 薛无兢 et al., noted, Liu, Yazi 柳亚子 et al., proof-read, *Contemporary High School Chinese* 《高中当代国文》, Shanghai: High School Bookstore, 1934.
20. Ye, Chucang 叶楚伧 ed., proof read by Wang, Maozu 汪懋祖 and Meng, Xiancheng 孟宪承, noted by Wang, Dingyi 汪定奕, *Chinese Textbook for Junior High School Students* 《初级中学教科书国文》, Nanjing: Zhengzhong Bookstore, 1934.
21. Noted by Zhang, Honglai 张鸿来 and Lu, Huaiqi 卢怀琦, *Chinese Readings for Junior High School Students* 《初级中学国文读本》, Beiping: The Chinese Society of The High School Affiliated To Beiping Normal University 北平师大附中国文丛刊社, 1932–1935.
22. Noted by Zhang, Honglai 张鸿来, Wang, Zhen 汪震 and Wang, Shuda 王述达, *Chinese Readings for Junior High School Students* 《初级中学国文读本》, Beiping: The Chinese Society of The High School Affiliated To Beiping Normal University 北平师大附中国文丛刊社, 1934–1936.
23. Zhao, Jingshen 赵景深 ed., *Mixed Chinese Text Books for Junior High School Students* 《初级中学混合国语教科书》, Shanghai: Beixin Bookstore, 1930–1932.
24. Zhu, Jianmang 朱剑芒 ed., noted by Han, Ailu 韩霭麓 and Han, Weinong 韩慰农, *Junior High School Chinese* 《朱氏初中国文》, Shanghai: World Bookstore, 1934.

25. Zhu, Wenshu 朱文叔 ed., proof read by Chen Tang, *New China Chinese Language and Textbook* 《新中华教科书国语与国文》, Shanghai: New National Bookstore, 1928–1929.
26. Zhu, Wenshu 朱文叔 ed, proof read by Shu, Xincheng 舒新城 and Lu, Feikuei 《初中国文读本》, Shanghai: Zhonghua Book Company, 1933–1934.

3. Modern Chinese articles and translations (including dictionaries) that have been cited:

 1. Cai, Ying 蔡瑛, "Liu Bannong's *Ta* 她 [She]" 《刘半农的"她"》, *Chinese People's Political Consultative Conference Report* 《人民政协报》, July 27, 2006.
 2. Chang, Jincang 常金仓, *Change and Continuity: The Theory and Practice of Cultural History* 《穷变通久：文化史学的理论与实践》, Shenyang: Liaoning People's Publishing House, 1998.
 3. Chen, Congyun 陈丛耘 and Li, Tong 李彤, "On the Language Gender Difference between '*Ta* 他' and '*Ta* 她'" 《谈"他"与"她"的语言性别差异》, *Modern Chinese* 《现代语文》(Language Research Edition), Vol. 8, 2011.
 4. Chen, Fukang 陈福康, "Also Regarding the Character '*Ta* (牠, it)'" 《也说"牠"字》, *Lu Xun Research Monthly* 《鲁迅研究月刊》, Vol. 6, 1996.
 5. Chen, Heng 陈恒 and Geng, Xiangxin 耿相新 eds., *New Cultural History, New History*, Vol. 4, Henan: Daxiang Press, 2005.
 6. Chen, Jianhua 陈建华, "City of Breasts and the Revolutionary Utopian Imagination" 《"乳房"的都市与革命乌托邦想象》, *Form and the Revolution: The Development of Modernity in Mao Dun's Early Novels* 《革命与形式－茅盾早期小说的现代性展开》, Shanghai: Fudan University Publishing House, 2007.
 7. Chen, Shaoming 陈少明, "What Is an Event in the History of Thought?" 《什么是"思想史事件"》, carried in the *Jiangsu Social Sciences* 《江苏社会科学》, Vol. 1, 2007.
 8. Gong, Shuming 贡树铭, "Liu Bannong and '*Ta* 她'" 《刘半农和"她"》, carried in *On Chewing Words* 《咬文嚼字》, Vol. 4, 2002.
 9. He, Xiang 贺祥, "The Character '*Ta* 她' Was Not Created by Liu Bannong" 《"她"字并非刘半农所造》, carried in *On Chewing Words* 《咬文嚼字》, Vol. 5, 1997.
10. Huang, Xingtao 黄兴涛, "The Story of the Character *Ta* 她: Invention, Debate and Early Circulation" 《"她"字的故事：女性新代词符号的发明、论争与早期流播》, Yang Nianqun 杨念群 (ed.), *New History* 《新史学》, Vol. 1, Beijing: Zhonghua Shuju, 2007.
11. Huang, Xingtao 黄兴涛, "'Mandarin Grammar' and 'English School Grammar' (The Earliest Dissemination of a Knowledge of English Grammar in the Late Qing Dynasty)" Part II 《〈文学书官话〉与〈文法初阶〉（晚清英文语法知识的最早传播）》（之二）, carried in *Wen Shi Zhi Shi* 《文史知识》, Vol. 4, 2006.
12. Huang, Xingtao 黄兴涛, "The First Chinese Book on English Grammar, *A Grammar of the English Language* 《英国文语凡例传》", carried in *Wen Shi Zhi Shi* 《文史知识》, Vol. 3, 2006.
13. Huang, Xingtao 黄兴涛, *In Search of a Cultural History: Taking China in Recent Years as Our Prospect* 《文化史的追寻－以近世中国为视域》, Beijing: Renmin University Publishing House, 2011.
14. Huang, Xingtao 黄兴涛, "Also Discussing the Invention of the '*Ta* 她' and '*Yi* 伊' Characters" 《也谈"她"字的发明与"伊"字》, carried in *Guangming Daily* 《光明日报》, July 26, 2005.
15. Jiang, Yinnan 蒋荫楠, "Superfluous Format of '*Ta* 他（她）'《画蛇添足的"他（她）"格式》, carried in *On Chewing Words* 《咬文嚼字》, Vol. 9, 1996.

16. Kong, Fanling 孔凡岭, "The Earliest Appearance of the Term May Fourth Movement and Its Connotations" 《"五四运动"一词的最早出现及其涵义》, *History Teaching* 《历史教学》, Vol. 7, 2000.
17. Li, Dongchen 李栋臣, "The Superfluous '*Ta* 她'" 《没有必要的"她"》, carried in *Building the Chinese Language* 《语文建设》, Vol. 4, 1995.
18. Li, Hongyan 李洪岩, "The Joy of Reading" 《读书逢喜事》, carried in *China Reading Weekly* 《中华读书报》, December 19, 2007.
19. Li, Ling 李玲, "Gender Consciousness and the Modernity of Modern Chinese Literature" 《性别意识与中国现代文学的现代性》, carried in *Research on Chinese Culture* 《中国文化研究》, Vol. 2, 2005.
20. Li, Ling 李玲, *Gender Consciousness in Modern Chinese Literature* 《中国现代文学的性别意识》, Beijing: People's Literature Publishing House, 2002.
21. Li, Qizhi 李奇志, "Qiu Jin and Lü Bicheng: The Quest for the Spirit of the Heroine in Their Lives and Writing" 《秋瑾、吕碧城其人其文的"英雌"精神追求》, *Hubei Social Sciences* 《湖北社会科学》, Vol. 11, 2008.
22. Ling, Yuanzheng 凌远征, "The History of the Creation of the Character '*Ta* 她'" 《"她"字的创造历史》, carried in *Linguistic Pedagogy and Research* 《语言教学与研究》, Vol. 4, 1989.
23. Liu, Chengyu 刘成禺 and Zhang, Boju 张伯驹, *Three Hong Xian Chronicle Poems* 《洪宪纪事诗三种》, Shanghai: Shanghai Classics Publishing House, 1983.
24. Liu, Danqing 刘丹青, "The Trichotomy of 'He, She, It' Is the Disadvantages, Root Causes and the Countermeasures" 《"他、她、它"三分法是弊端、根源与对策》, *Building the Chinese Language* 《语文建设》, Vol. 4, 1993.
25. Liu, Lydia He 刘禾, *Translingual Practice* 《跨语际实践》, translated by Song Weijie 宋伟杰 et al., Beijing: San Lian Shu Dian, 2002.
26. Liu, Xiaohui 刘小蕙, *My Father Liu Bannong* 《父亲刘半农》, Shanghai: Shanghai Renmin, 2000.
27. Liu, Youxin 刘又辛 and Bao, Yanyi 鲍延毅, "The Discussion over the Character '*Ta* 她'" 《关于"她"字的商榷》, carried in *Language Research and Teaching* 《语言研究与教学》, Vol. 3, 1984.
28. Liu, Zhaoji 刘兆吉, "A Brief Study on the Character '*Ta* 她'" 《"她"字略考》, carried in *Garden of the Chinese Language* 《语文园地》, Vol. 11, 1985.
29. Meng, Shuhong 蒙树宏, "On '*Ta* 她'" 《说"她"》, carried in *Lexicographical Studies* 《辞书研究》, Vol. 4, 1981.
30. Sun, Jiang ed., *New History* 《新史学》, Vol. 2, Beijing: Zhonghua Shuju, 2008.
31. Tian, Zhongmin 田仲民, "*Yi* 伊 and *Ta* 她 in Lu Xun's Fiction" 《鲁迅小说中的"伊"与"她"》, carried in *On Chewing Words* 《咬文嚼字》, Vol. 5, 1999.
32. Wang, Huayun 汪化云, "Him, Her and It" 《"他"、"她"、"它"》, *The Culture of Chinese Characters* 《汉字文化》, Vol. 2, 2000.
33. Wang, Yuanyuan 王媛媛, "Looking at '*Ta* 他' and '*Ta* 她' from the Standpoint of '*Ta*'" 《从"ta"看"他"与"她"》, carried in *Popular Literature* 《大众文艺》, Vol. 6, 2010.
34. Xia, Xiaohong 夏晓虹, "Heroines and Women of Distinction Probe Things Deeply: the Ideal Late Qing Female Personality" 《"英雌女杰勤揣摩"：晚清女性的人格理想》, *Literature and Art Research* 《文艺研究》, Issue 6, 1995.
35. Xiao, Yang 肖杨, "She: The 21st Century's Most Important Word" 《她：21世纪最重要的一个字》, *Nanfang Daily* 《南方日报》, January 10, 2001.
36. Yang, Hu 杨琥, "An Investigation into the Origin of the Name 'May Fourth Movement'" 《"五四运动"名称溯源》, *Journal of Peking University* 《北京大学学报》, Vol. 3, 2006.

References   223

37. Yang, Hui 杨慧, "Chinese Nation: 'Our Mother, the Motherland'" 《中华民族共有的最高诗情－"祖国母亲"考辩》, unpublished, 2007.
38. Yang, Jianmin 杨建民, "Liu Bannong and the Story of the Character '*Ta* 她'" 《刘半农与"她"字的故事》, carried in *China Reading Weekly* 《中华读书报》, February 6, 2002.
39. Yang, Nianqun 杨念群 ed., *New History* 《新史学》Vol. 1, Beijing: Zhonghua Shuju, 2007.
40. Yuan, Yidan 袁一丹, "The New Culture as a Movement" 《作为运动的新文化》, carried in *Modern China* 《现代中国》, Issue 12, 2009.
41. Di, Hua 翟华, *Western Men and Women Are Different* 《西式男女有别》, Carried in *Youth Reference* 《青年参考》, May 28 1999.
42. Zhang, Baoming 张宝明, "Where Does 'She' Come from: A Study on the Origin of Modern Women's Allegation 《"她"从哪里来－现代女性指称的源流考释》", carried in *Seeking Roots* 《寻根》, Vol. 1, 2008.
43. Zhang, Juling 张巨龄, "The Character '*Ta* 她' Is Not an Invention, But Rather Another Picto-Phonetic Character Taken from It" 《"她"字不是发明，而是借用成的另一形声字》, carried in *Guangming Daily* 《光明日报》, August 9, 2005.
44. Zhang, Zhixiang 张质相, "'*Ta* 她' and '*Ni* 妳' Should Not Be Used" 《不该用"她"和"妳"》, carried in *The Culture of Chinese Characters* 《汉字文化》, Vol. 2, 1994.
45. Zhang, Zhongmin 张仲民, "New Cultural History and Chinese Research" 《新文化史与中国研究》, carried in the *Fudan Journal: Social Science Edition* 《复旦学报》社会科学版, Vol. 1, 2008.
46. Research Office of the Works Compilation and Compilation Bureau of Marx, Engels and Lenin of the Central Committee of the Communist Party of China 中共中央马、恩、列、斯著作编译局研究室 ed., 《五四时期期刊介绍》, *Introduction to Periodicals of the May Fourth Era* 《五四时期期刊介绍》, Beijing: Renmin Press, 1959.
47. Zhou, Bing 周兵, "The Rise and Trend of Western New Cultural History" 《西方新文化史的兴起与走向》, carried in *Hebei Academic Journal* 《河北学刊》, Vol. 6, 2004.
48. Zhou, Lianhua 周联华, "*Ta* 祂 and *Ta* 他 in the Holy Bible" 《圣经中的"祂"和"他"》, carried in *Bible Quarterly* 《圣经季刊》, Vol. 21, 2007.
49. Zhu, Jinshun 朱金顺, "Regarding the Character '*Ta* (牠, it)" 《说"牠"字》, carried in *Lu Xun Research Monthly* 《鲁迅研究月刊》, Vol. 2, 1996.
50. Zhu, Jinshun 朱金顺, "Two Historical Items Relating to the Creation of the Character '*Ta* 她'" 《有关"她"字创造的两件史料》, carried in *Green Earth* 《绿土》, Vol. 38, April 1999.
51. Simone de Beauvoir, Tao, Tiezhu trans., *The Second Sex* 《第二性》, Beijing: China Book Company, 1998.
52. Appleby, Joyce et al., Liu, Beicheng 刘北成 and Xue, Xuan 薛绚 trans., *Telling the Truth About History* 《历史的真相》, Beijing: Central Compilation and Translation Press, 1999.
53. Leslie, A. White, Shen, Yuan 沈原 et al. trans., *The Science of Culture: A Study of Man and Civilization* (*Foundations of Anthropology*) 《文化的科学－人类与文明研究》, Jinan: Shandong People's Publishing House, 1988.
54. Ichirō Ishida 石田一良, Wang, Yong 王勇 trans., *Cultural History: Theory and Method* 《文化史学：理论和方法》, Hangzhou: Zhejiang People's Publishing House, 1989.
55. Burke, Peter, Li, Xiaoxiang 李霄翔, Li, Lu 李鲁 and Yang, Yu 杨豫 trans., *Languages and Communities in Early Modern Europe* 《语言的文化史－近代早期欧洲的语言和共同体》, Beijing: Peking University Press, 2007.

224 References

56. Peter, Burke, Yao, Peng 姚朋 et al. trans., proof read by Liu, Beicheng 刘北成, *History and Social Theory* 《历史学与社会理论》, Shanghai: Shanghai Renmin Press, 2001.
57. Maria Lúcia Pallares-Burke ed., Peng, Gang trans., *The New History: Confessions and Conversations* 《新史学：自白与对话》, Beijing: Beijing University Press, 2006.
58. J.S. Mill and Wang, Xi trans., *The Subjection of Woman* 《妇女的屈从地位》, Beijing: Commercial Press, 1996.
59. Đurđa Knežević, *Affective Nationalism* 《情感的民族主义》, referenced in Dai, Jinhua 戴锦华 (Selected and Edited), *Women, Nation and Feminism* 《妇女、民族与女性主义》, Beijing: Central Compilation and Translation Press, 2004.

4. Foreign works (including dictionaries) that have been used or cited

a. English
   1. Crystal, David, *The Cambridge Encyclopedia of the English Language*, Cambridge: Cambridge University Press, 1995.
   2. Simpson, John, and Weiner, Edmund, *The Oxford English Dictionary*, Second Edition, Oxford: Oxford University Press, 1989.
   3. Hunt, Lynn, *The New Cultural History*, Berkeley: University of California Press, 1989.
   4. Webster, Noah, *Webster's New, Twentieth Century Dictionary of the English Language, Unabridged*, Second Edition, New York: Simon and Schuster, 1983.
   5. Burke, Peter, *Varieties of Cultural History*, Ithaca, NY: Cornell University Press, 1997.
   6. Connell, R. W., *Gender and Power*, Redwood: Stanford University Press, 1987.

b. French
   1. Billequin, A. A., Dictionnaire Francais-Chinois, Peking: Typographie du Pei-T'ang, 1891.
   2. Séraphin Couvreur, Dictionnaire Chinois-Francais, Ho Kien Fou, 1890.

c. Russian
   1. Шахматов А.А., Историческая морфология русского языка. Москва, 1957.
   2. Иванов В.В., Историческая грамматика русского языка. Москва, 1964.
   3. Якубинский Л.П., История древнего русского языка. Москва, 1953.
   (I acknowledge the assistance of Dr. Ye Bochuan 叶柏川 in interrogating and interpreting the Russian materials)

d. Portuguese
   1. Michele Ruggieri and Matteo Ricci, Dicionário Português – Chinês. Direcção de Edição/John W. Witek, S. J., Edição/Biblioteca Nacional Portugal, Instituto Português do Oriente. Ricci Institute for Chinese-Western Cultural History, 2001.

e. Korean
   1. 고길섶, 『우리시대의 언어게임: 괴짜 '그녀'의 탄생설화』. "우리시대의 언어게임". 서울: 토담, 1995.
   I am grateful for the assistance of Dr. An Yuner 安允儿 in interpreting the Korean materials.

f. Japanese
   1. 挾間新太郎：「華語漫談（其の二）・他と她と牠」，『華北合作』第9巻第5期, 1943年.
   2. 柳父章：『翻訳語成立事情』，岩波書店, 1982年.
   3. 飞田良文：『明治生まれの日本語』，淡交社, 2002年.

Index of Translated/Transliterated Titles Referred to in This Work

Advance Together 48
Affective Nationalism 165, 173, 224
Against "Refuting the Research on the Character Ta 她" [or Should This Be "DON'T Refute the Research] 49, 66, 67, 215
Also discussing the Invention of the "Ta 她" and "Yi 伊" Characters 174, 206, 221
Also Regarding the Character "Ta (牠, it)" 113, 221
Analects 80
An Investigation into the Origin of the Name "May Fourth Movement" 45
Annihilate the Two Characters "Concubine 妾" and "Prostitute 妓" 94, 214
Annotations of Chronicle Poems of Yuan Shikai's Reign (Hong Xian) 166
Announcement on the Refusal to Use the Character "Ta 她" 88
Announcement: This Magazine Refuses to Use the Character "ta 她" xvii, 85, 200
Around the Stove 33, 34, 216
At the Performance 45, 212
August 15 Last Year 36, 46

Back Door Deals Among Native Place Associations in Beijing During the Beiyang Period: A Study of the Guangdong Native Guild 181
Banning the Study of the Classical Language and Ordering the Study of the Classics 136
Barriers 20
Battle of the Dragons and Tigers 138
Bei Xin 95
Bible Quarterly 173, 223
Bidding Her Farewell xi, 33, 39, 41, 47, 163, 199, 216

The Blandness of Chewing Words 117, 140, 215
Book of Han: the Empresses and Imperial Affines 166
A Brief Study on the Character "Ta 她" 174, 222
Brilliant Sister of Mine 43, 48, 213
Building the Chinese Language 174, 222
Burying the Chicken 107

A Certain Woman 116, 217
Change and Continuity: The Theory and Practice of Cultural History 175, 182, 221
The Character 'Ta 她' Is Not an Invention, but Rather Another Picto-phonetic Character Taken from It 174, 223
The Character 'Ta 她' Was Not Created by Liu Bannong 174, 221
The Chat 61
Chatting about Heroines of the Silver Screen 95
Chewing Words Is not So "Bland" 118, 140, 214
China Reading Weekly 6, 173, 222, 223
The China Times 2, 21, 35, 44, 46, 49, 73, 94, 108, 141, 217
Chinese and English Phrase Book 112
Chinese-English Grammar 9, 13, 14, 201
Chinese National Culture Quarterly 6
Chinese Teaching in Middle School 141, 213
Chrysanthemum 33, 46, 216
Chunlan's Letter to University President Cai 123
City of Breasts and the Revolutionary Utopian Imagination 172, 221
Coal in the Furnace – Nostalgia for the Motherland 173
Collected Jottings from the Kang Residence 174

226   *Index of Translated/Transliterated Titles Referred to in This Work*

Collected Works of Chen Wangdao 111, 112, 212
The Collected Works of Chen Yinke – Collected Letters 6
Collected Works of Liu Shi 95
A Collection of Experiments 173, 213
A Collection of New Poems 173, 217
Commemorating "May Four" 45
Complete Library of Textbooks of Normal, Middle and Primary Schools from Before Liberation Held by this Library 124, 141, 218
Complete Works of Bingxin 45, 218
Complete Works of Fu Sinian 45, 214
The Complete Works of Lu Xun 174, 214
The Compromised Position of Women 95
The Critical Review xix, 131, 142, 201, 211
A Cultural History of the Chinese Character "Ta (她, She)*" – Research on the invention and adoption of a new feminine pronoun* xxi, 184, 209
Culture and National Distress 89
The Culture of Chinese Characters 174, 222, 223
Current Opinion 27, 113, 133, 136, 142, 213
The Dahlia xi, 64, 69, 200, 214

Daily Jottings 174
Darling 17, 217
The Dawn 35, 215
The Debate over How to Read "Ta, 他*"* 68
The Debate over "Refuting the Research on the Character Ta 她*"* 69, 218
The Debate over the Question of the Character "Ta 她*"* 61
The Decameron xviii, 86, 90, 95, 200, 215
Declaration of a Student Strike 45
Declaration on the Construction of Standard Chinese Culture 137
Decrying Women's Rights in China 81, 94, 211
A detailed Critique of the Question of the Character "Ta 她*"* 49, 66, 72, 97, 212
Dictionary of the Chinese Language 7, 8, 113, 122, 125, 141, 214, 201
Dictionary of the National Language 129, 142, 217
Dictionnaire Chinois-Francais 14, 224
Dictionnaire Francais-Chinois 14, 214, 224
Discussing National Language Examination Topics with Professor Liu Wendian xix, 133, 142, 201, 203, 211

Discussion of the Differentiation between the Two Terms "He" (ta, 他*) and "They" (tamen,* 他们*)* 69, 101, 104, 105, 112, 113, 214
Discussion of "The Division of Ta 他*"* 112, 212
The Discussion of "he/she/it" (qu 佢*) and "Mr." (xiansheng* 先生*)* 112, 212
A Discussion of "Ta 他*"* 68, 215
Discussion of the Feminine Third Person Pronoun 93, 216
Discussion on the Use of Third Person Pronouns 98
The Discussion over the Character "Ta 她*"* 174, 222
The Discussion over the Translation of the English "She" ix, 22, 27, 199, 215
Divine Justice 79, 94, 213
Divorce 162
Dogs and Badges of Honor 33, 34, 216
Down with Yingci 83, 95, 216

The Earliest Appearance of the Term May Fourth Movement and Its Connotations 45, 222
Eastern Miscellany 44, 116, 118, 140, 141, 203, 211, 214
East of the Yalu 33
Emancipation Pictorial xii, 59, 63, 69, 77, 94, 155, 156, 157, 158, 159, 160, 161, 164, 172, 200, 202, 203, 204, 214, 217
The Empty Drum 26
English-Chinese Dictionary 12
English Grammar Explained 12
English Primer 10
English School Grammar viii, 11, 12, 14, 97, 199, 201, 212, 221
Enlightenment Magazine 39, 47, 50, 68, 69, 71, 93, 94, 98, 111, 112, 211, 213, 214, 215, 216
Essays from Qiejie Pavillion 174
Essays of [Liu] Bannong 26, 67, 97, 172, 213
Eternal Heroine Qin Liangyu 95, 216
Evening in a Small Peasant Household 40, 47, 214
Everyman's One Thousand Basic Characters 122
The Evolution of Gender 191
Excavation of Knowledge xxviii
Expanded and Annotated Pronunciation Dictionary of Common National Language Terms 142, 217

Index of Translated/Transliterated Titles Referred to in This Work   227

An Explanation of the Grammar of the
    Chinese Language 129, 142
The Exploits of Qiu Jin 82, 202, 217

Farewelling a Guest on the Huangpu 33
Fate and Faith 114
Fei Mu Perspicaciously Recognizes a
    Heroine 95, 212
Female Corpse 46
The Female Sex 191
The Female Third Person "Pronoun" 68,
    69, 98, 211
The Feminine Third Person Pronoun in
    Drama 93
Fire 140, 216
The First Chinese-English Work on English
    Grammar – "A Grammar of the
    English Language" 13
Flower of the Sea of Evil 82, 95, 217
Forced Marriage of a Heroine 82, 212
Foreword to Violets xix, xx, 139, 143, 201,
    203, 217
Form and the Revolution – The
    Development of Modernity in Mao
    Dun's Early Novels 172, 221
The Formation and Historical Practice
    of the Modern Concept of
    "Civilization" and "Culture" in the
    Late Qing and Early Republican
    Period xxvii
Forty Years in Journalism 137, 143, 215
Fragments 26, 82, 202, 217
Free Talk 68, 85, 143
From Arrogance to Deference 45
Fudan Journal: Social Science Edition
    171, 223
Further Discussion on "the Question of the
    Character Ta 她" 50, 55, 67, 68,
    202, 212

Garden of the Chinese Language 174, 222
Gender Consciousness and the Modernity
    of Modern Chinese Literature
    172, 222
Gender Consciousness in Modern Chinese
    Literature 172, 222
The Girl of His Dreams 122, 141
Goddess 27, 28, 109, 212
Golden Age 4
A Grain As Big As a Hen's Egg 106, 216
A Grammar of the English Language 8, 13,
    17, 218, 221
Grand Dictionary of Standard Chinese 128
Grandma's Heart 115, 140, 216

Grand Standard Dictionary 113, 215
Green Earth 6, 26, 223
Group Meeting Minutes: 18th National
    Language Teaching Group: Record
    of Proposal C 141, 217
Guangming Daily 174, 206, 221, 223
A Guide to the English Language 9, 13, 216
Guowen Weekly 121, 141, 213, 214

Hamlet 35
Handout on Composition 112, 211
Han Xiao's Song for the Qin 141
Happiness 46, 217
A Harbinger of Male-Female Relations in
    Peking's Student World x, 28, 30,
    45, 199, 213
Hebei Journal 171
Her Ideal Man 122, 141, 213, 214
Heroine of Chaos 82
Heroine of the Jade Watchtower 82
Heroine of Joffre's Camp 82
Heroines and Women of Distinction Probe
    Things Deeply: the Ideal Late Qing
    Female Personality 94
Heroines in Military Uniform 95, 216
Heroine's Mirror 82
He, She, It viii, 142, 199
The History of the Creation of the Character
    "Ta 她" 5, 222
History Teaching 45, 222
Honyakugo "kare" "kanojo" no rekishi
    [The History of the Translated
    Equivalent of "he" and "she"] 4, 5
Honyakugo seiritsu jijō [The Emergence of
    a Language of Translation] 5
How Could I Not Think of Her? xxi, 37, 39,
    41, 46, 47, 163, 173
How to Awaken the Everyday Chinese
    Woman 94, 212
How to use Ta 他, Ta 她, Ta 牝, and Ta 它
    113, 216
Huainan[zi] 51
Hubei Social Sciences 94, 222
Hubei Student's World 81, 211

Ideology in Goethe's Poetry 35, 36,
    46, 215
Immensee 109, 110, 113, 202
Inscription on a Photograph Taken at
    Keyan in Shaoxing 41, 47, 216
In Search of a Cultural History – Taking
    China in Recent Years as Our
    Prospect 3, 5, 221
An Integrated Dictionary 14

Interesting Language from the Academic World 95, 215
Interrogating the Character ta 她 93, 218
Interrogating the Highest Poetic Sentiment Shared by the Chinese Nation – "Our Mother, the 'Motherland'" 173
Introduction to Periodicals of the May Fourth Era 48, 172, 223
Invention and the Nature of Slavishness 108, 112, 202, 216
An Investigation into the Origin of the Name "May Fourth Movement" 45
In the Wine Shop 116
Is this a Person Too? 19, 20, 27, 216
It Is Not Necessary to Distinguish Between Male and Female So Distinctly 93, 214

Journal of Historiograhpy 182
Journal of Nankai University 27
Journal of Peking University 45, 222
Journal of the Women's Higher Normal School Literature and Art Society 116, 214
The Joy of Reading 173, 222

Kang Baiqing Notice 47, 213
Kunlun Slave 138, 139

Labor and Women 112
Lamplight 115, 140
Language and Literature World 4
Language Research and Teaching 174, 222
La Studentaro de la Stata Pekin-Universitato 47
Lectures on Chinese Grammar 112, 215
Letters Between Two 38
Letters from the Yinfeng Pavillion 138
Letter to All Female Graduates from Middle and Primary Schools 123
Letter to the Gentlemen of the Gongxueshe 108
Lexicographical Studies 5, 26, 222
Light of the Full Moon 42, 47, 218
Light of Learning 21, 26, 32, 35, 44, 45, 46, 49, 50, 60, 66, 67, 68, 69, 107, 108, 109, 112, 173, 211, 212, 213, 214, 215, 218
Linguistic Pedagogy and Research 5, 222
Literary Supplement to the Peking Gazettes 116, 118, 140, 214, 215
Literature and Art Research 94, 222
Literature and Art Series 27

Literature Weekly 94, 141, 217
Little Friend 120, 121, 141, 203, 213
Little Match Girl 17, 18, 26, 141, 201, 217
Liu Bannong and the Story of the Character "Ta 她*"* 6, 223
Liu Bannong and "Ta 她*"* 5, 221
Liu Bannong's Ta 她 *[She]* 46, 221
Liushugu 51
Looking at "Ta 他*" and "Ta* 她*" from the Standpoint of "Ta"* 174, 222
Love Letters Vol. 1 and *Love Letters Vol. 2* 38
Love Song 37, 38, 202, 214
The Lure of Death 44, 212
Lushan Travel Diary: 2nd of 37 Pieces 33
Lu Xun Manuscript Series 140
Lu Xun Research Monthly 113, 221, 223

Mainland 190, 198
"Mandarin Grammar" and "English School Grammar" (The Earliest Dissemination of a Knowledge of English Grammar in the Late Qing Dynasty)" Part II 14, 221
May Fourth 122
Meiji umare no nihongo [New Japanese Linguistic Creations in the Meiji Period] 4
Mencius 79
Meng Hun 26
Miss 73, 77, 94, 202, 217
"Miss" and "She" 94, 216
Missing pages from Guo Moruo's "Goddess" (1919–1921) 27
Model French-Chinese Dictionary 13, 14, 216
Modern China i, 143, 150, 151, 165, 180, 181, 184, 188, 189, 191, 196, 198, 213, 223
Modern Chinese 174, 221
Modern Chinese History Studies xxvii, 184, 185, 197
Modernity and the Recognition of the Character "Ta 她*"* 184, 210
Modern Woman 73, 94, 216
Modern Youth 95, 216
The Morning Post Supplement 67, 141, 146, 199, 213, 214, 215
The Morning Post x, 28, 29, 30, 35, 37, 38, 42, 43, 44, 45, 47, 48, 202, 213, 215, 216, 218
Mouse Plague 21, 27, 212
Movement for the Study of the Classical Language in Primary and Middle School 136

Index of Translated/Transliterated Titles Referred to in This Work

Murdered by Art 35
My Father Liu Bannong 47, 222
My Nanny, the Great Yan River 165
My Prose Poetry 46
My View on the New Poetry 32

Nanfang Daily 4, 26, 222
National Language Monthly 69, 101, 112, 113, 214
National Language Pronunciation Dictionary 122, 126
A National Language Reader 113
National Language Recordings 103, 122, 126
National Language Textbook for the New Education System 124, 125, 141, 203
Neighbor 155
A New Approach to Substituting fu 娘 *for fu* 婦 94, 217
New Cultural History 171, 221
New Cultural History and Chinese Research 171, 223
The New Culture As a Movement 143, 213, 223
New Dialects 126
New Dictionary of Literary Description 142, 214
New Education 141, 217
New Examples of Assigned Characters 99, 100, 105, 111, 112, 211
New Fiction 95, 107, 215
New History 45, 112, 171, 183, 206, 221, 222, 223
The Newlyweds 5
New Man 2, 26, 49, 50, 61, 65, 66, 67, 68, 93, 111, 137, 202, 211, 212, 213, 218
New Romanticism and Other Things 35, 46, 215
New Woman 94, 214
New Women's World of China Magazine 190, 198
New Year's Sacrifice 116, 118, 140, 162, 203, 214
New Youth v, viii, ix, 15, 16, 17, 21, 26, 27, 29, 40, 41, 43, 44, 47, 70, 138, 140, 173, 199, 201, 213, 214, 215, 216, 217
Nonsense 143, 217

Old Age 37, 46, 218
On Chewing Words 5, 116, 140, 174, 221, 222
The On-going Development of Comprehensive Research on Science and Art in East Asia 172, 206
On Male and Female 191
On National History – Responding to Mao Zishui 205
On Restoring the Power of Women 79, 94, 213
On the Dignity of Women 19
On the Language Gender Difference between "Ta 他*" and "Ta* 她*"* 174, 221
On the Question of the Character "Ta 她*"* viii, 15, 18, 26, 50, 53, 62, 66, 67, 72, 97, 144, 169, 199, 213
On the Refusal to Use the Character Ta 她 *and a Question for Reading Life* 91, 92, 95, 96, 202, 213
On "Ta 她*"* 5, 26, 222
Opinions on the Differentiation of the Character Ta 他 *(he)* 67, 112, 211
Organisational Principles of the National Language 123

A Parricide 18, 26
The Past and the Present of the Truth Association 47, 214
The Pei-yang Pictorial News xv, xvi, 83, 95, 135, 142, 200, 216, 218
People's Political Consultative Conference Report 221
Poets and Labor 35, 46, 215
Popular Language Theory 147
Popular Literature 174, 222
A Portuguese Chinese Dictionary 14
The Principle Behind the Publication of the Labour and Women Magazine 112
Probing the Original Meaning of the Character "Gui 鬼 *[ghost]"* 3, 6
The Pronoun Ta (他, he) *and Ta* (她, she) 67, 146, 147, 203, 213
Pronunciation Dictionary of Common National Language Terms 125, 126, 127, 131, 133, 135, 142, 203, 215, 217

Qie Yun 105, 126
Qiu Jin and Lü Bicheng: The Quest for the Spirit of the Heroine in their Lives and Writing 94, 222
The Question 33, 46, 213
The Question of "Modernity", a New Term and a New Concept in the Late

Qing and Early Republican Period – Revisiting China's Recognition of the Concepts of "Ideological Modernity" and Modern "Society" 171, 198
The Question of the Vulgar Scripted Ta 她 *and Ta* 牠 27, 113, 133, 134, 136, 142, 203, 213
The Question of Women's Personality 27, 216
Qu Rites 80

Raising the Whip 38, 214
Random Notes on the Zhao Family 173
Random Poems from Taizhou: Lamplight 115, 140, 217
Random Thoughts 105
Random Thoughts on the Question of Male-Female Relations 29
Random Travel Notes 94, 141, 217
Reading Life 86, 89, 95, 215
Recordings of the National Language Textbook 103
Record of Interview with Comrade Ji Chaoding 112, 113, 214
Red Magazine 82
Reflections on a Week in Shanghai 33, 47, 217
Reform 17, 26, 28, 217
Refusing to Use the Character Ta 她 86, 89, 95, 202, 215
Refuting Again the Research on the Character Ta 她 212
Refuting the Research on the Character Ta 她 *– If Liu Bannong Is Not Wrong Then Who Is?* 49, 66, 67, 212
Regarding the Character "Ta (牠, it)*"* 113, 221, 223
Regarding Ta 她 60, 68, 217
Regret for the Past 162
Remembering Liu Bannong 105, 174
Remorse 35, 215
The Renaissance Collection 26
The Renaissance xiv, 18, 27, 33, 35, 40, 41, 44, 45, 46, 47, 199, 200, 213, 216, 217
Reply to Mr. Gong Dengchao's Doubts Over "New Examples of Assigned Characters" 211
Republican Daily News xi, 39, 47, 50, 69, 71, 97, 98, 99, 199, 211
Research Methods of Vernacular Writing 123
Research on the character Ta 她 *– Is Liu Bannong Really Wrong?* 49, 66, 67, 68, 215
Research on Chinese Culture 172, 222
Research on New Western Cultural History 171
Research on the "Third Person Pronoun" 67, 68, 69, 93, 98, 111, 211
The Rise and Direction of Western New Cultural History 171
Rites of Zhou 80, 95
Romeo and Juliet 36
Rus' Justice 4

Salome 35
The Second Sex 94
Seeing Association Friends Wei Shizhen, Wang Ruoyu, Chen Jianxiu and Xu Chuseng off to Study in Europe 36
Seeing Mu Han off to Paris 32
Seeking the Moon 47
Self-Portrait of a Chinese Citizen 95
Self-Study 113
Separation 140, 216
Sequel 142
Sequel to the New Dictionary of Literary Description 142, 214
Seventeen Poems by Tagore 36
Shanghai Tan 95, 212
She? xi, 39, 47, 199, 213
She: the 21st Century's Most Important Word 4, 222
She and He 46
Shen Bao 37, 46, 60, 61, 68, 85, 121, 143, 217, 218
Shen Bao: Free Talk 68, 143
The Short Story Magazine xiv, 82, 107, 109, 113, 114, 115, 116, 119, 120, 140, 141, 200, 213, 216, 217
A Short Work on Grief 37
Shuowen 51
Shuowen Jiezi 60
Shūtei Sōzu Shōgakutokuhon [Revised Illustrated Primary School Reader] 4
Silver Box 68
Simon's Father 140, 214
Six Poems by Tagore 36
A Small Incident 43
Social Welfare newspaper 82
Society 32, 46, 201, 213
Society Reports 130, 142, 214
Some Reflections on Research into Cultural History 207

Index of Translated/Transliterated Titles Referred to in This Work 231

Song of the Seven Sons 165
The Soul of the Violin 15, 26
South of the Yangtze 32
Speech to the Beijing National Language Pedagogical Institute 58, 68
The Spirit of the Chinese People 79
The Spirit of the May Fourth Movement 45, 157
Spring and Autumn 85
Spring Excursion 19, 20, 21, 27, 201, 216
Standard Dictionary of Common National Language Sounds 127, 142, 218
Standard Student Dictionary of the Sounds of the National Language 113, 127, 128, 203, 217
Stones of the Jingwei Bird 81, 82, 202
The Story of the Character Ta 他: Invention, Debate and Early Circulation 45, 112, 183, 206, 221
Story of Li Chao 46, 213
Study 105, 107, 109, 112, 216
Study Magazine 105
Summer Daybreak 47
The Superfluous "Ta 她" 174, 222
The Swallow and the Butterfly 141

Ta 《他》 163, 172, 173
Taking One's Leave 45, 212
Tale of Bygone Years (Повесть временных лет) 4
Tale of the Campaign of Igor 4
Ta 他 [he], Ta 她 [she], and Ta 牠 [it] 130, 141, 142, 209, 213, 214
Ta (他), Ta (她), Ta (牠), and Ta (它) xvi, 135, 136, 142, 200, 218
"Ta 她" and "Ni 妳" Should Not Be Used 174, 223
"Ta 她" and the Women's Movement xviii, 86, 90, 91, 95, 200, 215
Ta 祂 and Ta 他 in the Holy Bible 168, 173, 223
A Team of Horsemen 140, 214
Telegram to the Teams in All Provinces 45
Tell Her (她) 141, 215
Tell Her (她) to Come Back 141, 215
The Theater 58
They Grind Exceeding Small 107, 113
The Third Person Feminine Pronoun in Drama 68, 69, 211
This Is Liu Bannong's Error 49, 61, 65, 66, 212
Three Dreams in the Desert 43, 44, 202, 217
Three Hong Xian Chronicle Poems 173, 222

Tianjin Social Sciences 171, 198
Tōsei Shosei Kishitsu [The Disposition of Students in the Present Day] 4
Trade Essentials 11, 14, 212
Translingual Practice xxiv, 5, 67, 170, 171, 173, 222
Travelling Companion 141, 213
Truth 47, 214
Two Historical Items Relating to the Creation of the Character "Ta 她 (she)" 5, 26, 223
The Two Unsightly Characters for Miss 94, 211

Universities Appropriately Lead the Way in Lifting the Ban on Female Students 31, 213
Universities Should Be Open to Women 30
Unofficial Biography of Liu Rushi 207

Violets xix, xx, 137, 138, 143, 201, 217
The Violin and the Rose 35
The Voice of the 20th Century 35, 215

Weekly Critic 17, 45
Wen Shi Zhi Shi 13, 14, 221
Western Men and Women Are Different 26, 223
West Wind 141, 211
What Happens after Nora Walks Out? 116, 214
What Is an "Event in the History of Thought" 5, 221
Whose Fault? Why Did She Commit Suicide?! xii, 156, 200
Why He Married Her 141, 214
Why She Died 35, 215
Why She Regretted the Marriage 172
Women, Nation and Feminism 173, 224
Women's Daily 140
The Women's Liberation Question Requires the Obliteration of the Boundary between Men and Women 93, 215
Women's Magazine 29, 94, 212, 217
Women's Voice xvii, xviii, 84, 85, 86, 89, 88, 89, 90, 91, 92, 93, 95, 96, 119, 131, 145, 148, 200, 202, 212, 213
Word Games of Our Times 5
Word Games of Our times: the Birth Story of the Odd [pronoun] "She" 5

232 *Index of Translated/Transliterated Titles Referred to in This Work*

Yi 伊 and *Ta* 她 in Lu Xun's Fiction 140, 222
Yi 伊 *and Ta* 她 *in Theatrical Scripts* 58
Young China Association xiv, 32, 35, 36, 37, 41, 46, 200, 213, 215, 217

Your Happiness 143, 213
Youth Reference 26, 223
Yu Pian 61, 126, 134, 168
Yu Pian: Qie Yun 134
Yupian: The Female Radical Section 60

Index of Proper Names Used in This Work (in Pinyin Order)

Ai Gu 162
Ai Qing 165
An Yuner 224
Arakawa Kiyohide 172
Aunt Xianglin 116, 118, 162, 203

Baidu 46
Bao Tianxiao 138
Bao Yanyi 174
Beijing Women's Advanced Normal School 140
Beijing Women's Normal University 140
Bing Xin xiv, 115, 119, 120, 200
Bu Zhuo 155

Cai Xiaozhou 122, 123, 209
Cai Ying 46, 221
Cai Yuanpei 50, 58, 68, 219
Cang Jie 86
Cao Xiang 10
Chang Jincang 175, 176, 177, 178
Chen Bao'e 45
Chen Congyun 174, 221
Chen Dabei 58, 68, 93
Chen Duxiu 65, 104, 138
Chen Fukang 113, 221
Cheng Xiaoqing 137, 138, 139
Chen Heng 171, 221
Chen Hengzhe xv, 120, 141, 200, 211
Chen Jianhua 143, 158, 172, 206, 221
Chen Jianlei 107
Chen Jidong 95
Chen Jitong 95
Chen Liwei 172
Chen Meiyan 6, 211
Chen Shaoming 5, 180, 183, 221
Chen Sibai 67, 100, 105, 109, 111, 112, 145, 211
Chen Wangdao 50, 62, 63, 64, 69, 97, 98, 99, 100, 105, 111, 112, 147, 171, 211, 212, 218

Chen Yaoming 4
Chen Yiming 68, 208
Chen Yinke xix, xxvi, 3, 6, 129, 131, 132, 133, 135, 136, 137, 142, 201, 203, 205, 207, 211
China Dictionary Editing and Compilation Office 129, 142, 217
China Education Reform Society 74
"China National Culture Construction Movement" 136
China Youth Association 29
Chu bei ying ci 94, 211
"Contributors to *New Examples of Assigned Characters*" 112
Correspondence 68, 69

Dai Jinhua 224
Dai Yi 142, 210
Da Tong 51, 52, 65, 68, 69, 72, 93, 98
Democratic Taiwan 95
Deng Chunlan 122
Deng Niudun 27, 46, 113, 212
Deng Yingchao 140
Deng Zhongxia 45
Di Hua 26
Ding Huang 133
Dong Yinhu 82
Duan Xipeng 45

Fang Ru 95
Fang Weigui xxviii, 172, 208
Fan Xiangshan 124, 218
Fei Xingzhi 30
Feng Tianyu 172
Feng Yunjun xv, 119, 200
Fudan University 65, 172, 212, 221
Fu Donghua 116
Fu Shuhua 94
Fu Sinian 28, 45, 214

234 Index of Proper Names Used in This Work (in Pinyin Order)

Ge Luofu 4
Geng Jizhi 115
Geng Xiangxin 171, 221
Gentleman from East of the River 207, 208
Gong Dengchao 60, 68, 101, 112, 131, 211, 212
Gong Shuduo 142, 210
Gong Shuming 6, 221
Gong Yuanchang 189, 198
Gu Hongming 79, 166, 167, 204
Gu Jiegang 124, 141, 218
Gu Mingdao 137, 138, 139
Guo Luogui 14, 212
Guo Moruo 21, 27, 28, 36, 44, 46, 100, 105, 107, 108, 109, 110, 113, 173, 202, 209, 212
Guo Zansheng viii, 10, 11, 12, 13, 14, 97, 199, 212

Han Bing 49, 50, 51, 52, 53, 55, 56, 57, 58, 60, 61, 62, 63, 65, 66, 67, 68, 69, 72, 73, 97, 100, 137, 143, 145, 168, 169, 202
Han Qiuhong 142, 210
He Xiang 174, 221
He Yongji [ji] 107, 108, 109, 113, 202
He Zhen 79, 94, 213
Hida Yoshifumi 4, 224
Hong Xi 37, 38
Hou Jue 113, 214
Huang Rikui 45
Huang Xingtao i, ii, iiii, iv, 5, 6, 13, 14, 112, 171, 174, 183, 198, 208, 210, 221
Huang Zhongsu 35, 36, 46
Hulan 131
Hu Shi or Hu Shizhi 17, 18, 24, 26, 38, 45, 85, 119, 124, 141, 143, 163, 169, 172, 173, 205, 213, 218, 219
Hu Yuzhi 44

Ichirō Ishida 175, 176, 182, 223
Iwazuki Junichi 172

Ji Chaoding 107, 112
Jin Dezhang xi, 39, 199, 213
Jin Dongren 5
Jin Fushen 146, 147, 171, 203, 213
Jing Rong 164, 204
Ji Shi 65
Ji Zhuman 91, 95, 96, 213

Kang Baiqing x, 28, 29, 30, 31, 32, 33, 35, 42, 45, 46, 47, 154, 166, 170, 199, 201, 213

Kawajiri Fumiko 172
King Meiwen 141
Ko Kilseop 5
Kong Fanling 45, 222
Kuang Qizhao 10, 14, 213

Leo Ou-fan Lee 194, 198
Liang Qichao 180
Liang Shiqiu 116
Liang Yimo 5
Liang Zhudong 5
Liang Zongdai 64, 115, 119, 141, 213
Liaozuobuyi 44, 48, 213
Li Changli 179, 181
Li Dazhao 64
Li Dingyi 143, 213
Li Dongchen 174, 222
Li Hanjun 64, 98, 99
Li Hongyan 173, 222
Li Jieren 116
Li Jinhui 120, 121, 141, 203, 209, 213
Li Jinxi 64, 65, 121, 218, 219
Li Jiye 39
Li Ling 172, 222
Li Lu 5, 223
Ling Xiaofang 122, 141, 213
Ling Yuanzheng 6
Lin Yutang 169
Li Peifen 142, 210
Li Qizhi 94, 222
Li Tong 174, 221
Liu Bannong viii, xxi, xxv, 5, 6, 7, 15, 17, 18, 22, 24, 26, 29, 37, 38, 40, 41, 46, 47, 49, 50, 51, 52, 53, 54, 55, 56, 61, 62, 63, 64, 65, 66, 67, 69, 85, 86, 97, 100, 104, 105, 126, 131, 138, 144, 145, 152, 163, 166, 168, 169, 170, 172, 173, 174, 199, 202, 212, 213, 214, 215, 221, 222, 223
Liu Chengyu 166, 173, 222
Liu Dabai 64, 99, 211
Liu Fu 38, 202, 213, 214
Liu Guisheng 113, 214
Liu He xxiv, 2, 67, 148, 149, 151, 152, 166, 168
Liu Jianhui 172
Liu, Lydia He 5, 222
Liu Qingyang 140
Liu Shi 89, 90, 91, 93, 95, 145
Liu Shipei 79
Liu Wendian xix, 133, 142, 201, 203, 211
Liu Xiaohui 47, 222
Liu Yazi 81, 218, 220
Liu Youin 174, 222

Index of Proper Names Used in This Work (in Pinyin Order)   235

Liu Zhaoji 174, 222
Liu Zhiqin 179
Li Wenhai 142, 210
Li Xiaotong 27, 113, 131, 133, 134, 136,
    142, 203, 213
Li Xiaoxiang 5, 223
Li Yitao 140
Lobscheid, Wilhelm 9, 13, 14, 201, 218
Lu Bohong 14, 214
Lujiangfengsheng 37, 46, 218
Luo Jialun 29, 30, 45, 46
Lu Qiuxin 94, 214
Lü Shuxiang 66
Lu Xun 20, 38, 43, 64, 105, 113, 115,
    116, 117, 118, 119, 140, 162, 169,
    170, 174, 202, 203, 209, 214, 221,
    222, 223
Lu Yin xv, 115, 119, 120, 200
Lu Yuan 214

Ma Junru 113, 214
Mandarin Ducks and Butterflies School xx,
    68, 115, 137, 143, 201
Mao Dun 44, 64, 115, 140, 172, 221
Mao Zishui 205
"May Fourth Movement" 28, 29, 30, 31,
    45, 46, 122, 141, 157, 222
Meng Shen 49, 52, 66, 68
Meng Shuhong 6, 26, 222
Ming Xi 48, 214
Mr Ma Er 121, 141

National Language Teaching Group 122,
    141, 217
New Fiction Period 5
New Man Society 65
New Youth faction 65

"Peking Middle and Higher Schools
    Student Association" 30, 45, 46
Puyi 143

Qia 130, 142, 214
Qian Junxu 109, 113
Qian Qianwu 142, 214
Qian Xingcun xii, 64, 200
Qian Xuantong x, 6, 17, 21, 22, 23, 24, 25,
    26, 63, 64, 65, 69, 101, 102, 103,
    104, 105, 109, 112, 113, 126, 129,
    143, 148, 169, 199, 201, 202, 214,
    215
Qian Yuan 117, 118, 119
Qin Hui 177
Qiu Jin 81, 82, 94, 202, 217, 222

Queen Kang 141
Qu Shiying 115

The Renaissance Society 19, 28
Ricci, Matteo 14, 224
Ruggieri, Michele 14, 224

Shao Lizi 50, 64, 71, 72, 78, 93, 99, 211
Shen Guowei 14, 206
Shen Jianshi 3, 6, 215
Shen Jie 68
Shen Wei 68
Shen Xuanlu 98, 99, 112, 211
Shen Yanbing 64, 115
Shen Zemin 37, 115
Shi Cuntong 76, 77, 94, 211
Shi Hun 107
Shi Pingmei xv, 119, 120, 141, 200, 215
Shi Song 142, 210
Shi Tong 89, 95
Shu San 86
Shu Xincheng 108, 221
Song Weijie 5, 170, 222
Song Wenhan 114, 220
South Society 81
Strategies of the Warring States Group 107
Study Group 105, 107, 216
Sun Fuyuan 118
Sun Hanbing 65, 137
Sun Hongyi 25
Sun Jiang 172, 206
Sun Lianggong 112, 215, 219, 220
Sun Xunqun 58, 59, 68, 101, 215
Sun Yu 65, 140
Sun Yuqi 65
Sun Zuji 49, 52, 53, 56, 62, 66, 67, 68, 215
Suzuki Masami 172

Tai Jingnong 140
Tan Daxuan 12
Tang Shichun 181
Tao Tiezhu 95, 223
Tao Zhixing 122
Tian 93, 215
Tian Han 28, 35
Tianjin Women's Patriotic Association 140
Tian Zhongmin 140, 141, 222, 223
Todam Publishers 5
Truth Association 43, 47, 105, 214, 216
Tsinghua University 43, 105, 107, 108,
    109, 113, 171, 202, 214, 216
Tsinghua University Study Group 107, 216
Tsubouchi Shōyō 5
Tsuchiya Hiroshi 5

236 Index of Proper Names Used in This Work (in Pinyin Order)

Wang Daocheng 142, 210
Wang Dewei xxviii
Wang Jingzhi, 115
Wang Maozu 136, 171, 218, 219, 220
Wang Qisheng 172, 206
Wang Renshu 116
Wang Rufeng 142, 210
Wang Sizhi 142, 210
Wang Tongzhao 28, 35, 36, 115, 201, 215
Wang Wuwei 50, 62, 65, 137, 143
Wang Xi 96
Wang Xinming 137, 143, 215
Wang Xiulu 141, 214, 218
Wang Yuanyuan 174, 222
Wei Hua 114, 216
Wei Ruowang 14
Wei Wanlei 171
Wen Yiduo 165
Women's Committee 88
Women's Higher Normal School, Beijing 116, 214
Wu Ke 95

Xia Mingfang 142, 172, 206
Xiang Baolun 95
Xiang Ru 83, 84
Xiao Yang 4, 26, 222
Xiao Ziqin 13, 14, 216
Xia Xiaohong 94
Xie Tihong 138
Xi Linxin 156, 157, 158, 159, 203, 204
Xiu Shui 66
Xuantong 143
Xu Deheng 45
Xu Dishan 115
Xu Ke 174
Xu Shen 22
Xu Shuzhong 22
Xu Suizhi 113
Xu Yanzhi 29
Xu Yonghong 107

Yamamoto Takuya 5
Yanabu Akira 5
Yan Fu xxv, 12, 166, 167, 204
Yang Baosan 47, 216
Yang Bojun 129, 142
Yang Hu 45, 222
Yang Hui 173, 223
Yang Jianli vi, 184, 210
Yang Jianmin 6, 223
Yang Lianggeng 123
Yang Nianqun 45, 112, 172, 183, 206, 221, 223
Yang Shaoping 9, 13

Yang Yinhang 60
Yang Yu 5, 223
Ye Bochuan 4, 224
Ye Chucang 99, 211, 219, 220
Ye Shaojun 18, 19, 20, 21, 27, 115, 124, 141, 201, 216, 218
Ye Shengtao ix, 18, 19, 27, 44, 64, 115, 140, 199, 201, 216
"Yi" 45
Yifan 105, 108, 202, 216
Yi Fan (Ivan) 113
Yi Fu 107, 113
Yi Keyi 45
A Ying 64
Ying Xia 157, 160, 161, 204
Yixuan 71
Yi Xuan 71, 72, 78, 93, 216
Yi Yin 25
Yoshizawa Seiichiro 172
You Luan 73, 94, 202, 216
"Youth Club" 66, 68, 215
Yuan Bi 37
Yuan Yidan 143, 213, 223
Yu Hualin 95, 210
Yun Zhen 37
Yu Pingbo 28, 33, 34, 35, 39, 41, 42, 46, 47, 163, 201, 216, 217
Yu Songhua 108

Zeng Pu 82, 217
Zhang Binglin 126
Zhang Boju 173, 222
Zhang Dongsun 108
Zhang Guotao 45
Zhang Juling 168, 174, 223
Zhang Shouan 172, 174, 206
Zhang Taiyan 134
Zhang Wentian 116
Zhang Wenzhi 113, 127, 142, 217
Zhang Xiping 14
Zhang Yiping 37, 38
Zhang Zhixiang 174, 223
Zhang Zhongmin 140, 141, 171, 210, 222, 223
Zhao Yuanren 47, 103, 122, 126, 173, 215, 217
Zhen 60, 68, 217
Zheng Boqi 35, 37
Zheng Zhenduo 115
Zhen Xin vii, 77, 78, 94, 217
Zhou Bing 171, 223
Zhou Gucheng 175
Zhou Huizhuan 94, 217
Zhou Jianyun 78, 94
Zhou Lianhua 168, 173, 223

Index of Proper Names Used in This Work (in Pinyin Order)   237

Zhou Shoujuan xix, xx, 68, 73, 115, 129, 137, 143, 201, 217
[Zhou] Shou Juan xx, 68, 73, 115, 129, 137, 139, 143, 201, 203, 217
Zhou Wu 35, 36, 46, 217
Zhou Yang 169
Zhou Zuoren ix, 7, 15, 17, 18, 19, 21, 22, 23, 24, 25, 26, 28, 43, 44, 49, 51, 62, 63, 64, 72, 101, 104, 115, 116, 141, 169, 172, 199, 201, 202, 215, 217
Zhuang Fu 50, 70, 72, 93, 218
Zhu Jingnong 122, 140, 141, 218
Zhu Jingwei 5, 206
Zhu Jinshun 5, 26, 113, 223
Zhu Xin 131, 142, 143, 218
Zhu Ziqing 47, 64, 74, 75, 76, 90, 94, 115, 123, 140, 141, 202, 217
Zijun 162
Zou Zhengjian 49, 52, 63, 69, 218
Zuo Yuhe 179

Taylor & Francis eBooks

www.taylorfrancis.com

A single destination for eBooks from Taylor & Francis with increased functionality and an improved user experience to meet the needs of our customers.

90,000+ eBooks of award-winning academic content in Humanities, Social Science, Science, Technology, Engineering, and Medical written by a global network of editors and authors.

TAYLOR & FRANCIS EBOOKS OFFERS:

- A streamlined experience for our library customers
- A single point of discovery for all of our eBook content
- Improved search and discovery of content at both book and chapter level

REQUEST A FREE TRIAL
support@taylorfrancis.com